GREAT VILLIERS

To

IVOR NOVELLO

GEORGE VILLIERS AT SIX MONTHS

From the Family Group by Gerard Honthorst in
the National Portrait Gallery

*Reproduced by permission of the Directors of the
National Portrait Gallery*

GREAT VILLIERS

A Study of George Villiers
Second Duke of Buckingham
1628-1687

By

HESTER W. CHAPMAN

LONDON
SECKER & WARBURG
1949

Martin Secker & Warburg Ltd.
7 John Street, Bloomsbury, London, W.C.1

First published 1949

Made in Great Britain. Printed at the St Ann's Press
Timperley, Altrincham
and bound by the Leighton-Straker Bookbinding Co. Ltd., London

CONTENTS

PART ONE: January 1628—June 1657
THE YEARS OF PREPARATION

PART TWO: June 1657—September 1670
THE YEARS OF TRIUMPH

PART THREE: September 1670—April 1687
THE YEARS OF INTRIGUE

CONTENTS—*continued*

LIST OF ILLUSTRATIONS

ACKNOWLEDGEMENTS

I AM indebted for so much help and kindness from so many people during my researches for this biography that I hardly know where to begin my acknowledgements. If it had not been for the encouragement and advice of my dear and honoured friend, Miss Rose Macaulay, it would never have been written at all. The courtesy and generosity of the Earl of Jersey in placing Buckingham's Commonplace Book at my disposal and allowing me to quote from it freely have enabled me to fill in my presentation of the Duke's personality with something much more satisfactory than theory or surmise. I have much pleasure in thanking Colonel Charles Grey, D.S.O., for his kindness and hospitality during my visits to Helmsley Castle and Kirkby Moorside. Especial thanks are due to Mr. and Mrs. J. F. Watson of Buckingham House, Kirkby Moorside, the Librarian of the Public Library in York, and the proprietress of the " Cock and Bottle " in that city. For constructive criticism and suggestions I am deeply grateful to my husband Ronnie Griffin, my cousin George Rylands, Mrs. H. E. Weatherall, Colonel Sir St. Vincent Troubridge, Miss Iris Morley and Mr. Noel Annan. For general criticism and advice I am indebted to Mr. Roger Senhouse and Mr. David Farrer. My grateful acknowledgements are due to the Directors of the Print Room and the Manuscript Room in the British Museum, to the Director of the National Portrait Gallery, to Captain Malcolm Wombwell of Newburgh Priory, to Sir Leigh Ashton, Sir Osbert Sitwell and, again, to the Earl of Jersey for his permission to reproduce the portrait of Buckingham by Simon Verelst. Finally I should like to thank all those friends who have listened so patiently and sympathetically to my prolonged and repetitive dissertations on the subject of this memoir.

HESTER W. CHAPMAN

Some of their chiefs were princes in the land;
In the first rank of these did Zimri stand,
A man so various that he seemed to be
Not one, but all mankind's epitome;
Stiff in opinions, always in the wrong,
Was everything by starts and nothing long;
But in the course of one revolving moon
Was chymist, fiddler, statesman, and buffoon;
Then all for women, painting, rhyming, drinking,
Besides ten thousand freaks that died in thinking.
Blest madman, who could every hour employ
With something new to wish or to enjoy!
Railing and praising were his usual themes,
And both, to show his judgement, in extremes;
So over violent or over civil
That every man with him was God or Devil.
In squandering wealth was his peculiar art;
Nothing went unrewarded but desert.
Beggared by fools whom still he found too late,
He had his jest, and they had his estate.
He laughed himself from Court; then sought relief
By forming parties, but could ne'er be chief:
For spite of him, the weight of business fell
On Absalom and wise Achitophel;*
Thus wicked but in will, of means bereft,
He left not faction, but of that was left.

John Dryden: *Absalom and Achitophel*

* *Absalom*: The Duke of Monmouth.
  Achitophel: The Earl of Shaftesbury.

PREFACE

TWO lives of the Second Duke of Buckingham already exist—a sketch, or rather an obituary, by Brian Fairfax, his cousin by marriage, written some years after his death, and a full length, well-documented study by Lady Burghclere, published in 1903.

As most amateurs of biography (of whom the present writer is one) begin by explaining what they do *not* intend to set forth, it is best to follow custom and state that this book is an attempt at a portrait rather than a Life and Times. Little or no effort at whitewashing the subject will be discovered, nor any tendency to reverse the judgement of history; one or two points in the Duke's character have been emphasised rather than slurred over or ignored altogether, as in the past. With great respect to the experts of to-day, it is proposed that Buckingham was something more than a buffoon, and in profound reverence for contemporary biographers and historians it is suggested that he was something less than the foolish and evil debauchee they saw fit to describe. The material for his life is copious at some points, meagre at others; no endeavour has been made to fill in the gaps with " fictionalised " history. Nothing has been invented. Scholars and historians are advised not to open this book, for they will find in it little that they do not already know.

The caprice and unreliability of Buckingham's behaviour can partly be accounted for by surmise, that most irritating and unsatisfactory of biographical methods, and partly by reconsideration of the facts. Here was a man who had riches, beauty, wit, power, the friendship of princes and the love of women: he threw away all these gifts with both hands. Why? Historical analysis should not be conjectural: there are a number of answers to some of the questions arising out of Buckingham's career.

How did Van Dyck's beautiful young cavalier become Lely's bibulous, pop-eyed courtier? How did Sir Thomas Fairfax's cultivated, delightfully amusing son-in-law become Anna Shrewsbury's lover and the murderer of her husband? How did the Buckingham of the Cabal become the dupe of Charles II?

How did the author of *The Rehearsal* become Dryden's victim and the laughing-stock of Whitehall? How did Clarendon's enemy become the puppet of the Earl of Shaftesbury? Finally, how did the richest nobleman in England become a down-at-heel country squire? Some of these problems can never be answered: some have been dealt with superficially, some not at all. It is the purpose of this memoir to set them out in as orderly and comprehensible a manner as may be achieved by a student, and to insinuate rather than propound the clues, with the hope that the reader will choose to share in the pleasures of investigation.

Pope's Great Villiers, and Dryden's Zimri, Butler's Duke of Bucks, Charles II's Alderman George—was one of these persons the "real" Buckingham, or can they be united into a single, solid figure? At least we may use them as signposts on the road back into the past. It is necessary to deliberate before choosing a guide for the mass of gossip, prejudice and deliberate falsehood which helps to form the substance of history. Neither the intellect nor the heart nor the memory nor the imagination should dominate where all may combine in the assessment and understanding of a character.

PART ONE
(January 1628 – June 1657)

THE YEARS OF PREPARATION

CHAPTER ONE

I

ON an August day in the year 1628, John Felton, a
lieutenant of infantry recently returned from the war in France,
bought a tenpenny knife at a cutler's on Tower Hill. He sewed
the sheath into the lining of his coat so that he could draw it out
easily and quickly with his right hand, his left being maimed and
useless. The knife was heavy and round-hafted.

He then set off for Portsmouth, walking most of the way and
sleeping in barns and under hedgerows, for he had very little
money. The army owed him eighty pounds and—so he considered—promotion; he had received neither.

Felton reached Portsmouth in the early morning of August
the Twenty-Third, St. Bartholomew's Day, and went immediately
to the house of Captain Robert Mason, Treasurer to the Army;
Captain Mason was also private secretary to the Duke of Buckingham, at that time Lord High Admiral and Commander-in-
Chief of the English forces, many of whom were pressed men.
At some point during his journey Felton had written some lines
on a piece of paper which he pinned inside the crown of his
hat.

Although it was not yet six o'clock a number of people were
passing in and out of Captain Mason's house. In the inner hall
the Duke of Buckingham and some of his staff were conferring
with the French generals. His wife and sister were still asleep
upstairs.

While they talked news came that the siege of La Rochelle
had been raised. The Duke ordered breakfast to be served at once
so that he might start for London to tell the good news to the
King. Meanwhile Felton had placed himself behind the hangings
of the passage between the hall and the parlour.

Presently breakfast was announced and the Duke got up,
followed by his gentlemen, and walked through the passage.
Within a few feet of the parlour door he paused to speak to Sir
Thomas Fryer; Sir Thomas was a short man and the Duke a very
tall one: he bent forward a little, and those with him waited
while the two conversed.

3

Felton now stood behind the Commander-in-Chief, who was between him and Sir Thomas Fryer. He stepped forward and drove the knife deep into the Duke's left side.

The Duke staggered into the parlour: he made a gasping exclamation and pulled out the knife. His staff surrounded him and two of them supported him as he leant against the table. Blood poured from his nose and mouth. He fell under the table and died immediately.

The passage was dark and narrow, and the persons in it so pressed together that no one had perceived Felton. Indeed for a moment or two those nearest the Duke believed him to have been seized with an apoplexy.

A few minutes later Felton was in the kitchen; in the crush of hurrying people his hat had been knocked off. Now it was known what had happened; the screams of the Duchess and her sister-in-law rang through the house as they knelt beside the body. "A Frenchman! A Frenchman!" somebody called out, remembering the sounds of altercation overheard during the conference between the allied generals. Felton mistook the word for his own name, and walked back into the passage.

It would have been quite easy for him to have left the house unseen, for the confusion was rising every moment. He declared his guilt, just escaped lynching and was committed to Portsmouth gaol. The paper he had pinned in his hat, so that in the event of his death by violence his motive should be known to his country and the world, read as follows:

"If I be slain, let no man condemn himself: it is for our sins that our hearts are hardened and become senseless, or else he had not gone so long unpunished. He is unworthy of the name of a gentleman, or soldier, in my opinion, that is afraid to sacrifice his life for the honour of God, his King and country. Let no man condemn me for doing of it: rather discommend themselves as the cause thereof, for, if God had not taken away our hearts for our sins, He could not have you so long alive."

During imprisonment Felton seemed to change his mind as to the value of his action, declared himself repentant and asked forgiveness of the Duchess of Buckingham. The slow, minutely recorded process of his trial revealed a mentality which the psychological experts of to-day would have described with greater detail and ampler surmise but with no less accuracy and detachment. Felton was of gentle birth but poor, unsuccessful and a younger son. He was of a deeply religious, melancholic temperament and either could not afford or did not wish to marry. He had endured his experiences during the retreat from the Isle of Rhé with fortitude; but he brooded long and bitterly over the injustice of the war, the inefficiency and waste of its administration and subscribed to the verdict of the House of Commons in pronouncing the Duke of Buckingham "the cause of all our miseries; the grievance of grievances." Furthermore, he had long been obsessed with the immorality of the Duke's private life, as exemplified by his power over both James and Charles I. Three months after his committal Felton was hanged at Tyburn.[1]

So perished George Villiers, Duke of Buckingham, in his thirty-seventh year, at the height of his greatness. A few months later the Duchess gave birth to another son whom she called Francis, after his grandfather, the Earl of Rutland. The eldest child, Mary, had been betrothed two years before to Charles, Lord Herbert, and now, at the age of six, she went to live with the Pembroke family. She was married soon after her twelfth birthday, widowed a year later and subsequently re-married to the Duke of Richmond and Lennox. At an early age Francis—and his elder brother George who was born on January the Thirtieth, 1628[2]—were adopted by Charles I, the King announced that he would be a father to the children of his friend. But the real reason for this breaking up of the little Villiers' family life was that the widowed Duchess had returned to the old faith and declared herself reconciled to the Church of Rome. That the children of the defender of the Protestant religion in Europe should run the risk of subjugation to their mother's influence was not to be considered: and so, "George, Moll and little Frank"[3] were bred up with the sons and daughters of the King.[4]

2

The history of the Villiers family begins with the history of England as a united kingdom in 1066–67, when William I, having to some extent consolidated his victory over the Saxons,

---

[1] Clarendon: *History*. Gardiner: *History*. A. J. Cammell: *The Great Duke of Buckingham*. Sir Dudley Carleton: *Correspondence*.

[2] He was born at Wallingford House at one o'clock in the afternoon. J. Aubrey: *Brief Lives*.

[3] Letter of the Duchess of Buckingham.

[4] Brian Fairfax: *Life of George Villiers, 2nd Duke of Buckingham*.

was joined by those of his followers who had waited upon success before leaving their homes for a strange country.

No member of the family of de Villiers de l'Isle Adam fought at Hastings; their descendants, unlike so many of their contemporaries, did not even bribe the monks of Battle Abbey to put their ancestor's name on the Roll: but shortly after the autumn of 1066 the progenitor of what may have been a junior branch came to England.[5] They settled first in Nottinghamshire. A hundred and fifty years later they had dropped their French patronymic and become de Villiers of Brooksby in the county of Leicester.[6] By the time that the Norman strongholds had made way for the manor-houses and castles of the Plantagenet epoch the Villiers had become part of England and grew with its growth; soon after the accession of Henry III they called themselves English, subscribing to the customs and manners of a strongly unified national life.

Slowly, as the face of England changed and the jungles of marsh and heath and forest shrank before the incoming tide of medieval towns and villages, the class to which the Villiers belonged became separated from the powerful and ambitious nobility from which it sprang and was transformed into that section of the gentry that possessed privileges without fame, land but little wealth. Presently the newly-born middle class was entrenched between them and the peasantry and their younger sons and daughters married into it; so the family of Villiers became a little less influential, a little more obscure in every generation.

They took no risks, and got no prizes. They went steadily on as country knights and Lords of the Manor Court, administrating, marrying, begetting, while across the firmament of English history such names as Runnymede, Evesham, Bannockburn, Crécy, Agincourt, Towton and Tewkesbury burst like shooting stars and destroyed as quickly as they illumined the fortunes of many who shared in the struggle for power. But the name of Villiers remained unlit, as it were a plant growing strongly and imperceptibly in a dark place. War and revolution, plague, anarchy and famine swept over England; but compurgation and ordeal had given way to Common Law, the villein was slowly becoming a

---

[5] The family of de Villiers de l'Isle Adam in Normandy continued to flourish and produced several men of note, the last being the poet, playwright and novelist, Philippe-Auguste-Mathias, born at St. Brieuc in 1840, who died penniless in the public hospital, in 1889.

[6] Burke: *Extinct Peerages and Baronetcies.*

freeman: scholarship, architecture and commerce had come to glorious life and the Dark Ages were gone before the noblemen and yeomen returned from the last campaigns of the Hundred Years' War. The Villiers and others like them were beginning to speak dialect English instead of Norman French: and by the time Wat Tyler was killed at Smithfield and Wycliffe died in his bed at Lutterworth, English was the common tongue. To the contemporaries of Chaucer, French had become the language of the enemy. Now the Villiers no longer needed clerks to indite their letters for them; their children were taught to read and write and keep accounts. The medieval microcosm in which their lives were set was culturally and artistically developed, yet at the same time quite cut off from the factions of those great families who destroyed one another in the Yorkist-Lancastrian strife that ended on Bosworth Field.

The mighty structure of the Church had shaken a very little at the onslaught of Lollardry; Dissent seemed to have been crushed: it was not to reappear till some thirty-five years after Caxton's death. Renaissance culture began to colour English life. Then the Tudor finger was on England's pulse as she struggled and fought in the fevers of the Reformation; and one day, some time in the first half of the sixteenth century, the Villiers—by this time they had dropped the *de*—unobtrusively ceased to go to Mass and embraced the Protestant Faith, as became a sensible and businesslike family.

Edward, Mary, and then—Elizabeth; the unlucky children of Henry VIII made way for the most splendid, subtle and fortunate of their race; and round the throne the names of Percy, Talbot, Bolingbroke and Bohun seemed to have faded behind those of Russell, Cavendish, Cecil, Gresham and Coke. Still the Villiers were only sheriffs of the county; some time between Shakespeare's first arrival in London and Marlowe's death, Sir George Villiers succeeded his father in that office; but soon a light was to shoot down into the darkness and the forgotten plant that had taken root in the days of the Conqueror put forth a magnificent flower.

Sir George Villiers had married twice; there were two sons and three daughters by his first marriage and three sons and one daughter by his second.[7] In 1592 his second surviving son by his last wife was born at Brooksby. The Villiers were not a strikingly handsome family, though well set up and healthy; this boy,

[7] See genealogical tree. Appendix I.

George, was remarkable for his grace and beauty; his mother, the formidable and calculating Mary Beaumont of Cole Orton, who was a connection of her husband's first wife and had originally come to live in the house as her waiting gentlewoman, became aware of George's potentialities and decided to give him a different education from that of her other children; at the age of thirteen he was sent to the French Court, where he remained for some years; and so, while his brothers received the training provided for those whose parents were too poor to send them abroad George was instructed in fencing, dancing and foreign languages by the best masters in Europe. John Villiers grew up oafish and eccentric: Christopher was a sot; George returned to England an elegant, fascinating and sophisticated young man soon after Robert Carr, whom James had created Earl of Somerset, was tried, with his wife, for the murder of Sir Thomas Overbury.[8]

Young Mr. George Villiers appeared—one might almost say he was produced—at a tournament, where he attracted the attention of James I who took him back to Whitehall and made him his cup-bearer. Thenceforth his rise to fame and power was extremely rapid. In 1616 he was made Baron Whaddon of Bucks, some months later Viscount Villiers, then Earl, then Marquis of Buckingham. He also became Lord High Admiral, Member of the Privy Council, Chief Justice in Eyre, Master of the King's Bench Office, High Steward of Westminster, Constable of Windsor Castle and Chancellor of the University of Cambridge. In 1620 he married Katherine Manners, sole heiress of the Rutland family; on the lady's side at least, this was a love-match; she remained passionately devoted to Buckingham: he had the reputation of a kind husband and an indulgent father. At about this time Buckingham partially re-built and entirely redecorated York House in the Strand and Newhall at Chelmsford; both these palaces were made ready at vast speed and expense, and both were pulled down before the end of the seventeenth century.

In 1623 Buckingham accompanied the Prince of Wales incognito to Spain in order to arrange a marriage with the Infanta; in spite of the failure of this expedition he was created Duke of

---

[8] The Earl of Somerset and his wife, Frances Howard, formerly Lady Essex, were condemned to death, but their rank and his past favour with the King saved their lives. Lady Somerset died in 1632 and her husband in 1645. Philip Gibbs: *King's Favourite*. E. Cobbett: *State Trials*.

Buckingham, Earl of Coventry, Warden of the Cinque Ports and
Steward of the Manor of Hampton Court.[9] After James's death,
some eighteen months later, Buckingham was as omnipotent as
before; he preceded the Queen in the favour of Charles I, and
when they disagreed took the opportunity to tell her that " Queens
of England had had their heads lopped off before now."[10] All
this time he continued to add to his collection of pictures, statues
and tapestries, which was only excelled in range and splendour by
that of the King. From 1625–28 Buckingham made a series of
warring sorties in Europe, the last being that organised to help
the Huguenots against the armies of Cardinal Richelieu at La
Rochelle. The common people felt an extreme bitterness against
this toll of men and money, and the news of the Duke's
assassination was received with great rejoicings all over the
country.

3

The " favourite ", male or female, of a monarch is at a dis-
advantage from the beginning, in the matter of reputation. Such
men as Gaveston, Leicester and Robert Carr were, of course,
disliked, not so much for the way in which they used their influence,
as for the ease with which they had jumped into success, instead
of struggling upwards by means of hard work or intrigue as did
those whose attractions were of a more ordinary kind. Their
contemporaries seldom did justice to their abilities, if they had
any:[11] and the biographers and historians who wrote of them in
the years to come were often as biased, as blinded by love or hatred,
as those who knew them personally. The relationship between
James I and George Villiers has been hotly debated and contemptuously dismissed; one biographer devotes several pages to
the defence of James and Villiers against slander: another assumes
that an idolisation by an unattractive and ageing man of a handsome youth needs no explaining. But whatever may be the
technical rights and wrongs of the situation, they are not in fact

[9] It was on his return from Spain that Buckingham stayed once more at the French
Court and temporarily gained the affections of Anne of Austria. This celebrated romance
has no real importance in the lives of either of the protagonists. *Memoirs* of Mme de
Motteville.

[10] *Ibid*.

[11] One contemporary was an exception to this prejudice; for his character of the first
Duke of Buckingham, see Clarendon's *History*.

of the slightest interest or importance except in so far as they
affect the subject of this memoir.

The Second Duke of Buckingham[12] was to hear a quantity of
talk about the wonderful father who had been killed before he
was a year old, all of it contradictory, most of it rather tedious.
He was to hear—and to read—of the elder Buckingham as an
upstart, a hero, a villain, a chivalric knight, a profligate catamite,
a sorcerer, a great statesman and soldier, and a muddling ninny.
The curious mixture of James's attributes, his sentimental-paternal
streak, his doting fondness for his protégé's wife and children, the
yearning admiration of the intellectual and neurotic for the man
of action—these were to be taken as much for granted by the
inheritor of the first Duke's titles and possessions as the extravagantly adoring letters and poems written by the King to his
" Steenie " and the stories of James's predilection for young and
beautiful men. The Howards' attempt to run Henry Monson for
the royal favour is one example of practical catering for the tastes
of the sovereign. As soon as Robert Carr fell the Howards set to
work on their cousin, " tricking and pranking him up, washing
his face every day with pousset-curd." The poor young man
endured these attentions for nothing; before his grooming was
half-way through, James's eye had fallen on George Villiers—
and so no more of Henry Monson . . .[13]

4

Two months after her husband's death a grant was drawn up,
giving the Duchess of Buckingham the wardship of ." the body
and lands, as of His Majesty's free gift ", of her elder son. It is
therefore probable that the little Duke of Buckingham was not
actually adopted by Charles I till his nursery days were over, that
is, shortly after his third or fourth birthday; he was two years
older than the Prince of Wales, whose tutors and governors he
was to share.[14]

[12] There had been Dukes and Earls of Buckingham in England ever since the time
of William Rufus. (See *Complete Peerage*.) The last Duke, Shakespeare's " poor Edward
Bohun ", whose grandfather, great-grandfather and great-great-grandfather all perished
in the Wars of the Roses, was beheaded at the instigation of Cardinal Wolsey in 1521. No
doubt James selected the title, in spite of its sinister associations, because of its connection
with an earlier Duke, Humphrey, who was the great-nephew of Edward III. For the
purposes of this narration, the subject is referred to as the Second, and his father as the
First, Duke of Buckingham.
[13] Sir Dudley Carleton : *Correspondence.*   [14] Brian Fairfax.

Thenceforth the gorgeous intricacies of Greenwich, Theobalds, Nonsuch, Hampton Court and Whitehall became his background; and court life, with all that it implied of formality, ritual and elaboration, took the place of contact with the world of every day. The bending knee, the hushed speech, the highly polished manners and graceful smoothness required for daily intercourse with majesty were thinly spread over a gruelling routine of lessons, religion, exquisitely artificial entertainments and violent exercise. The combination of such an upbringing and such antecedents was unusual. For twelve years the clever child of a murdered celebrity worked and played and appeared in public with a contemporary only a little less intelligent than himself whom he treated, except on occasions of ceremony, as an equal, but who would one day be King of England. In the royal family but not of it, of the aristocracy but not with it, Buckingham was doubly isolated and doubly orphaned. His mother remained on friendly terms with Charles I, but how much she saw of her children after her marriage to Lord Antrim in 1635 is not known.[15]

The directors of the Prince's early education—the Duke of Newcastle and Brian Duppa, Bishop of Chichester—were supposed to treat the two boys as brothers.[16] But did they? The sacrosanctity of monarchs was still inviolate when Buckingham was a child; and it is hard to believe that he did not feel as well as know that there was a confusing difference between the heir of the little, stammering King and the son of the great Duke, whom people still spoke of as a miracle, or a monster.

A portrait by Van Dyck of the royal children shows the future Charles II as a dark, plump little boy in a rose-coloured tunic and knee breeches; he stands squarely in the middle of the group of five,[17] his hand on the head of a huge mastiff, looking straight out of the canvas. His mouth is pouting and obstinate, his expression shrewd; his fringed hair falls lightly over a collar of point lace. He looks stolidly pleased with himself, perhaps because he has just reached the stage of grown-up dress, while his brother James is still in the bonnet and robe of babyhood. It is obvious that such a

[15] In a poem written many years later, Buckingham spoke of his mother as having been " whor'd " by the Earl of Antrim. This seems unfair, to say the least.

[16] Brian Fairfax.

[17] *Charles II*: (1630–1685). *Mary*: afterwards Princess of Orange (1631–1660). *James*: (Duke of York and afterwards James II) (1633–1701). *Elizabeth*: (1635–1650). *Anne*, who died in infancy. These were followed by: *Henry*: Duke of Gloucester (1641–1660), *Henrietta Anne*: afterwards Duchess of Orléans (1644–1670).

child might be difficult to rule; but his governors were, on the whole, well chosen.

Brian Duppa was appointed tutor to the Prince of Wales when Buckingham was six years old. He was a scholarly, serious-minded man of great strength of character and sweetness of disposition, who succeeded in attracting and holding Charles's affection. William Cavendish, Duke of Newcastle, installed as Governor at the age of forty-six, was also a serious but more sophisticated and worldly individual, in fact what is now known as the best type of Cavalier. He was an authority on horsemanship and horse-breeding, wrote plays and poems and translated Molière, corresponded with Hobbes and occupied himself with science and philosophy. Clarendon describes him as "a very fine gentleman".[18]

In view of his later development, it seems clear that it was on the Duke rather than on the Bishop that Buckingham inclined to model himself. Newcastle was witty as well as dignified, quick in repartee but slow to speak of himself; his adoring wife describes him as "courtly, civil, easy and free".[19] All these qualities would have been apparent and attractive to an intelligent child of nine. Three years later Newcastle was succeeded by William Seymour, Marquess of Hertford, a studious, elderly man, not nearly so well suited to the companionship of four vigorous high-spirited boys—for James, Duke of York, and Francis Villiers made up the quartette of pupils. These were the directors. There were also, among others, a French writing-master and a French tutor, an archery instructor, fencing and dancing masters, and Mrs. Wyndham, the Prince of Wales's old nurse. But the court of Charles I must be observed primarily through the characters and personalities of the King and Queen.

At the time of Buckingham's adoption by her husband, Henrietta Maria, sixth child and third daughter of Henri IV and Marie de Medici, was a lovely wilful creature of eighteen, distinguished more for her singing and dancing and her exquisite taste in dress than for stateliness, learning or elevated principles. Vitality and robust health were to help her during the miserable years ahead; when Buckingham first knew her she was proud of being the only Queen Consort of Great Britain who had refused

---

18 *History.*
19 *The Duke and Duchess of Newcastle*: by Margaret, Duchess of Newcastle. First published, 1667. Newcastle did not receive his dukedom till 1664.

to be crowned in Westminster Abbey and, paradoxically, prouder still of being the daughter of that King who considered Paris worth a mass.[20] Affectionate, hot-tempered and unscrupulous, she was to change for the better and to command the admiration of her bitterest enemies by showing an intrepidity and firmness which her delicate beauty seemed to deny. A fanatic in religion and a medievalist in politics, with no capacity to estimate, far less understand the feelings of others, she had neither the wit nor the intention to explore the vagaries of the English character; graceful, variable, spoilt, she could charm when she chose, which was not always; but like most pretty young women, she took pleasure in the society of attractive children, and it is certain that she was very kind to Buckingham and his brother.

From her husband the boy was to observe what regal dignity could be and, in later years, to learn how a majestic simplicity had masked the tortuous machinations of an obdurate and unteachable spirit. In the portraits of Van Dyck Charles I is nothing if not kingly; but the long nose with its pink-rimmed nostrils, the flaccid hands, the high calm forehead, the melancholy eyes, make him a baffling, pathetic figure, a person of promise rather than of achievement. He has the face of a man who in different circumstances might be a second-rate painter or a fairly reputable critic, but not an administrator or a leader, or even an able private individual. The traditional rites which accompanied christenings, marriages and other celebrations seem to have been unlit by any informality or touch of humour on his part, although on his own marriage night he had arbitrarily dispensed with some of the usual customs.[21] He graced all ceremonies—even that final ghastly scene outside the Banqueting Hall on a bitter January afternoon of 1649—but he was incapable of breaking the even flow of antique ritual with such joking comments and personal allusions as twenty years later were to make his eldest son an original and engaging figure.

So Buckingham was trained to the exigencies of prolonged and rigid ceremonial in throne-room, chapel and council-chamber. He became sufficiently accustomed to appearing in public to ignore the aspect or the mood of a staring crowd, and the resultant unself-consciousness and indifference were, in the long run, extremely harmful. To be one of the show figures in a pageant, that passes and re-passes before the popular vision like a stage army, is to acquire an imperturbability in which arrogance may have a share; if these characteristics are combined with a capacity for self-discipline, all is well; but Buckingham never achieved this combination, because, as a child, he became a freak product, a hybrid of royalty and nobility, sliding between the rules and habits which governed both those above and those below him. While Newcastle and Duppa were training the Prince of Wales for monarchy they could only assume that the young Duke, his education finished and his marriage arranged, would take on the responsibilities of a wealthy and privileged nobleman, governing his estates and inclining to politics or not, as he chose. They could not know that he was to be deprived of almost all he possessed, outlawed and defeated in battle before he was twenty-one, nor that he was to lose, in hideous circumstances, the younger brother who had been his constant and most intimate companion. But it is improbable, even if there had been no Civil War and Buckingham had taken up the position for which he was destined at the usual age, instead of achieving it by a clever trick after an interval of nine hazardous years, that he would have slipped into the conventional rôle of aristocrat and land-owner. The removal from his own sphere and the separation from family life had been drastic and complete. He was the King's ward; his trustees were appointed and his daily life conformed to a pattern set by the King; the disadvantages of the position were to increase as childhood gave way to youth.

The standard of taste at the court of Charles I was very high and the expenditure required to keep it so enormous. The scenery and dresses of the masques and pastorals performed either by or for the ladies and gentlemen of the household ran into many thousands; the entertainments themselves sometimes lasted six or seven hours at a time.[22] While the interlocking inspirations of Ben Jonson and Inigo Jones, the poetry of Waller, the music of Orlando Gibbons and Henry Lawes combined to illumine the hours of pleasure, the need for frivolity and relaxation found an outlet in telling fortunes, practising the new French dances and watching the antics of the Queen's dwarfs. The diversions of Charles II's circle have been widely advertised and much deplored; though less innocent, they were certainly a good deal cheaper than those of his father's court. In more than one sense the years that Buckingham spent there belonged to a golden age; by the time he was thirteen those years were numbered.

[22] Strickland.

Again, if he had been brought up by his mother he would at least have had the chance to learn the administration of his income, for the Duchess seems to have managed the complications of her estate with efficiency and care;[23] stewards and secretaries would have been there to help and advise the young Duke when he came of age. But he grew up among those who had the wealth of a whole prosperous country from which to draw; and the result was that fantastic standard of living so much commented on during his later years.

Among the better-known courtiers there was only one whose destiny was ultimately linked with Buckingham's. By the time the powers of such dignitaries as Archbishop Laud and Thomas Wentworth had ceased to exist Edward Hyde had become, first Buckingham's most dangerous critic, and then his bitterest enemy. But during the Duke's childhood the future Lord Clarendon was just a clever young lawyer of whose abilities only a few could speak with precision; by the time he had grown to be the friend and adviser of Charles and Henrietta—"What does Ned Hyde think?" the King began to say during the period of the troubles in Scotland[24]—Buckingham had left the court, possibly without even a childish recollection of the man whose ruin he had helped to achieve. But Clarendon's memory was as remarkable as his detachment; forty years later he sat down to write his memoirs: and his description of the Duke reads as if he had known him always.[25]

Suddenly, the world, or a piece of it, was before Buckingham and his brother, and the artificial restraints of a semi-royal, semi-courtly existence fell away. They were sent to the University and entered Trinity College, Cambridge. For the first time in their lives they were treated like other gentlemen of birth and breeding. Rich, handsome, privileged, they looked beyond the confines of the college and saw England as a pleasant, slow-moving place, where nothing ever changed.

[23] The first Duke left £61,000 worth of debts.

[24] Clarendon: *Life.* Hyde did not become Earl of Clarendon till 1660: to avoid confusion he is referred to by this title throughout.

[25] *Ibid.*

CHAPTER TWO

I

THERE is a false air of familiarity about many of the personages of the seventeenth century; during the latter half of it they begin to speak as it were colloquially, to say " won't " and " can't " and, even on occasions of ceremony, to abjure the stateliness of phrase with which their ancestors are associated; and we are further deceived by those historians who place the fatal adjective " modern " at the beginning of this period. In fact, to recreate even a particle of the life of the age is like peering into a dark pool whose contents and colours change and shift and vanish as we stare down into the shadows with aching, bewildered eyes. One element only is conspicuous; the rock which surrounds the illusive water has been shaped by the tides and tempests of religious controversy; it is upon this that we must base all our conceptions: in these outlines the history of the time is enclosed: and in this respect the story of George Villiers, Second Duke of Buckingham, is unusual.

Seventy years before Buckingham was born, the fires of Smithfield were extinguished; but they had not been forgotten by a people whose lives were still set in an Elizabethan mould. Old beliefs, old customs died hard; and the peasant who had annually celebrated the destruction of King Philip's Armada and the confounding of Guy Fawkes took no risks with his entry into the next world, secretly fingering the crosses sewn inside his shirt, or muttering an Ave while the parson read to him from the Prayer Book of King James I.[1] The Catholic gentry paid their fines for recusancy and hoped for easier times: the untaught fumbling for the old faith persisted, diminishing with the years; and the plant of Puritanism continued to put forth odder and stronger growths, spreading upwards from the poor and illiterate to those great families who were to lead the Parliamentarian armies in the Civil War. But whether Catholic or Protestant, the whole life of the English people was rooted in pious belief; the slightest outward deviation from custom was as weighty as it was noticeable to those who embarked on religious discussion as on a thrilling and dangerous quest. For some, to read certain books, to follow certain

[1] David Mathew: *The Jacobean Age.*

ideas to their conclusion, was to experience an intellectual and spiritual excitement impossible to withstand, to which all practical considerations must give way; to others, the place-hunters and adventurers, this juggling with conscience and eternity became a gamble for success. No man or woman, however cultured, remarkable or advanced, had as yet conceived of a world in which all could worship as they chose. The number of atheists was so small as to be negligible.

The social hierarchy of the seventeenth century was even more closely knit than that of earlier generations, because the landowners not only continued to marry into the merchant class, but were now in the habit of apprenticing their younger sons to the masters of industry. The divisions of caste that prevailed on the continent were therefore unknown in England: and the unquestioning acceptance of the power and privilege of rank entailed little or no reverence for the ancient lineage of the pre-Reformation aristocracy. The *nouveaux riches* of the Tudors had established the precedent of the country gentleman taking his place at Court with the great functionaries and their hangers-on.[2]

In such a society the arrangement of advantageous marriages was a matter of acute and far-seeing negotiation: and the resultant attitudes of men towards women and of parents towards their children are not easily assessed, because, between the interstices of the machinery the threads of human passion and caprice have sprayed out and covered the workings, as a creeper covers the outlines of a building. There were those happy and devoted wives and mothers in whom the historians of the nineteenth century delighted—Mrs. Hutchinson, Lady Verney, the Duchess of Newcastle, Dorothy Osborne; there were an even greater number of humble-minded, more conventional women whose lives were the unseen background of their husbands'. There were also one or two horrible stories; that of the Villiers–Coke marriage is the aptest example.

The First Duke of Buckingham's elder brother, John Villiers, asked, or was instructed by his mother to ask, for the hand of Frances Coke, the daughter of the great Sir Edward, some time during the year 1617. Both the girl and her mother were violently set against the marriage; there was something odd about John Villiers, and Frances Coke had a horror of him. Sir Francis Bacon, because of his jealousy of the Villiers family, did his best to prevent

[2] Mathew.

the marriage: but presently he received orders from James 1 and
Buckingham to further it, and, most unwillingly, he proceeded to
do so. Meanwhile Sir Edward Coke had discovered the house in
which his wife and daughter had barricaded themselves, and taken
it by storm with a troop of soldiers. The arrangements for the
marriage of Frances Coke to John Villiers (recently created
Viscount Purbeck) were put in hand and the settlements drawn
up. Frances remained obdurate: she vowed she would not go
through with the ceremony. Her father thereupon tied her up to
a bed-post and whipped her till she could bear no more; her consent
thus extracted, she was dragged to the altar and the marriage
accomplished. Shortly afterwards the newly made Viscount went
off his head; a little later Lady Purbeck and Robert Howard, fifth
son of the Earl of Suffolk, were impeached for adultery. Their
son, Robert, abjured the titles of both Villiers and Howard and
called himself by his wife's name; but many years later still, when
the Second Duke of Buckingham died without issue, Robert's
grandson claimed and was finally allowed to assume the title of
Earl of Buckingham.[3]

2

While the women of the seventeenth century were treated as
inferiors in every class, their place in the system was securely
established; there were no unwanted females in this compact and
rigidly controlled organisation. From the great woman of pleasure
whose powers, under Charles II, were to achieve an international
and political range, to the poorest village girl, the functions of each
and all were pre-ordained and assured. The wives of the landed
gentry had perhaps the best of both worlds, in that their control
of the domestic side was absolute and extended over an enormous
field. In houses which were largely self-supporting, where
unguents, medicines, linen, woollen stuffs, food, drink, and a
certain quantity of interior decorations were produced under the
supervision of the mistress, her standing was that of Prime
Minister to the autocracy of her husband. The dowerless and the
unmarriageable women moved from one to another of their
relatives' houses, helping or temporarily taking the place of a
sister or a niece in times of sickness. It was in this way that the
Second Duke of Buckingham's grandmother began by being

[3] Burke: *Extinct Peerages and Baronetcies.*

an unpaid companion and ended as Countess of Buckingham in her own right[4] and one of the most influential figures in the kingdom.

Young gentlemen were sent to the Continent at fifteen or sixteen in parties of four or five, or escorted by a tutor, and visited France, Italy, the Low Countries, South Germany and Switzerland. This final polishing took from two to three years and was often accompanied by further training in mathematics, music and fencing.[5] In Rome, Padua, Brussels, Paris or Munich, English youths learned what freedom could be; they made love in halting French or Italian;[6] they began to compose their own songs and fought their first duels, not often very bloody or dangerous affairs, but useful from the point of view of experience. Under Charles II the duel became a serious and deadly business; the fashion of fighting three or four a side had been brought back from France, with fearful effect; five years of civil war, too, had much to do with the ability to slaughter or disfigure a stranger, an acquaintance, or even a friend, with indifference to the possibility of revenge on the part of his family.

To look back, from the barbarism of one age to that of another, is hopelessly confusing; it is better to resist comparisons between the English people of to-day and those of three hundred years ago and to attempt an assessment, first of the disabilities and then of the privileges of our Jacobean and Caroline ancestors. The era of duelling, witch-hunting, pillory, stocks and torture-chamber[7] was also one in which the educated classes possessed natural appreciation of the arts of everyday life and delight in music, literature and painting. Similarly, those who could neither read nor write sang and danced and told stories in the vigorous and unspoilt tradition of popular taste; the man who had never set foot outside his own parish was as excellent a craftsman, as skilled a decorator, within his limitations, as those who worked for Inigo Jones, Christopher Wren and, later, Sir John Vanbrugh, in the newly erected palaces of the nobility. The shell decorations, the embroidery, the plaster-work and the carvings of a number of nameless men and women testify to their care for everything that

---

[4] The second Lady Villiers was created Countess of Buckingham in 1617, twelve years after the death of her husband.

[5] Sir John Reresby: *Memoirs.*

[6] *Ibid.* Sir John describes how at the age of seventeen or so he had a " particular acquaintance " with a pretty nun in a Carmelite convent in Lyons.

[7] In England the last attempt to extract confession by torture was in 1640. It was used in Scotland till the middle of the eighteenth century.

was fine, pure, intricate, rich and bold in the accomplishment, as in the conception, of a design.

The attitude of the privileged classes towards their dependents and inferiors was that of the farmer towards his prize stock or of the manufacturer towards his expensive machinery; such material was not easily replaced and required care and fair usage. A contented tenantry paid best, and it was therefore customary to help the sick and support the aged and " deserving " poor, in theory at least; this benevolence did not, of course, cover the floating population of unemployable vagabonds and beggars, who endured all the severities of the law. The attitude of the " undeserving " worker is not recorded, unless in the expression of discontent and rebellion; we shall never know the percentage of those who, born to labour, found happiness in doing that and little else; but there were plenty of village celebrations and gaieties for those lucky enough to live under generous and responsible landlords.

3

Describing the early years of the reign of Charles I, Clarendon speaks of " the happiness of the times ", and after a slightly ironic comparison of Continental unrest with English quiet, adds:

" When these outworks "—Scotland and Ireland—" were thus fortified and adorn'd it was no wonder if *England* was thought secure with the advantages of its own climate; the Court in great plenty, or rather (which is the discredit of plenty) excess and luxury; the country rich, and which is more, fully enjoying the pleasure of its own wealth, and so the easier corrupted . . . Lastly, for a complement of all these blessings they were enjoyed by, and under the protection of a King, of the most harmless disposition, the most exemplary piety, the greatest sobriety, chastity and mercy, that any Prince hath been endowed with (God forgive those that have not been sensible of, and thankful for those endowments)."[8]

When he wrote these lines Clarendon was looking back at a lost paradise from the bitterness of exile and disgrace. Although the court was elegantly luxurious, the country at peace and the reputation of the King very high abroad, by 1629 Charles had already been defeated in his first violent quarrel with a Parliament that did not sit again for eleven years. Still the surface of the national life remained almost untouched by the tides beneath; the old order prevailed; and here and there, in unimportant items of Court news, the name of Villiers reappeared. In 1633 the Lady

[8] *History.*

Mary Villiers[9] bore the train of the Marchioness of Hamilton, who was deputising for the Queen of Bohemia at the christening of the Duke of York; the following year there was a scandal about Eleanor Villiers, cousin of Mary, George and Francis, and Harry Jermyn; but after a short absence the lady resumed her duties at Court.[10]   Then John Villiers, Viscount Purbeck, apparently restored to sanity, married again; and three years after that Mary Villiers became Duchess of Richmond and Lennox with a portion of twenty thousand pounds. The wedding took place in August and the celebrations were on a large scale. The King and Queen dined and slept at York House; a play was presented, then there was supper and then dancing; their Majesties spent the night in rooms decorated with the lions and peacocks of the Villiers and Manners families.[11]

Before Mary's brothers went up to Cambridge the Scottish armies had defeated Charles I; the expedition to enforce the Prayer Book was a failure and first score to the King's enemies at home. A year later the Earl of Strafford was impeached for acts of tyranny in Ireland and suppressions of the law and liberties of the English people. The Prince of Wales, a boy of eleven, was sent to plead for his father's supporter, but in vain; a furious crowd surrounded Whitehall, and preparations were made to defend it; but after twenty-four hours' indecision Charles signed the warrant and "black Tom Tyrant" perished on Tower Hill. The Earl of Essex, who shortly afterwards became the Commander-in-Chief of the Parliamentary Army, took his pipe out of his mouth to remark, "Stone dead hath no fellow," thus unconsciously paraphrasing the ethics of the new age.

So, in early youth, Buckingham and his playfellow Charles saw what force could do and what royalty was worth without an army behind it; but very soon the young Duke and his brother were too much occupied with a new life and new friends at Cambridge— Abraham Cowley was one and Martin Clifford another—to see that the sands were running out in the palace of the kindly, stiff little man who had given them a home. In 1641 Buckingham was made president of the Council at York—most of his property was in Yorkshire—but it was, of course, a nominal honour; no one was interested in the opinions of a boy of thirteen.

---

[9] Although she was at this time the widow of Lord Pembroke's heir, the Lady Mary is referred to by her maiden name until she married again.

[10] Henry Jermyn was subsequently created Lord St. Albans.   [11] Brian Fairfax.

C

CHAPTER THREE

I

IN 1633, that is, in his sixth year, George Villiers achieved the position of Matriculated Fellow-Commoner at Trinity College. He did not graduate, partly, of course, because he was too young and partly because, as a nobleman, he did not have to go through the usual process of qualifying for a degree—then a matter of seven years' study—but was simply given one.[1] It may be assumed that the brothers did not enter the University till approximately 1641–42, remaining there for rather less than two years. They were in charge of a tutor, whose duty it was to report on their progress to their trustees, the Earls of Rutland, Newcastle and Pembroke, and Sir Robert Pye. They were no longer children. In their own eyes, it is certain, they were men. What did they look like? How did they appear to their contemporaries?

The exquisite, melancholy little creatures of Van Dyck's first portrait[2] have grown into tall, striking, rather sulky youths; they no longer seem to be twins. George's hair is still very fair; his hands, fine, strong and narrow, have more character than those of his brother, whose marvellous beauty has the austere, cool remoteness only found in very young persons; we know nothing of this boy but that he was famous for his looks and, finally, for his physical courage. Francis Villiers in his white satin doublet and blue mantle, with his dark love-lock and serene oval face, had seven more years to live when Van Dyck painted him for the last time. In this portrait both brothers appear frigid and haughty; but that may be because they were bored, weary of standing still and looking at the steady hand and sharp glance of King Charles's favourite painter.[3]

The site of Trinity College had been occupied by monastic institutions of learning since the fourteenth century; the charter of Trinity proper was granted by Henry VIII; by the time George

[1] Trinity College admissions. By courtesy of the Librarian, Mr. H. M. Adams.

[2] Facing page 36.

[3] This picture, No. 3605 in the National Gallery, is inscribed on the canvas as the portrait of the sons of the Earl of Lenox [sic]. In an article in the Burlington Magazine (February, 1922) Sir Charles Holmes makes it almost certain that the sitters are in fact George and Francis Villiers, and the portrait is so described by the Keeper of the Gallery, who has courteously supplied this information.

and Francis Villiers arrived there the pre-Reformation buildings had been pulled down and the Elizabethan and Jacobean architecture prevailed; the college appeared much as it does now, with the outstanding exceptions of Wren's and Gibbons' additions. Trinity was self-supporting, and its buildings included a woodhouse, swan-house, barber's shop, hen-house, malt-chamber, spice-house, housekeeper's chamber, and powdered meat-house. There was a tennis court, but no bowling green till some years after the Villiers' departure. Dr. Thomas Comber was Master and the Earl of Suffolk Chancellor.[4]

In 1636 Parliament petitioned for University Reform, and Archbishop Laud endorsed a report outlining some of the defects in the administration of the University in general and Trinity College in particular; here, it seems, the students were " negligent of their Chapel " and " some Fellows . . . scarce see the inside of the Chapel twice in a year ". The quire-men also were " unskilful ", the congregation leant, sat or knelt, each according to his whim, and worst of all, there was a rumour that the places of the Fellows and Doctors were for sale.[5]

The Quadrennium and Triennium into which the seven years' course was divided did not concern George and Francis Villiers; but they sat under nine different lecturers, eight of whom taught and examined for an hour and a half every day. In addition, the *Lector Humanitatis sine Linguae Latinae* gave a weekly discourse on rhetoric, and the other lecturers taught mathematics, elementary logic and thereafter higher logic and metaphysics. The day began with chapel at five o'clock, followed by a homily from one of the Fellows; then there was breakfast, lectures and public " disputations " (by those students preparing for degrees), then dinner in Hall at midday. After that there were more declamations in chapel or the schools, chapel again at six and supper at seven. Then the young gentlemen were free to enjoy themselves in their tutor's chambers and to converse in English instead of the Latin, Greek or Hebrew used during the hours of learning. The vacations were yearly and the undergraduates who had not attained a degree confined to the precincts. Cock-fights, dancing, skittles, taverns, dogs, cards and dice were forbidden; whippings were frequent and given in public. But nothing could stop the undergraduates smoking; they smoked all over the college.[6]

[4] Willis and Clarke: *Architectural History of the University of Cambridge,* Vol. 2.
[5] Cooper: *Annals of Cambridge,* Vol. 3.
[6] J. B. Mullinger: *Cambridge Characteristics of the Seventeenth Century.*

2

Abraham Cowley, the son of a wealthy London grocer, was ten years older than Buckingham; when his future protector arrived at Trinity he had been there several years and had already published—at the age of twelve—a volume of poetry; this was followed by more verse, a comedy in English and another in Latin: now he was working on an epic poem, the *Davideis*. Brilliant, fantastic, learned, Cowley was the first intellectual with whom Buckingham came in contact, and the two began a friendship which ended only with Cowley's death. In later years the poet let fall a number of embittered aphorisms on the emptiness of riches and rank and the pleasures of a quiet life; but that was after he had experienced, in common with other ageing Royalists, the disillusionments of the Restoration. Cowley's contemporaries, Milton among them, considered him the equal of Spenser and Shakespeare; he became the most celebrated poet of his day;[8] but when he first met Buckingham his apotheosis had not been reached and the boy's enthusiasm for his work and desire for his company must have added a feeling of security to the consciousness of success. Few poets, however popular, could afford to do without patronage: and Cowley saw in the impressionable, imitative young Duke the patron of his dreams. Readers of both Buckingham's and Cowley's works know now who was the lucky one of the two. The Duke could do no more than obtain a competence for the poet, a poor reward after years of hard work, exile and risk: the poet bequeathed to his pupil much of his own discrimination and culture and taught him how to improve the taste and technique he had helped to foster. Buckingham's wit would have been little more than a legend if he had never written *The Rehearsal*: *The Rehearsal* would not have been written at all if he had never seen and enjoyed Cowley's *Guardian*, which after the Restoration was re-written and acted under the title of *The Cutter of Coleman Street*; both versions were much admired and neither, except as a literary curiosity, has survived, while *The Rehearsal* was performed all through the eighteenth and nineteenth centuries and again as lately as 1925.[9]

---

[8] Cowley's *Works*: Cambridge University Press. Samuel Johnson's *Lives of the Poets*. Sprat's *Life of Cowley*.
[9] Montague Summers: *The Theatre of Pepys*.

Martin Clifford, buffoon, scholar and eccentric, was another kind of model whose influence on Buckingham was perhaps less desirable. Clifford's writings are no longer read; in his day he was what we now call a character, and his disregard of convention made him a conspicuous and entertaining figure.[10] Then there was John Cleveland, fellow and tutor of St. John's, a satirist and lyric poet, who, writing primarily under the influence of Donne, yet contrived to infuse a topicality into his poems that made them extremely popular in his own day and incomprehensible in ours.[11]

All these men were established, confident and rather destructive and cynical in their outlook than idealistic or strait-laced. Their shadows were to become a part of Buckingham's intellectual background during the whole course of his life; the echoes of their mockery, the exaggeration and fantasy of their conceits, their easy, intimate way of attacking a subject, inform everything that he wrote and much that he said. It was, in some degree, their combined influences that made his jokes meaningless or shocking to some of his contemporaries, who neither understood nor cared to understand the mingling of oddities, whims and droll fancy of which his humour was composed.

On March Twenty-First, 1641, the eleven-year-old Prince of Wales visited Cambridge, arriving at Peterhouse between nine and ten in the morning; with him were the Duke of Buckingham, Lord Francis Villiers, the Duke of Richmond and Lennox, Brian Duppa, Henry Seymour and a number of other gentlemen. The Vice-Chancellor received the Prince with a speech and gave him the honorary degree of Master of Arts; Buckingham and his brother also received their degrees on this occasion, though Francis is not recorded as having obtained his till a year later.[12] Charles was presented with two pairs of gloves, one from the Vice-Chancellor and another from Dr. Comber, and a bible from Dr. Collins, the Provost of King's. Then the Prince visited King's Chapel, where it was observed that he ignored the multitude of staring undergraduates and said his prayers looking straight ahead of him instead of into his hat; but this unconventionality was considered rather charming than otherwise. Then he had dinner in Trinity Hall and afterwards saw Cowley's *Guardian*, which lasted three hours and was preceded by a prologue addressed to himself. Another play, Vincent's *Paria*, followed *The Guardian* and then

[10] M. Clifford: *A Treatise of Humane Reason.* Albertus Warren: *Apology.*
[11] John Cleveland: *Poems* (1911 edition).   [12] *Annals of Cambridge*, Vol. 3.

the young prince left to join his father at Newmarket. During the
whole of his visit Buckingham and Francis Villiers attended him
bareheaded.[13]

This was on Saturday. On Monday, the King, accompanied by
the Prince, stopped outside Trinity on his way back to London
and was greeted with shouts of " *Vivat Rex!* " followed by a very
long speech from the Vice-Chancellor, the presentation of a bible,
another speech from Dr. Comber, a visit to Trinity Chapel and St.
John's Library, and a "travelling banquet", or stand-up meal.
There were two more speeches, one from John Cleveland, who had
the tact to confine his expressions of loyalty to a short and formal
address. At the banquet the King ate only a little and gave the
Prince some sweetmeats to put in his pocket for the journey. Then
the attendant noblemen, Buckingham and Francis Villiers among
them, fell to: they finished up everything in a few minutes.[14]

King Charles was not, on the whole, very pleased with his visit.
The behaviour of the University officials and undergraduates was
unexceptionable; but the common people of the town, women
among them too, had presumed to follow his coach, "humbly and
earnestly entreating that he should return to his Parliament or they
should be undone".[15] The entreaties of the Cambridge townsfolk
echoed those of a great many people who foresaw and dreaded the
final rupture between the monarchy and Parliament. Three
months after the King's visit to Trinity all serious attempts at
reconciliation on his side and of belief in his good intentions on
theirs were at an end. Parliament had been slowly forced to the
hateful conclusion that Charles was not fit to govern England; his
introduction of foreign troops into the seaports, his attempts to
impose the Prayer Book in Scotland and to employ lawyers,
bishops, soldiers and sailors as the instruments of monarchical
absolutism—in all these endeavours they saw the portents of continental dictatorship and the revival of hideous abuses. At the same
time the Royalist party perceived the abhorred spectre of anarchy
and ruin in the denial of the Divine Right by the fanatic, the
revolutionary and the crank; if such men as Prynne and Lilburne
were to go free, if the hatred and intolerance of Puritanism were
to assert themselves, then England would lose her greatness and
become degraded in her own eyes and those of the world. So the
crack widened, going down through all classes and types, splitting
even the solidarity of family life, before ever the fighting began;

13 Cooper.   14 *Ibid*.   15 *Ibid*.

when it did, the national genius for compromise seems to have reached its height: it became a common practice among fathers who had more than one son old enough to fight to send one to the Royalist and another to the Parliamentary army, so as to be on the right side when the end came. The Cavalier party believed that the war would be over in a few months and the Roundheads that the struggle would be prolonged. Neither army was large or well equipped and press-gang methods obtained on both sides.

On August the Ninth, 1642, the King proclaimed the Earl of Essex and all his followers traitors to the kingdom and a fortnight later convened his armies at Nottingham. The Prince of Wales, the nine-year-old Duke of York and the King's nephews, Rupert and Maurice, sons of the Queen of Bohemia, formed part of the group round their leader. Sir Edmund Verney, Knight-Marshal of England, carried the royal standard. The trumpets sounded and the herald stepped forward and began to read the King's proclamation. Charles, meticulous even in moments of drama and tragedy, took the parchment from him and scribbled in some corrections with a shaky hand. When the herald came to the altered messages he could not make out the words and so finished his reading in an uncertain, almost inaudible voice. A few weeks later the Civil War began.

3

It was very difficult for George and Francis Villiers to concentrate on their education. Cambridge was to become a keypoint in the war, and both sides were aware of this, with the result that in June, 1642, the authorities were ordered to collect money for the King and in the following month instructed to organise the defence of the city against him.[16] Oliver Cromwell, who had been elected member for Huntingdon two years before, kept a sharp eye on the dons: they were in fact planning to melt down the College plate for the King; Cromwell intervened just in time and imprisoned in the Tower those concerned in the scheme.[17] In September, 1642, both Houses of Parliament ordered the town and University to recruit men for the Roundhead armies: a month later Charles defeated Essex at Edgehill, and Prince Rupert, " that diabolical cavalier ", became the hero of the Royalist soldiers. In

16 Cooper.   17 *Ibid*.

February of the following year, shortly after Brereton and Sir
Thomas Fairfax had beaten the Cavaliers in the North, the
Cambridge undergraduates were excused from wearing surplices
or observing the "ceremonies" in the Chapel.[18] Then a thousand
Parliamentarian troops were quartered in the town, and many of
them began to destroy the statuary, glass and carving in the
colleges; the example had already been set by those members of
the Commons' committee who had torn down the images in the
Queen's chapel and thrown a Rubens, valued at five hundred
pounds, into the Thames.

Cambridge was in an uproar. There was fighting in the streets;
and the young Villiers' tutor was in a frenzy. But their guardians
were absorbed in duties of national import, their mother was in
Ireland and the officials of Trinity distracted by overwork and
the depredations of the Roundhead garrison.

It is not difficult to picture the state of mind of two energetic,
high-spirited boys, most of whose friends and relatives were
Cavaliers, who instinctively associated themselves with the interests
of the Stuarts and who were beginning to cap verses with and
share the politics of some of the most popular Royalist intellectuals of the day. The little princes, their juniors, were already
in the field: Rupert and Maurice were leading the King's armies
to victory—their cavalry charges were beginning to be talked
about; every day George and Francis woke up to hear that
another of their companions had run away to join the army. In
common with hundreds of other young men all over England
they believed themselves to have been born for this moment; the
years of training in horsemanship and fencing had prepared them
for the cruellest, most exciting, most horrible sport of all. The
hours of droning lectures and bored attendance on royalty while
dons sandwiched their presentations of bibles and gloves between
wedges of Latin oratory, the taboos of University life, were not
for them. They slipped away to join King Charles at Oxford and
were with Rupert and Lord Gerard at the storming of Lichfield
Close on April the Tenth, 1643. Here the Prince, with a force of
twelve hundred horse and seven hundred foot, had no difficulty
in taking the town; but the Close was heavily fortified, and two
mines were sprung before a successful assault could be made.
A few days later the Villiers' uncle, Lord Denbigh, was mortally
wounded.[19]

[18] Cooper.   [19] Clarendon: *History*.

Buckingham was fifteen and Francis Villiers a year younger when they first drew their swords against their own people. They were in magnificent health, entirely sure of themselves and wildly exhilarated at their escape from the tedium and irritation of University discipline. What their tutor felt, what despairing and expostulatory letters he sent off to his pupils and to their relatives and guardians, is not known. The Duchess of Buckingham upbraided Gerard; "but he told her," says Brian Fairfax, "that it was their own inclination, and the more danger the more honour."[20]

As soon as they heard that Buckingham and his brother had joined the Royalists, Parliament sequestered their estates. At this point their relatives set to work to put an end to their escapade. Such fiery young gentlemen were best out of the country, and it was agreed that they should be sent abroad to finish their education. Everyone assumed that by the time this was done the struggle would be over. The Earl of Northumberland was made responsible for them; a new tutor was appointed, William Aylesbury, brother-in-law of Edward Hyde, and George and Francis left England in his charge. They were not to return for nearly four years.

The remarkable mildness with which Parliament treated the young Villiers was characteristic of the spirit in which the Civil War began. Neither party was as yet desperate or weary enough to apply the merciless methods by which a war must be concluded; and many English gentlemen were resigning themselves to violence with a feeling of inevitability and consideration for the other side. This may be described as the old-fashioned, amateur's attitude, soon to pass away. Part of a letter from Sir William Waller to Sir Ralph Hopton expresses this chivalrous and anachronistic point of view.

"My affections to you are so unchangeable that hostility itself cannot violate my friendship. We are both upon the stage, and we must act the parts assigned to us in this tragedy. Let us do it in a way of honour and without personal animosities."

Both upon the stage . . . this was written in the summer of 1642. Neither the writer nor the recipient can have dreamed how pitiably, ludicrously inept such sentiments were to appear, both to the victorious and the defeated professional militarists of 1649, who perceived war as a matter of science and cunning, and who

[20] *Life.*

associated the playhouse with siege and rally and sortie rather
than with the amenities of a leisured existence.[21]

The England that Buckingham left in the summer of 1643
was still the England of king and courtier, of squire and peasant,
manor-house and preserve and common land; he was to return to
find it the England of stronghold and entrenchment, of burnt-out
villages and smouldering towns, of New Model soldiers and
reckless, hopeless, stubborn Cavaliers.

4

The usual route to the Continent was that via Dunkirk, Bruges,
Frankfort and the Rhine, then from Munich to Innsbruck, the
Brenner Pass and Trentino to Venice, where travellers of
Buckingham's kind generally stayed for a year before going any
further. Another way led from Paris along the Loire to Lyons
and Marseilles and by felucca to Genoa from Cannes, then a
fishing village. This route sometimes branched off from Lyons
to Chambéry and the Mont Cenis to Turin, where many young
gentlemen stopped for another year at the University.[22] Brian
Fairfax says that George and Francis Villiers stayed principally
in Florence and Rome. It is unlikely that they missed Paris on
their journey out: they were there on the way back in 1646. So
it may be concluded that they journeyed down the Loire and
stopped at Genoa before proceeding to Florence. Here, says Brian
Fairfax, " they lived in as great state as some of those sovereign
princes." In fact they were treated as became the sons of the
man whom the courts of Europe had once delighted to honour;
their status was that of guests rather than tourists. Here was
another twist to an unusual upbringing. From Whitehall to
Cambridge, from Cambridge to the army, from the army to the
court of the Medici—could the Earl of Northumberland really
have known to what influences he was subjecting this pair of
impressionable young men?

Ferdinando II, fifth Grand Duke of Tuscany, was a clever,
good-humoured, indolent man of thirty-three when the Villiers
came to Florence; the protector of Galileo,[23] the patron of artists,

---

[21] The " ordinance against stage-plays " was effected on September 2nd, 1642.
[22] L. Collison-Morley: *Italy after the Renaissance*.
[23] Galileo, sentenced by the Inquisition to retirement in Florence, died in 1642 and
was buried, at Ferdinando's command, in the chapel of the Medici.

scientists and intellectuals from all over Europe, he had inherited none of his Hapsburg mother's arrogance and bigotry, and his reign of fifty years covered one of the most peaceful periods of Tuscan history. Ferdinando was an extremely popular and economical ruler who managed to steer a skilful course between the belligerent powers of France, Austria and Spain, with the result that life in Florence achieved an elegance, sophistication and gaiety unknown in other European capitals. With his brothers the Grand Duke divided the administration of the kingdom, himself founding and presiding over the experimental, philosophic and mathematical societies, while he left the management of finance to one brother, the army to another, the arts to a third.[24]

No palace in Europe could compare with the vast magnificence of the Pitti; and though English gentlemen were pained at Ferdinando's frugal habit of selling his superfluous wine and advertising it by a wicker bottle hanging from the palace gates,[25] they had to admit that no other prince entertained on such a scale of fantasy, surprise and elaboration. The chariot-races, the fire-works, the illuminated barges in which violinists and *castrati* scraped and carolled their way along the Arno, the torch-lit tournaments, the mythological masques, the banquets, the pun-ning dissertations and improvised rhyming contests on the bridge of Santa Trinità, the hurry and profusion of daily life—these burst upon the young Villiers in a few days and nights of display and celebration.

The artists, San Giovanni, Lorenzo Lippi, Lucca Giordano— even the more orthodox Sustermans who painted the Medici family—took pleasure in exuberance, intricacy and sadistic humour: Giovanni covered the walls of Pratolino with a picture of nymphs castrating the Duke's favourite dwarf. Practical joking, noise, grossness, repartee and a remarkable disregard for their results combined in heightening the pace and fermenting the excitement of fresh invention. The correct, the conventional, the chaste in the persons of the Grand Duchess Vittoria and her mother-in-law the Archduchess Maria Maddalena were mocked or ignored. When his mother in shuddering horror gave the Grand Duke a paper on which were written the names of those young men whose versatile lusts had become common knowledge, he merely remarked that one title was missing from the list of powerful and

24 Harold Acton : *The Last of the Medici*.   Colonel Young : *The Medici*.
25 Evelyn's *Diary*.   Reresby.

distinguished noblemen, added his own in large capitals and threw the parchment in the fire. While treating his wife with great respect, Ferdinando continued to take his ease with a series of handsome pages; the Florentines shrugged their shoulders: the Grand Duchess, icy and impenetrable, had to shut her eyes to her husband's behaviour.[26]

These iconoclasms of outlook and custom were absorbed by Buckingham during what are now known as the formative years; in this society, that of Rome and, for a short time, Venice, he grew to manhood.

5

The Rome that Buckingham visited was ruled by the great Papal families of whom the most powerful were the Pamphili; Pope Innocent X was a member of this house, and he was governed by his sister-in-law, Donna Olympia Maldachini, a haughty and domineering widow in the fifties. Greedy, rugged, contemptuous, her face was one of the most familiar sights of the city, for every Cardinal and nobleman possessed her portrait and nearly every day she was seen leaving or entering the Vatican in a gilded litter. Her power was absolute and no office could be filled without her authority.[27]

Donna Olympia's Rome was a baroque city. The sinuous convolutions and dramatic effects of Bernini's genius were not confined to architecture and sculpture, but were also expressed in the witty and satirical plays he wrote for the Commedia dell'Arte. In the most successful of these, *I Due Teatri*, Bernini himself played the chief part as well as painting and designing the scenery and dresses. The informality, the easy, showy style of this production (in which a painted audience faced the real one) the divided stage, the topical cross-talk of the two principal actors, the beauty and elaboration of the final scene in which dancing peasants, gorgeously dressed riders and black velvet grooms carrying torches appeared by moonlight, followed by the figure of Death on a great ghostly skeleton of a horse, perfectly expressed the taste of the day, and may have been in Buckingham's mind when, many years later, he wrote the first draft of *The Rehearsal*.[28]

George and Francis Villiers entering Rome with their

---

[26] Acton.   [27] Collison-Morley.   [28] *Ibid*

attendant armed horsemen and muleteers, a party of some sixty or seventy individuals, were joining a concourse of wealthy and distinguished travellers from all over the world. Ambassadors with unpronounceable names and peculiar faces were to be seen every afternoon in the ante-rooms of the Vatican and in the halls of the Cardinals—Russians, Africans, Japanese. Rome absorbed them as easily as it absorbed Sir Kenelm Digby, who had come to borrow money for Queen Henrietta Maria, John Evelyn or the young Villiers, and taught them to enjoy Italian cookery and imitate Italian manners, then the most admired and the most courteous in Europe.[29] Shortly after his arrival Buckingham became acquainted with Abraham Woodhead, an Oxford scholar who had been deprived of his fellowship because he was a Catholic. He taught the young Duke and his brother mathematics, returned home with them and spent the next few years under Buckingham's protection.[30] But Roman society had so much to offer that was more exciting than mathematics—operas, oratorios, antiquities, processions; the palaces of the Aldobrandini, the Barberini, the Chigi, the villas of Borghese and Frascati; Italian, French and Spanish plays, Bernini's angels looking like dancing-girls and his Virgins like pagan nymphs; the studios of Rosa, Reni, Poussin and Lorrain; coach-racing, football, fountains of a thousand jets, exotic birds, wild animals. The colour and richness of Rome were spread out as a banquet for the favoured; among these Buckingham's place was high: and he was no laggard at this or any other feast.

6

Buckingham did not return to London till the spring of 1647; he was in Paris in May, 1646, having spent some time in Venice and Geneva. From Venice William Aylesbury wrote to the Villiers' cousin, Lord Denbigh, "We have this day begun our journey, so you may the better compute how long it will be before my lords can wait on you in London"; and a few months later, on the way to Paris, he says, "I am sure you will not let them lie there longer than is necessary, especially now the Prince is there."

[29] Mrs. H. M. Vernon: *Italy: 1494–1790.* Albion: *Charles I and the Court of Rome.*
[30] F. H. Jesse: *Memoirs of the Court of England.*

The Prince of Wales reached Paris in June; and the reason for their elders not wishing the young men to spend too much time together was that they were doing their best to keep George and Francis out of the war: it would have been very natural for Charles to demand their services. Later on Parliament rewarded Denbigh and Aylesbury by giving back the Villiers their estates in 1647. At this time there was some talk of Buckingham marrying Northumberland's daughter, the Lady Elizabeth Percy, a child of eleven.

Bishop Burnet's account of Buckingham's reunion with his old playfellow indicates that the harassed Aylesbury did not have an easy time. According to Burnet, who wrote about him many years afterwards, Buckingham deliberately "corrupted" the Prince of Wales, he himself "having already got into all the vices and impieties of the age." Furthermore, says the Bishop, Buckingham crowned his work by "possessing the young Prince with very ill principles, both as to religion and morality . . . with a very mean opinion of his father, whose stiffness was with him a perpetual subject of raillery." Burnet then describes how Buckingham "brought" Thomas Hobbes to the Prince, "under the pretence of instructing him with mathematics, and he (Hobbes) laid before him his schemes both as to religion and politics, which made a deep and lasting impression on the King's mind, so that the main blame of the King's ill principles and bad morals was owing to the Duke of Buckingham."[31]

This solemn and absurdly inconsequent denunciation is characteristic of Burnet, who was at the same time fascinated by Buckingham during his later years and bitterly ashamed of having been intimate with a person who had thrown away all his chances and fallen from favour. A brilliant writer and preacher, Burnet was also the self-righteous, hypocritical prig who has been caricatured all through literature from Shakespeare's Angelo to Miss Yonge's Philip Morville; the unctuous triumph with which he accounts for the "immorality" of a youth of seventeen by the influence of another of nineteen is typical of his repellently censorious attitude.

It is clear that Buckingham and Charles renewed their friendship in circumstances where the interest excited by the handsome face of the one and the unfortunate position of the other made the amenities of Paris as inescapable as they were absorbing. They

[31] G. Burnet: *History of My Own Time.* Ed. O. Airy.

began to sow their wild oats at the usual age and in the lavish style
that characterised them both: the difference between them and
some of their contemporaries was that they went on sowing them
till long past middle life ... At this time, Charles, never backward
in the ways of love, although mentally less developed than
Buckingham, was soon to be the father of a son (afterwards known
as James de la Cloche) by an unknown girl in Jersey.[32] It is
unlikely that his and Buckingham's jokes about the cold rectitude
and ungracious manner of Charles I only began during their
time in Paris; they could not fail to be renewed by the letters which
the Prince received from his father; pathetic to those who know
the King's destiny, their mingled peremptoriness and severity must
have been trying to a boy just beginning to realise what freedom
could be. Young people naturally tend to be cold and self-absorbed:
and the responsibilities and shocks of the Civil War—in which,
at the age of fifteen, he had been assigned the position of
Lieutenant-General of the Western Association—had already
caused Charles to acquire an apparently heartless imperturbability.
He had had time to think over and take in a number of unpleasant
and surprising facts: and he was never, all his life, to forget the
moment three years back when sitting with his little brother at
the roadside just beyond Gloucester, he heard the younger boy
ask innocently, "When are we to go home?" and his father's
frightening answer, "We have no home to go to."

There was at this time no alternative in Charles's case between
worrying himself sick and forgetting his troubles in the obvious
manner; that he chose this course rather than one more sensitive
and heroic had nothing to do with Buckingham's influence.

As to Hobbes, Burnet chose to forget that he had been the
friend of the boys' first governor and was one of the most sought-
after intellectuals then living in France. All their lives Charles
and Buckingham delighted in the company of clever men: and if
it really was the Duke who brought the philosopher and his future
King together, he did well. Not many young men could boast of
having had the author of *Leviathan* for a tutor. The tall figure of
Thomas Hobbes, with his ink-horn and notebook, was a welcome
sight to the young Prince; after the Restoration he gave Hobbes
a pension and their friendship lasted till the older man's death.

It was natural that Burnet and others like him should dis-

[32] O. Airy: *Charles II.* Sir John Pollock: *The Popish Plot.* D. Ogg: *England in
the Reign of Charles II.*

approve. Hobbes was suspected of atheism and disloyalty to the
Royalist cause; worst of all, his remedy for the political and social
evils of the time embodied the subordination of the ecclesiastical
power. His theory of absolutism—a " social compact " between
subjects and sovereign—savoured of foreign dictatorship, and his
witty, paradoxical yet lucid manner of writing was not at all to
Burnet's taste. Hobbes's influence over his pupil was good; he
taught him to think rapidly and express himself clearly. The
brand of absolutism formulated and desired by Charles in later
years had very little to do with the subtleties of Hobbes's
philosophy, for he never read *Leviathan*; he preferred Hobbes's
conversation to his writings.[33]

Meanwhile the Parliamentary Army, under the command of
Sir Thomas Fairfax, was rapidly getting possession of England.
Essex was dead; Prince Rupert had been deprived of his command: and a few weeks before the Villiers returned to York
House the Scots handed over the King to his enemies for the sum
of two hundred thousand pounds. At this time Cromwell's plan
was to place the King or one of his sons on the throne as a
constitutional monarch directed by a militarist oligarchy; he was
prevented from doing so by Charles himself, the Independents, and
the more extreme revolutionaries, of whom the Levellers now
seem the most interesting and remarkable section. Buckingham's
connection with this party was one of the incongruous and extraordinary elements in his career; it was effected later, when the
Levellers' influence had greatly diminished.

The story of the Levellers' movement is ironic and appealing.
With one unimportant exception their plans and ideals are now
realised by democracies all over the world, having first been put
into practice by the creators of the United States of America. The
value of their schemes is taken for granted and their prescriptions
for erring and unfortunate humanity adopted in all civilised
countries. In their own day they enjoyed a very moderate success
and are now, as a group, almost forgotten. They are called by
the name which they themselves rejected and they have sometimes been associated with the Diggers, whose theories contradicted theirs. The Diggers preached agrarian Communism,
while John Lilburne, the leader of the Levellers, constantly
asserted his belief in the private ownership of property.[34]

[33] Macaulay's *Essays*. T. Hobbes: *Leviathan* (Everyman ed.)
[34] Gardiner. T. C. Pease: *The Levellers' Movement*. John Lilburne: *Works*.

GEORGE AND FRANCIS VILLIERS AS CHILDREN
From the portrait by Van Dyck at Windsor Castle
Reproduced by gracious permission of H.M. The King

The Levellers' *Agreement of the People* consisted of four articles: (1) constituencies of equal size; (2) biennial Parliaments; (3) a "paramount law" to make, amend and repeal existing laws; and (4) manhood suffrage, irrespective of property. Their paramount law embodied free and universal education, trial by jury and the right of prisoners to counsel. It also advocated the abolition of ecclesiastical power and of imprisonment for debt and recommended the death penalty for murder and high treason only.

At the time of Buckingham's return to England, John Lilburne, a man of gentle birth and good education, was forty-three and had been Lieutenant-General of the Eastern Association for three years. He was known as free-born John and had been wounded, pilloried, whipped, fined and imprisoned without ceasing to defy while at the same time continuing to instruct his judges in his doctrines of democratic revolution and the return to Magna Carta. He wrote more than a hundred pamphlets, distributing one from the pillory, in another impeaching Cromwell and Ireton for high treason, in a third rejecting the authority of Charles I. Colonel Rainborough, one of his principal followers, declared that " the poorest He that is in England hath a life to live as the greatest He " and Lilburne amplified this with the statement that " all power is originally and essentially in the whole body of the people of this nation ", with the result that Cromwell eventually marked him down for destruction; but Lilburne's splendid courage, his qualities as an officer and the veneration he aroused in the common folk, the soldiers especially, made it impossible for the authorities either to confine or to punish him for long at a time. The tragedy of his position lay in the fact that the very people he was fighting for were at this time incapable of accepting the privileges he desired to give them. It was all very well for the crowds to sing,

> " And what, shall then honest John Lilburne die?
> Three score thousand will know the reason why."

The truth remained that " the poorest He that is in England " could not really conceive of an existence other than that he had accepted, complaining, for generations. There were ten thousand Levellers in London alone; but at this time they could neither organise nor be organised.

D

7

George and Francis Villiers found York House much as they had left it when going up to Cambridge nearly six years before. The Earl of Northumberland was living there and their father's old steward, Mr. Trayleman, was in charge of the household. This wonderful palace, with its Italian garden sloping down to the river and long gallery full of paintings, mirrors and statues, had just been the cause of a dispute between a Parliamentary Commission and the Villiers' guardian, over the pictures acquired by the First Duke of Buckingham that still covered its walls. These were valued at twelve thousand pounds and included nineteen Titians, seventeen Tintorettos, two Giorgione, thirteen Veronese, three Leonardo da Vinci, thirteen Rubens and three Raphaels, all of which the Commission proposed to sell.[35]

Northumberland, a judicious and deliberate nobleman, "the proudest man alive", according to Clarendon,[36] had been Lord High Admiral under Charles I and now acted for Parliament in the same capacity. Although he behaved more like a feudal potentate than a seventeenth-century aristocrat, he was honoured and trusted by all with whom he had to deal and at this juncture his vote in the House of Lords was of some moment to the Commission. He remained outwardly unaffected by their suggestions, merely pointing out that to take away the pictures round which the decoration of the rooms was planned was quite out of the question: the place would be unfit to live in: he would have to move, and should, of course, charge Parliament for his rent elsewhere. At this point an Independent member described a number of the pictures as lascivious and recommended that they should be destroyed. After a certain amount of grumbling and argument the Commission found it advisable to give in, and the Earl of Northumberland continued his serene and meditative tenancy of York House surrounded by some of the greatest masterpieces in the world.

Some time during the year 1647 Francis Villiers fell in love with Mrs. George Kirke, mother of that Colonel Percy Kirke who, nearly forty years later, achieved notoriety through the deeds of

[35] 4to Catalogue of the Curious Collection of Pictures of George Villiers, Duke of Buckingham, London 1758.
[36] History.

the regiment known as Kirke's Lambs. Mary Kirke was beautiful; at her marriage to a groom of the bed-chamber she had been given away by the King. Nothing else is known of her but that she was admired, free of her favours and, for a few months, the mistress of Francis Villiers.[37]

In the summer of 1648 the King was still a prisoner at Carisbrooke. The Prince of Wales had left Paris for the Hague, where he was staying with his sister, Mary of Orange. Shortly after their return from France, Buckingham and his brother had renewed their acquaintance with Henry Rich, Lord Holland, a friend and contemporary of their father. At the age of fifty-eight Holland still retained some measure of the good looks that had brought him the favour of James I. He was brave, charming and unreliable, " a very well-bred man and a fine gentleman in good times ", says Clarendon severely, " but too much desired to enjoy ease and plenty when the King had neither; and did think poverty the most unsupportable evil that could befall any man in this world ".[38]

Holland was, in fact, just the kind of dashing, superficial character likely to impress very young men; and because his record was shady (he had at one time acted for Parliament and was deeply distrusted by the King) he was all the more anxious to cut a figure and prove his loyalty. He had the self-confidence often found in the amateur soldier, and soon persuaded Buckingham and Francis Villiers that the three of them might turn the course of the war. He began to collect an army and ammunition; then, half-way through his preparations, he hesitated: was the risk too great after all? But—" the youth and warmth of the Duke of Buckingham and Lord Francis Villiers spurred him on."[39]

By July the Third, 1648, Holland, the Villiers and Lord Peterborough had collected an army of six hundred men. Buckingham was made General of the Horse; his plans had been confided to the Royalists who were waiting upon events overseas. William Aylesbury, then at St. Germains, received a letter beginning, " My Lord Duke of Buckingham hath many hearty wishers in France——" on the very day that his pupil left London.

For the first time in his career a light now falls on the tem-

---

[37] *Notes and Queries.* Mrs. Kirke's daughter, Mary, was the mistress of the Duke of York until the Duke of Monmouth displaced him.   [38] *History.*   [39] *Ibid.*

perament of Francis Villiers. Before leaving York House he put his affairs in order and paid some of his debts; there is no record of Buckingham having done anything of the kind.[40] Sanguine then and always—had he not come safely through the battle of Lichfield Close?—he set off without any fears for the future. But Francis gave a great dinner for Mary Kirke the night before he left London and presented her with a service of plate which had cost him a thousand pounds; when they said goodbye he asked for a lock of her hair: she sewed it into a piece of ribbon and hung it round his neck: and so they parted.[41]

8

Lord Holland took the precaution of engaging Dalbier, a Dutch mercenary who had served with the first Duke of Buckingham and been Quarter-Master-General to Essex during the Civil War, to organise and drill his men. On the evening of July the Fourth, the little army marched to Kingston where they ransacked the Parliamentary stables. Here Holland caused a proclamation, signed by Buckingham, Peterborough and himself, to be read to the people; it called for loyalty to the King and the return to absolute monarchy. Then they waited for the recruits who never came; Holland had told his supporters that five thousand at least would follow them from London. He moved on, and by the morning of the Sixth reached Reigate, held for the Parliament by Lord Monson.

By this time Parliament had been notified of these activities, and Holland, who was beginning to lose his nerve, withdrew to Dorking: so the afternoon and evening of the Sixth passed in gloom and uncertainty; Sir Michael Livesey, with a troop of Roundhead horse, was on Holland's trail and drove him back until he was forced to give battle near Surbiton Common.

Parliament followed Livesey's men with more troops from Windsor under Colonel Pretty. Then Holland perceived that all was lost and that there was nothing left to do but get to the coast and out of England with those who could not hide themselves from the Roundhead army. There was no time to consult his officers, who were scattered over the Common: the retreat was

---

[40] James II remarked that George and Francis Villiers were totally dissimilar, " both in face and in temper ". (Macpherson's *Memoirs of James II.*)
[41] Ludlow: *Memoirs.*

not organised: no orders were given. Buckingham, Peterborough and Holland cut their way out, hoping that their companions would follow.

No news of their movements reached Francis Villiers. He became aware that this was no longer a retreat, but a rout, when his horse was killed under him in a lane near the Common. He was then surrounded by a company of Roundheads who were intent on taking him prisoner.

It was nearly seven o'clock and long shadows striped the fields and hedges. Francis Villiers was wearing the breastplate and helmet that protected him from a frontal attack; he had his back against an oak which stood below the hedge. Now no one could come at him from behind and he had the advantage of those attacking from the side. The hours of fencing and mock duels with his brother and his friends, the years of training in sport and games, had made him quick and skilful: it was impossible to pierce his guard.

His opponents, enraged at this violent and stubborn display, called out to him to surrender: he refused. They could not waste any more time on the defiance of a headstrong and desperate youth: one of them instructed another to climb through the hedge and strike at him from the back of the tree.

The feeling of the sun-warmed trunk of the oak may have given Francis Villiers strength to go on. Reckless, mad with hatred and misery, perhaps hoping that even now some one might come to his help, he continued to resist the half-dozen troopers. Then his helmet was knocked off from behind. He staggered forward, to his death. His enemies closed round him. A few moments later they drew away to follow the pursuit. The body of Francis Villiers was left underneath the oak-tree. On his shattered breast hung a little square of shining ribbon.[42]

When the news of his death reached the Earl of Northumberland he gave orders that the corpse of his ward should be conveyed by water from Kingston to York House. This was done: and the body of the young Cavalier was oared down the weed-hung Thames and passed through the water-gate that Inigo Jones had built for his father and that has survived a greater holocaust than Francis Villiers could have dreamed of, even in the nightmare of his last moments alive.

---

[42] Ludlow. According to another contemporary historian Francis Villiers' body was submitted to " beastly usage " by his enemies. Walker's *History of Independency*.

He was buried in the Chapel of Henry VII in Westminster Abbey and lies there with his brother, his parents, and more than fifty members of that doomed and dangerous House for whom he died: among these are the young children of Charles I, James II and Queen Anne; and here rest Mary Queen of Scots, Charles II and Frances Teresa Stuart, afterwards Duchess of Richmond, whose beauty tempted Buckingham to one of his wildest political gambles and whose imperishable grace adorns our English pennies.

And, so capricious are the moods of human nature, there was greater mourning for this boy of nineteen than for any of those warriors and heroes who had preceded him into the halls of death. " A youth of rare beauty and comeliness of person ",[43] " the beautiful Francis Villiers ",[44] " the Lord Francis presuming perhaps that his beauty would have charmed the soldiers as it had Mrs. Kirke " (this from the contemptuous Ludlow) a number of doggerel elegies, an " F.V." roughly carved on the oak that had been his brief refuge and lastly, on his tomb in Latin, " The body of the illustrious Lord Francis Villiers, a most beautiful youth, the posthumous son of George, Duke of Buckingham, who in the twentieth year of his age, fighting valiantly for King Charles and his country, having nine honourable wounds, died the Seventh of July, 1648 "—these poor records and two portraits are all that have come down to us of Buckingham's younger brother.[45]

9

During the flight from Surbiton Common, Buckingham's helmet caught in the branches of a tree and he was nearly strangled; a young soldier, Tobias Rustat, turned back and saved him from this ignominious death.[46] Then the retreating army pressed on through Harrow towards St. Albans, reaching St. Neots on the evening of the Ninth. Here Holland collapsed and Buck-

[43] Clarendon: History.
[44] Aubrey. Brian Fairfax.
[45] Ludlow: Memoirs. Clarendon: History. John Aubrey. Manning and Bray's History of Surrey. Gardiner. Brian Fairfax.
[46] J. H. Jesse: Memoirs of the Court of England. Rustat later became Keeper of Hampton Court Palace and Yeoman of the Robes to Charles II: he was also the patron of Grinling Gibbons.

ingham interviewed the magistrates, to whom he read a slightly
modified version of the proclamation distributed at Kingston.
It ran:

" We come not hither to carry anything from you, but have given strict
order that neither officers nor soldiers take what is yours away. Nor are
our intentions to make a new war, but to rescue the kingdom from the
arbitrary power of the Committees of the several counties that labour to
continue a bloody war, to destroy you. Our resolution for peace is by a
well-settled government under our royal King Charles, and to bless God
that he hath made us as instruments to serve the King, the Parliament and
kingdom, in the way of peace."[47]

In the dark hours of the next morning Captain Scrope, now
leading the pursuit, burst into the little town. There was no time
to escape or to hide. Dalbier was killed. Peterborough got away:
Holland was captured beneath the archway of an inn.

A Roundhead officer, with his troop of horse, was still in the
process of cleaning up the town when he was told that Buckingham
and some of his followers were surrounded in the house where
they had spent the night. He made his way there. Suddenly he
was faced by another party of horsemen whose leader, a tall, fair
young man, charged into his troop. Before the Parliamentary
riders could draw together again, Buckingham's sword pierced
the body of their captain; he crashed down on to the cobbles,
dead: and the Duke shot through their ranks and rode on and
away beyond the shuttered windows and the staring people and
the dusty roads to the uplands, his Cavaliers streaming behind
him in the summer morning, breathless, desperate, free . . . There
was no more fighting in St. Neots that day.[48]

During the next fortnight nothing was heard of Buckingham;
it was said that he had fled to Lincolnshire: but all the time he
was hidden in London. At last news came that he had joined the
Prince of Wales at sea; Charles was very glad to see his friend
and received him with affection and sympathy. A few weeks later
Holland was executed, in spite of Fairfax's intervention, and the
Villiers' estates were sequestered again. Buckingham was alive
and unhurt: but he was ruined.

He never spoke of the brother he had lost. It would be facile
and pointless to draw upon the imagination for emotional results
of which there are no details or proofs. There is no way of finding
out if this silence was one of indifference or of rooted grief, or

[47] From a contemporary pamphlet in the British Museum.
[48] Clarendon's *History*. Brian Fairfax.

what affection, if any, existed between the brothers. They had always been together; if they had quarrelled or disliked one another they might conceivably have separated; that they did not separate shows unanimity of outlook, no more.

CHAPTER FOUR

I

THE exiled Royalists were divided into two camps, the Queen's, or the Louvrians, as the others called them, of whom Sir Harry Jermyn was the most influential, and that of the Hague, where the Prince of Wales set up a Council of which the principal members were Clarendon, Sir Edward Nicholas and Sir Francis Cottington, all elderly men. Nicholas had been Secretary to the Admiralty under Charles I and was a wise and moderate character, and Cottington, though he lacked Clarendon's wide range and Nicholas's experience, was equally conscientious and high-minded. These three rightly considered themselves experts in statecraft and were astonished and chagrined when the Prince included in the Council a group of much younger men—Robert Long, his private secretary,[1] the young Duke of Hamilton (whose elder brother was executed by Cromwell in February 1649), and Newcastle and Buckingham. Prince Rupert was one of the links between both exiled courts and the supporter of Montrose and Ormonde.[2] Montrose, with Hamilton and the Earl of Argyll, was responsible for the Royalist armies in Scotland; but he was at loggerheads with both Argyll and Hamilton, who were Presbyterians. Ormonde was Lord-Lieutenant of Ireland.

Montrose was thirty-six and Ormonde thirty-eight when they first visited Charles at the Hague; by tradition and temperament they inclined rather to the Clarendon-Nicholas-Cottington group than to the Buckingham-Hamilton-Newcastle faction. To the Scots contingent must be added a fifth member, John Maitland, Earl (afterwards Duke) of Lauderdale, an eccentric, uncouth but extremely sharp-witted nobleman, whom the young Buckingham was so foolish as to describe as "a man of blundering understanding".[3]

Of all these men Ormonde was the steadiest, Montrose the noblest and worst treated, Clarendon the nearest to genius, Argyll the most unscrupulous, and Buckingham, it must be owned, the oddest and most irritating. During these first months in Holland

---

[1] Younger son of Sir Walter Long of Draycot in Kent: created baronet in 1662.
[2] Ormonde was given his dukedom in 1660.   [3] Burnet.

the feuds that were to shadow their future intercourse were born in disagreement, impatience and strain; Buckingham never forgave Ormonde his dignified disapproval, nor Clarendon his sullen hostility, nor Charles his vacillations. Ormonde, who lost nearly a million pounds of which he ultimately recovered only thirty thousand, desired honour and peace, Clarendon orderliness and the old way of life, Buckingham power and ease. With reservations, and in profound disillusionment, all three were to achieve their ambitions: Montrose alone was spared the ambiguities and the disappointments of victory.

2

During the autumn of 1648 the Royalists, attempting conquest from Ireland, Scotland and the sea, were defeated by Cromwell. On September the Tenth of that year Lauderdale was received by the Prince of Wales on board *The Constant Reformation*, then at anchor in the Downs. With Charles were Rupert, Lord Gerard, Buckingham and several other noblemen. Lauderdale had come to suggest that Charles should join the Scots army and the young Prince "with great gallantry" accepted. Then came the conditions; these were that he should arrive unaccompanied by a chaplain and that from the moment of his setting foot on Scottish soil he should abandon the Prayer-Book which his father had tried to force on the Scots seven years before. By this time Charles had learnt how to temporise; he ignored the angry comments of Rupert and Gerard and proposed that he should first consult his father. Lauderdale shook his wild red head and replied that in that case he should return, without any answer at all, to those that sent him. There was a long and heated discussion in which Buckingham's point of view is not recorded but can be determined by subsequent events; two years later he and Henry Seymour[4] were the only English noblemen allowed to frequent Charles during his stay in Scotland; so it may be concluded that he advised, as on a later occasion, agreement to the Presbyterian demands, even to the exclusion of Montrose—whom the Presbyterians held in the greatest abhorrence—from the proposed expedition.

Charles finally agreed to the conditions, but the journey to Scotland did not take place just then, for the sailors were anxious

---

[4] Lord Beauchamp, known as "Harry Seymour", eldest son of the first Marquess of Hertford.

to give battle to the Earl of Warwick, who was in command of the Parliamentary ships in the Yarmouth Roads, and this was done. Lauderdale returned to Scotland and Charles reached Holland the next day. At the Hague the States-General agreed to vote him an allowance of a thousand guilders a day for ten days; after that he must shift for himself. His brother-in-law, the young Stadtholder, William II, suggested that Charles should spend the winter at the Hague as his guest, and the Prince thankfully accepted; he had no money to pay his soldiers and sailors or indeed to dress himself as became his station, so low were his funds.

Charles's fleet was reduced to eleven vessels, of which the Duke of York, a lad of fifteen, was the titular Admiral; when James escaped from England in May 1648 Charles withdrew this command from his brother on the perfectly reasonable grounds of his avoiding unnecessary risk; but James was bitterly chagrined by what seemed to him the spitefulness and jealousy of the precaution, and he and Charles remained on very bad terms until the Restoration.[5]

Shortly after Charles reached the Hague he fell in love with Lucy Walter, a " beautiful, bold, brown, insipid creature "[6] of nineteen who had followed her lover, Colonel Sidney, from London. Some time during the month of September 1648 she transferred her favours to the tall dark young Prince and she was still his mistress when two months later Charles fell ill of small-pox and had to put off his journey to Scotland again.[7]

Buckingham and Charles spent Christmas pleasantly enough with William and Mary of Orange and the long-exiled Palatine Stuarts, Rupert's family; Princess Sophia, especially, was delighted with Charles; but she got a little nervous when during a walk through the woods he told her that she was more beautiful than Mrs. Walter and the next day took care not to be left alone with her penniless cousin.[8]

During the last days of the Christmas festivities news came of the trial of Charles I. The Prince of Wales at once wrote to Fairfax, asking him to mediate; but times had changed since the Prince was last in England, and the great general could do nothing. Charles thereupon sent the Council of State a piece of paper on which was written his signature and nothing else, with an accom-

---

[5] E. Scott: *The King in Exile.*   [6] Evelyn.
[7] E. Scott. Lord George Scott: *Lucy Walter: Wife or Mistress?*
[8] *Memoirs* of the Electress Sophia.

panying letter saying that he would submit to any terms in return for his father's life.[9] There was no reply to this; and on the Fourth of February news reached the Hague that Charles I had been executed in the early afternoon of January the Thirtieth, 1649. Buckingham's twenty-first birthday fell on the same date as that of the King's death; it was well for him that he prided himself on his contempt for superstition.

The effect of the deed would seem to have been all in favour of the exiles, so great was the horror caused by the legalised murder of a king, although a few weeks afterwards both France and Holland were treating with Cromwell. A Dutch woman, hearing the news when in childbirth, died from shock;[10] Clarendon spent much of that day and many of its anniversaries in prayer and the composition of prayers: Montrose swooned away, and when he came to, burst into poetry. In March 1649 the English Parliament decreed that " Charles Stuart, James Duke of York and the Duke of Buckingham " were " banished as enemies and traitors, to die without mercy wherever they shall be found within the limits of this nation ".

3

It has been suggested that in view of his subsequent career Buckingham would have done better to share his brother's fate and that from the age of twenty onwards he achieved nothing but ridicule and dishonour.[11] Quite a good case can be concocted in support of this argument in spite of its sentimentality, to use no severer word. To die young and heroic is still considered suitable and desirable, even when the historical market is, so to speak, glutted with youth and heroism. No doubt Buckingham's escape and survival in the summer of 1648 were early examples of the bad taste for which he became celebrated in later life; and if this view is accepted we may the more conveniently branch off from it to the first recorded judgement of his character, given by Sir Edward Nicholas. "The Duke of Bucks is here still," he says, writing from the Hague, " ... Some of those about His Grace make him believe he is already wiser than his father. I wish he may be half so wise when he doubles his age. But, indeed, he hath wit enough, but I doubt he wants ballast."

---

[9] This paper is preserved in the Bodleian.   [10] Clarendon: *History*.
[11] Lady Burghclere: *George Villiers, Second Duke of Buckingham*. E. Scott.

Enough wit, according to seventeenth century standards, is sufficiently rare to justify some lingering interest in a young man who was so ill behaved as to avoid an early grave and the laurels that should have crowned the sacrifice of a life he generally contrived to enjoy, whatever the circumstances.

Buckingham's attitude, as expressed in a letter to William Aylesbury on April the Sixteenth, 1649, seems to disprove that he was at this time the self-seeking, gambling turn-coat from whom all right-minded readers and biographers naturally recoil. Aylesbury notes that Buckingham "wishes to compound for his estates in England, but such base submissions are required of him as he cannot submit to". Ten days later a Parliamentary agent in London wrote about Buckingham to a friend at Antwerp, saying that, "no oaths or mean things are required of the noble gent. if he will compound".

Buckingham did not compound. He declared his intention of following the Royalist fortunes into Ireland, where he hoped to have command of the Guards.

From August, 1648, to April, 1649, the Royalist outlook had been very black—though not so black as it was to become. During these months, Buckingham, in company with a number of other Cavaliers, could have returned to England without incurring more than temporary censure, and begun to lead the kind of life he had expected to lead, the kind of life that Northumberland, his guardian, Denbigh, his cousin, Richmond, his brother-in-law, and many other noblemen, still in some sort attached to the Royalist cause, were leading. Why did he not join them? Was his refusal to do so the result of his sanguine and arrogant temper? Or did he prefer to remain loyal, whatever the issue?

To attempt an assessment of Buckingham's character at this stage is to recall the succession of contrasts that made up his career until he reached Holland after the disaster of Kingston. He had never known family life, country life, or the responsibilities of his class; he left a palace for a college and a circle of esoteric intellectuals, only to break off that intercourse for the hardship and adventure of war, leaving these before he had had time to learn anything about them for the Courts of the Medici and of the Doges of Venice and the hospitality of the Papal families of Rome; returning once more to take up life in the station for which he had been born but not trained, he saw death and defeat, and escaped into exile with little but his looks and his wits to help him; it is not surprising that as disappointment, poverty and delay wore his endurance to the bone he sometimes used his powers ill and frequently incurred the disapproval of such men as Nicholas and Clarendon.

It was inevitable that those who had spent their youth in a lost world of security and responsibility should gaze in bewildered horror at the younger Cavaliers, who were growing up in an atmosphere of suspense, adventure and risk. Clarendon, Cottington and Nicholas were men of a steadier age and type whom misfortune could neither intimidate nor degrade, because their early years of orderly, hard-working English life were as a rock on which their convictions rested. Buckingham and his contemporaries mingled with cheats, spies and cut-throats as equals or at best as antagonists in a game which had to be played, while their elders used such creatures in deprecation and disgust, and then let them drop back into the gutters from which they came. Clarendon and Nicholas would work all day and half the night in stuffy or fireless rooms, thankful for one meal a day and a roof over their heads until the bad times were over; the younger men could not look so far ahead and snatched at pleasure with growing indifference and cynicism. Of one thing they were sure —if they ever did get back to England it would be to enjoy themselves for the rest of their lives. They did not dislike, in fact they favoured, soldiering; and keeping up appearances with an assortment of continental potentates who had to be flattered and cajoled was poor sport, but they did their best; what they could not stomach was the endless wearisome discussion at the Council table—were the Spaniards to be relied on? What did Mazarin's intercepted letters to Cromwell really mean? Were the Dutch likely to lend more money for ships and men this year? What was the news from Scotland, Ireland, the Louvre, London, Rome? It went on in a deadly grinding round until they grew weary, impatient, frantic with boredom and at last insupportable. " God help us," Nicholas burst out on one occasion, " When Hamilton, Mr. Long, Newcastle and Buckingham rule in Council!"

4

As soon as it was known that Buckingham had escaped into Holland, Richmond, Northumberland and Denbigh did their best to secure an act of indemnity for him; when this failed they were forced to accept the new régime and achieve such terms as they could for themselves; meanwhile the tradesmen were suing for Buckingham's goods in payment of his and his brother's debts —Francis Villiers having left several thousand pounds' worth of unpaid bills—and his relatives abandoned the young Duke to his financial difficulties.

Old Mr. Trayleman, still in charge of York House, was Buckingham's only friend in England. Aylesbury was in communication with him about the Duke's situation and the debts still owing in Paris; and Trayleman packed up and sent off sixteen chests of pictures and jewels from London to Amsterdam which the Dutch authorities allowed to go through the Customs duty free. This was in February, 1649; two months later one or two of these pictures and some of the agates in the first Duke's collection were pledged to a merchant in Antwerp for thirty thousand guilders.

At first, the store accumulated by his father seemed inexhaustible, and Buckingham's position was a much better one than that of his companions; this did not contribute to his popularity. But the train of followers that his position required, footmen, body-servants, grooms, a secretary—and a chaplain, whose duties were non-existent—had to be paid for; these expenses at length brought the Duke to the borderline of penury. Buckingham became anxious, then exasperated, and finally managed to ignore altogether the tedious question of his finances. Another exiled Cavalier, Lord Byron, suggested that Ormonde might be able to arrange something about the Duke's Irish property which was not yet under Parliamentary control. Buckingham and Byron were with the King in Paris when this was proposed, and the Duke said he would communicate with Ormonde: but he could not bring himself to sit down and write at length to a man with whom he had been unable to agree on matters of policy: and somehow, what with one thing and another, the business was never attended to . . . At last he was persuaded to make out a rough statement of his position in Ireland, and Byron wrote to Ormonde's secretary:

" This enclosed my Lord Duke of Buckingham hath desired me to send, which contains the condition of his estate in Ireland, being all for the present he is to rely upon . . . and he will take it for a great favour if you will please to acquaint my Lord Lieutenant with it and procure such ease for the tenants that His Grace may hope for some benefit out of it. He intended to have written to my Lord Lieutenant concerning this subject but was ashamed to burthen his first letter to him with a suit, and therefore enjoins me to that service. He is a person highly esteemed here [St. Germains] and notwithstanding his mother's follies (which no man censures more than he) a great admirer and honourer of my Lord Lieutenant's person . . ."

Poor Byron was doing his best; but his letter is that of a man who knows the weakness of his position. Buckingham should have written himself to Ormonde, instead of leaving his friend to say what an excellent fellow he was; this kind of letter is bound to irritate the recipient and do the sender nothing but harm.

Lady Antrim's "follies" consisted in her adherence to the Catholic faith and her inability to help her son; in October, 1649, she died, at Waterford. None of his relatives seemed to care what became of Buckingham's property: and he began to dislike his brother-in-law Richmond and his cousin Denbigh almost as much as the Parliamentary Commission who, in the following year, began to dispose of his English estates. Fairfax was given them all; he let some of the Duke's houses and properties to his friends and gave back the others; but he could not prevent Parliament settling four thousand a year on him, partly from Buckingham's estates and partly from those of the Marquess of Worcester. Meanwhile, Buckingham, with the violent irritation of the man who sees himself defrauded, determined to lay the blame nearer home: and he presently told the Council that he had some information "against" the Duke of Richmond; but this was all the revenge he could take on the brother-in-law who continued to live in easy circumstances while he struggled with creditors in Paris, Antwerp and the Hague.

5

In the year 1650, according to Burnet, "the man then in the greatest favour with the King was the Duke of Buckingham; he was . . . wholly turned to mirth and pleasure; he had the art of treating persons or things in a ridiculous manner beyond any man of the age . . ."

Burnet wrote these lines in the first decade of the eighteenth century, nearly fifty years after the period he describes and twenty years after Buckingham's death. Two hundred years later still, when Osmund Airy edited a new edition of the *History*, Burnet's alterations and erasures were all re-inserted, with the result that the second sentence of the passage quoted above runs as he first wrote it, thus:

" He was a man of noble appearance and of a most lovely wit, wholly turned to mirth and pleasure . . ."

The picture created by this, the original sentence, is one of gaiety and fascination; evidently Burnet thought so: and when he ran his pen through the flattering words he must have congratulated himself on his foresight and discretion, for in the eyes of this able divine seemliness counted higher than accuracy: and to have so praised the ruined and unrepentant reprobate who had once charmed him in spite of himself would have been as unsuitable as it was improper. But the brilliant creature that the nineteenth-century scholar released from the prison of Burnet's censorship lives now for ever in these unforgettable lines. Clarendon's description of Buckingham may here supplement Burnet's unwilling admiration:

" His quality and condescension, the pleasantness of his humour and conversation, the extravagance and sharpness of his wit, unrestrained by any modesty or religion, drew persons of all affections and inclinations to like his company . . ."[12]

It is difficult to consider such judgements as these without the bitterest regret. Buckingham had no Boswell; neither his friends nor his enemies, nor his boon companions, nor his mistresses, nor his wife, have left a single memento of his versatility in the most perishable of the arts. It is impossible, looking back across a gap of three hundred years, to recapture even the shadow of his allure or of the strange power he exercised over his critics and his foes. And there is fashion in wit, as in everything else; should we think Buckingham amusing, as we call it now, if we met him to-day? The very fact that little or nothing of his conversation has been preserved leads one to believe that his was the kind of humour expressed in gesture, look and intonation, and in his mastery of the unexpected, the inconsequent, the absurd. He was a clever mimic, too; but how uncomfortable mimicry can be if it is over-insistent or prolonged! Here again fashion must influence sensibility.

It remains to emphasise the cold disapproval of Burnet and the tragic resentment of Clarendon, their severity in matters of

[12] Clarendon: *Life*.

E

conduct, their narrowness of outlook on human affairs; yet both these men, in spite of all they knew and felt about Buckingham, show him as a person of irresistible attraction, splendid appearance and startling quickness of mind. How then must he have appeared to Charles II and others of his contemporaries when they were young men together, hopeful still, high-spirited, eager for pleasure? There is no answer but that which conjecture may provide.

6

In May, 1649, Clarendon and Cottington went to Madrid to get help for the invasion of England. Clarendon was determined that Charles should not be beholden to the Scots: the Dutch were equally determined that he should not stay on in Holland: and, at a hint from William of Orange, Charles and James went to Jersey, visiting Henrietta Maria on the way.

During the early months of 1650 Montrose visited all those courts in Europe from whom he hoped to get men and money for his master, while Ormonde prepared to meet Cromwell's armies in Ireland. When it became clear that neither were to be successful, Charles found himself in the unpleasant position of having to rely solely upon the Scots Covenanters, who were headed by Argyll and Hamilton, to gain his throne. The terms of the new Covenant comprised the installation of the Presbyterian faith throughout England, the abandonment by Charles of Ormonde and Montrose, the legality of the Scots Parliament and the establishment of penal laws against the Catholics.

No conditions could have been more odious, and for a long time Charles temporised and negotiated for better terms. But the Covenanters knew that they held the winning cards. " Now is the time," wrote one, " to pray that God the Lord will prevent the King with his tender mercies, for indeed he is brought very low. He has not bread both for himself and his servants, and betwixt him and his brother not one English shilling . . ."

When Henry Seymour returned from Ireland with the news of Ormonde's defeat at Drogheda and no word came from Montrose as to his progress on the Continent, Charles knew that he must either resign himself to exile for an indefinite number of years or betray the faith for which his father had died, destroy many of his followers' hopes and sacrifice two of his most valuable friends. Buckingham urged him to sign without further delay; so did Argyll, who offered him his daughter, the Lady Anne Campbell, in marriage; so did Lauderdale and Hamilton, who assured him that if he once appeared in Scotland, " he will find all his subjects compliant to his will ". Murray, Argyll's agent, added that Montrose would be spared and given " honourable employment " in Ireland.

Clarendon and Cottington were still in Spain; Nicholas was now excluded from the Council. Desperately Charles turned this way and that, trying to escape the Covenanters' toils; the Duke of Lorraine, the Queen of Sweden and even his brother-in-law of Orange advised him to sign. Buckingham made no secret of his exasperation at his master's dubious attitude; he swore that there was no dishonour, and added that Charles would be " in a capacity to recover all, in the end ".

Many historians have characterised this point of view as utterly contemptible and have cited Charles's behaviour and Buckingham's influence over it as examples of the blackest infamy and the most cynical indifference to the claims of conscience and principle. It must be remembered that the tenets of the age presupposed a disregard of scrupulous conduct as we understand it now and that the whole situation was, through the death of his father, forced on Charles who, at the age of nineteen, was only too ready to believe that he could adjust matters to everyone's —even Clarendon's—satisfaction, as soon as he was at the head of his armies in Scotland; and the Presbyterians themselves, as they showed by their conduct when he did arrive, were perfectly aware that Charles would dupe them if he could possibly manage it; in fact everybody's cards were on the table.

Furthermore, those who inveighed against the Covenant and abused Charles for signing it were non-combatants who put more trust in vague promises of mercenaries from Spain, Poland and Sweden, than did young men like Buckingham, who had fought against Cromwell's Ironsides and knew with what sort of adversary they had to deal. The Clarendon-Nicholas-Cottington attitude was: something must turn up, the collapse of the régime in England, a quixotic springing to arms from all over Europe to defeat " the beast, whom all the Kings of the earth do worship "[13] —while Buckingham and Argyll said that action must be taken

[13] Elizabeth of Bohemia.

before it was too late; delay was out of the question; as the weeks went by Royalists waiting in England were submitting to Parliamentary rule and their allies on the Continent losing interest in the cause. Before Oliver drew a steel ring round England they must strike: all the religious matters could be adjusted later. Such arguments are perhaps more easily understood by this generation than by those of the eighteenth and nineteenth centuries whose historians have set the fashion of condemning Charles's submission to his father's enemies.

The young King was in a state of deep distress. He hated the Presbyterians: but he was beginning to hate the insolence of the Dutch, the empty sympathy of the Swedes, the procrastination of the Spaniards, and the bland indifference of the French even more. He presented the Order of the Garter to Buckingham and later to Montrose almost as if he were filling in time with indifferent matters while his mind went over the ground again and again. Then he wrote a letter to Montrose, beginning:

" I will never fail in the effects of that friendship I have promised . . . and nothing that can happen to me shall make me consent anything to your prejudice . . ."

Fatal words from a Stuart to a servant of the crown—as Montrose read them did he remember the great Earl of Strafford and his single grim comment, " Put not your trust in princes "?

Presently the Covenanters were told that the army Montrose had collected was a large one, and with an alarm they could not conceal sent George Winram, Laird of Libberton, to lay their terms before the King. They met at Breda and Charles agreed to sign. Immediately this news was known a number of Royalists in England compounded with Parliament.

It was too late to turn back. Charles sent Montrose and Ormonde warning of his intentions, but Montrose did not receive the letter till after he landed in Scotland in April, 1650, with a much smaller army than had at first been expected; he was captured and hanged at Edinburgh a month later: no single word of reproach or blame escaped him. Meanwhile the Covenanters assured Charles that for his dealings with Montrose, " it will be Your Majesty's wish to acknowledge the sin and to humble yourself before God ".

Ormonde was more fortunate, reaching Caen, where he had left his wife and family while Charles was at sea. Just before he sailed from Holland, Charles received a communication from Lilburne, who was about to join the Royalists: he had begun to revolt against the military dictatorship under which England was sinking. But the Levellers must be temporarily relegated, as a last hope; and Charles, Buckingham and Henry Seymour landed in Scotland on July the Fourth, 1650, the Covenant having been signed the day before, at sea.

Charles was weighed down by the knowledge of Montrose's death and the disapproval of his supporters. But Buckingham was jubilant. He had again refused to compound, although Parliament had offered him his return and rehabilitation for thirty thousand pounds; he had now no rival near the King, and the Covenanters, deeply impressed by his influence, granted him the supreme favour denied to Charles—they gravely told him that he might bring his chaplain with him to Scotland; no one delighted in this sort of situation more than Buckingham. Yet with all his efforts to please, he did not trouble to hide his real nature; " his dissolute course of life was excessive scandalous; which to their great reproach they [the Covenanters] connived at, because he advised the King to put himself wholly into their hands ".[14] The point was, however, that Buckingham " took all the ways possible to gain Argyll and the ministers ".[15]

It would be interesting to know exactly how this mimic, courtier and man of fashion, still in his early twenties, set himself to exploit the " master-fiend, Argyll ",[16] and his covey of black-clad divines, or to see written down even a fragment of the conversations between Buckingham and Charles when they were alone, walking the deck or taking their ease in the cabin on board the man-of-war the Dutch had lent them. There are no such records. In later years Buckingham was not prone to dwell on this, his first diplomatic victory.

---

[14] Burnet.   [15] *Ibid.*
[16] Aytoun : *Lays of the Scottish Cavalier* (1849).

CHAPTER FIVE

I

ARCHIBALD CAMPBELL, eighth Earl and first Marquess of Argyll, was in his fifty-third year when Charles and Buckingham arrived in Scotland. He was swarthy, spare and rather lame, with a narrow bony face and a cast in his eye;[1] " a man of craft, subtlety and falsehood," says Clarendon, who "wanted nothing but honesty and courage to be a very extraordinary man, having all other talents in a great degree."[2]

Allowances must be made for Clarendon's natural prejudice. Argyll was a very extraordinary man indeed. His knowledge of human affairs and his gift for organisation amounted to genius; but he had many of the defects of genius, the disregard of the commonplace, the flashes of insolence, the sudden hesitations and withdrawals that may destroy the careful work of years. The twists of temperament that are the result of being a great deal cleverer than other people brought him to the heights of power, then to the depths of dependence upon others, and finally to his own ruin and death.

Argyll's greatest enemy, Montrose, had several times defeated him; their feud lasted all their youth. On one occasion Argyll had witnessed the systematic destruction of fifteen thousand Campbells by the forces of the man whom he at last succeeded in bringing to the scaffold. In the summer of 1650 Argyll placed the head of Montrose on a spike at the Tolbooth in Edinburgh and made himself master of Scotland. He could call to arms twenty thousand men, more than four times the number that Hamilton and Lauderdale were able to raise. Through Charles he hoped to consolidate his victories at home and extend his power into England. The King, throneless and penniless, was not so much his guest as his prey. A cunning and unscrupulous diplomat in his fifties was surely more than a match for a youth of twenty; and the Council, Buckingham among them, believed Charles to be entirely subjugated by the machinations of the McCallum More before ever the visit to Scotland began.

Charles was greeted with wild enthusiasm from the moment

[1] *Journal* of Sir Edward Walker. John Willcock: *The Great Marquess.* [2] *History.*

of his arrival at Garmouth on the Spey ; bonfires were lit and townsfolk and soldiers turned out to cheer him. This did not suit the Covenanters at all; never quite sure of their authority over the people, they, as it were, withdrew Charles from circulation as soon as they perceived how popular he was and made it impossible for him to have direct contact with any of the officers whose commander he was supposed to be. He was conducted to Aberdeen. When he reached this city on July the Seventh, the first sight that greeted him was the swollen and blackening right arm of Montrose, stuck over the principal gateway. Charles made no comment on this grisly reminder of the Covenanters' power and Argyll's supremacy, although it must have been pointed out to him that it was not the hand of an ordinary criminal that marked his entry into Aberdeen, but one he had clasped in friendship a score of times. The implication was obvious and depressing; here, " in the springe of the Kirk ", the presence of a King had no sanctity and no prestige without the authority of the Covenant behind it.

2

Meanwhile Cromwell also decided to invade Scotland; he had to do so in person, for Fairfax now withdrew himself from public life, sending in his resignation on the grounds of health in June 1650. The honeymoon was over. Indeed this cant phrase applies more accurately than in most cases to the political relationship existing between the two men. Cromwell, with his highly developed sensibility and vulnerable nerves was womanish in the conventional and flattering sense: Fairfax's unswerving judgement and his grasp of any situation characterises masculinity at its rarest and best. He disapproved on moral and practical grounds of the invasion of Scotland: and if he had long found Cromwell an uncomfortable bedfellow, he made no comment on the man with whom he had worked for nearly seven years.

Cromwell advanced into Scotland with little or no opposition and defeated the Scots at Dunbar at the beginning of September 1650. During these first months in his northern kingdom Charles's position had become " most sad and dangerous ".[3] He had to bear the increasingly heavy burdens of personal criticism from the

[3] Walker.

Covenanters, criticism which spared neither of his parents and reflected on every religious principle he had been taught to honour and respect. Lauderdale, Hamilton, Charles's physician, Dr. Fraser, and many more of his personal attendants had been dismissed from the so-called Court he held at the royal palace of Falkland. Buckingham and Lord Wilmot (afterwards Earl of Rochester and father of that more celebrated Rochester who was to collaborate with Buckingham in poetry and prose) were the only noblemen allowed near the King. Buckingham, the inseparable companion of Argyll, was Charles's sole support during the dreary and terrible months of three-hour sermons—on Sundays, both young men, assuming what gravity they could, had to sit through several of these—and constant lecturing and disapproval, of which Charles's " malignity ", or indifference to the Covenant, was the principal theme. Sometimes their tormentors let Charles and Buckingham alone to drink or to play cards, but not often, and then behind locked doors and shuttered windows;[4] sometimes they were allowed, even encouraged, to try their hands at golf; but as there is no record of either of them showing the least wish to return to this game in later life one may conclude that they found it only a little less wearisome than the sermonising and the crabbed punctilio which forbade even a smile on the Sabbath day.[5] (Buckingham's chaplain, Dr. King, stayed on at Falkland; it would be interesting to know how a man in such an anomalous position managed to fill in his time.)

Most humiliating of all, Charles was not allowed to be present at the meetings of the Covenanters' Council. Argyll's behaviour to the King was the perfection of courtesy and correctness; he approached him with reverential grace and received his demands with the profoundest respect: but when Charles made any proposals that he did not like, Argyll " gathered up his countenance " and left the room.[6] His eldest son was in charge of the royal guard of honour; Dr. Fraser and those grooms of the bed-chamber who had been sent away in July were still absent in the autumn. Finally, Argyll's suggestions for the King's marriage with the Lady Anne became at the same time more insinuating and more difficult to deal with every day and every hour. When Argyll quarrelled with the Duke of Hamilton, and Hamilton found it prudent to retire to his own estates, Buckingham did not hesitate to remain " wholly Argyll's ". Of the " two great jugglers " as Nicholas called Hamil-

[4] E. Scott.   [5] Burnet   [6] Clarendon: *History*.

ton and Argyll, George Villiers knew, none better, whose arm was the longer.

Adaptable though he could be, Buckingham was at once repelled and nonplussed by the mingled cunning, coarseness and sanctimony of the Scottish lairds whose way of life provided no resources for a young man of sophisticated taste and luxurious habit. The total lack of sympathy between Buckingham and these fanatical potentates made him turn to his fellow-exiles for companionship; of these one was Colonel Ellis Leighton, "a person of ready wit and promptness of speech" who contrived to hang on to the outskirts of the Covenanting party; Leighton, afterwards described by Pepys as a "mad, freaking fellow" and "a wonderfully witty, ready man for sudden answers and little tales", remained with the Royalists till after the Restoration.[7] Another member of Buckingham's group became useful to them, Colonel Silas Titus, formerly a Parliamentarian. Titus's contact with Charles I during his captivity at Carisbrooke had made him into a Cavalier, though no one quite believed in his conversion. The whole court, Covenanters and Royalists alike, had to be on their guard against Cromwell's spies. A report from one of these epitomises the atmosphere of chicanery and mistrust that increased from the time Charles left Holland to the moment of his return there two years later.

"They [the Scots] find nothing but vanity and lightness in him [Charles] and that he will never prove a strenuous defender of their faith; and it is evident still that he perfectly hates them . . . 'tis a matter of pleasant observation to see how they endeavour to cheat and cozen each other."[8]

By the beginning of October, Charles was at the end of his tether. Perhaps Buckingham's witty talk was wearing rather thin: perhaps the repetition of the Lady Anne's many virtues (she was said to be "a gentlewoman of rare parts and education") was beginning to alarm him, though he finally dealt with this particular problem in a way that was characteristic of his statecraft in the years to come; he sent Titus to France to ask his mother's approval of the marriage, secretly instructing the Colonel to come back with a refusal that would not wound Argyll's feelings and that no dutiful son could ignore. In spite of Buckingham's reiteration of everything that was to be gained from loyalty—if

---

[7] Leighton was also described as Buckingham's " own darling favourite ". T. Carte: *Life of Ormonde.*
[8] Gardiner: *Charles II and Scotland in 1650.*

the word can be used in such a connection—to Argyll, Charles
was beginning to realise his own strength and cunning.

For Argyll, over-reaching himself at last, had put into words
the thought that Charles for a time kept secret even from
Buckingham. When he came into England, the Marquess said to
Charles, "he might be more free—but for the present it was
necessary to please 'these madmen'"—the Presbyterians. These
double-edged words fitted neatly into the consciousness of the
aptest pupil Argyll ever had. Outwardly to agree with a body of
men whom he considered unbalanced and absurd was to become
a habit with Charles II. From Argyll—and from life—he learnt
what Buckingham could never learn: that to think of human
beings as fools or children is, mentally, at least, to assume an
absolute power over them: and his endeavours to achieve this
power were perfectly in the Stuart tradition. Buckingham, with
all his brilliance, had no bird's eye view of the world, no power
of detachment. It was in Scotland that Charles and Buckingham
began their separate courses—courses that were to leave them
enemies at last, one triumphant and weary, the other arrogant
and carefree, even in his own despite.

3

In September, 1650, Henry Seymour was sent away from
Falkland and the King moved to Perth with no companions but
his grooms of the bed-chamber, Wilmot and Buckingham.
According to Clarendon, Buckingham and Charles were on bad
terms at this time. "The Duke of Buckingham," he says, "had
lost much ground . . . by his having broken off all manner of
friendship with Duke Hamilton and the Earl of Lautherdale (to
whom he had professed so much) and had entered into so fast
a conjunction with the Marquess of Argyll . . . he was less dutiful
to the King than he ought to have been."[9]

Buckingham's irritation, freely expressed, was not surprising;
they had all agreed, many weeks ago, on the "conjunction" with
Argyll that Charles now wished to break. The King might have
been in a more reasonable frame of mind if the Covenanters had
not placed before him a new declaration, embodying expressions
of shame and regret for his own sins and his father's, condemnation

[9] History.

of his mother's "idolatry" and an assurance that he himself abhorred popery, prelacy and "superstition".[10] Charles at first refused to sign this document; the Committee insisted: he prevaricated: the Committee, through Argyll, told Charles that if he did not sign they would at once begin negotiations with Cromwell. The threat had its effect and Charles did as he was told with a bitterness of spirit that may be imagined. Shortly afterwards he had a secret interview with Mr. King, the Dean of Tuam, to whom he said he was "a true child of the Church of England and . . . a true Cavalier". While thus pacifying the Royalists, Charles at the same time promised Argyll a dukedom and the repayment of his loan of forty thousand pounds.[11]

Charles had decided to abandon the Covenanters. The defeat at Dunbar had weakened their power, and since retiring into the Highlands, Hamilton, Lauderdale and a number of other Scottish chieftains had been arming themselves against Argyll. Harry Seymour and Dr. Fraser were in touch with this new band of Royalists and they reported to Charles that he would do better to desert the Covenanters and ally himself with them.

Charles was delighted. For some time now he had felt he would rather be in Cromwell's hands than in those of Argyll. He told the Scots Royalists to meet him in Fife on October the Third.[12]

On the morning of October the Second, while Buckingham and Charles were riding out together the King told Buckingham what his plans were. The Duke said nothing for a moment or two. Then, making an excuse to leave his master, he rode back to Perth and told Lord Wilmot of this disastrous decision; for disastrous it certainly was. Argyll was still very powerful, while the Scots Royalists could only raise ten thousand men between them. When the King returned that evening Buckingham and Wilmot sought him alone in the bed-chamber and represented in the strongest terms the folly and risk of his new plan. For a long time Charles refused to listen to their arguments: some hours passed in heated discussion; then Charles appeared to give way and they parted for the night.[13]

Immediately Wilmot, who had had too much experience of the King's diplomacy to trust his word, informed Argyll of the scheme. Argyll set to work to banish or dismiss from the army all those noblemen with whom Charles had been plotting. After dinner the next day, Charles, who guessed what had happened,

---

[10] E. Scott.   [11] Willcock.   [12] E. Scott.   [13] Walker.

strolled nonchalantly into the garden; he was heading for the stables, but Buckingham stopped him. Another long discussion took place, and again Charles must have promised to submit to the Covenanters, for Buckingham left him and went indoors. Then it was discovered that the King had disappeared; he had not stopped to change his dress and had taken only three gentlemen with him.[14]

It was obvious that Charles was on his way to Fife; Buckingham, Dunfermline and another Covenanting nobleman ordered out their horses and gave chase. The pursuit lasted forty-two miles without a break; finally Charles was caught up and induced to return. On October the Sixth he and Buckingham slept at Huntly Castle and a few days later they were back in Perth.[15]

Charles's attempt to defy the Covenanters had one good result; they decided to let him attend the Council meetings. But the Scots Royalists blamed Buckingham and Wilmot for their defeat, Buckingham especially, because of his intimacy with Charles; their hatred and resentment were reported in Holland, and thereafter Buckingham was supposed to have "betrayed" his King; and all through the eighteenth and nineteenth centuries historians, describing the incident of the Start as the Scots called it, have followed this lead. It is possible that Dryden had the Start—besides one or two other incidents—in mind when he gave Buckingham the name of *Zimri* in his *Absalom and Achitophel*. Zimri, a usurper and a murderer, came to a terrible end.[16] So did not Buckingham; but the name of Zimri, coupled with that of traitor, is for ever associated with his.

In fact, Buckingham succeeded in preventing Charles from embarking on a double treachery. However deeply he distrusted Argyll, to have deserted him at this point would only have brought the King's name to further dishonour. Furthermore, Buckingham had enough knowledge of soldiering to realise the uselessness of attacking with a handful of men; he had seen the results of that at Kingston. He would have been perfectly right in using force to re-unite Charles and Argyll; as it was, he lost the King's favour, but not for long.

The Start was followed by the Coronation of Charles at Scone; the great Marquess himself placed the crown on his victim's head on January the First, 1651. The ceremony was preceded by two days of fast and mourning for the iniquities of the Stuart family

----

[14] E. Scott.   [15] *Ibid*.   [16] See Appendix III.

in which the King was forced to join; Charles, who had recovered his spirits a little by this time, was heard to remark at the end of the session, "I think I must repent, too, that ever I was born".[17] During the spring and summer of 1651 Charles and Buckingham forgot all their disagreements in the business of collecting and training a new army; Buckingham was made General of the Eastern Association. Preparations to march into England then began.

4

When Robert Long and Sir Edward Walker were dismissed from the Council, Buckingham was made Secretary of State. As soon as he realised that Argyll had temporarily abandoned the idea of marrying his daughter to the King he proposed for her hand.[18] This made Charles very angry, for it caused further awkwardness between him and Argyll. The Lady Anne, a nervous and delicate girl, sank into deep depression, whether for love of Buckingham or of Charles, or because of the uncertainty of her future, is not known, and died unmarried shortly before the Restoration.[19]

Charles and Buckingham, in the intervals of organising the campaign, enjoyed themselves at the Covenanters' expense, as usual; the Duke afterwards described how the Puritans "broke down the hedges and then bid the cattle not to wander", and how "at dinners they lay about 'em as fiercely as in the pulpit".[20] At this time he renewed his friendship and his interchanges of satirical comment with Abraham Cowley, who had become a messenger for the Royalists between Scotland and the Continent. In February Buckingham was busy collecting a picked troop of horse and generally occupying himself with plans for the invasion. One of his English agents reported that the Duke of Richmond was raising forces for the King and that Denbigh was ready to turn his coat again. Richmond refused a generalship on the grounds that he was no soldier and Buckingham persuaded Charles to give this position to his old comrade in arms, Lord Gerard.[21] Villiers' correspondence with his chiefs of staff shows him to be a careful, hard-headed administrator, but he did not

---

[17] Somers Tracts. [18] Willcock [19] Ibid.
[20] Commonplace Book of the Duke of Buckingham.
[21] Cary: Memoirs of the Civil War.

always share his followers' confidence in their abilities; when General Lambert routed the Scots Royalists on July the Twenty-Fourth, 1651, Buckingham merely referred to the disaster as " our late misfortune in Fife " and passed on to something else. His real opinion is shown in a letter to Newcastle, at this time his most intimate friend and ally, and reveals very low spirits. After reassuring Newcastle as to some money owed him by the King, Buckingham goes on to advise him—

". . . to make your peace, if it be possible, in England, for certainly your Lordship's suffering for the King has been great enough to excuse you if you look a little after yourself now, when neither is he able to assist you, nor you in a possibility of doing him service."

Going on to speak of the Scots Royalists defeated by Lambert, Buckingham describes them as " next to Cromwell the greatest enemies we had in the world ", adding—

" I hope now we shall agree and join to make a considerable army since they are defeated that were the greatest hindrance to it. If we can but unite among ourselves I am confident we shall yet make as brave an army as was ever raised in this kingdom, but whether we shall be so happy as that comes to or no, God knows . . ."

He concludes gloomily, " For my own part I am so weary of our ill fortune and the miserable condition we are in here that I do wish for some happy occasion of losing my life honourably in the King's service, and in the meantime all I desire is but to be well thought on by my friends, among whom I do reckon your Lordship as one of the first, and therefore do beseech you that you will continue me in your good opinion."

Those who accused Buckingham of inconsistency and frivolity chose to forget that his policy, with regard to the Covenant, was undeviating. He knew that the Covenanters were better soldiers than the Scots Royalists and he stuck to them, even after the shattering of all his hopes at Worcester. The courtier, the fribble, the nobleman who was " everything by starts and nothing long " was, in the sixteen-fifties at least, an energetic and able organiser and, as such, he found little support either from those above or those below him. His chief intelligence officer, Thomas Cook, who was in possession of all the Royalist plans and ciphers, was captured in Lancashire during the summer of 1651 and taken to the Tower. It was only necessary to show him the rack. The wretched man exclaimed " I do desire to unbowel myself in everything I can discover ", and proceeded to do so. Meanwhile Buckingham and the King, unaware of this misfortune, were quarrelling again, this time more violently than before.

No recruits joined the invading army during the march to the Border; by the time Charles's forces had been met by Buckingham and his rather unruly troop of horsemen in Lancashire it was quite clear that the invasion was extremely unpopular. Buckingham attributed some part of this failure to General Leslie, who got on badly with his English officers and whose gloomy demeanour and contradictory orders were having a disagreeable effect on the men.

Buckingham thereupon drew the King aside and began a long speech about Leslie's lack of success and the undesirability of employing a Scots general to command English soldiers; the King's business, he said, lay in reducing England to his obedience; he would never do this while Leslie was in command. Charles, rather taken aback, asked who, in Leslie's absence, was fit to take his place. Buckingham at once replied, " I hope Your Majesty will confer it upon myself."

Charles, deeply embarrassed, turned away without making any reply and, summoning one of his officers, began to ask him a string of questions. Buckingham said no more that day; on the next, during the march towards Worcester, he again approached the King and began by announcing that what he had proposed was so eminently suitable that Leslie himself would " willingly consent " to be put aside. Charles said coldly, " I can hardly believe you are in earnest or that you can in truth believe that you could be fit for such a charge." Buckingham fired up. Wherein, he demanded, did his unfitness lie? " You are too young ", was the short answer. " Harry the Fourth," said the Duke quickly, " commanded an army and won a battle when he was younger than I." He was going on to speak further when the King irritably announced that there would be no Generalissimo but himself; Buckingham, bitterly chagrined, withdrew from his master's side.[22]

He was extremely angry. For months he had been devoting all his energies to organising the Eastern Association and possibly without realising it had assumed that his promotion would not stop there; and the flatteries of his subordinates—over whom he held the powers of life and death—had made him sure of achieving the position of Commander-in-Chief and so outstripping his famous father, at the age of twenty-four. Now he was put down and denied by the man for whom he had twice sacrificed

[22] Clarendon : *History.*

his fortune. It was hard; and Buckingham, who had never before been refused anything he had set his heart on, behaved as foolishly as many other young men in similar circumstances. He did not attend the Council meetings: he went about unshaven and dirty and refused to speak to anybody. His fit of sulks lasted until the army reached Worcester at the end of August.[23]

5

From the start the march south had been a desperate risk. By the beginning of 1651 all Scotland south of the Forth and the Clyde, including Edinburgh, was in Cromwell's hands. It was greatly to the Roundhead advantage that by the time the march into England began, Argyll had withdrawn himself from the proceedings; he would have nothing to do with any step that entailed a risk; his retirement to Inverary was the signal for Hamilton's and Lauderdale's reappearance.

When the invaders approached Worcester they had only sixteen thousand men; Cromwell's pursuing army was more than double that number. The fact was that the English people disliked being invaded, even by their King, and even more than they disliked military rule. They rallied to Cromwell as soon as they realised that they were in danger from their ancient enemies.

Between August the Twenty-Second and September the Second, the result of the invasion was still uncertain; by the afternoon of September the Third, Cromwell's armies, under General Monk, had established themselves on both sides of the Severn; Charles, who with Buckingham and the rest of his staff had been watching the battle from the tower of Worcester Cathedral, decided to split his army into three; then he placed himself at the head of a small force of Highlanders and Cavaliers, and with Hamilton and Buckingham charged Cromwell's men on the south-eastern side of the city, so vigorously that he achieved a momentary success. During this sortie Hamilton was mortally wounded and Lauderdale taken prisoner.

The Royalist advance was stopped by an onrush of Ironsides, and, once broken, not even Charles's and Buckingham's gallant leadership and their disregard of their own safety could rally it again. Charles exclaimed that he would rather be shot than kept

---

[23] Clarendon: *History*.

GEORGE VILLIERS AS A YOUNG MAN

From the portrait by an unknown artist (school of Van Dyck)
at Newburgh Priory

Reproduced by courtesy of Captain Malcolm Wombwell

alive to see the consequences of defeat, but Buckingham, always cooler than he in such moments as these, advised cutting a way out of the burning city, and this, with one or two other Cavaliers, they managed to do. Then there was a brief consultation and it was decided to make for Scotland; Argyll, with his Campbells, was still available. Half-a-mile from Worcester Charles attempted to ride back, but Buckingham and Wilmot persuaded him that heroism was useless; the Scots were in total rout; there was no army left to rally.

Next morning the fugitives, now a party of some sixty horse-men, reached Newport, thirty miles from Worcester. They appealed to Lord Talbot, who knew the country, to guide them and he did so till they were nearing Kidderminster; here he confessed himself completely lost. Another member of the party, a Mr. Giffard, suggested that the King should take shelter at Whiteladies, an old Cistercian convent on the borders of Brewood Forest in the possession of the Giffard family.[24]

Here Charles and Buckingham seem to have parted company. Buckingham was conducted to Blorepipe Hall, whose owner, Mr. George Barlowe, advised him to lie up in the woods until the search-parties had gone by. The Duke came out of the woods as soon as it was dark to take refuge in a labourer's cottage where he remained hidden for six days and nights; he left his George, which had been given him by Queen Henrietta Maria, with his host and, disguising himself as a countryman, set out for Nottingham, to his sister's house.[25] For a short time the Duchess of Richmond sheltered the battered and exhausted ex-General of the Eastern Association. Then, somehow, after a number of unchronicled adventures, Buckingham reached the coast. By the middle of October, 1651, he was back in Holland.[26]

Cromwell's "crowning mercy", Clarendon's "fatal over-throw" were behind him. But the lesson was bitter. The elderly men, the Cavaliers of the old school, had been right after all. The Covenant that Montrose had declared would bring shame, ruin and dishonour had been signed for nothing. Estranged from the Catholic interest in Europe, routed in the field and almost penniless, the Royalists had now no hope at all—or so it seemed. Still Buckingham would not admit defeat. The Presbyterians, he said, were able to help them; he advised, and Nicholas was half inclined to agree with him, that when the King appeared "he

[24] E. Scott. [25] Jesse. [26] *Ibid.*

F

should walk entirely in the same steps of presbytery as formerly."
" And truly," added Nicholas, despairingly, " it is not easy to
advise what course His Majesty . . . should take." Clarendon
had returned to the Hague fulminating against the Spaniards,
whom he described as a " wretched, miserable, proud, senseless
people ", but he had no suggestions other than those he had made
before the Covenant had been signed.

Nothing could be settled until the King reappeared—and
where was he? Nicholas and Clarendon were horribly anxious:
Buckingham refused to see anyone " but his confidants, whereof
for your sake, I am none," wrote Nicholas to Clarendon; nevertheless, Nicholas went to see the Duke, who vouchsafed that the
King was " secure, but whether in France, Flanders or Holland
he cannot or will not tell." Buckingham had plans of his own:
he was still estranged from Charles, whom he had not yet forgiven.

CHAPTER SIX

I

ON the very day that Nicholas brought himself to wait upon Buckingham to get news of the King, Charles landed at Fécamp after a series of adventures which he never tired of describing. In the years to come hearts sank and glances of dismay were interchanged when His Majesty began on one of his Worcester anecdotes: and the names of those families who had staked their lives and fortune to save his—Giffard, Lane, Wyndham, Coningsby and Penderel—were as sign-posts on a weary road; for Charles was to acquire the unfortunate habit of telling many of his stories twice at a sitting.

Buckingham was not present at their first hearing at the family reunion in Paris, partly because he had not the money to make the journey;[1] he remained in Holland with Colonel Leighton, "one of the best companions at a meal in the world",[2] Titus, Lord Newburgh and a number of those mediocre hangers-on who generally attach themselves to highly placed persons; of these a certain Dr. Morley[3] seems to have attempted a reconciliation between Buckingham and Clarendon, naturally without success. "I am not at all deceived," wrote Clarendon, after he had joined the King in Paris, "by what Dr. J. Morley tells of the Duke of Buckingham, though the poor Dr. himself be."

The shock of this second defeat had been fearful, and Buckingham took longer to recover from it than from that of three years before; as he regained his spirits his resentment towards Charles fomented. He was aware, as he said long afterwards, that at this time he had but to make an advance and Charles would forgive him his "insolences".[4] But he did not do so, continuing to brood over the wrong done him before the battle of Worcester. There were plenty of sycophants to listen to his railings, and to agree with his theory that in General Leslie's place, so unfairly denied him, he might have saved the day. Always indiscreet, Buckingham soon became slanderously so: he impugned Charles's courage during and after the invasion, and went about the Hague

---

[1] Evelyn: *Hyde Correspondence*.
[2] Pepys.
[3] Afterwards Bishop of Winchester.
[4] Reresby.

saying that the King had "ill behaved himself in that conflict ".[5]
Mary of Orange, now a widow and regent for her infant son,
William, was told of this back-biting and forbade Buckingham
the Court, but he did not allow this state of things to last long.
He began to make himself extremely agreeable to Mary, who was,
according to Nicholas, "a very discreet and virtuous lady: and
if she had not the natural imperfection of her family, an unwilling-
ness to put herself to think of business, she would appear an
excellent princess."

A pretty, unattached young woman was the material best
suited to Buckingham's wiles; he now had in view a subtler and
more profitable revenge on Charles; he applied himself to pleasing
Mary, succeeded, and in January, 1652, was writing to Newcastle
on a very different note from that sounded in his letters from
Scotland.

"I should have written to you sooner but that I thought long before
this to have waited upon you myself . . . I do extremely long to have some
discourse with you concerning all our late misfortunes . . . The consequences
of our miscarriages is so sad that it is hard to think of them without
affliction, and yet I am confident your Lordship's natural good humour
joined to the ridiculousness of many passages I shall have to tell you, will
go near to make you laugh, but I shall defer the giving you that satisfaction
till I have the honour to see you . . ."

In default of Newcastle, Buckingham entertained the Princess
with the "ridiculousness" of his adventures; presently her aunt,
the Queen of Bohemia, began to find her quite cheerful, and noted
that she had renewed her interest in dress and fashions.

Then Nicholas told Clarendon that the Duke of Buckingham
had had the monstrous presumption to propose himself as a
husband to the Princess Royal. Clarendon replied in his most
devastating strain:

"Dear Mr. Secretary,
I never had speech with the King about that wild pretence you mention
of the Duke of Buckingham. But I have reason to believe he hath heard
of it and abhors it sufficiently, but takes no notice of it, upon confidence
that his sister disdains it. I have often had conference with the King
concerning the man, and find that he knows him as well as needs be. And
no doubt that the Queen is traduced in that report you have heard of her,
approving it; for besides the folly and madness of it, I know that she said
once upon the discourse, that if she thought it possible for her daughter
to have so base a thought, she would tear her to pieces with her own hands."

Queen Henrietta was not called on to carry out the threat which she was in the habit of making when any of her children displeased her; she was to use it again on the occasion of the Duke of York's secret marriage to Anne Hyde, and so often used it that it had become perfectly negligible. Charles, in fact, made no strictures on Buckingham's behaviour, and with the same apparent indifference heard from Nicholas that the Duke was now bent on making his " composition " in England. Clarendon added viciously that Buckingham " will no doubt marry Cromwell's daughter or be Cromwell's groom to save his estate ".

These were hard words for a young man who had twice refused to compound; yet Clarendon's hatred was very natural. He dreaded the renewal of Buckingham's influence over Charles and was far less tolerant of him than Nicholas, who, seeing the Duke more often, sometimes let fall a kinder phrase in his reports to Paris. Buckingham had qualities, certainly; but his friends, Tuke, Ascot, Titus and Leighton—what a druken, atheistical, sorry crew they were, and how repulsive was their mingling of rattle-trap bravado and casual corruption!

Then Nicholas's attention was suddenly diverted from Buckingham and the Princess-Royal. The legendary and menacing figure of the "infamous John Lilburne" rose from the cauldron of English politics and appeared among the exiles.

2

By the spring of 1652 Buckingham had given up all hope of winning the Princess-Royal; the discretion so much admired by Nicholas caused her to send the Duke an apologetic and courteous letter in which she told him that she had "suffered much for those civilities which she conceived convenient to a person of his rank" and begged him "not to take it ill if she entreated him . . . to forbear making visits to her."[6] On the receipt of this letter Buckingham immediately left the Hague and went to meet Lilburne in Amsterdam. Villiers gave no reason for this startling and—to the other Royalists—horrifying *volte-face*. His decision to affiliate himself with Lilburne shows that he had already acquired that disregard of the conventions that was to characterise his policy during his days of power. Lilburne had

[6] Francis Peck: *Desiderata Curiosa.*

declared that he could further the Royalist cause—very well: that was enough for Buckingham; any weapon, however dangerous or unusual, was better than none.

In spite of the fact that up to December, 1651, Lilburne had been on the friendliest terms with Cromwell, he reached Holland in January, 1652, under sentence of banishment for life, Parliament having used his latest piece of invective as an excuse to get rid of him. Buckingham's position made it impossible for him to seek out the Leveller himself: there had to be an intermediary; and it was at this point that one of the adventurers appeared who flitted between England and the Continent, getting what he could out of both sides. The shabby rake who becomes the creature of warring factions has always existed and always will exist, as long as what we call civilisation lasts; but in the seventeenth century such a man was at once a more recognisable and more lurid figure than his modern counterpart, who has had to acquire a veneer of respectability.

The individual who brought Lilburne to Buckingham at his squalid lodging in Amsterdam was called Captain Wendy Oxford (then, as now, the assumption of this particular rank was often the concomitant of seediness and pretension); and his wife was " a common whore " with whom he worked and lived on the best of terms. A picture of that first meeting—the shuttered house in a narrow street, the greasy, boisterous, out-at-elbows captain and his curtseying smiling partner, the elderly man in his plain worn dress, the young nobleman whose height and splendour seemed to fill the murky room—has been sketched by Lilburne,[7] who saw in Buckingham his last and only hope.

The two men dined, waited on by the Captain and his wife, and then they talked for a long time. Buckingham poured out most of his schemes to his new ally; he dwelt chiefly on his passionate desire to return to England " which he avowed he loved above all the places in this world "[8]—but how could he make his peace there? It must be honourably or not at all. (One can imagine Clarendon's bitter smile when many years later he came upon this phrase.)

Lilburne gave the young man what advice he could, none of it very helpful. Then Captain Oxford intervened; his connection with Parliament enabled him to obtain a pass for the noble Duke into England. But neither Lilburne nor Buckingham seemed par-

---

[7] John Lilburne: *A Defensive Declaration*.   [8] Lilburne.

ticularly anxious to conclude this part of the bargain and the question of the pass was temporarily abandoned.

A few weeks later Buckingham, Lilburne and Mrs. Lilburne met at Calais; in the absence of Captain Wendy Oxford both men spoke more freely; Lilburne's arrogance was apparent and the Duke's scepticism had increased; they were now, said a Cromwellian spy who reported their conversation, "very familiar together ".[9] The Leveller began with a diatribe against Cromwell and the Parliament, whom he described as a company of false and damnable rogues. To this Buckingham replied that he himself was willing to take the risk of coming into England as soon as a pass could be procured; he was not concerned with Cromwell's abandonment of Magna Carta: and he was ready to " fling himself into Parliament's hands to-morrow ". Lilburne answered, " My Lord, since you are so resolved, I would advise you not to stir in such things as yet," adding some further abuse of " the General " and his advisers, " those damnable villains ", whose overthrow he had already planned. " Let me hear which way you will do this," demanded Buckingham. " My Lord, I will tell you how," replied Lilburne, " first, I will set my press on work . . . and by my agents my papers shall be brought into the army . . . and so soon as these papers are spread [the soldiers] will fly in the faces of their officers, so that with the help of my particular interest the soldiery shall do all themselves, and I will do nothing but sit in my chair and use my pen." The Duke expressed disbelief in this simple scheme. " Why, then," exclaimed Lilburne indignantly, " I perceive you take the General for a wise man? " Buckingham assented. " No! " persisted Lilburne angrily, " heretofore all his business was managed by Ireton and is since by others, and as for the General himself, he is as false a perfidious rogue as ever lived in the world. I know no reason," he went on with rising bitterness, " why I should not vie with Cromwell, since I had once as great a power as he has, and greater too, and am as good a gentleman, and of as good a family." To this strange and pathetic outburst Buckingham made no answer, merely repeating, " Sir, if you have any interest in England, as you say you have, I pray you use it for me, for I have a great desire to be reconciled to my native country." " Do not stir in it yet," urged the older man; and as the Duke remained noncommittal he continued to speak his thoughts aloud. " So, if Cromwell keep himself above the law, that I cannot have my right

[9] State Trials.

by the law, I may kill him how I can—I am resolved to have one fling more at Cromwell. . . ."[10]

In spite of the underlying division between them, Buckingham and Lilburne continued to keep in touch with both Levellers and Royalists in England, and made Calais their headquarters; all this time the estrangement between Buckingham and the King continued. During the Christmas festivities the Duke appeared at the French Court and took part in a masque; for a day or two he was ill and confined to his room in the Palais Royal, but Charles made no enquiries, and when he was about again received him very coldly.

Buckingham's friendship with Lilburne was censured by both Clarendon and Nicholas, Clarendon, as always, expressing himself with greater severity. Charles made no comment on the connection and no response to Lilburne's offer "to bring in the King within six months if he had but ten thousand pounds". As far as Charles's finances were concerned the sum required might as well have been ten million: for he was again the pensioner of the French Court and had had to borrow a few thousand pistoles here and a suit of clothes there, as occasion offered.[11]

Meanwhile the older Cavaliers viewed with disgust the incongruous spectacle of Lilburne and Buckingham as intimates and allies; Clarendon believed that Lilburne was merely using the younger man for his own revenge on Cromwell. But Lilburne was incapable of planning a personal vengeance, vindictive though he could be in the cause of his ideals. As the months went by he began to realise that he ran as great a risk of being murdered in Holland as of being "clapt up" and tried for high treason in his own country; both Parliament and the Royalists wanted him out of the way: and some of the Cavaliers approached Captain Wendy Oxford with a view to disposing of him.

The jolly Captain was as ready to slit a throat as to share a bottle or the favours of his wife: but Buckingham heard of the scheme and persuaded the Cavaliers to leave Lilburne alone; Buckingham was then told by Oxford that only he stood between the Leveller and his enemies on both sides of the Channel: the Duke had but to give the necessary information for Lilburne to be extradited and brought to justice, while he himself would be rewarded by the pass into England. For the third time Buckingham refused the terms offered for his return.

Lilburne was safe, but not for long. A fiercer enemy than

---

[10] State Trials.   [11] *Memoirs* of Cardinal de Retz.

Cromwell, Oxford or the Cavaliers—his own restless spirit—
urged him towards his fate: unable to endure the inactivity and
aimlessness of exile, he reappeared in England in the summer of
1653 and was brought to the bar.

The course of that celebrated and significant trial is too well
known to be recounted here. In his *Defensive Declaration* Lilburne
described the Duke of Buckingham as his greatest benefactor, spoke
of his " reason, sobriety, civility, honour and conscience " and
offered to be his pledge. He added:

"I do as immediately and instrumently owe my life to him as ever
David ought to his Jonathan; his powerful influence among the desperate
Cavaliers being such that instrumentally under God he principally preserved
my life from the many complotted designs that the said Oxford had
cunningly laid by their hands to get me murdered . . . I judge myself bound
and obliged in conscience and gratitude to travel in his errands a thousand
and a thousand miles upon my feet."

Lilburne could be as ungrateful as most fanatics to those who
had protected him; Cromwell, though he had more than once stood
between him and Ireton's and the Commons' wrath, never
received praise of this kind. The fact was that Buckingham had
made another conquest, perhaps the oddest he ever made.
Quarrelsome, credulous, entirely selfless and always in deadly
earnest, Lilburne found in George Villiers the complement of his
own difficult nature; the Duke's inexhaustible vitality and quick
understanding rose to meet Lilburne's flights of moody eloquence
and furious denunciation, stimulating, encouraging, scheming;
and the man who believed all men equal under God paused in his
weary struggle against authority to contemplate the brilliant world-
ling who was neither dedicated to a cause nor crushed by tyranny
and saw that he, too, was wronged . . . The England of Lilburne's
dreams was a place in which there was as much room for the
cultured fine gentleman as for the merchant, the apprentice, the
soldier or the labouring man; in that kingdom of the imagination
all contributed and benefited, and all were free.

It is possible that Buckingham, at the age of twenty-six, was
worthy of the friendship of this great man; at this time even
Nicholas realised the Duke's qualities and was concerned for his
future, deploring his circle of flatterers and his tendency to atheism,
heartily wishing " that he had some good people about him; for I
very much doubt," he added, " that Leighton (who is a very
vicious man) will undo him."

Nicholas also noted the impression that Lilburne made on the exiles; others besides Buckingham, Lord Percy, for instance, whose opinion he respected, believed that the Leveller " was more able to set the crown on the King's head than ever Scotland was, if His Majesty will follow his advice ". But he could not bring himself to believe in Buckingham's integrity, disapproved of his following Lilburne to England in July 1653 and continued to find fault with the Duke's joking, carefree ways. That Buckingham took his liberty and perhaps even his life in his hand on the English expedition was not considered; his attitude was all wrong, and his frivolity unforgivable.

It was perhaps this very lightheartedness that appealed to John Lilburne; for gaiety had had little place in the series of embittering conflicts that made up the Leveller's career; by the time he reached Holland he was old and broken: and it is unlikely that he had ever before met a man of the Duke's calibre, one in whom intellect and daring were combined with a derisive and original humour; a man who could laugh at his own failures and make a dinner-table story out of misfortune. This seeming superficiality, anathematised by the older Royalists, was a stimulus to such a temperament as Lilburne's, whose principal weakness lay in his tendency to make a tragedy out of disappointment or misadventure.

Clarendon remained inexorably hostile. " The Duke of Buckingham is here at the old rate and is good for nothing," he remarked when the Duke again arrived in Paris. By this time Lilburne had been acquitted of high treason and imprisoned in Jersey, where he was " more trouble ", according to the Governor of Elizabeth Castle, " than ten Cavaliers ".

3

Many years after the Restoration, Catherine de la Mothe, Comtesse d'Aulnoy, visited the English Court and fell in love with the Duke of Buckingham. Mme d'Aulnoy was then an extremely pretty young woman and a successful novelist; her relationship with Buckingham must have been all that she desired, for he is in effect the hero of the *Mémoires de la Cour d'Angleterre*, an historical romance, full of incident and humour, but almost entirely lacking in characterisation; the elegant beings that flit through its pages bear no more relation to life than the princes and princesses in the charming fairy-stories that their creator dedicated to Madame, Charles II's youngest sister. The " Memoirs " are not even gossip, far less fictionalised biography: and the title is purposely misleading. But here and there one or two facts help to make a background for the writer's manipulation of celebrated personages, many of whom, Buckingham among them, were alive when the book was published.

Mme d'Aulnoy knew that Buckingham had made several secret and dangerous journeys into England during his exile; and she often heard him recount the adventures that had befallen him there; so when she composed her book she dressed up the real hardships and risks in the fanciful attire that suited the taste of the day. Thus we are told, through Buckingham's own lips, how he duped the Roundheads before the Battle of Kingston by disguising himself as a clown, how in this way he conveyed to his sister Mary some " important documents "—Mme d'Aulnoy is far too good a storyteller to bore her audience with the nature of these apocryphal papers—and how, as a common player with a black patch over his eye, the Duke was secretly entertained by Cromwell's eldest daughter, Mrs. Ireton.[12]

It has been suggested that Buckingham himself invented these stories and that they were naïvely recorded for posterity by the credulous lady-novelist.[13] The reply to this contention is that none of the incidents bears the mark of Buckingham's peculiar genius; they are at the same time too conventional and too far-fetched to be attributed to the Duke who, if he had taken the trouble so to deceive Mme d'Aulnoy, would have added fantasy to verisimilitude and yet precluded obvious silliness, as in *The Rehearsal*, where he achieved the perfect combination of realism and nonsense.

Nothing is known of Buckingham's adventures in England, except that they were, like everything else he attempted at this time, unsuccessful. Lilburne's schemes had failed: the Duke was out of favour at the Hague and in Paris: his friends in England were able to do nothing for him: he had very little money. This would have been the moment to compound or at least to desert the Royalists and try his fortune elsewhere. Buckingham did neither. He joined the Dukes of York and Gloucester as a volunteer under Turenne and fought against the Spaniards at Mouzon, Arras and Valenciennes. Outside Mouzon he fell ill of a fever and had to withdraw from the siege.

---

[12] Mme d'Aulnoy: *Mémoires de la Cour d'Angleterre.*   [13] Burghclere.

4

Buckingham had only to take up soldiering to regain the favour of the older Cavaliers. In this guise he appeared at his best, while in Clarendon's mind at least there was always the hope that he would be killed. As a politician and a schemer the Duke irritated and bewildered those whom he could not dazzle or amuse: as a soldier he compelled their admiration.

Active service in the seventeenth century was a baroque display of the magnificent, the sordid, the horrible and the luxurious. The great noblemen of England, France and Spain went into battle in elaborate and costly full dress: their tents were as fancifully and expensively decorated as their armour: their mistresses followed them in gilded coaches. The atmosphere of a beleaguered stronghold or a conquered city was that of a *fête champêtre* in a nightmare, with gentlemen smoothing out their laces before going into action and ladies coquettishly posing against a ruin while a few yards away the cries of the wounded and the dying rose above the rumble of the cannon and the rattle of matchlock and steel. George Villiers was perfectly suited to the incongruities, the contrasts and the grotesque confusion of such a setting. During the relief of Arras he and a number of other English volunteers " behaved so as none were better spoken of . . . and little Mr. Harry," as the senior Cavaliers called the fifteen-year-old Duke of Gloucester, " did his part well."

Clarendon and Buckingham might have agreed on one point: that the years with Turenne were well spent, not wasted or embittered. But it was not in Buckingham's temperament to resign himself to the life of a professional soldier. When the Spaniards were driven out of France he turned again to " the old rate ", to the deceptive, twisting path that led back into England. It is difficult to understand what he hoped to effect when he left the French wars for underground intrigue. His two great allies, Argyll and Lilburne, were relegated; Argyll had been ruined, partly by Cromwell and partly by his eldest son: Lilburne had finally abjured political strife to become a Quaker. The number of discontented Royalists, among them many men of power and substance, was increasing in England; but Buckingham's widowed sister Mary, who had chosen to join Henrietta

Maria at the French Court with her only son, the five-year-old
Duke of Richmond, had no other cheering news to tell her restless
brother.

By the spring of 1656 Cromwell had been Lord Protector of
England for three years and defeated his enemies all over the
world. This was the moment that Buckingham chose to begin
scheming against him once more; Titus, Leighton, Morley, a
Catholic priest called Father Talbot, and the English Lady Abbess
of a Benedictine convent in Ghent were among his helpers. A
secret society of Royalist insurrectionists who called their organisation The Sealed Knot had been in action, or what they
thought of as action, since 1653. Buckingham was in communication with them and he believed that their numbers also
were rising steadily. It only remained to make sure that the King
and the older members of the Council were behind him.

5

During the year 1656-57 Charles and Buckingham were in
opposite camps. Since his return into exile the King had been
entirely dominated by Clarendon, who never missed an opportunity of poisoning his mind against the Duke. Buckingham's
impertinences were many and needed no emphasis from the
Chancellor. Charles's enmity could always be revived by the
reminder that Buckingham had dared to attempt marriage first
with the Lady Anne Campbell and then with the Princess-Royal;
there was also the memory of that embarrassing scene on the
march towards Worcester which appeared, in perspective, only a
little less monstrous than the Duke's affiliation with the unspeak-
able Lilburne.

In addition to this, Buckingham's criticisms of the King had
all been repeated, by Clarendon's instructions; and Charles, outwardly imperturbable but inwardly sensitive to fault-finding,
remembered and resented the contemptuous comments that gained
in spitefulness at second hand. One of Nicholas's correspondents
had said that " his ink was not black enough to express the base
and horrid language Buckingham did belch out concerning our
Master " and that Herbert and Lord Gerard were " unsufferable
concerning the King's person and his affairs, and none can excel
them but the Duke of Buckingham ". This was bad enough; but

the Duke made matters worse by complaining that he had received
none of the moneys due to him from Charles during his service
with Turenne and "continued extravagant in his carriage"
towards the King. Nicholas added rather smugly, "These great
wits are none of the best servants or friends. They may be good
company for a time: but they are uneasy to live with."

It is not hard to believe that Buckingham was "uneasy to live
with" at this time. At twenty-eight he was a weary and disappointed man; but although he was defeated in all he set his
hand to, he continued to work—so he declared—for the restoration
of the monarchy in England. He had no military forces to draw
upon save those promised by the heads of The Sealed Knot;
and their numbers varied maddeningly from month to month;
he had sold the last of his father's pictures to Queen Christina of
Sweden in order to fit himself out for his war service: and all
he had gained from this service was the friendship and admiration
of Turenne, who could not help him against Cromwell; nevertheless he struggled on with his little band of plotters, irritable,
obstinate, absorbed.

During these years of hopeless exile the strain had begun to
tell on the scattered groups of Royalists who circulated, spying,
back-biting and tale-bearing, between the Low Countries and
France. Depression and suspense had given way to quarrelling
and drunkenness: duels, brawls and scandals were the result. "I
may truly say," wrote one of Cromwell's spies from Holland,
"that no greater abominations were ever practised among people
than at this day at Charles Stuart's Court. Fornication, drunkenness and adultery are esteemed no sin amongst them." It is
noticeable that the reports of Buckingham, hostile though they
are, fail to show him as a sot or a fire-eater. Many unpleasant
characteristics were to spring out of his easy, genial temper in the
years to come: now he concentrated all his energies on one object,
and—quite naturally—was accused of treachery for his pains.

Everything the Duke did was wrong, according to Nicholas,
Clarendon and their supporters; the chorus of censure, disapproval
and suspicion makes sad reading. They believed that he was
playing his own hand, irrespective of the Royalist interest; it is
more likely that Buckingham thought he was working for his
master when all the time at the back of his mind was the picture
of the life for which he longed—the return to that power, wealth
and ease of which he had been deprived and which he had three

times denied himself; yet, although he could at any moment have put an end to the poverty and dreariness of exile by compounding with Parliament, he hung back from taking so definite a step. The comments he let fall at this time and a little later show a total confusion of purpose: at one moment he was threatening to destroy the Protector, at another abusing the King. The effect on Clarendon was the same in either case. When Buckingham was "civil and free" with him, the gouty, carping Chancellor only sneered; when the Duke was silent he was suspected of pride or deceit; when he became estranged from Leighton it was because of Leighton's loyalty to the King: when he took up with Sexby, another Leveller, it was for his own purposes: when he was in Antwerp he should have been in Cologne, when he went to Calais he should have remained in Bruges (Clarendon disapproved of "gadding ways", even in his own family), when he was robbed as he left M. de Schomberg's lodgings in Paris it was no more than he deserved.

Buckingham's attempts to gain Charles's support were frustrated by Clarendon again and again. The Chancellor did not trust his young master any more than he did the Duke of Buckingham: no Stuart could be trusted; so he bombarded him with admonishing letters, imploring him to be more open with his followers and warned him against playing off one against another. Charles seemed to agree; but he consented to receive the Duke in spite of Clarendon's frenzied reiteration that "Buckingham could do the King better service by not going to him."

The interview was a failure from Buckingham's point of view; he was unable to conceal his disgust and irritation at Charles's evasive attitude; and Charles could not forget how often he had been the subject of Buckingham's sarcasms. Then Nicholas and his correspondents began again on the Duke's worthlessness and unreliability. He had shown great presumption in approaching the King: all his group, Sexby in particular, were suspect; he was "after the old way, no church or religion"; he pretended to be a Catholic one day and a Presbyterian the next (his aunt, Lady Denbigh, was sure that he affected Presbyterianism, and she should know): he had used disgraceful language of the King "and those about him whom he values", i.e. Nicholas and Clarendon: he was plotting with Cromwell and degrading his "gallant father's" name (the first Duke would never have "run these ways"): he was in Dover as Mr. Billing, in London as Mr.

Browner, in Breda as Mr. Barcott, at Paris in consultation with
the Queen, "passing by creeks to and fro between England and
France", and—worst of all—"busy with the Papists".[14]

6

Cromwell's attitude towards Buckingham was that of the
man who neglects nothing in order to consolidate his position.
During the last years of the Protectorate the question of a Cromwellian dynasty had been debated, with the result that the
Parliamentary rulers began to consider alliances with the Royalist
aristocracy. The enormous prestige of the land-owning classes
had been little affected by their defeat in the field; and during the
sixteen-fifties it became as necessary to cajole them back into
England as to defeat their attempts at invasion. Any kind of
connection with Buckingham made it easier for Cromwell's spies
to determine the movements of the Royalists and to stamp out
their schemes for the overthrow or the assassination of the man
on whose life their powers depended.

It is certain that Cromwell and his advisers did everything
they could to use Buckingham, while he in his turn tried to give
them the impression that he might at any moment act as a reporter
between them and their spies on the Continent in order to travel
to and from England with greater ease. To this end Cromwell
granted the Duke a permit to establish himself anywhere in the
kingdom. That until the summer of 1657 Buckingham only used
this pass as a means of travel was entirely ignored by those who
accused him of treachery.

As soon as Buckingham's movements were known the worst
possible motives were assigned to them, not only by Clarendon,
Nicholas and Ormonde, but by almost everyone in the Royalist
party. For one Cavalier to accuse another of offering himself up
to Cromwell was the commonest form of abuse; even Clarendon
was at one time suspected of this particular treachery; it was,
therefore, inevitable that Buckingham, an independent and
extremely active young man, should fall under a suspicion that
became a certainty as the months went by. As early as 1655 it was
thought that he had already "made his peace" with the
Protector and was to marry one of his relations.

---

14 All the accusations in this paragraph are from Nicholas.

In fact at this, the saddest and most hopeless period of the exile, Buckingham was the sole Cavalier who—if only for his own ends—was still making a serious attempt to re-establish the monarchy. The Cromwellian delegates were received in all the courts of Europe; the two greatest Continental powers, France and Spain, were too much occupied with their own quarrels to spare men or money for what was now generally thought of as a lost cause; and the dignitaries of the Royalist court were, therefore, reduced to interminable correspondence about their financial problems and the possibilities of a revolution at home. While they were sitting at their desks, Buckingham ventured his reputation and his hopes of fortune trying to organise the revolt that the older men were waiting for; that he did not succeed has further blackened his fame.

The attitude of the King is hardest to define, perhaps because Clarendon so seldom allowed him to think or speak for himself. That curious, deadening apathy, characteristic of the Stuarts, seems to have descended on him during these years. Outcast, derided, ignored, Charles appears to have sought such distractions as were available to a king with an unpaid retinue and a short purse; long afterwards, when he remarked to Burnet that he believed "God would not make a man miserable for taking a little pleasure out of the way", he may have been thinking of the weary days and feverish nights that he spent in Cologne, Brussels, Breda, Ghent and the Hague when England seemed further away than the Barbadoes and Whitehall a mirage in the desert of foreign intrigue and hope deferred ... Buckingham's activities, Clarendon's lectures, his brothers' grumbling, all were unendurably tedious; he only woke to action when his mother tried to force the Duke of Gloucester into Catholicism; at this point he dashed off one or two admirably forceful letters and then sank back into lethargy, preferring to have his decisions made for him.

In this way Buckingham met with discouragement from the man who had been his closest friend and his greatest debtor. He had no one on whom he could rely; for Clarendon, following the old, evil practice of setting one double-dealer upon another, now bribed Colonel Titus and Father Talbot to follow the Duke's movements and report on everything he did; the result was not very satisfactory. Father Talbot, who met Buckingham in Brussels and persuaded him not to go over into England again, said that

G

" the Duke's interest was very considerable " and that " he must be kept satisfied, or at least not made desperate " through lack of help.

The Chancellor changed his tactics upon this recommendation. Buckingham was given to understand that he was representing the King's interest, but quite unofficially, so that in the event of failure or disgrace Charles's name should not appear in any of the negotiations. There was no harm in using such a creature as George Villiers: but it must be clearly understood that he took all the risks.

Titus did not trouble himself with watching the Duke too closely, for he was engaged in the more congenial task of distributing Saxby's pamphlet against Cromwell, *Killing No Murder*, which Clarendon read and pronounced " as witty an epistle as he had seen ".

Then, on June the Seventeenth, 1657, Clarendon reported that " the Duke of Buckingham is believed to be in England upon some desperate design, for a rising in the City or against the Protector's person."

Buckingham's design was desperate indeed. He arrived in London in mid-June and remained there for three months in close seclusion. He was promised an act of indemnity, but got no audience of the Protector; nor is it likely that he desired one. Some time ago it had occurred to him that Fairfax, not Cromwell, was the man to raise up both himself and his cause. Fairfax and Cromwell had divided the Villiers estates between them; and, by allying himself with Fairfax, Buckingham could at one stroke recover most of his property and the power to collect an army for the King—an army commanded by the General and led by himself that would sweep over England. Two years before Buckingham had approached Charles with what he said was a message from Fairfax to this effect, only to be rebuffed.[15]

The bond between himself and Fairfax must be intimate and indissoluble. The General's daughter Mary, his only child, was still unmarried. During the months that he lay hidden in London, Buckingham planned a way, through the daughter's heart, to the father's favour.

15 Nicholas himself denied that any such message was conveyed to Charles.

PART TWO
(June 1657 – September 1670)

THE YEARS OF TRIUMPH

CHAPTER ONE

I

THE Fairfaxes had been established in Yorkshire several hundred years before the Villiers came over from Normandy, but like the Villiers, they acquired no fame until the seventeenth century. During the reign of Henry VII, Sir William Fairfax married a sister of Lord Manners of Roos; and so his descendants were related to Buckingham's mother. Thomas Fairfax, son of Sir Ferdinando, afterwards Lord Fairfax, and Lady Mary Sheffield, was born in 1612, educated at home and subsequently at St. John's in the University of Cambridge; he saw some war service abroad and then travelled in France; in 1637 he married Anne Vere, daughter of Lord Vere of Tilbury; a year later their daughter Mary was born at Bolton Percy in Yorkshire.[1]

In 1648 Sir Thomas succeeded his father as Lord Fairfax: but the exigencies of his profession and his principles made it impossible for him to retire into the intellectual pursuits and family intercourse for which he longed. It was not only for themselves that Mary's parents desired the quiet days and nights and the opportunity for study of country life; at five years old she had been carried away from the advancing Royalist armies and left for dead in a farm-house; next day her father heard that she and Lady Fairfax were alive and safe. But from that stormy summer of 1643 until the spring of 1650 he seldom saw his " little Moll ", although he never forgot to send his love to her; he had to leave her early training to her mother.

Anne Fairfax was a deeply religious woman, high-minded and fearless as became a Vere of Tilbury and the wife of a great commander; she was famous in later life, and in history, for her outburst during the trial of Charles I in Westminster Hall; she may have been severe and uncompromising in her politics, but she was an indulgent mother; she brought up Mary with loving care, teaching her to take notes of the sermon when they went together to the parish church of Bolton Percy, where Lord Fairfax's uncle was Rector, and placing her against that background of wide culture, social responsibility and unostentatious piety in which she herself had been educated.

[1] C. F. Markham: *Life of Fairfax*. Complete Peerage.

When at last the war was over and the Fairfaxes were able to lead the life to which their tastes and traditions inclined them, they returned home. The General had no wish to establish himself in any of the houses given him by Parliament from the Villiers estates; he preferred his own land; so the devoted family of three settled at Nun Appleton in Yorkshire, originally a convent acquired by the Fairfaxes during the Reformation which had been re-built by Mary's grandfather; the ruins of the old nunnery still extended from the south side of the main building to where the gardens and meadows met the river Wharfe.

This beautiful manor-house was of red brick, E-shaped and crowned by a cupola; the great hall or gallery where Lord Fairfax kept his collections of coins, medals and engravings was fifty yards long, occupying all the central section and decorated with pictures, marble chimney-pieces and thirty carved wooden shields bearing the family escutcheons.

The high pointed roofs of Nun Appleton looked over a deer-park of oak-trees, but the garden—the General's favourite outdoor hobby—was one of the most unusual in the neighbourhood, for the flowers were massed in beds shaped like fortresses of five bastions apiece. From the library windows Lord Fairfax could observe these examples of modern taste and military training whenever he looked up from his writing; for he was occupied with a metrical version of the Psalms and composed a good deal of forthright if not very remarkable poetry.

The Reverend Henry Fairfax of Bolton Percy had several children; one, Brian, a clever studious boy, five years older than Mary, became especially attached to his distinguished cousin and spent a great deal of time at Nun Appleton during the General's retirement there—a retirement which was to be interrupted soon after Mary's nineteenth birthday.

Both Lord and Lady Fairfax, outwardly conventional in behaviour and generally inclining to custom in matters of tradition, were inconoclastic in their treatment of Mary. They startled their friends and neighbours by keeping her at home when all her contemporaries were long since married; and they engaged a tutor for her when she was twelve, just as if she had been a boy. This tutor was the son of the Rector of Swinestead in Holderness, and his name was Andrew Marvell. He stayed at Nun Appleton for two years.

2

When Buckingham arrived in London in June, 1657, he was entirely friendless. Suborned by Clarendon, the King had cast him off, though during their last interview he had been moderately agreeable, advising the Duke to make his peace in England, the better to serve the Royalist cause. The man who had engaged himself to travel "a thousand and a thousand miles upon his feet" on Buckingham's errands had made his last journey: the Duchess of Richmond, once more in England, had no influence: Lord Denbigh was entirely devoted to the Parliamentary interest. But the tide was beginning to turn against Cromwell; his grasp on England had been loosened by the expenses of his wars with France and Spain, even by his victories at sea. The standard of living had fallen and the Protectorate was now as unpopular with the heavily taxed merchant classes as with the ruined Cavaliers.

For the first three months after his arrival Buckingham saw no one, and his servants were instructed to say that he was too ill to receive. But he was in touch with Abraham Cowley and his wife, and with a Mr. Robert Harlow, a friend of the Fairfaxes. At last he consented to see Colonel Bamfield, a Parliamentary agent, who had his correspondence tapped and reported on the letters that were passing between him and Lord Fairfax. Bamfield knew that his superiors were unlikely to believe in his story of a betrothal between Buckingham and Mary Fairfax, for the rumour of an engagement had arisen before, nearly four years ago, and died down. He was, therefore, extremely cautious in his attempted summary of Buckingham's attitude. "It is thought," he wrote to Thurloe, Cromwell's Secretary of State, "that the Duke of Buckingham is in England privately, with your consent, and is to marry Lord Fairfax's daughter. This seems romantic . . ."[2] In fact the Colonel was not of the opinion that Buckingham would be so foolish as to try again.

Then Lord Fairfax came to London. "The Duke has put his business into a better position," said the next report, "and will do something, but not so well as was believed on his first appearance in public." It is probable that Buckingham's first public appearance was at Whitehall, where Cromwell, who knew that

[2] i.e. a falsehood.

he had not long to live, was trying to place the future of England in reliable hands; in spite of great opposition he was still considering the plan of placing the young King on the throne as a puppet ruler; but the reports from the Continent were unfavourable; Charles Stuart was "already too debauched", and the complications were too many. The Protector could not bring himself to believe in the rumours that Lord Fairfax was giving his only child to the disgraced, suspect and penniless George Villiers: nor was Fairfax himself quite sure of his intentions, in spite of his increasing appreciation of Buckingham's gifts. But one member of the Council, a cousin of the Fairfaxes, who was aware, though no one else seemed to be, that Mary was already betrothed to Lord Chesterfield and that the banns "had been twice asked in church", told them that the Duke was still paying great court to Fairfax and that the Chesterfield match had been broken off; he added bitterly, "I think the sole design to be a Duchess made them forbid the banns".[3]

Lord Fairfax had not the least wish to see his daughter a duchess, rightly considering that to be a Fairfax was quite good enough; but his own health was beginning to fail and he wanted her settled. Presently his wife, his daughter and some other members of the family, Brian Fairfax and old Lady Vere among them, joined him in London, and Buckingham was given his chance.

He took it. A few weeks later he was betrothed to Mary, privately, on account of the Protector's certain disapproval, but with the consent of her parents and of her grandmother, an extremely severe and puritanical old lady.

Clarendon, hearing the news, refused to believe it: the Cromwellian agents continued to look on the Duke as an unsuccessful suitor: Charles made no remark: nor are Lord Chesterfield's comments recorded. Brian Fairfax's explanation is, "The young lady could not resist his charms, being the most graceful and beautiful person that any Court in Europe ever saw . . . all his trouble in wooing was, he came, saw and conquered."

The story of George Villiers' marriage to Mary Fairfax is perhaps romantic, in the modern sense; but it is not quite so simple as Brian Fairfax—who was immediately and completely subjugated

---

[3] It is doubtful if Mary would have been happier married to Philip Stanhope, third Earl of Chesterfield, who died in 1714 in his eightieth year and was described by Swift as "very subtle and cunning . . . the greatest knave in England".

by Buckingham—would have us believe. In order to account for
Lord Fairfax's action in this, the matter nearest his heart, it is
necessary to examine rather more closely the subject of Buckingham's reputation at this point in his career.

3

For thirteen years Buckingham had visited England only
at long intervals and for very short periods; during this time of
involuntary exile the reports on his behaviour were all made,
with the exception of John Lilburne's, by his enemies. And very
censorious they were; though able, versatile, energetic and cour-
ageous, he was considered, as has been seen, a disloyal, arrogant
and untrustworthy young man. To emphasise this judgement is
to "point" the unreliability and one-sidedness of all historical
knowledge; there is no record, for instance, of Argyll's or the
Earl of Newcastle's opinion of Buckingham, let alone that of the
Princess of Orange, Charles II or Turenne, to name only a few
of those whose liking for him was undoubted. Furthermore,
during the latter part of Buckingham's time abroad his reputation,
in regard to women and the bottle, is inextricably bound up with
that of his master and it has been impossible, hitherto, to separate
them. Buckingham and Charles are paired off as debauchees,
cynics and idlers, in spite of the fact that during early manhood
they were estranged for months at a time and saw little or nothing
of one another.

It is therefore desirable to recapitulate the censure of Clarendon,
Nicholas and the Puritan spies in order to show their hatred, and
indeed their fear, of Buckingham; in their opinion he might do
anything, and everything he did was detestable.[4] But in the
entire course of their condemnations there is only one comment
on his insobriety and his predilection for the pleasures of the
alcove. While Charles, as we know, was early celebrated for his
susceptibility and its consequences, there is no linking of Buckingham's name with that of a mistress; he tried to marry Anne
Campbell and Mary of Orange for reasons of ambition and no
doubt made himself very agreeable to both ladies in the process.
In the Thurloe correspondence we read that in April, 1656, he
spent three days at the house of Mme de Nieuport, who was the

---

[4] In 1651 the Parliamentary spies reported on Buckingham's " lasciviousness ", but
were unable to substantiate the charge. Whitelocke's *Memorials*.

wife of the Dutch Ambassador in France and a Royalist agent; beyond that, there is nothing to show that he had acquired the reputation that became his during the early years of the Restoration and reached its climax in his later life.

All this is a little disappointing; it would be simpler and much more suitable to think of Buckingham as breaking hearts and begetting illegitimate children all over Europe while he was still a young, handsome and unsuccessful adventurer, and then to see him established as a rake during middle age. If this had been so —and if one can be certain of anything it is that both Buckingham's paramours and his drunkenness would have been fully described as soon as his enemies discovered them—neither Lord nor Lady Fairfax would have considered him as a son-in-law. That they accepted him presupposes not so much his conquest and their subjugation as his general desirability as the husband of a beloved child and a great heiress.

George Villiers came of a house that was ancient indeed, and noble; but his father's connection with the Stuart family was not such as to recommend him to a man like Fairfax, who could look back on a line of ancestors of unsullied respectability. The blackest mark against the Duke was the question of his disloyalty to Charles II, but as Fairfax himself, though unwillingly, had deserted the father, he cannot be blamed for his condonation of Buckingham's desertion of the son;[5] and it will be seen that between the autumn of 1657 and the spring of 1660, Buckingham and his father-in-law laboured unceasingly for the return of Charles, not as the passive instrument of the Puritan party but as the Defender of the Faith and the hereditary monarch of Great Britain and Ireland.

Finally, in Fairfax's eyes, Buckingham was no penniless outcast but the owner of estates by which the General himself had refused to profit; he did not consider that Parliament had a right to dispose of the Villiers' or anybody else's property, and from the moment of the trial of Charles I had been against the régime, giving up his command in order to show his disassociation from it; now, for some years, only his services and his popularity had saved him from persecution by the Puritan extremists. Buckingham's appearance gave him the chance to put things right, and he did so.

[5] Fairfax had approached Charles I in a final attempt at a negotiated peace in York in the year 1645, but was denied admittance.

In spite of all these considerations there was much against the Duke: his rumoured atheism and unconventionality, his leaning towards low company and, worst of all, his connection with Argyll and the Presbyterians, those wicked men who had sold their King to his enemies. These disadvantages had to be overcome: how Buckingham overcame them is not known. His persuasiveness and adaptability have already been demonstrated; they can never have been tried higher than in the weeks of his probation with the General and his family. Buckingham not only cleared himself: he swept the Fairfaxes off their feet. How was it done? Brian Fairfax's " he came, saw and conquered " tells us nothing.

The most powerful weapon in Buckingham's armoury was his effect on Mary. She fell in love with him at first sight; and she loved him always, in spite of the unhappiness he caused her. As Brian Fairfax says rather sadly, " She patiently bore those faults in him which she could not remedy." So, although the course of Buckingham's almost magical installation and his triumph cannot be described in detail, all the characters in the drama may be seen—the dazzling hero, fresh from hardships and dangers, poverty and exile: the severe but ultimately indulgent parents: the boyish, adoring young cousin: the formidable grandmother—all are there.

And the heroine? It only needs that she should have a little beauty, a modest appeal, to fit into such a setting. The lady in this kind of romance is not really important, as long as she possesses some looks, and a certain distinction.

Alas! Alas! Mary Fairfax—" a most virtuous and amiable lady "—was uncompromisingly, distressingly plain, even ugly, with the kind of ugliness that cannot be overlooked or disguised. She had inherited none of her father's melancholy, high-bred beauty, none of her mother's fire and spirit. A cheerful, intelligent, sensible young woman, she was remarkable, in an age of elegance and wit, for her total inability to shine either in appearance or conversation. "A little round crumpled woman, very fond of finery," says the Vicomtesse de Longueville, seeing her a few years after she became Duchess of Buckingham. Poor Mary— like many clever people, she inclined rather to the ridiculous, covering her dresses with gold lace and her neck and arms with heavy jewels, just when a voluptuous and calculated disarray, that expensive substitute for simplicity, was coming into fashion.

She was no fool. She knew what she was doing when she married a Villiers, and it is unlikely that she complained. As the first lady in England after the Queen and the Duchess of York, she enjoyed gaiety, and—when it came her way—the society of her husband. Little more is known of her.

4

The marriage was celebrated at Bolton Percy on September the Seventh, 1657, a fortnight after the Duke, through Robert Harlow, made his formal proposal for Mary's hand. He had prepared the way by the following effusion—there is no other word for it—to Lady Fairfax.

" Madame,

I shall hope from the intercession of the person that does me the favour to deliver this to you, what I could hardly have expected upon any other account: that your ladyship will be pleased to pardon me the boldness of writing lately to your daughter. Mrs. Worsnam was the first that gave me the confidence of making my addresses to her, and it was by her means only that I had the happiness of waiting upon her, and if that interview had made me so little master of myself as not to be able to refrain laying hold of an opportunity offered to me of letting her know the pain I endure for her sake, I hope your ladyship may be persuaded to make a true interpretation of it, and to believe it could proceed only from an excess of that respect and devotion I shall ever bear Mistress Fairfax (whom if my fortune were in any way proportionable to my affections) I should have the impudence to pretend to deserve at least as much as any other body whatsoever, since I am sure it is impossible to love or honour anything more than I truly do her and to wish for anything with greater longing or impatience than I do for some means of giving both her and your ladyship undeniable proofs of it, being confident that if your ladyship knew the nature of the passion I have for her, you could not be so ill-natured (however averse to me soever she might be) as not to pity my condition or to refuse the endeavouring to further me by your favour to the enjoying of what only in this world can make me perfectly happy. That is, Madame, the honour of being your ladyship's most dutiful son as I shall forever (whether your ladyship will or no) challenge eternally that of being, Madame—Your ladyship's most humble and most obedient servant,

BUCKINGHAM."[6]

Abraham Cowley was Buckingham's best man and composed an Epithalamium—not a very good one—for the wedding feast. The Reverend Simon Harcourt had the prescience to exclaim to

---

[6] From the original manuscript in the British Museum.

Lady Fairfax that he "saw God in the Duke's face", when he was reading the marriage service: this remark went the rounds of county society. After the junketings were over the Duke and Duchess settled down at Nun Appleton, now part of Mary's dowry. Buckingham had to remain in seclusion even here, for the Cromwellian agents were once more on his trail, the Protector having expressed himself, with ominous restraint, as "not pleased" with the marriage.

The Fairfaxes were in ecstasies with their fascinating son-in-law. "He is the oracle of his father, mother-in-law and wife— who is the best of the four," commented Clarendon, sourly, after the news of the Duke's marriage had been verified; he concluded that Buckingham must have done the Protector "some great service" for the marriage to have been allowed. Here, as so often before, Clarendon's prejudice led him astray. During the months before his marriage when he lay hidden in London or at his sister's Buckingham almost certainly ventured upon that double-dealing of which he had been accused in the past. The course of his actions is obscure; but the correspondence concerning it indicates his willingness to let the Protector believe that he wished to marry, not Mary Fairfax, but either Mary or Frances Cromwell.

It is unlikely that Cromwell, who was a devoted father, would have allowed either of these girls[7] to marry the man who had so recently threatened his destruction, but neither did he like, says Brian Fairfax, speaking of the Fairfax marriage, "such a conjunction of Mars and Mercury"; Cromwell therefore encouraged Buckingham by allowing him to visit his daughters at Whitehall, although he himself did not receive the Duke, making appointments with him and then breaking them. Before the Duke's marriage became known he was allowed a pardon under the Great Seal and put forward—by some unnamed members of the Privy Council—as a suitable husband for one of the Protector's daughters. The most likely solution of the mystery is that certain members of the Council were trying to make mischief between Fairfax and Cromwell by means of Buckingham's intrusion into their joint lives; they did not succeed.

At a Council meeting which took place during the summer of 1658 the old suspicions flared up again and it was suggested that the Duke should be exiled to Jersey. By this time he and his wife

[7] Mary Cromwell married Lord Falconbridge and Frances Lord Rich in November 1657.

had left Yorkshire and were living at York House. Buckingham was on his way to Cobham to visit the Duchess of Richmond when he was arrested by Colonel Gibbons, who recognised him at once, although the last time they had met was for a fleeting moment during the battle of Kingston. On being asked his business the Duke glibly replied that he was about to visit the Countess of Pembroke, " to reconcile her with her lord", thus clearing his sister of complicity in anything of which he might be accused; he was then conducted to the Tower.

As soon as he heard of his son-in-law's arrest Lord Fairfax, accompanied by Brian, went to London and interviewed the Protector at Whitehall. The General was bursting with indignation at what he considered a personal insult, but he restrained himself at first, merely asking that the Duke might be released as soon as possible. Cromwell, also determined not to quarrel, " dealt friendly but plainly " with Fairfax, remarking that before allying himself with " those who were enemies both to his honour and interest " he should have consulted with " his old friends, that had went along with him in all the wars ". Lord Fairfax then began on his defence of Buckingham, pointing out that the Duke was " a better man than he (Cromwell) took him to be ". But the Protector would not listen to this, and Fairfax, losing his temper, " turned abruptly from his old acquaintance " and followed by the awe-struck Brian, strode away down the gallery, " cocking his hat and throwing his cloak under his arm as he used to do when he was angry ". Everyone, Brian included, expected the General's arrest to follow that of his son-in-law after this, but " the Protector was wiser in his passion ", and Fairfax returned to York House unmolested. Buckingham was sent from the Tower to Windsor, stopping, " at his earnest request ", to see his wife and her father and mother on his way, and he then remained at Windsor with the Cowleys; but when Cromwell's last illness began he was again arrested and sent to the Tower, where he was treated as a very dangerous prisoner. His release came just in time; his own account of it was found by Brian Fairfax after his death and preserved among the Fairfax papers.

" As soon as Oliver was dead, they proclaimed his son, Richard Cromwell, Protector of England, with the same solemnities that ever Kings of England were proclaimed Kings. I was then close prisoner in the Tower, with a couple of Guards lying always in my chamber and a sentinel at my door. I confess I was not a little delighted with the noise of the great guns, for I presently knew what it meant, and if Oliver had lived for three days longer I had certainly been put to death."

The Duke rejoined his wife at York House, and from that time onwards they were always together, either in London or at Nun Appleton. On the Twenty-Third of February, 1659, Buckingham appeared at the bar of the House of Commons and engaged himself, upon his honour, " that he should not abet any of the enemies of this Commonwealth ", while Lord Pembroke stood bail for him for twenty thousand pounds. He then returned to Yorkshire. At about this time, Buckingham translated Horace's Ode, *Fortuna saevis laeta negotiis*, as being suitable to his circumstances.

5

Like many of his contemporaries, Buckingham possessed a Commonplace Book. One was found in his pocket after his death, and in 1792 came into the hands of Lord Carlisle, who gave it to Lord Jersey; in the archives of the Jersey family it is still to be seen, a thick black book measuring four inches by two and a half with gold ornamentation and silver clasps; it can be reversed and written in from either end.[8] Buckingham has made his entries under different headings, of which there are sixty-nine in the first half of the Commonplace Book; the second half contains the opening scenes of a very indifferent play, in the classical manner, which was never finished. Most of the headings are generic—Love, Beauty, Poverty, Policy, Solitude, Anger, Life, Fame and so on—some are in rhyme and some are unfinished jottings of no interest or value. There is only one entry under " Women " and several under " Love ", " Lust ", " Confession ", " Death " and " Sorrow ". Buckingham refers with some contempt to soldiers, modesty, divination and confession and seems to have approved of poverty, fickleness and wit—an odd selection out of so many subjects. Here, in his small neat hand, is one of his first poems; it is on the death of Oliver Cromwell:

> " Deep in his flesh, deep struck th'Almighty's dart.
> The terrors of the great one stormed his heart.
> Thus in his height of sin and shameless pride
> Thus by God's hand the British Gracchus died."

[8] In January 1898 there appeared an article on the Second Duke of Buckingham in the *Quarterly Review* (No. 373) by an anonymous author, who reproduced some half-dozen passages from the Commonplace Book. The greater part of the excerpts given in this biography are here published for the first time.

This is an unsuccessful experiment; and the highly conventional verses of gallantry—

> " All that I do, all that I say,
> All my night, and all my day,
> Shall be the constant tribute that I pay "

—seem to connect themselves to this period, the period of his early married life. His opinion of marriage was quite different. " Wives we choose for our posterity, mistresses for ourselves. . . . Marriage is the greatest solitude, for it makes two but one and prohibits us from all others." These thoughts were concealed from his wife, whose character best fits another of his little rhymes:

> " Find me a woman fair and wise and kind—
> Let me but one such woman find—
> And on that screen my thread of life I'll wind."

" This was the happiest time of all the Duke's life," says Brian Fairfax, speaking of the months that Buckingham and Mary spent " orderly and decently " before the curtain went up on the glittering extravaganza of the Restoration and they took their places at the Court of Charles II. He adds, " Now he lived a most regular life, no courtships but to his own wife, not so much as to his after-beloved and costly mistress, the philosopher's stone."

Buckingham's passion for chemistry had not yet superseded his love of hunting; but the greater part of his leisure was spent with his father-in-law, whose life he was thinking of writing. Neither Buckingham nor Fairfax dreamed that the coming revolution was to be bloodless; they were preparing to risk their lives for the last time.

And Mary? Had she begun to feel beneath the wit and the gaiety and the good humour of her splendid husband the cold indifference of the man who had married out of policy? It is unlikely that she demanded more than she received; at this time Buckingham's life was too busy and too exciting for him to resent the presence of the stumpy, dark little woman to whom he was bound: and his affection for his father-in-law extended to the whole Fairfax family, with whom he was on the best of terms. Perhaps, as the months went by and there was no prospect of an heir, they were all a little disappointed; but the Duke and his wife were young, vigorous and healthy, and there was plenty of time. . . .

At the end of December 1659 Lord Fairfax, who was spending Christmas at Nun Appleton, received a letter from General Monk,

THE DUCHESS OF BUCKINGHAM

By an unknown artist

asking for his consent to the rising against General Lambert, then in command of the Roundhead army. Brian Fairfax came into the room just as Lord Fairfax, Buckingham, another Fairfax cousin and the Reverend Mr. Bowles were discussing the best way to send an answer and the General exclaimed, " Here is my cousin Brian, I undertake he will do our business for us." Brian accepted and was given his instructions for the journey to Scotland. He was disguised by Buckingham as " a young country clown " and advised by him to travel unarmed; but his brother insisted on his carrying a rapier concealed in a cane.

At Coldstream, Brian was well received by Monk, who promised " to watch Lambert as a cat watches a mouse ". Meanwhile Fairfax and Buckingham collected their forces and prepared to meet Monk at York on January the First. Christmas week was spent by Buckingham at Malton, where he drilled and organised the volunteers who poured in from all over the countryside. Then he moved to Knaresborough, where he was to join up with his father-in-law and take over the troops commanded by Sir Henry Cholmely, Immediately he arrived a number of ex-Parliamentary officers refused to serve under a " malignant " and a Cavalier, and Buckingham was relegated to a subordinate position on Lord Fairfax's staff, entering York at his side to the shouts of " A Fairfax! A Fairfax!" from the people. There were no shouts for George Villiers; and when Monk arrived, having accepted the submission of Lambert's armies, and went on to London to declare a free Parliament, he was accompanied by Buckingham, while Fairfax returned to Nun Appleton, refusing the command which Monk had offered him. The Duke was not among those noblemen who were received by Charles II at Breda; but he was at Dover for the King's arrival on May the Twenty-Fifth, 1660, and the French Ambassador reported that Charles received his old friend very coldly.

The rebuffs of Cromwellian officers, the coolness of the Stuart family, left Buckingham unperturbed. He was not sensitive; and he knew exactly how he was going to succeed. When the royal coach set off from Dover Charles and Monk sat facing the horses: the Dukes of York and Gloucester were opposite; but the boot— the huge semi-circular cover of the back wheel containing an outside seat for one person—was empty: and before anyone could stop him Buckingham had placed himself in it. Two miles from Dover Charles left the coach and continued his journey on horseback; his

H

brothers and General Monk rode on either side of him. Buckingham, bare-headed, was just behind.   From Dover to Rochester,
where Charles spent his first night in England, his progress was
slow and fatiguing. By the time they all left Rochester for London
on the following day Buckingham was reinstated—no one knew
how—in Charles's favour.[9]

6

Charles II was thirty years old when his enraptured people
drank his health kneeling in the streets of London and lit bonfires
and rang the church bells to celebrate his return. His younger sister,
Elizabeth, had died in 1650 at the age of fifteen; Mary of Orange
and Henry of Gloucester died of smallpox during the first winter
of his reign; of the seven children of Charles I and Henrietta
Maria only three—Charles II, James Duke of York and Henrietta
Anne—lived to enjoy the triumph of the Stuart family. The
Princess Henrietta Anne was gentle, foolish and vain: James was
vain, obstinate and debauched: and Charles was obstinate, clever
and unscrupulous. Charles disliked James, but was endlessly
tolerant of him; James was jealous of Charles and both were
deeply attached to Henrietta Anne, who idealised her brothers—
for she had seen very little of them and was no judge of character.
All three were patient with but intensely irritated by their mother:
her influence over her sons was negligible.

Charles had outstripped Buckingham since the days of their
childhood under the care of Brian Duppa and the Duke of Newcastle. The slow-witted, awkward boy had grown into a subtle,
deep and cunning man, whose intellect had been sharpened in a
hard school, harder than any Buckingham knew, and whose
pleasant ways and idle humour concealed a sleepless determination
to outwit his enemies and have his own way, whatever the cost.
Buckingham—" the finest gentleman of person and wit I think I
ever saw," says Sir John Reresby, who came to know him at this
time[10]—with his high spirits and quick-firing repartee, his careless

---

[9] Sir Edward Walker.
[10] The legend of Buckingham's elegance reappeared during the summer of 1947
in a daily paper in an advertisement from the firm of Messrs. Moss Bros. of King
Street, W.C.   It runs as follows: " George Villiers, 2nd Duke of Buckingham, childhood friend of Charles II and popular in gay Covent Garden society was described by
one contemporary as ' The finest gentleman of presence. [sic] and wit I think I ever
saw.' Although to-day this elegant is but a historic memory, Moss Bros. of Covent
Garden still carry on this English tradition of good clothes."

grace and his general effect of magnificence and recklessness and dash, had succeeded easily, too easily, in spite of his setbacks and misfortunes; Charles, still apparently subjugated by Clarendon, was learning, remembering, storing up all that his brains and observation taught him; he could read men, and women too, because he had trained himself to wait and watch and listen while others blundered and talked and gave themselves away ... Even while he seemed to give in he was collecting himself to attack and undermine; as a very young man indeed, he had known how to defeat a discarded mistress, Lucy Walter for one; his son by her whom he called James Crofts and later created Duke of Monmouth had been kidnapped and taken away from his termagant of a mother when Charles himself was little more than a boy. There is no doubt at all that he was right to remove the child from a young woman who tried to murder her maid by piercing her ear with a bodkin and who was believed to have perished miserably " of a disease incident to her profession "[11] without a penny to bury her—but Charles's instructions to those whom he entrusted with the work have an extraordinarily cold and merciless tone; and this very detachment, with its accompanying astuteness, was entirely lacking in Buckingham's helter-skelter, impulsive character. Again and again George Villiers burst out of all control and lost his head, his temper and his manners, and made himself intolerable and then veered round and begged to be forgiven: again and again Charles watched him rush to his destruction, waited for him to turn and held out his hand—until at last his old friend went too far and snapped the thread that bound them and the King shrugged his shoulders and let him go. . . . But in the summer of 1660 that separation was a long way off and Charles was easy and kind. Buckingham's pretty cousin, Barbara Villiers, had followed Charles from the Hague with her husband, poor foolish Roger Palmer.[12] The King loved Barbara; perhaps her appalling temper reminded him of Lucy Walter and his early youth; and presently everyone in London knew that she was his mistress and began to notice her and when they could to pay court to her; only Clarendon refused to acknowledge her existence.

[11] *Life of James II*: Clarke. It is by no means certain that Lucy Walter died of venereal disease; Clarke's version of her relationship with Charles II is both spiteful and unreliable, as has been shown by Lord George Scott in his fascinating book, *Lucy Walter: Wife or Mistress?*

[12] Barbara Villiers was Buckingham's second cousin once removed. See Genealogical Table, Appendix I.

For quite a long time Barbara Palmer and the Duke of Buckingham were friends; rapacious, gross and stupid though she was, he could always amuse her: and they were united in their hatred of Clarendon.

CHAPTER TWO

Because the aristocrats and statesmen of the Restoration were, generally speaking, venal, cultured, socially accomplished, elaborately dressed and sexually uninhibited, a veil of romantic illusion has fallen between them and a generation whose attributes are in marked contrast to theirs. Nevertheless, somewhere in the obscurity which nostalgia for the past, ill-digested information and tabloid learning have helped to create, the men and women of the Court of Charles II are waiting to be discovered again; and one of the surest ways of getting at them is through the realisation that they do not really resemble ourselves. Our degeneration, our wickedness, our hypocrisy are not theirs; many of our aspirations and achievements are as far removed from theirs as from those of the Ninevites or the predynastic Egyptians.

To swallow this premise is like gulping down a dose of medicine; it is so much easier and pleasanter to think of Nell Gwynn, Rochester, Hortense Mancini, or even Titus Oates, as people not unlike ourselves, in fancy dress, using a picturesque and unusual turn of phrase; but if we can forget our own world and the worlds that lie between us and our seventeenth-century ancestors and take their manners and habiliments for granted, we shall come infinitely nearer to them and to the point of view of the great historians and scholars who have shown us the way back into the past.

Buckingham's character and career are typical of his age; they contain a scale of contrasts which is both repulsive and bewildering, judged by the standards of to-day; the tape-measure of the twentieth century shrivels up as it touches this man. Rank and privilege were his at birth; then, during the first thirty years of his life, he became a soldier of fortune when he was not a fugitive or a prisoner: in 1660 he acquired political power and an income of twenty thousand a year. The effect on his character was, in the end, disastrous. The first half of his life reads like an adventure story: the second half is a study in corruption, and although it is the more interesting of the two it is not for the squeamish. In Buckingham's day men of noble birth and good education looked on political life as a gamble for personal supremacy. The stakes were high: the players stood to lose wealth, reputation, life itself; and the game was played out against a background of squalor, splendour, violence, cruelty, highly cultivated intellect and luxurious taste. By modern standards, Buckingham appears as a murderer, a cheat and a bully. He was also kind, generous, good-tempered and amusing. Brian Fairfax, who loved him till the day of his death, must here speak again in his defence:

"The world has been severe in censuring his foibles, but not so just in noting his good qualities.

"For his person, he was the glory of the age and any court wherever he came. Of a most graceful and charming mien and behaviour; a strong, tall and active body, all of which gave a lustre to the ornaments of his mind; of an admirable wit and excellent judgement; and had all other qualities of a gentleman. He was courteous and affable to all; of a compassionate nature: ready to forgive and forget injuries . . . but when he was provoked by the malice of some and ingratitude of others, he might show that a good-natured man might have an ill-natured muse . . .

"The faults objected against him were, that he loved women and spent his estate.

"His estate was his own. He had often lost it for the king, and might now be allowed to enjoy it himself . . .

"His amours were too notorious to be concealed, and too scandalous to be justified, by saying he was bred in the latitude of foreign climates, and now lived in a vicious age and court; where his accusers of this crime were as guilty as himself. He lay under so ill a name for this, that whenever he was shut up in his chamber, as he loved to be, *nescio quid*, or in his laboratory, *meditans purgarum* over the fumes of charcoal, it was said to be with women . . ."

In another volume of papers Brian Fairfax has left a less flattering but more informative sentence about himself and his patron.

"He would employ me in receiving his rents and paying all his money, till, my friends advising me of the danger, I gave it over and thought I escaped well that I was not oppressed under the ruins of his fortune."

It took Buckingham quite a long time to get through his vast wealth; but he did it in the end.

2

The Privy Council of the Restoration consisted of thirty members, twelve of whom had been Roundheads; Clarendon may be said to have headed it as Lord Chancellor and chief director of public affairs; Ormonde was High Steward and Lord-Lieutenant of Ireland, the Duke of York Lord High Admiral, and Nicholas —who was succeeded two years later by Arlington—Secretary of State. There was a smaller committee or cabinet which sometimes made decisions without the knowledge of the Privy Council. All the officers of State were responsible to the King, who called himself his *premier ministre*; but as he continued to show that disinclination for business already commented on by Nicholas, the principal authority was Clarendon's.

There was no unity of action among the ministers; they often opposed both the King and one another in Parliament while they were in office; but they were liable to instant dismissal from Charles, who thus became the fountain-head of departmental and court intrigue; and as he himself was much influenced by persons who had no official standing at all, it was often necessary for his ministers to approach him through the companions of his leisure. Of these, Buckingham was one of the most privileged; he did not become a Privy Councillor till 1662: till then his position was undefined, but not in the least precarious. Charles could not do without him: and his cousin Barbara, in whose apartments the Ministers frequently met, delighted in his company.

All the Ministers of the crown lived and worked in the old palace of Whitehall, of which nothing now remains but the Banqueting Hall, built by Inigo Jones in 1622; the rest was destroyed by fire in 1698. By the time Charles II came to the throne Whitehall was not so much a palace as a series of buildings of Tudor and Jacobean date, all connected with one another, and spreading, quite unsymmetrically, from the river front along Parliament Street and Whitehall Street as far as Scotland Yard on one side and what are now the Admiralty Arch and St. James's Park on the other. Roughly in the centre was the Privy Garden, lying behind the Banqueting Hall, between the Cockpit and the Thames. The Cockpit, originally built by Henry VIII, was a large octagonal building containing several suites of rooms occupied by those who were most intimate with and necessary to the King. Clarendon, Barbara Villiers (whose washing sometimes hung out to dry in the Privy Garden),[1] Monk, now Duke of Albemarle, Monmouth, the Duke of York, and Buckingham all lived there at different times.

[1] Pepys.

At the far end of Whitehall stood Buckingham's birthplace, Wallingford House, which had been built for Viscount Wallingford, Treasurer to the Household under Queen Elizabeth and James I. This building, on the site of which the Admiralty now stands, was first connected with the Navy during the occupation of Buckingham's father who, as Lord High Admiral, rebuilt the house and held his Council of the Sea there. In 1660 his son sold it to the Government, who used it for the Offices of the Fleet; it was destroyed in 1770. A few hundred yards away stood York House, just outside the precincts of Whitehall. Buckingham pulled down this palace, which his father had built on the ruins of Cardinal Wolsey's, in the sixteen-seventies; it seems odd that he should have left the Water Gate standing, but there it is.[2]

When Buckingham came into his heritage he was a gambler, and he lost a great deal of money at play; he gave up cards and dice a few years after the Restoration and spent his fortune on building, women and chemistry. He sold Newhall to Albemarle in 1662 and a few years later built the wonderful river palace of Cliveden, of which only the terrace now remains. He possessed some ten or twelve country places in Yorkshire and elsewhere, as well as rivers, coal-mines, and forests all over England; he also owned a large house in York itself and the half-ruined but still habitable castle of Helmsley, where he spent his last years.

With all these splendid possessions, the friendship of the King and great wealth, Buckingham was one of the most envied men in the kingdom;[3] there were some indeed who declared that he had not done enough, during the years of exile, to deserve his good fortune; and one disgruntled Cavalier, Lord Bristol, said as much to his face. "High words passed," says one who was present, and a challenge was given and taken; but Charles, who was determined to stop duelling and brawls in the neighbourhood of Whitehall at least, confined Bristol and Buckingham to their lodgings until their tempers had cooled down.

This happened in August 1660. A few months later Buckingham was giving trouble again. On November the Sixth, he and Henry Jermyn, now Lord St. Albans, were sent to Calais to escort

Queen Henrietta Maria and the Princess Henrietta Anne to England. The Princess was now betrothed to Monsieur, who had recently succeeded his uncle[4] as Duke of Orléans. Everyone was delighted with the match, the Princess most of all, although she came to dislike her husband intensely within a few weeks of marriage. She was a pretty and reasonably accomplished girl: but her health was delicate and one of her shoulders higher than the other. Hitherto she had led the secluded life of a poor relation with her dominating and unreasonable mother; now she was a great lady and a leader of fashion. Charles, who had seen almost nothing of her, treated her more like a sweetheart than a sister; and Buckingham fell in love with her—so he declared—from the moment of their meeting in Calais.[5]

3

The Queen-Mother and her youngest daughter arrived in England in time for the last act in the drama of the Duke of York's marriage to Anne Hyde, Clarendon's eldest daughter. There was no getting out of it; neither the Chancellor's outbursts of rage and grief, nor the Queen-Mother's fury nor the attempts to blacken the young lady's honour by four of the Duke's friends could release him from his bonds. Anne Hyde was Duchess of York; and Charles told his brother that " he must drink as he had brewed and live with her whom he had made his wife."[6]

Anne Hyde's triumph did not affect Buckingham in 1660; but he used it in his campaign against her father during the years that followed. Now all his thoughts were for the Princess Henrietta. He quarrelled with a gentleman in her drawing-room, perhaps to draw her attention to himself, perhaps because he really was in a state of frenzy; and when she and her mother left England in January 1661 he rushed on board the ship that was carrying them to France without any luggage or change of clothing.[7] At sea the Princess became very ill, and for a time it was believed that she had small-pox. She was taken back to Portsmouth, followed by Buck-

---

[4] Gaston, father of La Grande Mademoiselle.
[5] Mme de Lafayette: *History of Madame.* C. Hartman: *Charles II and Madame.* Strickland: *English Princesses.*
[6] Burnet.   [7] Mme de Lafayette.

ingham, who was "behaving like a madman" and "suffering",
so one of her ladies reported, "from an inconceivable despair".[8]
When her illness was diagnosed as measles and they were able to
set forth again, Buckingham accompanied them as far as Havre-de-
Grâce, where the Princess halted for a rest.[9]

- At Havre-de-Grâce there was a fearful scene between Buckingham and Admiral Sir Edward Montagu.[10] During a game of
cards the Duke accused Sir Edward of cheating and gathered up
the money he had lost to him. The Admiral said no more that
night; the next day he sent a friend to ask Buckingham "whether
he did remember what he said . . . and whether he would own
it with his sword and a second".[11] Buckingham accepted the
challenge; but this time the dispute was settled by the Queen-
Mother, who commanded him to proceed at once to Paris, to
inform Monsieur of the Princess's safe arrival.[12]

When Buckingham and the Princess met again at the French
Court he made it clear that he was still in love with her, and she
encouraged him by holding conversations with him in English,
to the rage of Monsieur, who could not understand a word of
what they were saying and from their looks suspected the worst.
On one of these occasions the Princess asked Buckingham what
he thought of Mme de Chalais, the mistress of the Comte de
Guiche; Buckingham made the reply expected of him, and the
conversation appeared to take on a very intimate tone indeed.
This was too much for Monsieur, whose plump painted face
became convulsed with rage; he rushed to his mother and
hysterically demanded the instant dismissal of the odious English-
man.

Anne of Austria could not really be angry with Buckingham—
he was so like his father! She managed to soothe her younger son
(Louis was merely amused by his desperation) and, after some
delay, asked King Charles to recall the Duke to England.[13] The
romance, for it was no more, was over. When Buckingham and
the pretty Princess met again, nine years later, they met as
politicians, almost as rivals. The comments of the Duchess of
Buckingham on her husband's French expedition have not survived; perhaps she did not make any.

---

[8] Mme de Lafayette.   [9] Ibid.
[10] Cousin and patron of Samuel Pepys: afterwards Lord Sandwich and Master of
the Wardrobe.
[11] Pepys.   [12] Mme de Lafayette.   [13] Ibid.

4

In the autumn of 1660 the spectral figure of Argyll suddenly appeared in one of the ante-rooms at Whitehall. Ruined by Cromwell's seizure of his property and abandoned by his eldest son, the " great juggler " had decided to risk everything in a last appeal to the man he had crowned at Scone and betrayed at Worcester. But Charles's celebrated clemency did not extend so far; he refused to see his old enemy, who was hustled out of the palace and taken to the Tower. In the spring of 1661 he was sent to Edinburgh and there tried and executed; and presently the news reached England that his head had been placed on a spike at the Tolbooth—the same spike that had been used for the head of Montrose.

It is unlikely that Buckingham gave more than a moment's thought to this hideously apt retribution. Argyll had played and lost; and Buckingham, faced with the enormous accumulation of his own winnings, was chiefly occupied, during the first two years of the Restoration, in putting his affairs in order. His position entailed vast expenses: and he turned from attempting to regulate these to order a magnificent suit of clothes—there was a rumour that it cost him thirty thousand pounds—for the coronation.[14] He then set up a laboratory at Wallingford House; in a few years' time he counted on discovering the philosopher's stone: when he could turn other metals into gold there would be no need to worry about his finances.

On the Twenty-Second of April, 1661, King Charles went by water to the Tower, where, according to the ancient custom, he spent the night before his coronation. There the procession collected and passed over Tower Hill, through Crutched Friars, Aldgate, Leadenhall Street, Lime Street, St. Paul's, Whitefriars, Temple Bar, the Strand and Whitehall, and so reached the Abbey at ten o'clock in the morning. Buckingham rode alone, the other dukes behind him and in front Norroy and Clarencieux Kings-at-Arms and two noblemen in medieval dress representing the duchies of Normandy and Aquitaine. At the door of the Abbey the procession reassembled and the newly-made regalia was borne before the King into the quire, Ormonde carrying the crown,

---

[14] It was quite possible for one suit to cost as much as this, for on special occasions the material used would be thickly sewn with jewels.

Albemarle the sceptre and Buckingham the orb; the sword was carried by Lord Shrewsbury; seven years later he and Buckingham were to meet for the last time in a deserted field at Barn Elms. The regalia was then laid on the altar and a pall of cloth-of-gold held over the King by the Barons of the Cinque Ports—Buckingham, Albemarle, Lord Berkshire and Lord Sandwich.

The Abbey was filled with splendidly dressed officials and courtiers. Looking down at the slowly moving figures in the quire were nearly all those men and women whose destinies touched Buckingham's in the years to come—Clarendon, Arlington, Clifford, Ashley Cooper, Lauderdale (recently created a Duke and Lord-Lieutenant of Scotland), St. Albans, the Killigrews, Bab May, Lord Ossory, George Saville; among the women the most admired was his cousin Barbara, now Lady Castlemaine, and the most notorious, Anna Maria Brudenell, Countess of Shrewsbury, a silky, tigerish beauty in her twenties.[15] Dryden had no place there: Rochester, Sedley and John Churchill were schoolboys still, Mme d'Aulnoy and Frances Stuart in Paris: but perhaps, somewhere in the crowds outside, were two dirty little girls, already known in the brothels of the town as Moll Davis and Nelly Gwynn.

When Charles had been annointed, crowned and proclaimed King of Great Britain, France and Ireland he sat enthroned to receive the homage of his peers; York came first, then Buckingham, to touch his crown and kiss his cheek and swear allegiance. Then followed the banquet in Westminster Hall. Northumberland (an old man now), Suffolk and Ormonde rode in before the courses which were served on the knee by the Gentlemen of the Bed-Chamber, of whom Buckingham was one, Albemarle tasting the dishes before they reached the table. There was the inevitable hitch at the King's departure from the Hall, when his footmen tried to wrest the canopy from the Barons of the Cinque Ports: but Albemarle intervened. It was all very noisy and exhausting: but at least the weather had been moderately kind. Late in the afternoon the King returned privately in his barge and landed at Whitehall Stairs.[16] The illuminations, the shouting and the feasting continued all night long. Evelyn, who had stood in the Strand

---

[15] She became the second wife of Francis, eleventh Earl of Shrewsbury, in January 1659, and had one surviving son by him who succeeded his father in 1668.

[16] Pepys. Evelyn. Sir Edward Walker. All three differ slightly in their account of the procedure; Sir Edward, as Garter-King-at-Arms and part organiser and recorder of the ceremonial, has been the most closely followed.

and blessed God when the King came back to London, went soberly home and copied out his *Panegyric*, which he presented to Charles the next day in the Privy Chamber; and Pepys took his wife and Mrs. Franklin to see the bonfires in Axe Yard, where he was forced by the uproarious crowd to drink His Majesty's health kneeling, and " wondered to see how the ladies did tipple ". The age of licence had begun.

CHAPTER THREE

I

A PORTRAIT of John Lacy, the favourite actor of Charles II, shows him at three separate angles in strikingly dissimilar roles. If we are to see Buckingham clearly during the first seven years of the Restoration, we must visualise him in much the same way, presented as it were in three successive panels, all of which have different backgrounds. In the first he appears as the viceroy of the King in the West Riding, with Sir John Reresby at his side; in the second against the ornate richness of Whitehall between Frances Stuart and Barbara Castlemaine; in the third we see him facing Clarendon and Ormonde in the Gothic gloom of the House of Lords. Each panel is darkened by the shadow of Lady Shrewsbury and crowned with a medallion of Charles II, who contemplates his old friend and enemy with his familiar look of secrecy, irony and power.

In 1661 Buckingham was created Lord-Lieutenant of York-shire and made his official entry into York, " where ", says the *Mercurius Publicus*, " all the nobility and gentry came to wait upon His Grace and the town received him with all the joy and best music they could make ". The Mayor and aldermen gave him a banquet and after accompanying them to church twice in the one day he was escorted to his lodgings by a " gallant troop of volunteers " while the cannon and the church bells mingled in a deafening welcome. Here Buckingham renewed his acquaintance with Sir John Reresby, whom he made his deputy-lieutenant. Sir John, who admired him enormously, noted that " he could not be long serious or mind business " and, on another occasion, described how the Duke " behaved himself with some insolence towards His Majesty ".

From the summer of 1662 till the autumn of 1663 Buckingham was occupied in putting down two Puritan rebellions in the north, one in Leeds and Wakefield, and a more serious and extensive rising organised by Rymer and Oates, two ex-Parliamentary officers, whose plan was to raise the countryside against the King and then march on London. It is unlikely that this simple scheme would ever have succeeded; but that it was disposed of quickly and with comparatively little loss of life was due to Buckingham, whose correspondence with Charles and Arlington shows him as a skilled, conscientious and careful organiser. His reports to Arlington arrived daily and covered all the aspects of a campaign in which he himself had to be magistrate, judge, quartermaster, recruiting serjeant and general adviser. Arlington,[1] now Secretary of State in Nicholas's place, was a pompous, extremely able man who intrigued against Buckingham when he did not support him. Only once, throughout the long, complicated, mutually courteous correspondence of the Northern Rebellion, is there a flash of irritation. On the way to Doncaster Buckingham sent the King a full account of his plans. He ended with:

"I give Your Majesty the trouble of reading this tedious letter, having the fortune to have so many about Your Majesty that I know will censure everything I do, that I am resolved to make Your Majesty yourself the judge of my actions and the director of them, and I hope Your Majesty will have the justice to protect me from the malice of my ill-wishers, since I have no ambition in this world but to serve Your Majesty to the utmost of my power . . ."

The Duke knew very well that the moment he left the Court not only Clarendon and Ormonde, but Arlington too, would work against him. Immediately Buckingham reached York he asked for full powers and was given them; Arlington's next letter was not answered by return and the Secretary ended a long list of instructions with, "I most infinitely applaud Your Grace's punctuality in writing, but complain at the same time that you do not answer one of mine."[2] Arlington was determined to make it clear who was giving the orders; at the same time the tone of his letters shows that he had read Buckingham's first communication to Charles and taken the hint conveyed in it to himself. Lord Fairfax also wrote to his son-in-law, urging clemency for the rebels, many of whom had been his comrades in the Civil War. The Duke was merciful; of the thousands of prisoners only eighteen were executed, the judges who had been sent to Yorkshire were recalled, and when Buckingham returned in the autumn of '65 to put down a minor rising he did so on a wave of popularity which carried him over his preparations for the coastal defences against the Dutch a year later. At such times as these he was at his best, able, energetic, open-handed and gay. One Yorkshire gentleman wrote to another:

[1] He became Lord Arlington in 1664.   [2] Arlington: *Letters*.

"The Duke of Buckingham's prudent management has made all sorts of persons in the city and country show the greatest readiness to serve on occasion. He has mustered his troop, which is well equipped, and those who came in hopes to be listed outnumbered those entertained; he dismissed them kindly with ten shillings a man for the charge of their journey. It is wondered by his gentlemen that nothing is said of him publicly, so I beg that this may be in the next Gazette."

It must be emphasised that nearly everyone who served under or worked with Buckingham spoke well of him and became devoted to his interests; but the praise of such men as Sir John Reresby and Brian Fairfax weighs little against the condemnation of his more celebrated detractors, Clarendon, Ormonde, James II and Dryden. If Buckingham had been content to remain a local administrator and the friend of Charles, if he had confined his versatility to music, poetry and plays, and his tastes to building, chemistry and venery he would have escaped the censure of his contemporaries and the shocked disgust of the eighteenth and nineteenth century historians. That he was too easily swayed, too anxious to excel and too much indulged by those he subjugated is his tragedy, the old tragedy of the silver spoon.

2

In the summer of 1662 Catherine of Braganza, "a very little . . . modest, not handsome lady",[3] arrived in England with a train of three hundred attendants, including some very odd looking maids of honour, "six frights", according to Anthony Hamilton,[4] escorted by a duenna and a number of gentlemen of whom one, Don Pedro da Silva, was called Peter of the Wood by Buckingham. When poor Don Pedro left England in disgust at the tricks played on him by Buckingham "the happy Duke," says Hamilton, "inherited [from him] a Portuguese nymph . . . whose appearance was still more appalling than that of the Queen's maids of honour."

Hamilton and his brother-in-law were both old men when they composed the most fascinating of all *chroniques scandaleuses*; and the lack of information about this episode from other sources leads one to believe that Buckingham's affair with the Portuguese

---

[3] Evelyn. Pepys. Reresby.

[4] *Memoirs of the Comte de Gramont*, by Anthony Hamilton, Intro. and Notes, C. H. Hartmann, new translation by Peter Quennell (1932).

nymph was rather in the nature of an elaborate joke than a reality.

Buckingham went to Portsmouth for the marriage of Charles and Catherine. And then, shortly after his first return from Yorkshire, the Queen gave a Candlemas masquerade to which all the Court were invited. The Comte de Gramont's account of the evening and of the elaborate practical jokes that he, his fiancée Elizabeth Hamilton—a very remarkable young lady[5]—and Buckingham played on Lady Muskerry,[6] Miss Henrietta Blagge[7] and the Marquis de Brisacier do not sound uproariously amusing after an interval of nearly three hundred years. But we are assured that the King "split his sides with laughing" at Lady Muskerry in her sixty ells of gauze and silver tissue and Miss Blagge in her four yards of yellow ribbon with gloves to match. Lady Muskerry was stout and slightly deformed: Miss Blagge had white eyelashes and spoke shocking French: Brisacier dressed ridiculously; so these three unfortunates became the victims of their more sophisticated contemporaries. So did Colonel John Russell[8] when he appeared in a slashed doublet and an old-fashioned high-crowned hat with an oil-skin cover—Gramont could not get over the oil-skin cover. And as for the skipping and stumping of the English country dances called for by King Charles ("The old dance of England—Cuckolds All Awry"[9]) Gramont could hardly keep his countenance when he saw them for the first time; but he approved of the King as being more Bourbon than Stuart. "And as for the beauties," he says, "you could not turn round without seeing them."

Illuc heu miseri traducimer! Posterity contemplates these celebrated ladies in embarrassed silence. With one exception, the women who sat for the Court painters of the seventeenth century are now seen as so many armfuls of flesh, drapery, pearls and hair: and yet, looking at them, and remembering what they stand for and what they were, it is difficult to look away, especially from the portrait of Frances Stuart, the least representative of the

---

[5] Sister of Anthony Hamilton and grand-daughter of the First Earl of Abercorn; before marrying Gramont, she refused, among others, Sir John Reresby, the Duke of Richmond, Henry Jermyn, Henry Howard (afterwards Duke of Norfolk) and Richard Talbot—" lying Dick Talbot "—afterwards Duke of Tyrconnel.

[6] Only child of the Marquess of Clanricarde; her third husband was Robert Villiers, alias Danvers, who took the title of Earl of Purbeck. (See p. 18.)

[7] Daughter of Colonel Blagge: she married Sir Thomas Yarburgh, by whom she had sixteen children.

[8] Third son of Francis, fourth Earl of Bedford.   [9] Pepys.

I

women whom we now think of as the Windsor beauties. A
distant cousin of the King and the protégée of Madame, she
became maid of honour to Queen Catherine at the age of eighteen.
Her serene and dazzling fairness contrasted strangely with her
romping ways. "It would have been difficult to imagine," says
Hamilton, "less brain, combined with more beauty . . . She was
graceful, an accomplished dancer and spoke French better than
her native tongue; besides she was polished, and possessed that
air of fashion which is always so much run after and which it is
so hard to acquire, except it has been learned in France from very
early youth."

The King fell violently in love with Frances. Partly in
defiance and partly because it was the fashion of the day, Lady
Castlemaine, set on showing that she had no fear of her as a rival,
made a pet of her; she kept Mrs. Stuart to sleep in her own bed
and gave parties for her. "And at night," says Pepys, "began a
frolic that they two must be married, and married they were, with
ring and all other ceremonies of church service, and ribbands and
a sack posset in bed and flinging the stocking; but in the close it
is said that my Lady Castlemaine, who was the bridegroom, rose,
and the King came and took her place."

The frolic might well have turned into a tragedy for the Lady,
as Clarendon called her; but Frances, while encouraging the King
to court her in public, avoided the final proofs of his love: though
she agonised him by these last-minute refusals, they yet remained
on excellent terms. No doubt Charles believed that she must give
in at last. At his command she posed for the medal designed by
Philippe Roettier, whose study of her as Britannia was reproduced
on the coin of the realm; thanks to Frances Stuart, Britannia
(whom we should rather incline to think of as an ageing and
battered female) sits looking out over the waves in deathless
youth and beauty.

Buckingham immediately set himself to subjugate Mrs.
Stuart in order to strengthen his influence over the King, and for
a time he divided his attentions between her and Lady Castlemaine; but when the latter quarrelled with Charles the Duke
and Duchess of Buckingham gave a ball for the King and Queen
at Wallingford House to which the Lady was not asked. "Well,
much good may it do them!" exclaimed Barbara. "For all that,
I will be as merry as they," and gave orders for a late supper in
her own house, where the King spent the rest of the night after

staying for a very short time at the ball; nevertheless her influence was thought to be on the wane.[10]

Meanwhile Buckingham advised Frances Stuart " not to marry, except for some great fortune." Already the idea was in his mind —and there is no doubt that he put it into hers—that Charles might divorce the Queen, for she had miscarried once and was believed incapable of further child-bearing. English kings had married their subjects before now—and the old game of keeping off and tempting on could be played by one who was herself a Stuart, as well as another. Frances seemed to listen: but there was something curiously imponderable and fluid about the surface of her character. Her tastes were childish, and only the simplest kind of joke or game held her attention.[11] The Duke's culture and learning were therefore put aside in his dealings with this enigmatic creature, whose delight it was to build castles of cards and to play blind man's buff. She liked music, gossip and mimicry too: but card castles came first.

Every night, as soon as the candles were lit, high play began in Mrs. Stuart's apartment, as in those of all the Court ladies: and at the biggest table she sat, dressed in black and white, with diamonds in her hair and on her shoulders,[12] surrounded by ambitious and eager courtiers, the Duke of Buckingham at her elbow, building card castles. She sometimes entertained young architects who tried to imitate her: but she had eyes only for George Villiers, who built higher and more skilfully than anybody else. It was useless to compete; the climbers and the schemers and even the architects soon resigned themselves to handing the cards to their hostess and admiring the Duke. " God knows," Gramont exclaimed, " what a manager he was, and what a head he had for instructing another!" When he was building card castles Buckingham had a very cool head indeed.

Then, when the last frail structure had fluttered and fallen came the time for music: and Frances Stuart, the King's dark hand on hers, listened to Buckingham singing his own songs in French, English and Italian.[13] Then they danced—a Bransle, a Coranto and the new French dances; but music and dancing had to stop soon, for nothing must go on too long; and Buckingham would begin on his imitations. Perhaps this was the most generally enjoyable part of the evening: for nobody quite knew what

[10] Pepys.   [11] Gramont.   [12] Pepys.

[13] Pepys describes Buckingham's music as " the best in the world " and seems to have been in the habit of playing or singing it for his own and his friends' entertainment.

was going to happen. There was the old favourite, that of Chancellor Clarendon, whom Buckingham showed in all his official pomposity, carrying the shovel for the mace and marching up and down while Colonel Titus went behind him carrying the bellows for the privy purse (it is only necessary to give one glance at Clarendon's picture in the National Portrait Gallery to reconstruct this particular bit of fooling). Then the Duke would deliver one of his mock sermons or take off someone else— Arlington perhaps, or Lady Muskerry—or, best of all, he would begin what seemed an ordinary conversation with another courtier, reproducing him, not to himself, but to the room in general, so that everybody was laughing except the victim. In fact Buckingham was irreplaceable and inimitable: and if he were not in the room when Frances's parties began she would send " all over the town " for him to come to her.[14]

So these two were drawn together; and one day Buckingham made his first and, in Mrs. Stuart's case, his only error. All his life he had been allowed to feel that he was irresistible and that he had but to advance in order to conquer. He received, on this occasion, a very sharp and definite rebuff, and abandoned at once all personal designs on his pupil.[15] For a time he fell from favour; and Arlington, who had been waiting for his chance, began to try his hand at influencing the young lady. He made good progress with her at first; his self-important manner and flow of speech— perhaps even the scar on his nose which he emphasised with a long black patch—were in the nature of a novelty. But Buckingham, before he left the field, had scorched up the territory that the Secretary sought to gain.

One day, Arlington, primed with wordly maxims and historical analogies, obtained an audience of Mrs. Stuart and began to address her in his usual prosy and pontifical manner about her attitude towards the King; he offered her " his very humble service and best advice ",[16] and pointed out the singular advantages of her position and the mutual benefits to be derived therefrom . . . but he was not half-way through his discourse before Frances, crimson with suppressed giggles, burst into peals of laughter. Buckingham's caricature stood between her and Arlington in grinning mockery; she could not help herself, had no excuses and continued to laugh: the enraged minister abruptly left the room.

14 Gramont.   15 *Ibid*.   16 *Ibid*.

Frances followed her first mentor's advice in her treatment of the King; when Lady Castlemaine, in desperation, declared she would miscarry of her child by him if she did not get the very latest thing in glass coaches presented to Charles by Gramont, Mrs. Stuart counter-attacked with the threat that she would never be with child if the coach was not given to her;[17] at the same time, says Clarendon, "she never seemed disposed to interfere in the least degree in business, nor to speak ill of anybody"; this increased Charles's delight in her company, for "he did not in his nature like a busy woman".[18] Lady Castlemaine on the other hand, was always intriguing and had a shrewish tongue. So the duel went on. Pepys, formerly in ecstasies over the little Stuart, described her as a cunning slut, who was trying to climb up on to the throne.

In February, 1664, Lord Sandwich, Buckingham and Arlington formed a committee—their own phrase—to "get" Frances Stuart for the King;[19] to this end the Duchesses of Richmond and Buckingham gave a ball for her and Charles, in the hope that a climax of drinking, dancing and horseplay would find Frances off her guard; but Queen Catherine, warned by Lady Castlemaine, arrived unexpectedly at three o'clock in the morning and the King returned with his wife and the lady to Whitehall.[20]

Frances Stuart had become one of the most talked of and envied women in Europe; the French Ambassador called on her as soon as he arrived in England and, finding her with the King, begged to be allowed to see the legs which Charles had publicly declared to be the most beautiful in the world.[21] Mrs. Stuart obligingly exhibited these exquisite objects to the knee: and the representative of the greatest monarch in Europe sank, in silent adoration, on his own.[22] The Duke of York, who alone of those present was in a position to speak his mind, remarked sourly that Mrs. Stuart's legs were, in fact, too slender: he would give nothing, he added, warming to the subject, for a leg that was not plump, short, and most important of all, clothed in a green stocking.[23] There was no doubt an awkward pause at this point: but it is certain that Frances, at least, remained unmoved.

The Duchess of Buckingham's share in these intrigues was subordinated to her husband's interests: she gave balls or made

[17] Gramont.   [18] Clarendon : *Life*.   [19] Pepys.
[20] Hartmann : *La Belle Stuart*.
[21] Gramont. Forneron : *Louise de Kéroulle*.   French State Papers.
[22] Gramont.   [23] *Ibid.*

visits, as he required; no one was sorry for her, for she was immensely rich, at the head of English society and the most intimate friend of the Queen, with whom she played games and went expeditions in disguise.[24] When Arlington wrote that he had spent the Christmas of '65 at Lord Crofts' with Buckingham and the young Duke of Monmouth and " passed it merrily . . . with warm country dances " he did not mention Mary. No doubt she was with her father, who was recently widowed and very anxious about the way her husband was treating her. When Buckingham, returning from Newmarket races, spent the night at the Sun Inn at Aldgate and was there attacked by one of his servants with a sword, everyone was perfectly transfixed—not at the attempted murder nor that Buckingham had disarmed the poor mad creature: the Duke was always at his best in an emergency—but at the fact that he had been found, *alone with his wife*, getting ready to go to bed at nine o'clock in the evening! For a time it was thought that there was something seriously amiss with His Grace of Buckingham.

The bias of such comments and of Gramont's anecdotes is against Buckingham; most historians have seen him only in the Whitehall setting and he has come down through history as a rattle and a buffoon. It is perhaps because the card castles and the blind man's buff and all the other frivolities are symbolic that they are remembered, while Buckingham's ability as a man of action and an administrator has been passed over and forgotten. His virtuosity has been his undoing.

3

From the moment of the King's return, Buckingham began his war against Clarendon. The Chancellor's supporters—Ormonde, and the Duke of York—were also attacked by him; though he never succeeded in overthrowing James, whom the King abused in his cups and supported publicly and officially. If Buckingham had been asked he would have said that it took him seven years to defeat Clarendon: and the Chancellor himself believed that George Villiers had worked his ruin. The fact was that Clarendon's unpopularity and inability to move with the times made it impossible for the King to protect him indefinitely: by the

[24] Pepys.

beginning of 1667 the whole country was against him; he neither understood nor cared to understand the new age in which he found himself. As soon as he realised how powerful the Duke was he wrote to him politely, almost sycophantically: but even here he could not forbear to find fault and suggested that Buckingham should keep "a stricter guard" upon himself—with regard to whom, or to what, is not known. Though he knew that he was mocked, Clarendon could not believe that no one wanted to listen to him: he continued to harangue and lecture the King, whom he still treated as a schoolboy, at greater and greater length. He condemned Charles's friendly, casual, or as we should now call it, democratic behaviour, his accessibility to petitioners, his liking for eccentrics and rakes, his passion for "sauntering", tennis, swimming and yachting; he contemplated with horror the drunkenness, high play and duelling of the King's immediate circle. And the women were as bad, in Clarendon's eyes—they dressed indecently, wore wigs as if they were fashionable young men and made scenes in public—the Duchess of Richmond, for instance, falling out with her cousin Barbara, called her "Jane Shore", and "hoped she would come to the same end".[25] (But the twice-widowed Mary Villiers was beginning to settle down now; she had lost her only son, the eleven-year-old Duke Esmé, who had been succeeded by his drunken cousin Charles.)

No effort of Clarendon could part the King from Buckingham, who disgraced himself at the outbreak of the second Dutch war by quarrelling with the Duke of York; he demanded that he be given a flagship and, when he was refused, went on board the *Unicorn* as a volunteer, got round the captain and started giving orders and sending despatches; this was bad enough; then Clarendon recorded with solemn horror that Buckingham had asked for a seat on the Naval Council at War at sea. But did the King reprimand him? Not at all—Charles merely remarked that he was fickle and sent him to Yorkshire to arrange against a possible invasion.[26] It was intolerable.

Technically and according to the rules of the day, Buckingham was within his rights in this affair; as a Privy Councillor he was eligible for the Naval Council at War, and as a peer he was morally and traditionally bound to give his services either as a soldier or a sailor in the event of enemy action; if he had had the sense to curb his arrogance and dissemble his contempt for James he would

[25] Pepys.   [26] Clarendon: *Life*.

not have put himself in the wrong. James—whose stupidity has become a legend—had disliked Buckingham ever since their service under Turenne, when his brother's too versatile friend presumed to give him advice and even to find fault with his direction of the siege of Arras;[27] he never forgot this piece of insolence and his refusal to give Buckingham a flagship was instinct with the resentment and irritation that had been accumulating for years and that Clarendon had helped to foster throughout the exile. James must have been aware too, that anyone who had a grudge against him turned to George Villiers for support; Lord Bristol, who made up his quarrel with Buckingham in order to do so, solemnly told him that by means of astrology he could prove to the King that the Duke of York meant to destroy him and so succeed to the throne. "I am sure," he added, "that this would work with the King." "It would so," replied Buckingham, contemptuously, "but in another way than you expect—for it would make the King so afraid of offending him that he would do anything rather than provoke him." Bristol persisted: he laid his information before Charles; and the result was exactly what Buckingham had foretold.[28]

Neither James nor the Chancellor could persuade Charles to put his foot down when Buckingham formed an unofficial Opposition in the House of Lords, the nucleus of the party that ten years later was led by himself, Halifax and Shaftesbury against the King; the fact was that whenever George Villiers was suppressed he burst out somewhere else. The quarrel with the Duke of York was patched up during the plague year, when the Court left London and Buckingham entertained James and his wife in Yorkshire.

In the summer of 1666 the Court returned to Whitehall. Arlington and Buckingham seemed to dominate the King; but when they abused Clarendon, Charles made some evasive reply: the old man was too useful to be discarded entirely. "There goes your schoolmaster!" Buckingham exclaimed as the Chancellor left the room, and the King would answer with a shrug or a smile. At night in the bed-chamber when Charles spoke of his plans for the next day Buckingham would remind him of his dependence: he could do nothing without the Chancellor's permission: he was no king, but the servant of Clarendon.[29] The other gentlemen of

---

[27] *Memoirs of James II*. Ed. J. S. Clarke.
[28] Burnet.   [29] Clarendon: *Life*.

the bed-chamber were amazed at these familiarities: the King
remained tolerant and amused; but surely the very fact of his
allowing them meant that the Chancellor's days of power were
numbered? Then, just as Buckingham's mockery seemed to be
having effect he had to leave London. He had been occupying
himself with the installation of a large glass-works at Lambeth,
the first of its kind in England;[30] he was forced to abandon this
and all his political intrigues to arrange for the defences against
the Dutch along the northern coast. And now, in the summer of
his fortieth year, his life was touched with the shadow of coming
disaster. Lady Shrewsbury joined him in Yorkshire.

4

Of all Lely's sleepy goddesses Lady Shrewsbury is the most
nonchalant and the most imperial. He painted her several times—
at full length in green velvet, glancing sidways in rose-coloured
satin, and as Minerva in a wonderfully fantastic head-dress of
ostrich feathers with a spear in her plump hand and a look of
insolent languor in her heavy eyes. Her tolerance was as remarkable as her caprice. "Though nobody," says Gramont, "could
brag that he alone had been kindly entertained by her, equally there
was no one who could contend that his suit had been ill received."
Colonel Thomas Howard, Lord Arran, Henry Killigrew and the
younger Henry Jermyn, St. Alban's nephew, all preceded Buckingham in her favour; Jermyn and Howard fought a duel for her
in which Jermyn's second was killed. Both the principals survived,
Howard to become the Dowager-Duchess of Richmond's third
husband in 1664 and Jermyn to follow James II into exile twenty-
seven years later. And yet not very much is known about Anna
Shrewsbury: her reputation has obscured her character. "I would
take my oath," Gramont said to Hamilton, "she might have a
man killed for her every day and she would only hold up her head
the higher on account of it; you would think that she received
plenary indulgence for everything she did." (Lady Shrewsbury
was born and brought up a Catholic.) "There are three or four
gentlemen," he went on indignantly, "who wear each of them
a yard of her tresses by way of bracelet, and nobody cares a pin."

[30] The Venetian Ambassador—who described Buckingham as " a very peculiar man
and difficult to deal with "—later declared that the glass trade in Venice had been completely ruined by the success of the Duke's factories in England.

That her influence over Buckingham was evil is undoubted. From the moment that he became her lover he changed into a bully and a fire-eater; his restlessness, his excitability turned to a raging fever that drove him from one excess to another. During the first months of his intimacy with this lady—from October, 1666, to July, 1667—he was involved in public brawls and challenges with five different people and was three times sent to the Tower for insufferable rowdiness and general belligerency. In middle life he was passionately in love for the first time—his tenderness for Madame may be dismissed as romantic and sentimental—and his love was, as far as one can tell, returned; he was Lady Shrewsbury's acknowledged paramour for eight years and they went everywhere together. What means she used to goad and infuriate him so, what suffering she caused him, can never be known. But there are one or two entries in Buckingham's Commonplace Book which make it possible to guess at her methods.

In the first place Lady Shrewsbury's attitude towards her religion appears to have been in some respects orthodox and traditional; however little she allowed the process to interfere with her pleasures, she went to confession much as a drunkard or a glutton takes a cure in order to prepare for his next bout. Her professions of piety infuriated Buckingham, and were no doubt meant to do so. He made more comments under the heading, " Confession ", than under any other; he seems to have returned to it again and again with infuriated disgust, observing, " 'T'is dangerous, methinks, for priests to know the sins of others, for 't'is but an easy step for sin out of the memory into the will." Was Anna Shrewsbury in the habit of taunting her lover with the secrets, hidden from him, that she revealed to her confessor? It may be so. Here is Buckingham's opinion. " I should be afraid that she should not deny the secrets of her body to whom she discovers the secrets of her soul . . . Upon the condition of absolving a woman from a thousand old sins 't'is easy to persuade her to commit one new one . . . Those that love their sins will love those that know and are acquainted with them, and they who hate them will love those who pretend to take 'em away."

Certainly Lady Shrewsbury was a trouble-maker; whenever she appeared, duels, quarrelling and scandal followed. One can only conclude that she enjoyed the scenes, the unpleasantness, the degradation that her vanity required. The cold and sluggish temperament of a heartless and permanently dissatisfied woman can be discerned beneath Lely's flattery; supercilious, idle, bored, she was capable of driving anyone near her into maniacal despair for the sake, not of a new sensation, but of any sensation at all. She employed, with callous adroitness, all the tactics that make love into an ordeal and a test; icy harshness, shuddering acceptance, wild abandon, all were hers. Buckingham's remarks under the headings, "Kisses", "Lust", "Love", and "Sleep" give a momentary impression of her moods.

"Such a woman was made to punish man, and the Devil to punish such a woman . . . Men should declare their love, women should hide it, as those parts that serve love are outward and apparent in men, but inward in women . . . Love's like a game of chess, if both be cunning gamesters they'll ne'er make an end . . . It would content me if you did but dream of me; or if I could dream that you did so, but I will never sleep enough for thinking of you to dream at all . . . Sharp-headed kisses that go to wound desire . . . Joy would have killed me, but that I could not die upon the lips of my life . . . You are in everything a Goddess: but that you will not be moved by prayers."

The easiest enchantment that exists—the enchantment that turns human beings into greedy stupid animals—was this woman's; when Reresby speaks of Buckingham's "fatal amour" for her, he refers not only to the miserable Francis Shrewsbury, but to his own friend and patron. Henceforth Villiers was like a man who has been poisoned by the claws of a man-eating tigress: and he bore the marks to his grave. His good days were over from the moment that Lady Shrewsbury, with the exaggerated caution sometimes shown by violently reckless persons, came to York chaperoned by her husband, two brothers and a sister-in-law.

5

No picture of seventeenth-century life is complete without its background of music. "All the officers," says Sir John Reresby, speaking of Buckingham's troop, "loved music so well that the Duke had a set of violins, Sir Henry (Bellasis) had another, and I also had three musicians that played very well, one on the hautboy, and one on the bass viol." In fact, Sir John was enjoying himself in York, even more than the year before when the Duke was " diverting himself at nights with his deputy-lieutenants and officers, or dancing with the ladies." Then Buckingham's guests arrived and everything changed.

Lord and Lady Cardigan, Lord Brudenell and the Shrewsburys arrived with " a great retinue " and Buckingham took a house for them in York and entertained them " at vast expense ". Sir John Reresby, who had recently married, found it advisable to send his wife away, although she was in attendance on the Duchess of Buckingham; he considered the Duke's house-party " no good school for a young wife ". Lady Reresby's wishes were not, of course, consulted, and she left, while her husband continued to to spend " the days in visits and play and all sorts of diversions that place could afford and the nights in dancing, sometimes till day the next morning ". Sir John was of the opinion that Lady Shrewsbury first became Buckingham's mistress during this visit; but it is possible that their relationship had already been established in London and that it was the reason for her coming north.

Sir John was under the impression that the Duchess of Buckingham had no knowledge of her husband's infatuation. This is unlikely. The Duchess was not only a good but an intelligent woman; she had been nine years married and was prepared to shut her eyes to most things.

Lord Shrewsbury was not ready to play the complacent husband; usually " so well bred as to be disinclined to reproach his wife ", he made a scene on this occasion.[31] No one—except Reresby, who seems to have been in Buckingham's confidence— was quite sure how far matters had gone. Lord Brudenell's suspicions were confirmed one evening, when he walked quickly through the dining-room and saw a couple standing in the twilight whom he recognised; they were both so tall . . . it could only be the Duke and his sister. He hurried on, pretending not to have seen them; very late that night he was sent for to support his brother-in-law during a " great quarrel of jealousy concerning the Duke ". The dispute ended in the defeat of the poor cuckold, who was persuaded by his wife to stay on in York for her pleasure.[32]

Then they all went away, leaving Buckingham, who was bound by his duties, to his recollections. The thought of Lady Shrewsbury haunted and maddened him. " If contemplation be

[31] Gramont.   [32] Reresby.

the manna of love," he wrote, " give me the fleshpots . . . I can no more live by past favours than the air can be enlightened by the beams of yesterday . . . Thy power is so absolute, that I think the Devil's promise was made good to women, when he said, You shall be like gods . . . I am much mistaken, if our weakness be not all your strength and our nakedness all your armour." Could he trust her? Was she false? Was she in the power of her confessor? " It cannot choose but make priests lascivious to feel thus the privy parts of women's souls . . ."[33]

He was in a frenzy of impatience and ready to pick a quarrel with anybody. A few days after Lady Shrewsbury's departure, Lord Falconbridge came to dine, bringing with him Sir William Frankland and the future Lord Halifax, then Sir George Savile; Savile was the nephew of Shaftesbury and just the sort of brilliant young man most likely to please and amuse his host. During the course of the evening Falconbridge and Buckingham drank more heavily than usual, quarrelled—what about, we are not told—and a challenge was conveyed to Buckingham through Sir George. Next morning Reresby offered to be the Duke's second, was told that he had already accepted Savile and that " he did not know whether it would come to fighting or not ". A few hours later Sir George came to find Reresby in the Minster; he wanted to borrow a longer sword, his own being more for ornament than use. Then the two young men hurried off to a field outside the city and there found Buckingham and Falconbridge in conversation, their swords still in the scabbard. After all, what had been said? Neither could quite remember: tempers had cooled and the duel was abandoned.

Sir John, a stickler, was shocked; in his eyes to relinquish a duel was a confession of cowardice. " I was sorry to see my Captain come off so calmly in this matter ", he said to Sir Henry Bellasis, and the remark went the rounds, finally reaching Buckingham, who gave his lieutenant a good talking to for his disloyalty. Sir John was ready to fight anyone who had repeated his stricture—how else could he prove himself blameless? Buckingham prevented an outbreak of challenges and, though he and Sir John were reconciled, their friendship never regained its first warmth. Shortly after this the Duke was able to leave York and join Lady Shrewsbury in London. But there was as little happiness for him with her as without her.

[33] Commonplace Book.

6

As soon as Buckingham returned he renewed his fight against
Clarendon. This time he ignored the Chancellor and concentrated on his allies; he could do nothing to discredit the Duke
of York: so he began by attacking the Duke of Ormonde.

Handsome still, urbane, dignified and " decent even in his
vices ",[34] Ormonde was not the kind of man whose personality
lends itself to ridicule; it was difficult and dangerous to impugn
his reputation, which was, unlike Clarendon's, firmly established;
but as the representative of a people whom Parliament looked on
as barbaric and hostile, he could be assaulted officially.

The weapon used by Buckingham against Ormonde was the
Irish Cattle Bill. The strength of his case lay in the flooding of
the English market with cheap Irish meat, thus enriching, at the
expense of the home trader, the detested Irish farmers. The
discussion of the Bill was long and heated; no compromise, such
as that of " powdering " and packing the meat in Ireland and
shipping it in casks or barrels was acceptable; both Houses " were
as angry with the cattle when they were dead as when they were
alive ", says Clarendon.

Buckingham took this opportunity of attacking the Ormondes.
He placed himself at the head of those who were against the
import of Irish cattle " with a marvellous concernment ".[35] He
arrived early at the debates and stayed till the last. His efforts
were rewarded with the passing of the Bill and the defeat of the
Lord-Lieutenant of Ireland after a series of arguments and scenes
of extraordinary bitterness. The consumer of cheap meat seems
to have had no representative in this affray: and the English
butchers obtained their triumph through a personal feud; for,
apart from his support of Clarendon, Ormonde had gained
Buckingham's hatred by marrying his fifth son, Lord Arran, to
Mary, the Duchess of Richmond's only surviving child, who was
the heiress-presumptive to the Villiers estates.[36]

During the course of one of the debates Buckingham, " who
assumed," says Clarendon, with unwilling admiration, " a liberty
of speaking where and what he would, in a dialect unusual and
ungrave, his similes and other expressions giving the occasion of

34 Burnet.   35 Clarendon: *Life*.   36 See Appendix I.

much mirth and laughter . . . said . . . that whoever was against that Bill had either an Irish intellect or an Irish understanding."

As soon as the debate was over, Ormonde's eldest son, Lord Ossory, approached Buckingham and asked him to walk into another room. There a challenge was given and accepted; it was agreed that the business should be concluded within the hour, at a place in Chelsea Fields.

Buckingham went home to change his sword and, a little late, crossed the river to find, not Ossory, but two other gentlemen waiting for him. They told him that they were there to stop the duel and added that two more interveners had just left Chelsea Fields in the company of Lord Ossory.

Buckingham said no more and went away. Next day, as soon as the Peers had taken their places, he gave them an account of what had happened: his discourse was several times interrupted by the infuriated Ossory. Then Lord Arlington spoke. What had caused the challenge? What provocation had the noble Duke given the noble Lord? For a long time Ossory refused to say. The house was getting restive, but several hours passed while the matter was "bandied up and down".[37] Ossory at first denied having made the challenge: but Buckingham taunted him almost to the point of renewing it then and there. Finally Arlington, speaking with some sharpness, insisted on Ossory's repeating what Buckingham had said. There was a pause, and then the young man blurted out in his undulating brogue, "The Duke of Buckingham made many sharp railleries and unhandsome reflections upon my relations".[38]

After some further discussion Arlington polished off the dispute in his most business-like manner by sending Buckingham before the Black Rod—that is, appointing a time and place for a public apology to the House—and Ossory to the Tower. Both offenders were severely lectured in separate rooms as soon as the House had risen.[39]

A few days later the Marquess of Dorchester, an elderly, intolerant member of the Clarendon-Ormonde faction, "jostled" Buckingham, not quite inadvertently, as they took their places for a conference in the Painted Chamber. The Duke replied by pushing

[37] Arlington: *Letters*.   [38] *Ibid*.
[39] Arlington. Clarendon, writing some years after this incident, says that both Buckingham and Ossory were imprisoned: but Arlington's letter, giving an account of it only twenty-four hours later, says that Buckingham was excused the heavier disgrace as he had not given the challenge.

Dorchester's elbow aside and asking him in a loud voice, " if he were uneasy ? " " Yes," replied Dorchester fiercely. " You would not dare do this if we were anywhere else." " Yes, I would," retorted Buckingham. " I am a better man than you." " You lie ! " Dorchester exclaimed, and Buckingham immediately knocked off his hat and then his perriwig. Dorchester was the shorter and less agile of the two; but he afterwards boasted that " he had as much of the Duke's hair in his hands to recompense for his pulling off his perriwig . . ."[40] This ridiculous scene was concluded by the forcible separation of the two peers, and both were sent to the Tower.

A couple of days later Buckingham quarrelled with the Marquess of Worcester at a committee meeting. He leant across the table, took Worcester by the nose and " pulled him about ". The exasperated members interposed: Buckingham went back to the Tower.

But in or out of the Tower Buckingham could still count on the King's favour; when he and Prince Rupert quarrelled over the stabling of their chargers and the Prince pulled Buckingham off his horse and challenged him " in the public street ", Charles himself intervened and pacified his infuriated cousin.

It is permissible to see behind the outlines of these passages the figure of Lady Shrewsbury, to whom violence was as the breath of life. Buckingham was sitting with her in a box at the play when Henry Killigrew, either in jealousy or in drink or both, began an attack on him from the next box, abusing and grimacing at him. Buckingham, who knew that he had supplanted Killigrew, behaved with unusual restraint and merely told him to mind his face and his language. Killigrew thereupon struck the Duke on the head with the flat of his sword. Buckingham jumped out of his box and chased Killigrew across the theatre; when they got to the benches Killigrew's perriwig fell off and he began to cry for mercy.

After a short imprisonment Killigrew left for France; before he departed he made a formal apology to the Duke and Lady Shrewsbury. Buckingham thought no more of the matter; but his mistress was unappeased.

Such brawling as this shows George Villiers at his worst to a modern audience; of his contemporaries Clarendon records it in disgust, Pepys with gloating disapproval, Arlington in matter-of-

40 Clarendon. Pepys.

GEORGE VILLIERS IN HIS LATE THIRTIES
From the portrait by Simon Verelst at Osterley Park
Reproduced by courtesy of the Earl of Jersey

fact acceptance, and Reresby—a delightful character—in simple satisfaction; the King, whose point of view can be more closely identified with Buckingham's than with those of the other four, wrote to Madame:

" For Harry Killigrew, you may see him as you please, and though I cannot commend my Lady Shrewsbury's conduct in many things, yet Mr. Killigrew's carriage towards her has been worse than I will repeat; and for his *démêlé* with my Lord of Buckingham he ought not to brag of, for it was in all sorts most abominable. I am glad the poor wretch has got a means of subsistence, but have one caution of him that you believe not one word he says of us here, for he is a most notorious liar, and does not want wit to set forth his stories pleasantly enough . . ." In another letter he adds: " My Lord of Buckingham is so afraid that you should think that he is the cause that Harry Killigrew does not return hither since you have desired him to forgive what is past, as he has again desired me to tell you that there is nothing of what relates to him in the case . . ."[41]

7

In March 1667 Frances Stuart made a runaway match with a drunken nincompoop—Charles Stuart, Duke of Richmond.[42] The King—who had told her " that he hoped one day to find her ugly and willing "[43]—was bitterly angry. Buckingham told him that he had Clarendon to thank for this, and Charles, remembering Clarendon's attitude towards his pleasures, was half-inclined to believe that it was so; Buckingham added that the Chancellor had been well aware of Queen Catherine's disability and had married his master to a barren wife in order to make Anne Hyde Queen of England; but Charles ignored this far-fetched accusation.

It was the right moment to begin a final and crushing attack on the Chancellor; but Lady Castlemaine, angry with Buckingham for his continued support of Frances Stuart, persuaded the King to send him away from Court for a time; and the Duke with his wife and Lady Shrewsbury retired to Owthorpe, his estate in Northamptonshire,[44] where he consoled himself with chemistry, violin-playing and the composition of some new songs against his return. In his absence Barbara, who knew how dangerous her cousin could make himself by his " merry tales " of life at Whitehall, grew very

41 Hartmann : *Charles II and Madame.* 42 See p. 123.
43 Burnet. (Note by Lord Dartmouth.)
44 Formerly the seat of Charles Brandon, Duke of Suffolk and second husband of Mary Tudor, sister of Henry VIII.

K

uneasy; and Charles, who had been excessively irritated at Buckingham's discourtesy in not coming to take leave, began to wish
for his company. Clarendon was amazed that in such circumstances as these the Duke continued to have a large following. How
could a man who made mock of God Almighty's creatures, knew
no method and, worst of all, seldom got up before eleven o'clock
in the morning, command respect or even attention? An early
riser and a tireless worker, the Chancellor could hardly believe
that Villiers counted for anything with serious people. And yet—
" It cannot be imagined," he says, " how great an interest he had
in both Houses of Parliament . . . He found a respect and con-
currence from them of different tempers and talents, and had an
incredible opinion with the people." The common folk detested
Clarendon for his religious persecutions, his avarice and his supposed share in the sale of Dunkirk to Louis XIV, whom they were
already beginning to look on as the national enemy. Buckingham's
friendly manners, his magnificence and spendthrift ways made him
a popular spectacle; his reiterated belief in liberty of conscience
brought him supporters from all parties. Levellers, Presbyterians,
Anabaptists, all saw in the Duke a friend, even a leader, although
no one took him seriously when he stood up for the freedom of
the very few who had no religion at all. Respectable citizens were
delightfully shocked by his eccentricities, his amours and the
garbled versions of his witticisms. And his power over the King
seemed almost magical. " I suffer him . . ." Buckingham was
reported to have said of his master, " that I may hereafter better
command him."[45]

During the later part of the exile Buckingham had made a
friend of Major John Wildman, whom he afterwards described as
the finest statesman in England.[46] Wildman, formerly a Leveller,
now a republican, was also a lawyer and a very able business man;
he exerted great influence whenever he cared to exercise it, never
betrayed a friend and plotted against despotism for fifty years and
through five reigns; he crowned his long career by becoming
Postmaster-General under William III. He was five years older
than Buckingham, " in whose bosom," says Pepys, he was " entertained " and whom he met almost daily during 1667; but when
the Duke was consorting with Wildman and his other republican
protégés " he made the King believe that he was with his
wenches ".[47] After Buckingham retired from politics Wildman

45 Pepys.   46 Ibid.   47 Ibid.

attached himself to Shaftesbury; but he was still Buckingham's friend and, with Bishop Sprat and Sir Robert Clayton, a city knight, became one of the trustees of the Duke's estate soon after 1670. After Buckingham died, Parliament allowed Wildman to sell his estates in order to pay his debts.[48]   There is no doubt that Wildman was the only person—with the possible exception of Sprat—whom the Duke trusted through all his vicissitudes; many of his republican allies were as greedy and unscrupulous as his enemies round the throne.

One of these false friends was a man called Braythwaite, whom Buckingham had made his steward; he was also a Leveller and had had to fly beyond seas at the Restoration. One evening, before the Duke's departure for Owthorpe, Charles reproached him for consorting with such a fellow: Buckingham apologised and then said that Braythwaite was, in fact, a remarkable man, now entirely loyal and well worth meeting; in a very short time he persuaded Charles to give him an audience. He arranged a supper-party at Wallingford House and presented Braythwaite to the King, who seemed interested in his knowledge of popular opinion in England and impressed by his declarations of loyalty.[49]

Then the Duke left London and Braythwaite, dazzled by the favour shown him, proceeded to climb on his patron's shoulders to a position nearer the throne; he turned informer and, obtaining a private audience of the King, accused Buckingham of high treason; the Duke, he said, had forecast the King's death by means of astrology. Charles handed Braythwaite over to Arlington, to whom the spy gave further information against the astrologer, Dr. Heydon; Heydon's correspondence was seized while he himself was imprisoned. A number of letters from him to the Duke were found in which the astrologer apostrophised his patron as "Mighty Prince", "Highness" and "the Darling of the People". None of these letters had been posted. There was one from the Duke himself in which, says Clarendon, "there were many unusual expressions", but nothing which bore out the accusation of high treason.

Nevertheless a warrant was made out for Buckingham's arrest and Serjeant Bearcroft arrived at Owthorpe to take him. He was greeted by Brian Fairfax, who denied him admittance. Somewhat overawed, he went away and came back again next day with some aldermen, the Mayor of Stamford and a justice of the peace; by

[48] M. Ashley: *John Wildman*.   [49] Clarendon: *Life*.

this time Buckingham had fled and when the party searched his cabinet all they found was " some tunes pricked on several papers with the Duke's own hand ". Meanwhile Buckingham had left in a coach and six " and six led horses " for London.

A proclamation was issued for his arrest, forbidding anyone to shelter him from justice. The Duke, who was flitting about the city, hidden by day and changing his refuge by night, sent several messages and letters to the King, and his secretary, Martin Clifford, to interview the Chancellor. Clarendon behaved with great correctness to Clifford; but he noted with alarm that the King " seemed to be weary of the prosecution ".

Dr. Heydon wrote from the Tower to the Duchess of Buckingham—who had followed her husband to London—that

" the Duke is wronged, and with my life I will let the world know it. I pray let not my lady be afraid, and when His Majesty hears the truth, he will be restored to more favour than ever, and his enemies ashamed of their actions . . . the Duke is most unjustly abused, and I am kept a close prisoner, tortured in these dungeons to forward their designs against him, but Death shall close on the scene before I will be found to damn my soul for a witness to their wicked designs . . ."

The search for Buckingham continued. Then it was heard that one of the witnesses for the crown had died of small-pox and that another had withdrawn his evidence. Buckingham immediately wrote as follows to the King:

" May it please Your Majesty—
Though I could not but be afraid of Your Majesty's anger, yet I dare trust your kindness, and now I understand that Your Majesty thinks your honour is concerned with my surrender, I will have no longer consideration, since that comes in question, but as soon as I am in a posture fit to appear before Your Majesty I shall come and throw myself at your feet to be disposed of as Your Majesty shall think fit, being, with great humility, may it please Your Majesty—Your Majesty's most dutiful and most obedient subject and servant—

BUCKINGHAM."

Charles would have liked to conclude the matter at once, but Clarendon insisted on a prosecution and Buckingham, having given himself up, was taken to the Tower; on the way there he stopped at the Sun Inn at Aldgate, where he was " mighty merry ",[50] sending a message to the Lieutenant of the Tower that he would come to him when he had dined; then he showed himself

[50] Pepys.

on the balcony to the cheering crowds who had come to applaud
the Chancellor's enemy.

The King continued "very impatient to be rid of the
business"[51] and desired that the Duke should be freed immediately,
but Clarendon was firm. Charles then had to submit to one of
Lady Castlemaine's semi-histrionic, semi-hysterical displays of
temper. "You are a jade that meddles with things you have
nothing to do with at all," he said impatiently. She screamed at
him—"You are a fool! And if you were not a fool you would
not suffer your business to be carried on by fools—and cause your
best subjects and those best able to serve you to be imprisoned."[52]
The Lady, very naturally, was terrified of what Buckingham
might say about her if he became her enemy.

On June the Third, 1667, Buckingham was interviewed by the
Lords of the Privy Council in the Tower; he then appeared before
them at Whitehall as a prisoner and was again examined. His
manner to the King was perfection: but he answered the questions
put to him about Dr. Heydon in a joking manner. He was
"bitter, sharp and very slighting"[53] to Arlington when the latter
desired "that His Grace would give a positive answer to the
questions commanded by the King", and replied sharply, "I
hope you'll believe what I say, otherwise I shall have but an
unequal part of this business". He then described Heydon as a
man who could not be "trusted with a tallow candle". During
the second interview he denied that he had ever written to Heydon,
saying that he knew him well and had had dealings with him in
"distillations" for chemical research; but he looked on the poor
Doctor as "cracked in his brain and fit only to be laughed at".[54]
He was asked whether he had ever cast the King's nativity, then
a treasonable offence. The incriminating paper was handed to
him and, after looking at it, he said to Charles "Sir, this is none
of my hand, and I refer it to Your Majesty whether you do not
know this hand." The King took the paper; there was a pause;
then he remarked, "It is indeed none of yours, I know whose
it is, but cannot recall it." Buckingham replied, "Why, it is my
sister of Richmond's, some frolic or other of hers about some
certain person—and there is nothing of the King's name in it,"
he added, turning to the lengthening faces round the Council
table, "but it is only said to be his, by supposition."[55] The King

[51] Clarendon: *Life.*   [52] Pepys.   [53] *Ibid.*
[54] Clarendon: *Life.*   [55] Pepys.

took the letter again and recognising the Duchess of Richmond's writing, " seemed much out of countenance ".[56]

The Duke was told to withdraw. Charles declared with some irritation that he had been deceived and that there was no need to press the matter further. Buckingham was released. It was another nail in Clarendon's coffin.

Buckingham remarked that " a person was only to be committed to prison by my Lord Chancellor or my Lord Arlington and there is little doubt of his becoming extremely popular."[57] But he had the tact to keep away from Court for several weeks. Towards the end of September he was allowed to kiss the King's hand and resume his place at the Privy Council and as Gentleman of the Bed-Chamber.

A month later Clarendon interviewed his master for the last time. As he limped across the Privy Garden, the tears pouring down his face, Lady Castlemaine ran out into her aviary in her dressing-gown with her long dark hair about her shoulders to see him go; Bab May and Arlington were behind her. Standing there among her paraquitos and her love-birds, she crossed herself and thanked God, believing that she had now no rival in all the world.[58] That night in the bed-chamber the King told Buckingham to ask what he pleased, and he would grant it. It was characteristic of George Villiers that he asked for nothing, not even the Chancellor's head on a charger. His greatest enemy, the man who had stood between him and the King for more than twenty years, was ruined and that was enough.

Bristol and Buckingham forced the Lords to deprive Clarendon of all his offices and impeach him on seventeen counts, of venality, treachery and illegal assumption of power.[59] Warned by his friends, he left England, which he was never to see again.[60] From France he sent a petition to the House of Lords containing his answers to the charges made against him. Buckingham presented it to the Commons, remarking, " The Lords have commanded me to deliver to you that scandalous and seditious paper sent from the Earl of Clarendon; they bid me present it to you and desire you in convenient time to send it to them again; for it has a style they are in love with, and they desire to keep it."[61]

The rights and wrongs of Clarendon's ruin have little to do with Buckingham's career. The Chancellor was that odd but not

---

[56] Clarendon: *Life.*   [57] Jesse.   [58] Pepys.   [59] Burnet
[60] He died in Rouen in 1674.   [61] Kennet: *History of England.*

rare type—the fascinating writer and superb stylist who is an intolerable and unattractive bore in social intercourse. The sound of his voice, going on and on and on, in admonition, self-righteousness and exhortation, rings through the sombre and ironic cadences of his writings like a gong struck by a clumsy hand. Entirely lacking in imagination, sympathy or charm, he loved his country and his master without vision, without thought of self, obstinately, faithfully, to the end. He persecuted Catholics and Dissenters on the highest principles: he kept a magnificent and formal state in his great house in Piccadilly—Dunkirk House, the people called it—because he considered it due to his position: he forbade his wife to call on Lady Castlemaine when the most perfunctory acknowledgement of her power would have brought him safety from his enemies. He ruled the Royalist party for twelve years and England for seven; yet after the Restoration he could not influence our history; he could only stand on the river's brink and shake his fist at the course of the stream.

As Ossory, Dorchester, Worcester, Killigrew, Clarendon and finally Ormonde[62] were defeated, one by one, no comment fell from the lips of the man who best knew the whole range of Buckingham's character and all his possibilities. One historian has remarked that while Henry VIII would have sent Villiers to the block, Charles II kept him as a curio[63]—and there exists no apter definition of Charles's attitude. Yet, as so often happens in the assessment of Buckingham's place in history, something is missing. Charles was capable, in rare cases, of deep and lasting affection. Buckingham, the living symbol of his boyhood, of his youth and of his misfortunes, held a unique position. He was the familiar friend, to whom Charles could speak of old days as to another self. Disagreement, mistrust and treachery might separate these two; but between them, always, lay the shared territory of the past.

[62] See p. 154.   [63] Ogg.

CHAPTER FOUR

THE fall of Clarendon saw Buckingham's triumph. By the
end of 1667 he was principal Minister of State, supreme in the
King's favour[1] and on the old friendly terms with Lady Castlemaine. He had overcome all his enemies with the exception of
Arlington, to whom he was now openly hostile, and York, whom
he contrived to insult without reproof. His wife was acquiescent
and devoted: his mistress was kind: his sister was in waiting at
the French Court, ready to look after his interests when the time
came. He was surrounded by a group of brilliant younger men
of his own rank and his "creatures", as York called them, all
obtained preferment in their various spheres; of his old Cambridge
friends, Cowley was pensioned with a farm in Chertsey and
Clifford given the mastership of Charterhouse. The Duke's
chaplains made profitable marriages and became bishops; he was
popular with the people, emulated by the wits and feared by the
politicians. Yet although he towered head and shoulders above
his rivals the shadows were thickening round him. He was forty:
he had no legitimate heir: and his intellectual powers, more
dazzling and versatile than ever before, were diffused, blinding
his judgement, weakening his application and generating further
caprice and instability. Lady Shrewsbury may have had something to do with this: her nature tended to destroy such balance
as his possessed. And he could not trust her or guess at her
thoughts; was she a mystery, or just a mass of vanity? "My
believing in you and you believing your glass will undo us both",
was his comment, made, perhaps, when he gave her the heavily
embossed silver table and mirror that are still to be seen at Osterley
Park. "If you allow me only your fair and outward dress," he
added, "I am no more beholden to you than you are to your
looking-glass."[2]

The mingled self-indulgence, absent-mindedness and effrontery
of Buckingham's behaviour were extremely irritating to most of

---

[1] " The King is now become . . . a slave to the Duke of Buckingham." (Pepys.)
[2] Commonplace Book.

his contemporaries. Reresby—from whom he was now completely estranged—says:

"The King consulted him chiefly in all matters of moment; foreign ministers applied themselves to him, before they were admitted to have audience of the King; but he was so unfit for this character, by reason of his giving himself up to his pleasures, that (turning the night into day and the day into night) he neglected both his attendance upon the King, the receiving of ministers, and other persons that waited to speak to him . . ."

Burnet is naturally more censorious:

"He had no principles, either of religion, virtue or friendship. Pleasure, frolic, and extravagant diversions, was all that he laid to heart. He was true to nothing; for he was not true to himself. He had no steadiness nor conduct; he could keep no secret, nor execute any design without spoiling it. He could never fix his thoughts nor govern his estate, though then the greatest in England."

The judgement was passed on to the generation succeeding Buckingham's, who condemned him at second-hand, in such terms as these:

". . . A man of great parts and an infinite deal of wit and humour: but wanted judgement, and had no virtue or principle of any kind. These essential defects made his whole life a continued scene of inconsistencies. He was ambitious beyond measure and implacable in his resentments: these sometimes were the effects . . . of his pride which, whenever he pleased to lay aside, no man living could be more entertaining in conversation. He had a wonderful talent in turning all things to ridicule; but by his own conduct made a more ridiculous figure in the world than any he could, with all his vivacity of wit and turn of imagination, draw of others."[3]

Dean Lockier told Spence that when Buckingham came into the presence-chamber, "it was impossible not to follow him with your eyes, he moved so gracefully",[4] and M. de Verville, in his *Memoirs of the Court of England*, supports this view with

"He was one of the finest gentlemen that Europe ever saw; his conversation was easy and charming, serious when occasion required it, but generally facetious, and turning upon mirth; he had a genius that fitted him for the highest posts of the State; but pleasure, which was his predominant passion, made him ridicule all manner of business: and as ill habits are not easily left off, this at long run made him incapable of it."

Pepys remarked that it was "pretty to see how people do speak kindly of the Duke of Buckingham as one that do enquire into faults; and therefore they do visibly favour him." And lastly

[3] Carte: *Life of Ormonde.*   [4] *Anecdotes of Men and Books.*

Mme d'Aulnoy, who came to England at about this time, exclaims:

"Never had there been a man better made, nor more regularly beautiful; and in his conversation there was something so engaging that he pleased even more by his intellect than by his person and one would have found it difficult to say which of the two created the deepest impression. All his words went straight to the heart; he was born for gallantry and magnificence; and he carried it further than any other lord in England."[5]

She adds naïvely, "He had great powers of persuasion", and her praise was supplemented by that of Louis XIV, who described the Duke as the finest, in fact the only English gentleman he had ever met.[6]

Hovering about Buckingham like a ring of poisonous dragon-flies were Sedley, Buckhurst, Etheredge and Rochester—young men who were as delicately discriminating in their aesthetic appreciations as they were bestial, predatory and violent in their pursuit of pleasure. They turned from the composition of graceful verse or acute and sensitive dialogue to toss a poor fiddler in a blanket, rape a girl or insult a helpless old man; two of these exquisites, these connoisseurs, subtle and perspicacious in so much that they wrote, set themselves to turn the stomachs of the brutal London mob during an evening's amusement, and succeeded; they organised attacks on unprotected citizens, slit noses to the bone, and spent hours concocting tedious scurrilities on those ladies who had been so misguided as to withhold their favours. The Earl of Rochester is said to have been consistently drunk for five years:[7] Sir Charles Sedley caused his servants to waylay and horsewhip an actor who had caricatured him on the stage:[8] Lord Buckhurst carelessly murdered a tanner by mistake, but "made himself a very good tale" and was acquitted.[9] Intellectually these men could hold their own with such as Otway, Samuel Butler and even Dryden; when engaged on what they chose to describe as a prank or a frolic their behaviour was that of the worst type of juvenile delinquent, vicious, unlovely and boring.

A little apart from this group was the political circle, of which the principal members were Sir Thomas Clifford, Sir William Coventry, the Duke of Lauderdale, Halifax, and Sir Thomas Osborne, afterwards Lord Danby. But there was one greater in

---

[5] *Mémoires de la Cour d'Angleterre.*
[6] Mignet: *Négociations Rélatives a la Succession d'Espagne.*   [7] Burnet.
[8] V. de Sola Pinto: *Sir Charles Sedley.* Edward Kynaston was the actor in question.
[9] Pepys.

spirit and capacity than any of these, greater even than the powerful and privileged George Villiers: one who pulled the strings and made puppets of the ablest men in England—Anthony Ashley Cooper, Earl of Shaftesbury and Chancellor of the Exchequer from 1661 to 1672.[10]

2

Two hundred and sixty-seven years ago the " pigmy body " of the wise Achitophel was brought back from Holland and entombed in the vault of his ancestors. Since that time his enemies and his admirers have taken the stage in turn. In life, as in death, he has been the victim of superb artists; his seventeenth and nineteenth-century biographers have had to defend him against fearful odds: for the man whom Dryden lampooned and Charles II outwitted and Macaulay condemned has little chance of a fair hearing.

It is perhaps presumptuous to add yet another nosegay to the massed bouquets of invective and appreciation that ornament Shaftesbury's grave; but in so far as he was for more than twenty years the supporter and ally of the subject of this memoir, his peculiar and unforgettable genius demands some slight reconsideration. Praise and blame are, in both senses, impertinent: to attempt analysis is to grope in the dark: to recreate the personality of a statesman who so seldom gave himself away an impossible task. His nicknames—" Count Tapski ", " Little Sincerity ", " Lord Shaftesbury ", and " The Alderman "—show him in a wavering light; his portrait by Greenhill,[11] that of a man of fashion and culture whose keen sweet smile has nothing to do with his thoughts, only fascinates and bewilders; his letters, easy, vivid and succinct, display an enormous range but little emotion; his speeches, whether trenchant, dramatic, or merely bland and formal, give the impression of a screen for the speaker's secret opinions; fragments of his conversation show him as imperturbable, humorous and ruthless. He had thousands of followers— and one friend, John Locke, his son's and grandson's tutor; his enemies were as the sands of the sea, but he found their company more stimulating than that of his own circle. He has been

[10] He became Baron Ashley in 1661 and Earl of Shaftesbury in 1672.
[11] Now in the National Portrait Gallery.

described as a man without ideals, faith or honour; but he had two objects—the liberty of the English people and his own direction of that liberty; for these he sacrificed health, fortune, fame and peace of mind.

As a boy in his teens Shaftesbury helped to defeat his enemies in a lawsuit over his property; as an undergraduate in his first year he led a successful revolt against the older students; as a young officer he managed to demolish the stronghold of Corfe Castle for the Parliamentary Army. He never completely recovered from the injuries he had received in a carriage accident and probably owed his life to Locke, whose treatment—the insertion of a silver tube to drain the poison from a permanent abscess— was a favourite subject for jest among his enemies. Shaftesbury's greatest gift was his prophetic intuition; he was able to alter the shape and colour of his schemes long before change had become inevitable and acceptable to others. He was aware, instinctively, of the moment when power begins to corrupt: he set himself against dictatorship before the dictator could perceive what he himself had become. He could afford to defy Charles I, Cromwell, Clarendon, and finally Charles II, because he was a very rich as well as a very able man; but it must be emphasised that in turning against these rulers, one by one, he was fighting the same battle, a battle which his judgement and intellect eventually told him he must lose; yet he never sheathed the sword: even when he left England for the last time he was withdrawing in order to advance again, although he must have known that he was dying and that he had been, for a short time, insane from ill health and over-exertion. He was without fear, without illusions and without vanity; he struck with whatever weapons came to hand— Buckingham, Monmouth, the French Ambassador, the scum of Newgate, the toss-pots and hacks of the Green Ribbon Club, it was all one—and he was as merciless, as unscrupulous in his dealings with informers, blackmailers and pimps as with the martyred Russell, the insinuating Halifax, and the mischievous Ferguson.

To this self-contained and fiery fanatic the English people owe some of the freedom about which they have been so voluble during the past two centuries. His less skilful followers were often persuaded that he was showing them the way to personal supremacy, and in imitation of his adroitness they rushed head-long to their destruction. Shaftesbury's taunting, mocking smile urged Buckingham to his political ruin: and his ghost rose to beckon Monmouth across the Channel to Bridgwater, Sedgemoor and Tower Hill. This tiny, delicate creature with his huge fair perriwig and elegant dress, his piercing wit and clear soft voice[12] brought not peace but a sword to the unruly people he had organised: and he taught them how to use it before he died, defeated and alone.[13]

By the time that Buckingham became principal Minister, he and Shaftesbury were already close allies; Shaftesbury had advised his release from captivity in 1658 and supported his intrigues against Clarendon during the ensuing years. Shaftesbury was consistently useful to Buckingham in public and private affairs, and there is no record of any split or estrangement between them until Shaftesbury's final defeat in 1682; mutual admiration, agreement, understanding and convenience bound them to one another for more than a generation; in statesmanship Achitophel was the master and Zimri the pupil: but there is no evidence that affection or even friendship existed between the inconstant courtier and the relentless politician.

3

In the middle of September, 1667, Lady Shrewsbury, with only one maid, left England and went to live in a convent in France.[14] Her departure was a danger signal; for although Buckingham, "brisk as ever",[15] seemed entirely absorbed in affairs of State, he and his mistress were as a rule inseparable.[16] There was some reason for her withdrawal; at the beginning of the following year the King heard that Lord Shrewsbury had sent a challenge to Buckingham.[17]

Some weeks passed before the duel could take place, for the arrangements involved not only the principals but four other

---

[12] " Lord Ashley . . . spake . . . with great sharpness of wit, and had a cadence in his words and pronounciation that drew attention." Clarendon: *Life*.
[13] Martyn: *Life of Shaftesbury*. Christie: *Life*. H. D. Traill. Ogg. Macaulay: *Essays* and *History of England*. Trevelyan: *England Under the Stuarts*. Foxcroft: *Life of Halifax*. Dryden's *Works*. Marvell: *Works and Correspondence*, etc., etc. Fargo: *The First Earl of Shaftesbury*.
[14] Pepys.   [15] *Ibid*.
[16] At about this time he is supposed to have consoled himself for Lady Shrewsbury's absence by an affair with Lady Norwich: but as Mme d'Aulnoy—who is said to have had a child by him—is the authority, the story is probably apocryphal.
[17] Pepys.

gentlemen—Shrewsbury's seconds, Mr. Bernard Howard and Sir John Talbot, and Mr. Jenkins and Sir Robert Holmes, who were to appear for Buckingham. Charles told the Duke of Albemarle to confine Buckingham to his own house or at least "to take security that he should not do any such thing as fight".[18] Albemarle misunderstood his instructions and waited for the King to let him know of Buckingham's movements: Charles believed that Albemarle was already on the alert and thought no more of the matter: and so Buckingham and Shrewsbury were able to make their plans unmolested.[19]

On the Twenty-First of January, 1668, they met in a close at Barn Elms. All the combatants engaged simultaneously. After a few minutes, Buckingham, seeing that Jenkins was in difficulties, tried to prevent Howard closing in on him. Howard managed to keep the Duke off: then he "ran furiously" upon Jenkins, and killed him. Meanwhile Sir Robert Holmes wounded Talbot in the arm and they both retired.

Buckingham and Shrewsbury were now left to fight it out alone. Although Buckingham never afterwards made any comment on his own actions, it is possible that he intended merely to disable Shrewsbury and so conclude: it is equally possible that he and Lady Shrewsbury had decided that her husband was better out of the way. One thing is certain—that she held the strings in her hands and could have prevented the duel if she had wished.

By this time Buckingham had received a slight wound, no more than a scratch, but enough to shake his usual coolness. He parried Shrewsbury's attacks, feinted and straightened his arm. His sword pierced Shrewsbury's right breast and came out at the shoulder.

Panting, bleeding, Buckingham drew away. He had a house near by, to which he retired; it must be presumed that his servants disposed of Jenkins's body, for nothing more was heard of him. Meanwhile Talbot and Howard carried Shrewsbury to a coach, drove to Arundel House and sent for a physician. His report was favourable; the wounded man was gravely hurt but likely to recover.[20]

It now remained to set the legal machinery going, and Shrewsbury, through his relatives, applied for a pardon for "accidentally" causing the death of Jenkins. Six days after the duel he obtained it and was pardoned for "all assaults and

[18] Pepys.   [19] Ibid.   [20] Ibid.

batteries " on Buckingham and Sir Robert Holmes. On the same day Buckingham was pardoned for his attack on Shrewsbury and for Jenkins's collusion, " whether they had died or shall die of the same ". Howard and Talbot were also pardoned.

Meanwhile Shrewsbury continued to progress; he was believed to be out of danger.[21] There was a fearful scene at the Privy Council, where the King had to plead " the eminent services done by most of the persons . . . engaged . . ." and to promise the extreme penalty in the event of another duel.[22] Pepys observed bitterly that " this will make the world think that the King hath good Councillors . . . when the Duke of Buckingham, the greatest man about him is a fellow of no more sobriety than to fight about a mistress . . . My Lady Castlemaine," he added, ". . . will, it is believed, keep all matters well with the Duke of Buckingham."

A week later Shrewsbury was still alive—though the doctors were not so hopeful—and Buckingham went to the first night of Sir George Etheredge's *She Wou'd If She Cou'd* with Sedley and Buckhurst; all three gentlemen condemned the play as a " silly, dull thing ".[23] On February the Tenth, Buckingham appeared at the opening of Parliament; his speech urging toleration for Dissenters was concise, sincere and closely reasoned: there were no fireworks: he merely made an appeal to the common sense and humanity of his hearers. " He leads the fanatics and thinks to be another Oliver . . . and the House of Commons is swayed by him as a favourite or *premier ministre* ", remarked one nobleman angrily. The Duke's Bill was thrown out by a large majority. On the Sixteenth of March, Lord Shrewsbury died. His widow stayed on in France.

The shock and disgust caused by the murder of Shrewsbury and Jenkins were out of all proportion to the standards of the day. It must be remembered that far greater disapproval would have been shown if Buckingham had been so unconventional as to ignore a challenge of this kind. Charles realised it, and irked though he was by the grim results of the Shrewsburys' quarrels and Buckingham's bad management, he allowed the Duke to keep his position. How was it then, that the circumstances of this duel were coloured, in the public imagination at least, with a peculiar horror, a melodramatic significance? For generations to come almost the only thing remembered about the Second Duke of Buckingham was that he had killed the husband of his mistress;

---

[21] Pepys.   [22] *Ibid.*   [23] *Ibid.*

for years, historians repeated and students believed that Lady Shrewsbury, dressed as a page, held her lover's horse and watched the slaughter and that he spent the night with her in the shirt that had been spattered with the dead man's blood.[24] The solution lies in Lady Shrewsbury's hideous reputation and Buckingham's utter recklessness. A few months after the duel she came back to England and was escorted by him to Wallingford House. Then, for the first and last time, the Duchess of Buckingham protested. It was not for her " and that other ", to live together in a house, she said. Lady Shrewsbury had spent some time with Buckingham by then, and he had his answer ready. " Why, Madam, I did think so," he replied, " and therefore have ordered your coach to be ready to carry you to your father's."[25] " A devillish speech, but, they say, true," remarked Pepys, " and my Lady Shrewsbury is there, it seems."

At this point Lady Shrewsbury saw fit to go through the motions of a broken-hearted widow; Buckingham's comments on this singular tribute to convention are extremely acid. " He died out of necessity," he remarks, " and she grieves out of custom." He added bitterly, " She weeps and beats herself; aye, she had need strike the rock to get water out of it." Yet he could not help being aware of the effect that this strange grief had upon himself and wrote a rhymed description of his mistress's histrionics—

" Disciplined tears which still in ambush lay,
    Expecting but the word to march away . . ."

Incredulous, cynical, he was still fascinated. " Her sadness," he noted, " became her so well, that it bred delight in everybody else." No hypocrisy, however monstrous, could diminish Anna Shrewsbury's power. Drying her tears, he observed that they " seemed like crystal returning to its first principle ",[26] and continued to " run out of all " with her, regardless of criticism.[27] On a later occasion he had to speak up for her in the Queen's bed-chamber in front of the King, the Duke of York and a number of other gentlemen. Lady Shrewsbury was known to have set a gang of footpads on her old enemy, Harry Killigrew, who had returned from his brief exile in France proclaiming that

[24] Lord Peterborough, Spence, Echard, Andrew Lang, etc. As lately as 1931 Mr. Montague Summers repeats this story in his Introduction to Dryden's *Dramatic Works*; with the addition of: " When her husband fell, the lady rushed forward and embraced the Duke, all clotted and spattered with the poor cuckold's blood."

[25] Pepys.   [26] Commonplace Book.   [27] Marvell: *Correspondence*.

LADY SHREWSBURY

By Sir Peter Lely, in the National Portrait Gallery

*Reproduced by permission of the Directors of the National Portrait
Gallery*

she was once more his mistress, or any man's, for the asking. He was attacked on the way to his house at Turnham Green and left for dead with nine wounds in his body: his servant was killed: and Lady Shrewsbury was there, in a coach and six, to see it done.[28] "They did not mean to hurt but to beat him," broke in Buckingham hastily, "and he did run first at them with his sword."[29] The Duke of York thought that Buckingham "was of conspiracy" with Lady Shrewsbury in the business and that "it might cost him his life in the House of Lords". York spoke to Pepys of this possibility in great glee: but Buckingham continued to "rule all", in spite of York's and Prince Rupert's furious complaints of his insolence.[30]

There is no proof that Buckingham had anything to do with the attack on Killigrew: the French Ambassador exonerated him completely; but he was bound publicly to support Lady Shrewsbury, whose responsibility for the death of three more men— her husband's, Jenkins's, and Killigrew's bodyservant's—is unquestioned. It would be absurd to attempt any exculpation of Buckingham for his share in Shrewsbury's murder: but it is curious that Shrewsbury, having shut his eyes to his wife's conduct for ten years, should suddenly challenge her lover. Why had he ignored Colonel Howard and Harry Jermyn and left them to fight one another? He may have rejected, at long last, the role of cuckold; Lady Shrewsbury and Buckingham may have discussed the possibility of his divorcing the Duchess: or Lady Shrewsbury's vanity may have required yet another tribute to her powers of fascination. The fact remains that Buckingham was not the kind of man who follows up a challenge at all costs, as he had shown by his treatment of Falconbridge, Ossory, Dorchester and Killigrew; nevertheless the only defence that can be made for his actions is that he was conforming to the customs of his time. "'T'was her husband grieved whilst he was living, 't'is reasonable she should do it now he is dead," he noted long afterwards when he remembered Lady Shrewsbury's attitudinizing.[31]

4

As soon as the scandal began to die down Buckingham did his best to establish himself as a respectable public figure. He

---

[28] Pepys.   [29] *Ibid*.   [30] *Ibid*.   [31] Commonplace Book.

L

entertained Cosimo de Medici, the son of his old friend and patron, with his usual extravagance,[32] attended church with his wife.[33] and put up a memorial to Abraham Cowley in Westminster Abbey for which he composed the inscription.[34] He bought the Mastership of the Horse—then the most important of all the Court places—from the Duke of Albemarle for twenty thousand pounds, and was elected High Steward of the City of Oxford. At the East India Conference in May, 1668—which lasted five hours[35]—he addressed the House of Commons in a brief, sober, mildly satirical discourse, making his effect with the man-to-man, common sense appeal that had brought him so much consideration from the Lower House in the past.

None of these efforts at consolidation was really successful. Buckingham's views on religious tolerance, his connection with Lady Shrewsbury and his freedom of manner with the King, made him an object of mistrust.[36] He therefore turned towards foreign affairs; and here, almost at once, he made progress.

England was now virtually ruled by that cabinet council known as the Cabal, of which the members—Clifford, Arlington, Buckingham, Ashley and Lauderdale—were divided into three religio-political groups, for Arlington and Clifford were Catholic in sympathy, and Buckingham and Ashley supporters of the Dissent which Lauderdale had abjured.[37] Buckingham, Clifford and Ashley were at this time united in their pro-French policy, while Arlington, who was married to a Dutchwoman, was in favour of continuing the alliance with Holland; Lauderdale concerned himself little in foreign affairs.

In order to negotiate a commercial treaty with France, Buckingham sent over Ellis Leighton—recently knighted—and Ralph, Baron Montagu, as his envoys to Madame, whom Louis had made the principal agent in his dealings with Charles, believing her influence to be greater than was in fact the case; Montagu, who detested Buckingham, became Arlington's spy and did everything he could to discredit the Duke with the French King and his ministers.

---

[32] Magalotti : *Travels of Cosimo de Medici*.   [33] Pepys.

[34] Cowley lay in state at Wallingford House and was, by Buckingham's orders, carried to his grave on a hearse with six horses " and all funeral decency." Evelyn.

[35] Marvell : *Correspondence*.

[36] " On Monday (Nov. 25, 1669) at the Committee of Information, the discourse ran of something obliquely girding upon the Duke of Buckingham, but without making that impression which some apprehended." Marvell : *Correspondence*.

[37] Of Presbyterianism Charles said to Lauderdale, " Let that go, it is not the religion for a gentleman." Burnet.

Early in 1669, Buckingham's sister Mary, who was in attendance on Queen Henrietta Maria at Colombes, discovered that other negotiations, having nothing to do with the commercial treaty, were being made without his knowledge and that he had become the dupe of the French Ambassador—Colbert de Croissy—Charles and Madame. She at once wrote to her brother and told him all she knew.[38]

Buckingham realised how useless it would be to complain to his old friend, Charles Stuart; he went at once to Colbert de Croissy and called his bluff. The Ambassador protested in vain; His Grace's sister was mistaken—but here he was interrupted by the infuriated Duke, who accused Madame of treachery to her brother and himself, and of adultery with the Duke of Monmouth during the latter's recent visit to France: he would make her double-dealing public and discredit her for ever in the eyes of Louis XIV; the horrified Colbert told his master that he simply dared not transcribe all that the "Duc de Bouquinquam" had said.[39] Buckingham refused to accept any explanation from Colbert and Madame herself had to send over Sir Ellis Leighton with a flattering, imploring message, to which he replied:

"You must excuse this bearer if he has stayed here too long, for it has not been his fault. I was desirous to have sent along with him a man capable of treating upon our affair, but that was impossible, and I own to you that I foresee difficulties enough in finding a person who knows the language and is versed in business, in whom I can confide: nevertheless I will do anything in my power to accomplish it, and shall be very sorry, if not daring to send Leighton to you, and not being capable to find another, I must be reduced to the necessity of entering into the matter with the Ambassador here, as it will greatly lengthen the affair. I have been with him as you ordered, and told him that you commanded me to communicate everything to him, but that I did not dare to do it without the King my Master's leave, and for this reason desired him to ask your pardon on my part. I have also burnt your note and beg you will believe that the strongest desire I have in this world is to obey you.

For the love of God don't be impatient; and consider that in a place where every measure must be taken to gain the good will of the people, one cannot act with so much despatch as might be wished."[40]

It was a sign of his growing instability that Buckingham allowed himself to be thus cajoled. In fact the commercial treaty was being used by Charles for a much more drastic scheme. On January the Twenty-Fifth, 1669, he summoned the Duke of York,

[38] Mignet.   [39] Ibid.
[40] Sir John Dalrymple: Memoirs of Great Britain and Ireland. Original in French.

Arlington, Clifford and Lord Arundel of Wardour and told them that he had decided to follow his brother's example and become a Catholic; he spoke with tears of his convictions[41] and solemnly asseverated his intention that England should return to the old faith. Thereupon Arlington was won over to the French alliance and Colbert informed of what had happened, with the result that Louis agreed to help Charles to destroy the Dutch power and establish Catholicism in England—though he was rather taken aback when his cousin demanded two hundred thousand pounds down for his public declaration of the faith and eight hundred thousand a year for his share of the attack on Holland.[42]

Nothing of this was revealed to Buckingham and Ashley, who were now occupied with home affairs; their principal object was, ironically enough, the establishment of the Protestant succession. They were again considering the King's divorce and re-marriage; in spite of the Queen's unblemished reputation they planned that he should divorce her for adultery;[43] failing this, they were going to prove Monmouth's legitimacy and run him as Protestant favourite against the Popish James. So Zimri and Achitophel worked upon poor Prince Absalom and made him " drunk with honour and debauched with praise ".[44] It was Andrew Marvell's opinion that Lauderdale " at one ear talks to the King of Monmouth, and Buckingham to the other of a new Queen ". Buckingham afterwards told Burnet of his most fantastic scheme for Charles's divorce; if the King would give him leave, he said, " he would steal [the Queen] away and send her to a plantation where she would be well and carefully looked to, but never heard of any more ". It would be given out that Catherine had wilfully left her husband: then she would be divorced for desertion. It is possible that Buckingham was not perfectly serious when he put forward this plan; he was unable to resist entertaining his friends with it, and the Queen was warned to be careful of her movements in the event of being kidnapped. Then Buckingham had another idea— why should not Her Majesty become a nun? At this point Charles told him sternly to hold his tongue and the Duke returned to the attack on the heir-presumptive; he and Ashley began by discredit-

---

[41] James II: *Memoirs.*

[42] Ogg. Mignet. Charles afterwards reduced his price for arming against the Dutch to £300,000.

[43] Lord Roos's divorce, on the grounds that his wife had foisted on him her illegitimate son (whom she tactfully christened Ignoto) had set the precedent for this.

[44] *Absalom and Achitophel.*

ing Sir William Coventry, a member of the Council and the Treasury and secretary to the Duke of York.

Coventry—" a sullen, ill-natured, proud man, whose ambition had no limits "[45]—was the ideal butt for George Villiers. The Duke set to work to write a play, in which the chief comic character was made up to look exactly like Sir William and discovered sitting at an enormous circular writing table of his own invention: its drawers were labelled " Affairs of Spain ", " Affairs of France ", " Affairs of Holland ", etc., etc., and Coventry's prototype muddled about in front of it with pieces of paper on which his official memoranda were inscribed. There was, very naturally, a good deal of talk about the piece; and the outraged Coventry made a formal complaint to the King.[46]

Charles sent for the comedy, read it and said that it contained nothing offensive; this was not surprising, as the writing-table scene had been removed before the play was sent in to him. Coventry, aware that he had been fooled again, sent a challenge to Buckingham by Henry Savile. Buckingham requested Sir Robert Holmes to act for him, but Savile refused to deal with anyone but the Duke himself; before they had time to make any arrangements they were interrupted. Meanwhile Colbert implored Buckingham " not to hazard his valuable life . . . an action . . . singularly unnecessary after the proofs of courage he had so lately given ", and Buckingham held his hand.[47] The rehearsals of the play continued, although Coventry and York's adherents threatened to have the actors publicly whipped if they dared to put it on.[48] Then, at a Council meeting, the King enquired of Buckingham, " upon his honour ", if he had received a challenge from Coventry. Buckingham gave the reply expected and Coventry was sent to the Tower and deprived of all his offices, while Buckingham was shown special favour by his master.[49] Colbert assured the Duke of Louis' support with regard to Coventry, and a few days later Charles wrote to Madame:

" I am not sorry that Sir Will: Coventry has given me this good occasion by sending my Lord of Buckingham a challenge, to turn him out of the Council. I do intend to turn him also out of the Treasury. The truth of it is he has been a troublesome man in both places, and I am well rid of him."[50]

York's anger with Buckingham grew to a frenzy; the feud between them was now a public matter. Buckingham's next attack

45 Clarendon: *Life*.   46 French State Papers.   47 Burghclere.
48 *Ibid*.   49 Pepys.   50 Hartmann.

on York was characteristic and unanswerable; he pretended to be in fear of his life from the Duke's vengeance: when he drove out in his coach he was protected by seven " musquetoons ", a gesture which Charles found almost as amusing as his Prime Minister's imitations. York raged and protested: but there was nothing to be done.[51] Buckingham's ostentatious terror was neither actionable nor treasonable: it was merely provocative and added to his popularity with the people, whose hero he continued to be.

5

In 1669 Buckingham at last succeeded in displacing Ormonde; his governorship was given to Lord Berkeley of Stratton, and Ellis Leighton, now Berkeley's secretary, left France in order to look after Buckingham's interests in Ireland.[52] Louis XIV—whose eye for detail was only equalled by his capacity for hard work and his love of conquest and the Catholic Church—looked about for an agent who could ingratiate himself with the English Court circle in general and with Buckingham in particular. His choice fell on the Abbé Pregnani, an Italian monk, skilled in chemistry and astrology; the Duke of Monmouth had returned from France full of praises of his gifts.[53]

The Abbé started off well enough with some suitable prophecies about the future greatness and indissolubility of France and England; then Charles and Buckingham took him to Newmarket, where he was so unfortunate as to pick three losers in succession.[54] The Duke of Monmouth, who persisted in following his tips, lost a great deal of money; and " the poor Abbé," wrote Charles to Madame, " was very much troubled for fear that the railleries about foretelling the horse-matches may have done him some prejudice . . . he was only trying new tricks which he had read of in books and gave as little credit to them as we did," he added kindly.[55] Shortly after the Newmarket disaster Pregnani was recalled; he had failed all along the line, even to the point of rousing Buckingham's suspicions again, although he had spent hours alone with the Duke in his laboratory at Wallingford House.[56] Buckingham expressed his doubts in the following letter to Madame:

---

[51] *Memoirs* of James II, ed. Clarke.   [52] Carte. Ogg. Burnet.
[53] Hartmann.   [54] Burnet.   [55] Hartmann.
[56] Buckingham became an F.R.S. in 1663; but his interest in science seems to have been confined to the discovery of the Philosopher's Stone.

" The Abbé on his arrival here having given me a letter from Your
Royal Highness I offered him my services and asked him if he had orders
to speak to me of any business: he answered that he had no other business
save that of seeing the country. But not being able to believe that he had
undertaken this journey only through curiosity to learn our language and
being besides informed that he was making confidences to others about
certain things which he would not communicate to me, I confess that it
made me begin to suspect that Your Royal Highness had not so much
confidence in me as I had tried to deserve . . . If the Abbé on his arrival
had spoken to me with the same frankness as he employed on his departure
I should have had no trouble in entering into relations with him, for I
assure you, Madame, that, besides the absolute power you will always have
over me to make me obey you in all things, I find in him qualities which
I greatly esteem . . . I am in despair . . . at finding myself always in danger
of passing for a rascal or a visionary through the eagerness and mistakes
of certain people who do not understand our business. Nevertheless I hope
that in the end Your Royal Highness will be satisfied with my efforts . . ."[57]

Buckingham did well to be suspicious, for Charles was continually reminding his sister that the Duke was completely in the
dark as to the real nature of their plans: writing in cipher, he
says:

" (Buckingham) knows nothing of (my) intentions towards the (Catholic
Religion) . . . and (you) need not fear that he will take it ill that (you) do
not write to him, for I have told him that I have forbid (you) to do it for
fear of intercepting of letters."[58]

" (Lord St. Albans) told (Buckingham) that I had forbidden you to
write to him by which he believed there was some mystery in the matter
but (Buckingham) was not at all alarmed at it because it was by his own
desire that I writ to you . . . It will be good that you write some time to
(Buckingham) in general terms, that he may not suspect that there is farther
negotiations than what he knows of, but pray have a care you do not say
anything to him which may make him think I have employed anybody
to (Louis XIV) which he is to know nothing of, because by the messenger
he may suspect that there is something of (Catholic Religion) in the case
which is a matter he must not be acquainted with; therefore you must have
a great care not to say the least thing that may make him suspect anything
of it."

" I have seen your letter to (Buckingham) and what you write to him
is as it ought to be; he shall be brought into the business before he can
suspect anything except that which concerns (Religion) which he must not
be trusted with. You will do well to write seldom to him, for fear something
may slip from your pen which may make him jealous that there is something
more than what he knows of."[59]

[57] Hartmann. Original in French.
[58] *Ibid*. The words in brackets are represented by numbers in the original.
[59] *Ibid*.

6

For some time Buckingham had urged upon Charles the importance of dealing more directly—" as gentleman to gentleman "—with Louis.[60] This could only be achieved by the long planned visit of Madame to England; Monsieur, furiously jealous of her power, did everything possible to prevent its taking place, and for a time he succeeded. Finally, his brother commanded his permission, and on the Sixteenth of May, 1670, Madame arrived at Dover. She had been seriously ill, was extremely unhappy in her marriage and heart-broken by Monsieur's niggardly allowance of three days' holiday with the brother she had not seen for nine years.[61] She was looking very pretty, however, and her diplomatic talents were at once put to the test. Buckingham and Arlington, officially allies, were again " striving against each other ",[62] and a split in the Cabal must be avoided. Madame succeeded in reconciling them, though not permanently.[63] On the Twenty-Seventh of May the Secret Treaty of Dover, the *Traité de Madame*, was signed by Arlington, Clifford, Arundel and Sir Richard Bellings (Queen Catherine's secretary) on the one side and Colbert de Croissy on the other. Unknown to Buckingham, Ashley and Lauderdale, Charles had agreed to make England into a dependency of France and bound himself to enforce the discarded and dreaded Romish religion upon his people; for this he was to receive financial and military support from Louis against his enemies at home and abroad.[64]

Charles's acceptance of the Treaty had nothing to do with

[60] Mignet. Ogg.   [61] This was afterwards extended to seventeen days.
[62] James II.   [63] *Ibid.*

[64] Clause 2 of the Treaty runs: The King of England, being convinced of the truth of the Roman Catholic Religion is resolved to declare it, and to reconcile himself with the Church of Rome as soon as the state of his country's affairs permit. He has such confidence in the fidelity and affection of his subjects that none of them, not even those who (as yet) have been denied a full outpouring of the divine grace, will fail in their due obedience to their sovereign. But as there are always unquiet spirits who mask their designs under the guise of religion, the King of England, for the peace of his kingdom, will avail himself of the assistance of the King of France, who, on his part, as he is anxious to contribute to a design glorious not only for the King of England, but for the whole of Catholic Christendom, promises to pay to the King of England two million livres tournois, the first half payable three months after ratification of the present treaty, the other half three months later. In addition, the King of France undertakes to provide, at his own expense, 6,000 troops for the execution of this design, if they should be required. The time for the declaration of Catholicism is left entirely to the discretion of the King of England.

Madame's influence. His share in it has been variously described; some historians would have us believe that it was a black-hearted and unscrupulous betrayal: others see it as a brilliant diplomatic manœuvre: others again—though these are in a minority—declare that Charles captained a poor team successfully and proved himself a patriot as well as a ruler.

Charles was, in fact, so hard-pressed for money that he had only three collar-bands in his wardrobe and no ink or paper for his Council table.[65] The financial arrangements made at the Restoration had been quite inadequate, and though the King was far from being a good manager he was not as extravagant as his father nor as war-like as Cromwell: he reaped the bad harvest sown by both. That he eventually cheated Louis as well as his own ministers by sliding out of his religious obligations has been marked up to his credit; but this rather dubious asset was only part of the inescapable heritage bequeathed him by his exile and his dependence on such men as Argyll. "*When you come into England, you may be more free—but for the present it is necessary to please these madmen.*" To Charles all proselytising, whether Protestant, Presbyterian or Catholic, was the work of madmen: but he was willing to please them so long as it was convenient to do so. This friendly, affable man was quite ready to pocket his people and gamble with their lives and liberties—and equally ready to defend them, if he was not put to too much trouble. About three things he was adamant: he would not go on his travels again, he would not tamper with the succession, and he would not " give up an hour's divertisement for the sake of any man ".

Three weeks after her return to France Madame died of a perforated duodenal ulcer. Charles's tears at their parting and his passionate grief at her death caused Burnet, and others after him, to reflect upon the nature of his attachment to his sister. The borderline between passion and love no longer appears as clearly defined as in Burnet's day; that Charles and his frail, pretty youngest sister strayed into the No Man's Land between the one and the other is undoubted and not the least attractive trait in their characters.

Presently Charles roused himself to deal with the panic caused by the death of Madame. It was necessary to show his disbelief in the rumours that she had been poisoned, presumably by her husband, that absurd and pathetic figure, and even more urgent to

[65] Burnet.

provide for another treaty, which the duped members of the Cabal might sign. So the *Traité Simulé* was put in hand and Buckingham sent to St. Germains on an official visit of condolence. He took his chaplain, Thomas Sprat, Buckhurst and Sedley with him and remained in France from July to September of the year 1670.

7

Buckingham himself suggested the visit to the French Court after a conference with the other ministers of the Cabal.[66] Arlington pretended to hesitate, although in fact nothing could have suited him better, for the secret of the Dover Treaty was not so well kept as it ought to have been; too many people had been privy to it in the first place and Parliament was already suspicious of a Catholic alliance. But if the great Duke of Buckingham, the Dissenters' champion and the ally of Ashley, went to France, it would be a sign that no religious interference was impending.

Buckingham's progress at the French Court is chiefly recorded by Arlington's agent, Ralph Montagu; blighting though his comments are, it is Montagu, not Buckingham, who emerges as a disagreeable and sinister figure. Louis was pleased with Buckingham, both personally and as a " man of importance and consideration " and had Madame's apartments ready for him at St. Germains; he also provided the Duke with one of his own coaches, eight footmen and all his living expenses. Louis, as ever, thought of everything; besides his present to Buckingham of a sword of which the hilt was set with diamonds, he arranged for a pension of four hundred pounds a year to be paid to Lady Shrewsbury, who told Colbert " that she would make Buckingham comply . . . in all things ";[67] Louis also sent over a large bribe for Lady Castlemaine.

The Duke made very leisurely progress to St. Germains, stopping at the tailor's in Paris to fit himself out for his reception. Then at last he reached the palace and met again the formal, solemn, consciously majestic young King. Buckingham adapted himself to the rarefied atmosphere of stately entertainment and ritualistic display with characteristic ease; his " noble presence and graceful mien " were " very acceptable, and even captivating, to many that beheld him ".[68] With some complacency he wrote to

[66] Christie.   [67] Jesse.   [68] L. Echard: *History of England*.

Arlington that he had had more honours done him "than ever were given to any subject", and that

"Nothing but our being mealy-mouthed can hinder us from finding our accounts in this matter." Later he added, "I am every day convinced of the happy conjuncture we have at present in our hands, of any conditions from this Court, that we can in reason demand. The King of France is so mightily taken with the discourses I make to him of his greatness by land that he talks to me twenty times a day; all the courtiers here wonder at it, and I am very glad of it . . ."

Buckingham did not mention—though Montagu's secretary did —that the richness of the dishes had been a little too much for him and that he was ill for several days as a result of the "collation" served on the canal at Versailles after a mock sea-fight in which a flag-ship was attacked and sunk by an elaborately decorated fleet of smaller vessels.[69]

One night, soon after his arrival, Buckingham and his companions were asked to a supper-party given by the diminutive and eccentric Comte de Lauzun, at that time the most intimate friend of the French King. When the feast ended and the guests were sitting over their wine, a masked cavalier, accompanied by two masked ladies, suddenly appeared. Immediately the music changed its rhythms and the three swept into a stately *pas de trois*. During the ballet the ladies, with delicately persuasive gestures, urged the gentleman to give up his jewelled sword; but he would not yield until the music ceased. Then all three dancers unmasked. The recalcitrant cavalier was Louis XIV and one of the ladies his *maîtresse en titre*, Madame de Montespan, who, with her companion, now approached the Duke of Buckingham and presented him with the sword. This scene of elaborate and charming artifice was in perfect contrast to the casual manners and rather muddled splendour of the Court represented by George Villiers; but he played his part in it with the graceful and winning courtesy for which he was noted, while his hosts looked on complacently. It is permissible to assume that he had been prepared for this intricately devised compliment and that he was rather amused than awestruck by its ingenuity.[70]

The Duke was a little put out by the theft of some of the jewels from the hilt of his presentation sword by the younger courtiers. There was a story that he tore off the diamonds from his hat and scattered them amongst those ladies who had been so ill-bred as to

[69] French State Papers.   [70] Ravaisson, *Archives de la Bastille.*

declare that they must be paste, exclaiming, "See if they are or
no!"—but this anecdote may rather be regarded as an illustration
of the effect he was making than taken literally.[71]

When he had attended the funeral of Madame and made his
appearance as the guest of honour at masques, balls, comedies,
operas and a pastoral acted in an illuminated grotto, the Duke was
promised the command of the English armies then preparing to
invade Holland. The States-General were alarmed by the reports
of his visit; John de Witt, one of the few who kept his head in the
gathering storm, dryly remarked to Sir William Temple that His
Grace was surely not sent to France to see the country or to learn
the language.[72] Meanwhile the Duke's "wonderful gaiety and
address"[73] continued to delight the French nobility and to alarm
Ralph Montagu, who had had to lend him some money on his
return and wrote almost hysterically to Arlington that he himself
was "quite broke" and must have five hundred pounds immediately. Montagu flattered Buckingham as well as he was able,
but was thankful to see him go. George Villiers was not his friend,
he knew that very well; some of the French over-rated him: others
mistrusted him and did not want him to command the army;
Louvois, hearing of his Presbyterian and anti-monarchist ten-
dencies, had said, "Le Duc de Bouquinquam est un homme incom-
patible, et nous ne voulons point qui'l fasse le méchant ici, comme
il fait en Angleterre." Of course Buckingham "pretended to be
very fair" to Arlington, but that was His Grace's detestable habit,
to make himself pleasant to everybody. Nevertheless, Montagu
thought there might be serious trouble if the Duke did not get his
generalship after all the flatteries he had received, and then, who
would be blamed? The poor, unfortunate, hard-working English
Ambassador.

Buckingham, unconscious of Montagu's agitation, returned to
Paris with a miniature of Louis XIV set in diamonds, his sword
and belt and the agreeable consciousness of having refused a bribe
of forty thousand pounds from the King for persuading Charles to
allow the French fleet to occupy British seas and harbours;[74] he
had ignored Shaftesbury's suggestion that he should break off the
negotiations altogether.[75] It now remained to attend to his own

---

[71] Oldmixon: *History of the Stuarts*. This story has also been attributed to Buckingham's father.
[72] *Ibid*.   [73] *Ibid*.
[74] He afterwards told Burnet that he believed Arlington to have accepted this bribe.
[75] Burnet.

affairs, the clothes that his servant Douty had been buying for himself and Lady Shrewsbury, and the coaching of one of his musicians by a Parisian master, before returning to England with the draft of the false treaty. Everything had gone well. He was delighted with himself and perfectly unaware that the difficulties made by Charles and Arlington during his dealings with Louis had been entirely fictitious and only raised to cover up the full extent of their own duplicity. Louis' plan was to begin the invasion of Holland in the spring of 1671; then, as soon as the Dutch were crushed, Charles was to declare himself a Catholic and start the religious campaign at home.[76]

[76] Christie. Ogg.   Mignet.

PART THREE
(September 1670 – April 1687)

THE YEARS OF INTRIGUE

CHAPTER ONE

I

TEN years of wealth and power and four years' association with Lady Shrewsbury had brought out the worst in Buckingham's character. By the end of 1670 he was politically at the zenith of his fortunes and morally degraded. During part of the next twelve years he was to climb out of the mire and associate himself with a better cause than that provided by Continental and palace intrigue; but before he plunged into the struggle that followed the rise and fall of Shaftesbury's leadership he had become the dupe of those more cunning, the tool of those more painstaking, than himself. At intervals, and unaccountably as it seemed, he found the political avenues blocked; so he let ambition go and turned to another world—the world of the theatre.

It is well for posterity that he did so. If George Villiers had been a little more hard-working than Arlington, and a good deal abler than Charles Stuart, he would have neglected his greatest gift. That he, from time to time, deserted Clio for Thalia is something to be thankful for; had he been faithful to the sterner Muse he would have had no leisure for Mr. Bayes of *The Rehearsal* and English literature would have been the poorer.

Between 1663 and 1686 Buckingham wrote seven dramatic pieces: *The Chances* (a revised version of Beaumont and Fletcher's play for which he composed new Fourth and Fifth Acts), *The Country Gentleman* (his skit on Sir William Coventry, written in conjunction with Sir Robert Howard, which has not survived), *The Rehearsal, The Restoration, or Right Will Take Place* (a new edition of Beaumont and Fletcher's *Philaster*), *The Battle of Sedgemoor, The Militant Couple*, and *A Conference*. The last three were not intended for the stage, being short dialogues written to amuse the author and his then dwindling circle; they will be dealt with as fragments of autobiography in their proper order.[1]

The Rehearsal falls into a different category from the other surviving plays, for it is a work of art; but in so far as *The Chances* and *The Restoration* respectively lead up to and fall away from the standard set by Buckingham's masterpiece, they are worth a brief

[1] George Villiers, Second Duke of Buckingham: *Works*, 1715 ed.

reconsideration. *The Chances*, a romantic drama first produced in January 1667, with Charles Hart and Pepys's mistress, the beautiful and celebrated Mrs. Knipp—who made a great hit with her song, "All Night I Weep"—was entirely successful, being revived during the seventeenth, eighteenth and early nineteenth centuries and performed in London as recently as 1922. For all that, *The Chances* is not interesting: the dialogue is easy and unaffected, the action rapid; but the characterisation is conventional and flat. Here and there is a flash of the gaiety that was to reach its apotheosis in *The Rehearsal*, but not enough to light up the intricate course of mistaken identity and general misunderstanding which compose the whole. The epilogue contains a charming allusion to Nell Gwynn and gives Buckingham's reasons for adapting an old favourite instead of producing an original work.

> "The end of plays should be to entertain,
> And not to keep the auditors in pain.
> Giving one price, and for what trash you please,
> He thinks, the play being done, you should have ease.
> No wit, no scene, no freedom and a box
> Is much like paying money for the stocks.
> Besides, the Author dreads the strut and mien
> Of new praised poets, having often seen
> Some of his fellows, who have writ before,
> When Nell has danced her jig, steal to the door,
> Hear the pit clap, and with conceit of that
> Swell, and believe themselves the Lord knows what."

Buckingham's second adaptation, *The Restoration*, was written more than twenty years after *The Chances* and some fifteen years after *The Rehearsal*; the author took it with him on his last journey to Yorkshire in 1686, and there is no record of its ever having been performed. Its chief interest lies in the topical allusions of the prologue and epilogue. In the prologue Buckingham speaks of his recent—and final—political overthrow.

> "Nothing is harder in the world to do,
> Than to quit what our nature leads us to.
> As this our friend here knows, who, having spent
> His time and wealth for other folks' content;
> Though he so much as thanks could never get,
> Can't, for his life, quite give it over yet;
> But, striving still to please you, hopes he may,
> Without a grievance, try to mend a play.

> Perhaps he wished it might have been his fate
> To lend a helping hand to rule the State:
> Though he conceives, as things have lately run,
> 'Tis somewhat hard at present to be done."

In the epilogue there is a jibe at his own folly and a bitter allusion to Shaftesbury who, in Buckingham's view, had recked as little of ruining his followers as of destroying himself :

> " If, by my deep contrivance, wit and skill
> Things fall out cross to what I mean them still,
> You must not wonder; 't'is the common fate
> Of almost all grave governors of late:
> And one would swear, as every plot has sped,
> They thought more with their elbows than their head;
> Yet they go on as brisk and look as well,
> As if they had outwisdom'd Machiavel:
> So curs will wag their tails and think they've won us,
> At the same instant they make water on us.
>
> .   .   .   .
>
> Yet, faith, the little Lord when hence he ran,
> Did compass one thing like an able man:
> For since he could not living act with reason,
> 'T'was shrewdly done of him to die in season."

The resigned contempt of these last lines has taken us a long way from the wild absurdity and reckless exuberance of *The Rehearsal*. This play was conceived as a means of attack on a certain kind of drama and finally used as a weapon against an unconquerable adversary. The story of its creation is the story of a contest in which the honours were divided.

2

John Dryden, who was three years younger than Buckingham, succeeded Sir William Davenant as Poet Laureate and Historiographer-Royal in 1668. The rise of his fortunes had synchronised with everything that was new, popular and elaborate in the Theatre of the Restoration. As early as 1662 Dryden's reputation was nearly made; but he perceived that the demand for plays was likely to be greater than the supply and that the quickest way to achieve wealth and fame was by connecting himself with the rulers of the theatrical world. Here the monopoly was divided between Sir

Thomas Killigrew[2] and Sir William Davenant. These gentlemen had each a company of players, for whom they built theatres on the latest Continental model; Killigrew's was the Theatre Royal in Bridge Street and Davenant's The Duke of York's in Lincoln's Inn Fields. Sir Robert Howard, son of the Earl of Berkshire, was one of the most prolific and popular playwrights; Dryden allied himself with Sir Robert by marrying his sister, Lady Elizabeth Howard, collaborating with him in the production of plays and sharing a house with him in Lincoln's Inn Fields. Thus established, he made it his business to give the theatre-going public—a more sophisticated and wealthier public than that of the early seventeenth century—what they wanted.

At this time comedy and farce were not as popular as they were to become. The great demand was for heroic dramas on the grand scale. Expensive and complicated productions, with painted scenery (this was first used by Sir William Davenant in 1663), incorrect but gorgeous costumes, mechanised devices, enormously variegated " perspectives " and startling *coups d'œil* were the rage; to this end Dryden followed up his witty and lightly moving comedies with splendid and majestic dramas of which the inspiration was the Continental romance of the late sixteenth and early seventeenth centuries; some of the most celebrated and popular of these novels—or *romans à clef,* for they presented royal and other famous living personages and historical events under fantastic pseudonyms—were *Le Grand Cyrus* of Scudéry, *L'Astrée* of d'Urfé and *Polexandre* of Gomberville; these stories, with their ineffably noble heroes, virtuous heroines, high-sounding sentiments, and prolonged discourses, provided the "light" reading of the educated classes during the greater part of the seventeenth century.

On the English stage the current predilection for ghastly and terrifying realism was catered for by placing the actors in scenes of blood and torture (sometimes mangled and gory bodies, modelled in wax, were used for the backgrounds) and causing the characters to suffer horrible agonies upon the stage—as, for instance, in Dryden's *Indian Emperor*, where Michael Mohun as Montezuma defied the Spanish general (Charles Hart) from the rack and argued with the proselytising Jesuit missionary in rhyming couplets of sustained and formal eloquence during a phenomenal run of fourteen nights.[3] Some stage directions from

[2] Father of Harry Killigrew.
[3] This play was first produced at the Theatre Royal in April 1665, and subsequently dedicated to the Duchess of Monmouth.

two of Dryden's operas, *The State of Innocence* and *Albion and Albianus* give an impression of the elaborate standards then obtaining for productions of this kind.[4] *Albion and Albianus* opens with:

> The Scene is a street of Palaces which lead to the Front of the Royal Exchange; the great Arch is open, and the view is continued through the open part of the Exchange, to the Arch on the other side, and thence to as much of street beyond as could properly be taken.
> Mercury descends in a chariot drawn by Ravens.
> He comes to Augusta and Thamesis. They lie on Couches at a distance from each other, in dejected postures: She attended by Cities, he by Rivers.
> On the side of Augusta's couch are painted Towers falling, a Scarlet Gown and Gold Chain, a Cup of Maintenance thrown down, and a Sword in a Velvet Scabbard thrust through it, the City Arms, a Mace with an old useless Charter, and all in disorder. Before Thamesis are broken Reeds, Bull-rushes, Sedge, etc., with his Urn Reversed.

During the course of the opera
> The Clouds divide, and Juno appears in a Machine drawn by Peacocks; while a Symphony is playing, it moves gently forward, and as it descends, it opens and discovers the Tail of the Peacock, which is so large, that it almost fills the opening of the stage between scene and scene.

Then—
> The cave of Proteus rises out of the Sea, it consists of several arches of rockwork, adorned with mother of pearl, coral and abundances of shells of various kinds: Thro' the arches is seen the sea, and parts of Dover pier: in the middle of the Cave is Proteus asleep on a Rock adorn'd with Shells, etc., like the Cave. Albion and Acacia seize on him, and while a Symphony is playing, he sinks as they are bringing him forward and changes himself into a Lion, a Crocodile, a Dragon and then to his own Shape again; He comes toward the front of the Stage and sings.

In *The State of Innocence*
> The First Scene represents a Chaos, or a confus'd mass of matter; the Stage is almost wholly dark: A symphony of war-like Music is heard for some time; then from the Heavens (which are opened) fall the rebellious Angels wheeling in the Air, and seeming transfixed with Thunderbolts; The bottom of the Stage being opened, receives the Angels, who fall out of sight. Tunes of Victory are played and a Hymn sung: Angels discovered above, brandishing their Swords: the Music ceasing and the Heavens being closed, the Scene shifts and on a sudden represents Hell: Part of the scene is a Lake of brimstone or rowling Fire: the Earth of a burnt colour: the fall'n Angels appear on the lake, lying prostrate: a Tune of Horror and Lamentation is heard.

[4] *The State of Innocence* was never performed. The music of *Albion and Albianus*, performed in 1685, was by Louis Grabu, Master of the King's Music.

Subsequently

From that part of the Heavens, where the Sun appears, a Chariot is discovered, drawn with white horses; and in it Uriel the Regent of the Sun. The Chariot moves swiftly towards Lucifer; and, at Uriel's approach, the Sun recovers his light.

At the same time the works of the Elizabethan and Jacobean playwrights were continually revived and benefited by the simple elegance of the newly built theatres, where the changes of scene were provided for by movable flats, an apron stage some seventeen feet deep and little windows or balconies on either side of the proscenium arch. The audience no longer faced the rigours and uncertainties of the weather, for they were roofed in by a dome from which hung chandeliers with wax candles; the stage itself was lit by chandeliers hanging from the proscenium arch and foot-lights in oil lamps. Most important of all, from the public's point of view, the theatre was now the resort of respectable persons. Gentlemen unaccompanied by ladies sat in the pit, round the three-sided stage, on benches: then came the first tier containing the boxes, the most expensive seats, the central and largest box being reserved for royalty; this was surmounted by the second tier, where the ladies of the town sat in vizard-masks with their gallants, and crowned by the cheapest seats in the third tier or gallery, where the gentry sent their lackeys to sit among the roughs and workfolk. The musicians' gallery was either above the proscenium arch or just below the stage. The orange-girls stood in the pit with their backs to the audience.

The players were in the most literal sense the King's servants and the servants of the public. Seventeenth-century audiences had no notion of sitting in well-bred, attentive silence; the actors had to make their effects as best they could above the din of late arrivals and drunks, the penetrating drawl of court gentlemen's criticisms and the screaming sallies of the Vizards or Fire-ships, as the women of pleasure were called. They must be prepared to dance the jigs, heys and canaries which so often concluded a scene[5] without stumbling over wax droppings, orange-peel or a lice-ridden periwig thrown by a tipsy nobleman from the benches; they must sing their ballads and choruses through a barrage of tobacco-smoke from the same quarter. The comedian had to be very careful of his own gags and the interpolations of the author—if these turned out

[5] The hey was danced by the entire company, divided into rows; the canaries was a jig danced by two persons.

to be politically offensive the play was taken off and the actor, whether reprehensible or not, sent to the Porter's Lodge at White-hall, where he was flogged: and a flogging generally meant a crushed rib or two and a week out of work. The most celebrated and successful of the men—Lacy, Kynaston, Hart, Mohun—were as sure as anyone could be in those uncertain times of a pension in old age; the women had to rely on more personal support in the hey-day of their youth and fame. There was neither pity nor care for ageing, feeble players—they were hissed and pelted from the boards. Both men and women had to be on view behind the scenes to receive the criticisms of patrons and authors and the advances of the stage-struck while they changed their clothes and took off their make-up; they must be ready to face enraged, abusive audiences when the play struck a wrong note and to wait half an hour or more for the Court party to arrive; they had to appear in the dangerous splendours of dead people's clothing and so risk small-pox or the plague.

Theatre folk did not then receive the reverential treatment now given them: but then, as now, they were followed, adored and spoilt if they pleased their public: then, as now, older people sometimes remembered their past glories and mourned their failing powers: then, as now, they lived in a separate world and spoke a language of their own.

3

Dryden's dramas and comedies followed one another with bewildering lustre and assured success; by 1668, surrounded and supported by such lesser stars as Orrery, Settle and Crowne,[6] he was supreme in the theatre. His enemies were of the Court party, led by Buckingham and enforced by Rochester, Etheredge, Buckhurst and Sedley, who considered him an unworthy successor to the great playwrights of the past; of these, Jonson was their hero: they admired him "to idolatry" and caused his plays to be revived again and again. This made no difference to Dryden's popularity;

---

[6] Roger Boyle, first Earl of Orrery (1621–1679), statesman, soldier and author of *Mustapha, The Black Prince*, etc., etc. Elkanah Settle (1648–1724), lampooned by Dryden as Doeg in the second part of *Absolom and Achitophel* (to which he replied with *Absolom Senior* or *Achitophel Transposed*) and author of *The Empress of Morocco*, etc. John Crowne (d. 1703?) author of *Juliana* and other plays and of the celebrated court masque, *Calisto*.

there was plenty of room for him and Ben Jonson in the English theatre.[7]

Some time in 1663 Buckingham, with the help of Sprat, Cowley and Martin Clifford, had begun to write a skit, taking as his butt the impresario of the heroic drama; to him the attack was in the nature of a campaign; he saw nothing valuable or entertaining in the plays then beginning to be popularised by Davenant and Sir Robert Howard, who, in his view, substituted pretension for poetry and bombast for dramatic effect. The sketch, for it was no more, took Sir William Davenant as the central comic figure: he was called Bilboa, and great play was made with the fact that his prototype had lost a portion of his nose and covered the scar with a piece of black paper. This was as far as Buckingham got; he soon became too much occupied with political and other affairs to bother with the piece; then, just as he had finished the first draft —by now some of Sir Robert Howard's mannerisms and tricks of speech had crept into Bilbao's dialogue—the plague broke out and the theatres were closed. After another long interval—or a series of intervals—Buckingham set to work again; Joe Haines, a popular comedian and a protégé of his[8] made some suggestions; between 1668 and 1670 Dryden's Laureateship, his complacency, his prodigious output, and above all, his condescending criticisms of Jonson, caught Buckingham's attention; he had tried, and failed, to defeat the heroic drama by organising a scene during the first performance of Colonel Henry Howard's *The United Kingdoms* and barely escaped with his life from the resultant mêlée: now there must be no mistake. He re-christened his central character Mr. Bayes, dressed him in black velvet (Dryden's preferred wear) threw in some references to the Laureate's mistress, his liking for stewed plums and snuff, called the play—it was now a full length farce—*The Rehearsal* and interpolated some scenes in which a quantity of Dryden's best effects were brutally and brilliantly caricatured.

On December the Seventh, 1671, *The Rehearsal* was produced at the Theatre Royal with John Lacy (coached by Buckingham himself in Dryden's mannerisms and intonations) as Mr. Bayes, the voluptuous and beautiful Edward Kynaston, so moving in boys' and women's parts, as Prince Volscius, Cartwright doubling

---

[7] Buckingham was nine when Jonson died; it is possible that he may have seen him or heard him talk when Jonson was helping to produce his masques at the Court of Charles I.

[8] He accompanied Buckingham to France in 1670.

Thunder and the Second King of Brentford and the lovely but
not very talented Mrs. Ann Reeves, Dryden's mistress, as
Amaryllis.[9] The King was present, and all the Court: the audience
laughed till they cried: and Dryden was known henceforward as
Mr. Bayes.

4

The outline of *The Rehearsal* is extremely simple. Mr. Smith,
who lives in the country, has come up to London for a round of
pleasure: he falls in with his old friend, Mr. Johnson, a playgoer,
and, as he himself thinks, a wit; they have just begun to discuss
the new plays, and their authors, when Mr. Johnson catches sight
of one of these very persons, Mr. Bayes. " Godso, this is an
Author: I'll go fetch him to you . . . Here he is, I have caught him,"
he says. Mr. Bayes is only too willing to give the two gentlemen
an account of his methods and success and follows it with an
invitation to come and watch the final rehearsal of his newest
drama, *The Two Kings of Brentford*. All three go along together
to the theatre. During the course of the rehearsal the characters of
the town and the country playgoer are fully developed and contrasted with the ineffable complacency of Mr. Bayes and the
bewildered recalcitrance of the players, who hardly know what to
make of his latest masterpiece. They struggle on while Mr. Bayes
explains to the increasingly bored and bewildered Smith and the
consciously knowing Johnson the mechanics of his art and the
transcendant quality of his inspiration; at the same time he
rehearses a whispering scene, a banqueting scene, two fights, a
battle and several dances; some of the characters descend from the
clouds to music, others rush on from the wings, others shoot up
from the trap-doors, invariably knocking over Mr. Bayes, who loses
his spectacles and the script alternately, but never ceases talking.
The climax is reached in a series of madly farcical, utterly disastrous
scenes of which Mr. Bayes is the victim: finally he threatens to take
his play to the other house, where it will be properly appreciated.
Mr. Johnson and Mr. Smith leave in disgust. Mr. Bayes runs
desperately after them—they positively must not miss the treat of

---

[9] It is characteristic of the humour of the day that Mrs. Reeves played herself in *The
Rehearsal*. It would be interesting to know if this actress—who shortly afterwards retired
to a convent abroad—appeared willingly or under pressure, or with complete indifference
to the feelings of her lover. John Lacy was succeeded by Joe Haines as Mr. Bayes.

treats, his final scene—and the actors, left alone, combine in refusing to appear in a play of which they can make nothing. They do a dance for another play, set up the bills to advertise it, and the curtain falls.

The effect of *The Rehearsal* is cumulative. The author keeps his shock tactics for the climaxes. It is at once conveyed that Mr. Smith is a sensible, truthful fellow and that Mr. Johnson is rather pretentious; then, after a page of dialogue, Mr. Bayes " passes over the stage " and as soon as he has spoken with the other two we perceive that he is absurd, long-winded and vain, but little more. He explains three rules, to which he attributes his success.

Mr. B. Why, Sir, my first rule is the rule of Transversion, or *Regula Duplex*; changing Verse into Prose or Prose into Verse, alternative, as you please . . . My next rule is the rule of Record, by way of Table-Book. Pray observe.

Johns. We hear you, Sir: go on.

Mr. B. As thus, I come into a Coffee-house, or some other place where witty men resort, I make as if I minded nothing (do you mark?) but as soon as anyone speaks, pop I slap it down, and make that too my own . . . My third rule I have here in my pocket . . . When I have anything to invent, I never trouble my head about it, as other men do; but presently turn over this book, and there I have, at one view, all that Persius, Montaigne, Seneca's tragedies, Horace, Juvenal, Claudian, Pliny, Plutarch's Lives, and the rest, have ever thought upon this subject; and so in a trice, by leaving out a few words, or putting in others of my own, the business is done.

This sort of thing seems rather thin material for a whole play—that is the first impression. Then, as the rehearsal continues and Mr. Bayes directs the players and alternately condescends to and lectures Johnson and Smith we realise that there is something epic about his silliness. He is going through one of his opening scenes:

Mr. B. Come out, Thunder and Lightning. (*Enter Thunder and Lightning.*)

Thun. I am the bold Thunder.

Mr. B. Mr. Cartwright, prythee speak that a little louder, and with a hoarse voice. I'm the bold Thunder! Pshaw! Speak it out in a voice that thunders it out indeed: I am the bold Thunder.

Thun. (*very loud*). I am the bold Thunder.

Light. The brisk Lightning, I.

Mr. B. Nay, but you must be quick and nimble. The brisk Lightning, I. That's my meaning.

. . . . .

Thun. I strike Men down.

Light. I fire the town.

Thun. Then let critics take heed how they grumble,
         For then begin I for to rumble.
Light. Let the ladies allow us their graces
         Or I'll blast all the paint on their faces.

.   .   .   .

Thun. Let the critics look to't.
Light. Let the ladies look to't.
Thun. For Thunder will do't.
Light. For Lightning will shoot.
Thun. I'll give you dash for dash.
Light. I'll give you flash for flash.
Both. Look to't, look to't; we'll do't, we'll do't: Look to't, we'll do't.
(*Twice or thrice repeated & Exeunt.*)
Mr. B. There's no more. 'T's but a flash of a Prologue: A Droll.
Smith. Yes, 'tis short indeed: but very terrible.

After the scene between the two Kings of Brentford Mr.
Johnson exclaims:

This is a majestic scene indeed!
Mr. B. Ay, 'tis a crust, a lasting crust for your rogue critics, egad ...
It was I, you must know, that have written a whole play just in this very
same style; it was never acted yet.
John. How so?
Mr. B. Egad, I can hardly tell you for laughing—ha, ha, ha—'t'is so
pleasant a story: Ha, ha, ha.
Smith. What is't?
Mr. B. Egad, the players refus'd to act it. Ha, ha, ha.
Smith. That's impossible.
Mr. B. Egad, they did, Sir, point-bank refused it, egad, ha, ha, ha.
John. Fie, that was rude.
Mr. B. Rude! Ay, egad, they are the rudest, uncivilest persons and all
that, in the whole world, egad; egad, there's no living with them; I have
written, Mr. Johnson, I do verily believe, a whole cart-load of things, every
whit as good as this, and yet I vow to gad, these insolent rascals have turned
'em all back upon my hands again.
John. Strange fellows indeed!

Presently follows the celebrated Boot Scene, which was interpolated in the second edition, in 1672.

Mr. B. Here now, Mr. Johnson; you shall see a combat between love
and honour. An ancient author has made a whole play on't; but I have
despatched it all in this scene.
  (*Volscius sits down to pull on his boots; Bayes stands by and over-acts
the part as he speaks it.*)

Vol.   How has my passion made me Cupid's scoff?
         This hasty boot is on, the other off,

And sullen lies, with amorous design
To quit loud fame, and make that Beauty mine.

. . . . .

My legs, the emblem of my various thought,
Show to what sad distraction I am brought.
Sometimes with stubborn honour, like this boot,
My mind is guarded and resolved to do't;
Sometimes, again, that very mind, by love
Disarmed, like this other leg does prove.
Shall I to honour or to love give way?
Go on, cries honour; tender love says, Nay;
Honour aloud commands, pluck both boots on;
But softer love does whisper, put on none.
What shall I do? What conduct shall I find
To lead me through this twilight of my mind?
For as bright day, with black approach of night
Contending, makes a doleful, puzzling light
So does my honour and my love together
Puzzle me so, I can resolve for neither.

(*Goes out, hopping, with one boot on and the other off.*)

. . . . . .

Mr. B. I remember once in a play of mine, I set off a scene, egad, beyond expectation, only with a petticoat, and the belly-ache.

Smith. Pray, how was that, Sir?

Mr. B. Why, I contrived a petticoat to be brought in upon a chair, (nobody knew how) into a prince's chamber, whose father was not to see it, that came in by chance.

John. God's my life, that was a notable contrivance indeed.

Smith. Ay, but, Mr. Bayes, how could you contrive the belly-ache?

Mr. B. The easiest i' the world, egad . . . I made the Prince sit down upon the petticoat, no more than so, and pretend to his father that he had just then got the belly-ache; whereupon his father went out to call a physician, and his man run away with the petticoat.

Smith. Well, and what followed upon that?

Mr. B. Nothing, no earthly thing, I vow to gad.

After rehearsing a dance ("Pray dance well before the Gentlemen; you are commonly so lazy—you should be light and easy, tah, tah, tah ") Mr. Bayes explains:

But Mr. Johnson, egad, I am not like other persons, they care not what becomes of their things, so they can but get money for 'em; now egad, when I write, if it be not just as it should be in every circumstance, to every particular, egad: I am not able to endure it, I'm out of my wits and all that, I'm the strangest person in the whole world; for what care I for money? I write for Reputation.

During the funeral scene Mr. Bayes cannot trust the actors to do justice to his verses; he begins to read, but breaks off to say:

And what do you think now, I fancy her to make love like, here in the paper?

Smith. Like a woman, what should she make love like?

Mr. B. O, my word, you are out, tho', Sir: egad, you are.

Smith. What then, like a man?

Mr. B. No Sir, like a humble-bee.

Smith. I confess, that I should not have fancied.

. . . .

Mr. B. Yes, I think for a dead person, it is a good enough way of making love; for being divested of her terrestrial part, and all that, she is only capable of these pretty amorous designs that are innocent and yet passionate.

After the coffin has opened to disclose a banquet provided by Pallas Athene and gobbled up by the hero, Bayes orders the stage to be filled for his big scene between the two Princes, Prettyman and Volscius. The whole point of this scene, he says, is that Prettyman and Volscius are *not* in love with the same woman, " a new conceit " with which he is extremely pleased. During the dialogue he is unable to help bursting in with such exclamations as " Antithesis! " " Simile! " " There's a great verse! " " That is as well, egad, as I can do," " Now, mark! " " Now, the rant's coming," "Ah, gadzookers, that's well writ! " and finally in a crescendo of excitement and self-congratulation loses his perriwig.

After this the action hurries to an end with the two Kings of Brentford " descending from the clouds singing in white garments: and three fiddlers sitting before them in green." There follows a battle, a jig danced by the Earth, Sun and Moon, and another battle in which all the soldiers are slain by the hero. Mr. Smith, who has been bursting with irritation for some time, protests—

But Mr. Bayes, how shall all these dead men go off? For I see none alive to help 'em.

Mr. B. Go off! why, as they came on: upon their legs: how should they go off? Why, do you think the people here don't know they are not dead? He is mighty ignorant, poor man; your friend here is very silly, Mr. Johnson, egad, he is. Ha, ha, ha. Come sir, I'll show you how they shall go off. Rise, rise, sirs, and go about your business. There's go off for you now. Ha, ha, ha . . .

Any quotation, long or short, must detract from the general effect of *The Rehearsal*, which is so closely knit that it seems to have lasted a bare half-hour; it should run for less than two hours, if taken at the proper speed. The epilogue pleads for a release from the influence of such writers as Mr. Bayes.

> The play is at an end, but where's the plot?
> That circumstance the poet Bayes forgot.
> And we can boast, tho' t'is a plotting age,
> No place is freer from it than the stage.
>
> .   .   .   .   .
>
> Let's have, at least, once in our lives, a time,
> When we may hear some reason, not all rhyme:
> We have this ten years felt its influence;
> Pray let this prove a year of prose and sense.

5

The cruelty of the attack is terrifying; but with the passage of time Mr. Bayes has become an endearing figure. The success of *The Rehearsal*, far from causing Dryden's literary downfall, increased the popularity of his plays and inspired the wonderful description of Buckingham quoted at the beginning of this memoir, of which the poet afterwards wrote:

"The character of Zimri in my *Absalom* is, in my opinion, worth the whole poem: 'T'is not bloody, but 't'is ridiculous enough. And he for whom it was intended was too witty to resent it as an injury."

Elsewhere he says:

"I answered not *The Rehearsal*, because I knew the Author sate to himself when he drew the picture, and was the very Bayes of his own fame."

Buckingham replied to Dryden's attack in the following lines:

> "As witches images of wax invent,
> To torture those they're bid to represent,
> And as the true live substance does decay,
> Whilst that slight Idol melts in flames away,
> Such, and no better witchcraft wounds my name,
> So thy ill-made Resemblance wastes my fame.
> So as the charmed brand consumed i' the fire,
> So did Meleager's vital heat expire.
> Poor name! what medicine for thee can I find
> But than with stronger charms thy charms t'unbind."[10]

[10] Commonplace Book.

There was no charm powerful enough to destroy the heroic drama, which continued to flourish long after Buckingham was in his grave. For many years a story was handed down of the Duke's final victory over Dryden. It has been disproved: but it is worth repeating because it throws a light on the reactions of contemporaries to this great literary duel. It was said that during one of the performances of Dryden's dramas a female character came down to the front of the stage and declaimed, with an agonised look and an appropriate gesture, the following lines:

"My wound is great, because it is so small."

Buckingham instantly stood up in his box, and shrilled out in ludicrous mimicry:

"Then t'would be greater were it none at all!"

The house burst into a roar of laughter and the play had to be taken off, with the result that the author lost his "benefit", due on the third night of the run. In fact Dryden never wrote such a line; he may have written the riposte attributed to Buckingham: or both lines may have been written by the Duke: or the whole story, like Ouida's apocryphal "none rowed faster than stroke", may have been one of the popular jokes of the day.

The Rehearsal transcends parody. It is not necessary to read what it caricatures in order to enjoy it nor to remember what scholarship has discovered, that almost every line has a reference to another writer's work and that more than seventy plays have been dredged to make a single farce. The fact remains that Mr. Bayes can be placed among the great comic figures of our literature; though not of their stature, he bears comparison with Malvolio, Mr. Collins and Mr. Micawber, because his creator has made him generic and typical. Every writer has something of dear, delightful Mr. Bayes in his nature, conceal it how he may: everyone connected with the theatre shares his capacity for self-delusion, his child-like, unself-conscious excitement over his own work, however modest and sensible he may be.

Mr. Bayes rather resembles the characters created by Edward Lear and Lewis Carroll than Sheridan's Mr. Puff, that shameless theft of a hundred years later; he reminds us of the Mock Turtle, Humpty Dumpty, the Young Lady of Sweden and the Old Person of Annerley; he derives from Bottom the Weaver, and his modern counterpart is Groucho Marx—while Mr. Puff, amusing though he is, bears no relationship to either of these outsize figures. The fact that *The Rehearsal* gave birth, first to Fielding's *Pasquin*, and then to Sheridan's *Critic*, has nothing to do with the general tone of Buckingham's play, which is one of maniacal inconsequence and staggering unexpectedness, tedious to some, incomprehensible to others, rapture to those who relish this particular form of fun—for such expressions as humour and wit savour too much of premeditation and intellectual exercise to be used in connection with Mr. Bayes, his bursts of ecstatic conceit and his appalling energy.[11] For a long time his name and his conversation were as familiar as are those of the Mad Hatter or Mr. Pickwick to-day; now they are almost forgotten: but then, how often are the heroic dramas of Dryden and his contemporaries revived? Perhaps one day they will all rise again together. There is a story, not from a reliable source, that Buckingham and Rochester invited Dryden to sit with them in their box at the first night of *The Rehearsal*, the better to enjoy his confusion. If it is true—well, the black velvet Laureate has been long since revenged.[12]

[11] It cannot be too much regretted that, as recently as 1945, the accomplished and discerning Sir Laurence Olivier chose to revive *The Critic*, when *The Rehearsal* had been so long ignored.

[12] Buckingham's *Collected Works*. Thomas Brown's Preface to Buckingham's *Works*, 1715 ed. Montague Summers: *The Restoration Theatre* and *The Theatre of Pepys*. V. de Sola Pinto: *Sir Charles Sedley*. John Hayward: *Collected Works of the Earl of Rochester*. Thomas Davies: *Dramatic Miscellanies*. Dryden's *Poetical Works*. Dryden's *Dramatic Works*, edited by Montague Summers. John Downes: *Roscius Anglicanus*. B. Dobree: *Restoration Comedy* and *Restoration Tragedy*. Pepys. Evelyn. Macaulay's *Essays*. Malone. Ben Jonson: *Dramatic works*. Andrew Marvell: *Works and Correspondence*. Spence: *Anecdotes*. Beaumont and Fletcher: *Dramatic Works*. *The Rehearsal*, edited by Montague Summers. Scudéry: *Works*, etc., etc.

CHAPTER TWO

I

BUCKINGHAM left St. Germains as the sponsor of a treaty which he believed to be genuine. He was given another and much more important trust—the escort of Louise de Kéroualle who, at the age of twenty, was to take Madame's place as French agent at the Court of Charles II. She had been in attendance on Madame during her last visit to England; when Charles was asked by his sister to choose a farewell present from her store of trinkets he replied, perhaps not quite seriously, that the only jewel of hers he coveted was her Breton lady-in-waiting; Madame answered that she was responsible for Mlle de Kéroualle to her parents, and no more was said. But the image of Louise, connected now with his last farewell to his sister, remained in the King's mind; he made it clear that he wished to see her again —and what more fitting cavalier for this new beauty than the great Duke of Buckingham, the friend of the French and the English Kings?

For some time the Duke had been aware that a change of mistresses was impending, for Lady Castlemaine, recently created Duchess of Cleveland, was no longer young and her influence over Charles had begun to weaken. For George Villiers it was the work of a moment to ingratiate himself with Mlle de Kéroualle; he did this before the journey to England had even begun: and there yet remained three weeks of travel to strengthen her dependence on his company.

When Buckingham left St. Germains he sent some of his gentlemen with Louise as far as Dieppe, where he proposed to meet her; meanwhile he promised to see that a yacht should be ready for the last stage of the journey, which they would make together: he expected to reach Dieppe before she did: but there were one or two little matters that he must deal with in Paris . . .

Louise got to Dieppe after a fortnight's travelling. Where was the Duke? He had not yet arrived. And where was the yacht? There was no sign of it in the harbour. She was not sorry to rest a little, and settled down to wait. Twenty-four hours passed. (There was a rumour that the Duke had gone ahead and was bringing back the yacht himself.) Two days went by, and then a week. Still there was no news of His Grace of Buckingham. (But the weather was rough; no doubt he was still at sea.) Louise waited on. Then, after nearly a fortnight, she heard that Buckingham had arrived in England from Calais, some ten days before. He had forgotten all about her.[1]

She never forgave him. From that moment Buckingham's fortunes began to decline. His negligence gave Arlington the opportunity he needed; he told Montagu to send over a yacht, and as soon as Louise arrived the Arlingtons took care of her. "So," remarked Burnet, in joyous condemnation, "the Duke of Buckingham lost the merit he might have pretended to, and brought over a mistress whom his own strange conduct threw into the hands of his enemies." Strange conduct indeed: Buckingham made no explanation of it to Louise or to anyone else; nor shall we ever know if he forgot about her because she bored him—if she had not, surely he would have accompanied her all the way to Dieppe?—or because he felt he could do without her.

Until this moment his relationship with the mistresses of Charles II had been variable, but, on the whole, satisfactory. His connection with these celebrated women is part of his career. Buckingham's story is, to some extent, the story of Barbara Villiers, Nell Gwynn, Moll Davis, Louise de Kéroualle and Hortense Mancini.

2

Barbara Villiers' ungovernable temper and total disregard of convention, though excessively unattractive in themselves, made Charles forget he was a king; when she screamed and stamped and vowed she would set fire to his palace or dash out his child's brains on the hearthstone of the Matted Gallery—when she called him names, "made a slighting puh with her mouth"[2] and cried for the moon (or failing that, another two or three thousand a year) she was treating him as she treated all her lovers, of whose existence he was cynically aware. Her healthy, glowing beauty, her airs and graces, her refusal to accept defeat in any circumstances—when the Thames rose and flooded her kitchen, she swore she would dine, if she had to set the furniture alight[3]—swept

---

[1] Burnet.   [2] Pepys.   [3] *Ibid.*

him along and compelled his admiration, even when her behaviour disgusted and embarrassed him. There is no proof that she cared for anything but money, jewels and possessions; she was brutal—especially to her children—predatory and uncultured; if she opened a book, it was to see whether her name appeared in it: if she went to the play, it was to show herself to the crowd: if she took a hand at cards she must win, or the King pay her losses.

All these extravagances were permitted her; her children were ennobled, her caprices indulged, her lovers allowed to frequent the Court; of these Buckingham was the only one who openly shared her favours with Charles. She had to make some show of discretion when she took up with Charles Hart, in revenge for the King's affairs with Nelly and Moll Davis; he chose to ignore her relationship with Jacob Hall, the rope-dancer, just as he ignored her conversion to Roman Catholicism (he never meddled with the *souls* of ladies, he said, when Barbara's relatives implored him to save her from Popery). Charles's attitude was clearly defined; he was stimulated by her transports, of whatever nature, and as long as she delighted his eyes he could forgive her inconstancy.

Buckingham's relationship with his cousin was more mercurial; they came to know one another too well to keep up a façade. He generally had the upper hand, for Barbara had the vain woman's terror of mockery, and Buckingham did not care a pin what people said about him. He could never make up his mind whether to ruin or support her: and his vagaries must have agitated her considerably. For a long time they were allies; then he deserted her for Frances Stuart. Mrs. Stuart became Duchess of Richmond, returned to Court and was forgiven by the King; once more Buckingham and Barbara were inseparable. He brought Moll Davis and Nelly to his master; still Barbara could not do without him. Then she took a fancy to handsome, penniless John Churchill and gave him—they were distant cousins—five thousand pounds. Buckingham warned Charles, who broke into his mistress's room to find the future Duke of Marlborough like the lover in a farce, half in, half out of the window. "I forgive you, for you do it for your bread", he said contemptuously; and a few days later both Barbara and the young guardsman were forgiven.[4]

---

[4] Burnet. Dartmouth. In 1676 a novel, entitled *Hattigé, ou les Amours du Roy de Tamaran*, reproduced this incident as its central theme. The King of Tamaran was Charles II; the heroine, Hattigé, Barbara Villiers; Rajep, John Churchill; and Osman, Buckingham.

She must have felt that she could, as we say now, get away with anything; yet when she swept down on Wycherley, whose good looks had caught her eye, Buckingham, in the character either of a rival or a watch-dog, interfered again.

This was in 1671. The playwright, terrified of the Duke's displeasure, asked Sedley and Rochester to plead for him. When they did so, Buckingham replied, " I do not blame Wycherley, I only accuse my cousin." "But," said Rochester, "you are about to ruin a man with whose conversation you would be pleased above all things." The Duke said no more. Two or three nights later Sedley and Rochester arranged a supper-party; Wycherley exerted all his powers, Buckingham exclaimed, "By God, my cousin was in the right of it!" and became Wycherley's friend and supporter.[5] The consequences were so favourable to Wycherley, that other, less successful, writers were apt to approach the Duke through him. In this way he persuaded Buckingham to see the ruined and failing Samuel Butler, whose *Hudibras* had once so pleased the King that he always carried a copy in his pocket. Buckingham agreed to accompany Wycherley to Butler's lodging; on the way there he saw a pair of pretty girls, and was gone before his companion realised what had happened; and so poor Butler never got the help he needed.[6]

Wycherley's gifts had nothing to do with his conquest of Barbara; he was a fine figure of a man, and that was enough for her. Her final overthrow was not Buckingham's responsibility; she failed because she was no longer young and lovely. She was not amusing, like Nelly, nor gently feminine, like Louise, nor intellectually sophisticated, like the Duchess Mazarin. With her beauty her charm disappeared; but before she left the Court in 1677 she had collected from the easy-going Charles a quarter of a million pounds and Nonsuch, one of the most splendid palaces of the English kings, which she at once pulled down.

Nell Gwynn, "brought up", in her own words, "in a bawdy-house, to fill strong waters to the gentlemen,"[7] was a more congenial character. She is, with Alfred the Great, Henry VIII and Queen Elizabeth, one of the most widely advertised persons in English history, and, rather unfairly, the most popular. "A bold, merry slut,"[8] "the indiscreetest and wildest creature that ever was in a court,"[9] she was also clever enough to realise her

[5] John Dennis: *Original Letters.*   [6] Macaulay.
[7] Pepys.   [8] *Ibid.*   [9] Burnet.

limitations. Mrs. Nelly was a clever buffoon; but she played the part both on and off the boards of the Theatre Royal. She hammered in her originality, her daring and her guttersnipe repartee remorselessly and without ceasing. Those who had to listen to her night after night, day after day, must have got rather weary of Nelly and her "merry gang",[10] Nelly and her good heart, Nelly and her nick-names, her surprisingly clean petticoats,[11] her dancing, her crude imitations of her rivals and her roars of laughter. She was nothing if not practical; she got sixty thousand pounds out of her Charles the Third, as she called the King, in four years. (Her Charles the First was Hart, whom she shared with Barbara Villiers: her Charles the Second, Lord Buckhurst, who kept her for some years before she passed into more exalted hands.[12] "He never used her with the decencies of a mistress", remarks Burnet, as if in extenuation of the King's passion for her.[13] It is possible that casually, and by the way, she became Buckingham's mistress also; but she had a much better developed sense of propriety than he; when he "attempted some gallantries" with her in the King's closet, she promptly boxed his ears.[14] Nelly, in so far as she had any beliefs, was a Protestant; she supported Buckingham when he became a member of the Opposition and pleaded for him with the King on more than one occasion; if she had a political slogan, it was "No Popery and wooden shoes"—but her interests had nothing to do with public affairs.

Of Moll Davies little is known but her exquisite singing and dancing. Charles first saw her in *The Two Kinsmen*, of which her song, "My Lodging is on the Cold Ground", was the principal attraction.[15] She was his mistress for four years and then, having made her pile, retired.

After these three harsh, reckless creatures, came Louise de Kéroualle, quiet, humourless, well bred and tenacious. In spite of her monstrous expenditure—she received an allowance of forty thousand pounds a year as soon as she had been created Duchess of Portsmouth in the summer of 1671[16]—she became an institution, not a popular one. Madam Carwell, as the English people called her, was faithful and untiring in her allegiance to her real master, Louis XIV; but she behaved towards Charles with propriety and made him happy during their later life; though there is a story of

[10] Marvell: *Correspondence*.   [11] Pepys.   [12] Gramont.
[13] "Pray what decencies are those?" was Swift's comment upon this statement.
[14] Venetian State Papers.   [15] Pepys. Gramont.   [16] Forneron.

her staging an illness to get something out of him which he would not grant, and of his contemptuous comments on her machinations.[17] For fifteen years this plump, baby-faced little woman helped to rule England. Buckingham stood for everything that she disliked most in English life, its informality, disorderliness, eccentricity and freedom of speech and opinion; they could never have become friends: and Louise was a pitiless enemy.

Hortense Mancini, niece and heiress of Cardinal Mazarin, whose name she took on her marriage to the Marquis de la Meilleraye, was a voluptuous Italian beauty, with a temperament and a tragic past. Her husband, eccentric to the verge of insanity, had made life unendurable for her and she ran away from him and from her four children to wander across Europe in man's clothes with a train of lovers of both sexes and a menagerie of dogs, monkeys and birds.[18] She arrived in England in November, 1676, at the age of twenty-nine. She took no interest in politics and managed to become the friend, simultaneously, of Arlington, Buckingham, Gramont and even, after some tremendous battles, of Louise. The Seigneur de St. Evremond, a grotesque, idle, clever exile of sixty, fell desperately in love with her; he, Buckingham, Lord d'Aubigny and Hortense made a literary group of their own within the Court circle and met almost every day. Burnet found St. Evremond and Buckingham very similar in " their copiousness of invention, pleasantness and variety of conversation." St. Evremond used to compare Buckingham to Petronius; although he had as little to do with state affairs as Hortense he was not above accepting payment from Louis for turning the Duke's attention towards French interests. Hortense also took money from Louis; but her chief source of income came from Charles, who settled four thousand a year on her. " Si votre Roi la baise seulement une fois, je tiens la de Portsmouth pour foutue " predicted a Frenchman who knew all three: but Hortense never supplanted Louise, possibly because she had no wish to do so.

These were the principal ladies of the King's household. Behind them flitted a number of shadowy, elegant figures—Jane Roberts, Winifred Wells, Catherine Pegge—who are memorable only because they sat to Lely or momentarily attracted Gramont's attention.

With the possible exception of Hortense Mazarin, who

---

[17] Lady Cowper's *Diary*, 1715.
[18] Hartmann: *The Vagabond Duchess. Memoirs of the Duchess Mazarin.*

appears to have been a woman of taste, personality and culture, the mistresses of Charles II were a dull lot. Beauty, expenditure, a series of fearful scenes and, in Nelly's case, some specimens of that celebrated Cockney humour of which we are all getting a little tired, alone remain to enhance the sumptuous presentations of Lely, the acid wit of Gramont, the disgust of Evelyn and Burnet, and the covert longings of Pepys. As the chosen companions of one of the cleverest men who ever exploited the English people, they are remarkable from the point of view of contrast only; that Charles saw through their various affectations is undoubted. (His penultimate thought for Nelly shows no deep, romantic affection, but rather that obsession with the trivial that characterises most death-beds; soon after he had asked his brother not to let poor Nelly starve he remembered that one of his eight-day clocks needed winding.)[19] Charles II knew his women for the shallow, selfish, rather pathetic creatures they were; they helped him to pass the time: they gave Buckingham and all those who were trying to use them a great deal of trouble and very little help: and that is all that need be said about them.

3

As soon as he returned to England Buckingham continued his negotiations with Louis XIV by correspondence. In addition to the subsidy granted for the attack on Holland, the Duke demanded, and presently obtained, the promise of the islands of Woorne and Goree off the Dutch coast.[20] Although he had declared that he would not observe any contracts made through his Protestant representatives, Charles supported this and any other requirements suggested by Buckingham that happened to suit himself; he double-crossed Louis over the real and the false treaty, while continuing to deceive the Protestant section of the Cabal.

Buckingham's letters to Louis were full of loyalty and gratitude; he implied that Lady Shrewsbury's "pension" was super-rogatory; he told Colbert de Croissy that he was already aware of Louis' boundless munificence and that there was no danger of his failing His Most Christian Majesty. He wrote to Louis imploring him to ratify all the articles of the Treaty before Parliament met at the end of October. He added that the Dutch Ambassador was

[19] Ailesbury.   [20] Mignet.

already bribing him to change his alliance: there was, of course, no question of that; nevertheless he would be "furieusement inquiet" until the matter was concluded.[21] Parliament voted a subsidy of two and a half millions for the defence of the English coasts and the strengthening of the navy; Charles replied by issuing a veto on all Jesuits and Roman Catholic priests, who were to leave England before May the First, 1671; at the same time he conveyed to Louis his regret that he must put off his declaration of the faith.[22]

Meanwhile Buckingham—conveniently, perhaps—fell ill; some of the more important meetings were held at Wallingford House; but he was unable to attend Parliament. He wrote to Louis that he would be in despair "if Your Majesty could doubt my zeal and fidelity", adding that he was very much disturbed by the delays over the Treaty; he hinted that Montagu and Colbert de Croissy were secretly working against him, and concluded:

"If we consent to the dishonour that is daily thrust upon us, Your Majesty will miss the finest opportunity in the world to employ those talents with which God has endowed you and which are capable, at the lowest estimate, of ranking you as equal with the greatest in all history. Sire, I speak as I feel . . ."[23]

Louis replied most graciously. His letter, assuring Buckingham that no one was deceiving him, began "Mon Cousin" and had the effect desired.[24] It was then agreed to postpone the war against Holland until the spring of 1672. Colbert de Croissy was afraid that Lauderdale and Shaftesbury who, he said, "n'avaient pas l'étourderie du Duc de Buckingham",[25] might suspect the existence of the real treaty; but they were still deceived.

During all these negotiations Buckingham seems to have been haunted by the shadow of his father's glory. The first Duke had been Lord High Admiral and Commander-in-Chief at the age of thirty—his son was now forty-three and had nothing but a Lord-Lieutenancy and the Mastership of the Horse, in spite of all his power and influence. Buckingham knew himself to be abler and more experienced in warfare than his father—how was it then, that he was perpetually superseded? The promised generalship of the English forces had been ratified by Louis and his ministers, yet the King of England had said nothing about it . . . Was it

[21] Mignet.   [22] Ogg.   [23] Mignet.   [24] *Ibid.*   [25] *Ibid.*

possible that Charles would not be governed by Louis in this matter? Could he be planning to put aside his chief Minister for somebody else? And time was getting on; "Methinks I see the wanton hours flee, And as they pass, turn back and laugh at me," was Buckingham's private comment.[26]

It was not until the false Treaty was signed on December the Thirty-First, 1670, that Buckingham had leisure to look into his own affairs. His finances were in a bad state; the French expedition had cost him more than he had received; of his income of nineteen thousand six hundred a year, he now paid out fifteen thousand annually in wages, taxes, interest and fee-farm rents.[27] He represented the hardship of his case to Charles, who gave him a pension of two thousand five hundred a year for twenty-one years and one of one thousand five hundred for life, upon the northern excise; he had been receiving the excise upon all imported glass, but this grant was now rescinded; in the following year he was given a patent for enclosing common land in Yorkshire and all the new building ground near Wallingford House. It was characteristic of Buckingham that the moment his financial burdens were a little eased he began to make preparations for entertaining sixty French noblemen who visited England in May, 1671. He had barely recovered from this when he was given the Chancellorship of the University of Cambridge; he leased back his own property, York House, from the French Ambassador, in order to entertain the Cambridge dignitaries in a suitable manner, and spent several hundreds of pounds on a present of plate, inscribed with his arms, for the University. Later in the year Charles was received by Buckingham at Cambridge; gravely the Duke presented his old friend and boon companion with "a fair Bible".[28]

In the first months of 1671 Buckingham was accused of employing the infamous Captain Blood to murder the Duke of Ormonde, who was set upon by a gang of roughs near his house in Piccadilly and only escaped through his own vigorous resistance and the bravery of his coachman. Lord Ossory accused Buckingham, in the King's presence, of setting Blood upon his father, adding, "I therefore give you fair warning; if my father comes to a violent end by sword or pistol, if he dies by the hand of a ruffian or by the more secret way of poison, I shall not be at a loss to know the first author of it: I shall consider you as such: and

[26] Commonplace Book. [27] Pepys. [28] Echard.

wherever I meet you, I shall pistol you, though you stood behind the King's chair."[29]

There is no proof at all of Buckingham's guilt in this matter. He was capable of the most outrageous behaviour; but he avoided murder unless, as in the case of the Shrewsbury duel, it was thrust upon him. Blood had already made an attempt on Ormonde in Dublin, eight years earlier; he had a grudge against the Lord-Lieutenant, who had confiscated his estate when he put down the anti-monarchist risings of the sixteen-sixties. Having failed to revenge himself in Ireland, Blood came over into England and associated himself with any rebellious movements that appeared to want a leader. He escaped after his second attack on Ormonde but was arrested later, during his most celebrated exploit, the attempted theft of the Crown jewels from the Tower. He was tried and condemned to death. Then, to the horror and amazement of his more responsible ministers, Charles consented to give Blood an audience. This was tantamount to granting him a reprieve; the robber was emboldened to defend himself with calculated frankness and effrontery. He confessed to his share of the attack on Ormonde, and gave his reasons. He then proceeded to tell the King that he had planned to kill him when he went to bathe at Battersea; "but when he had taken his stand in the reeds for that purpose, his heart misgave him out of awe of majesty". Charles showed no surprise or disgust at this remarkable statement and Blood went on to plead for his own life and those of his associates. If His Majesty "would spare the lives of a few he would make hundreds of malcontents and conspirators loyal".[30] This adroit mixture of flattery, sauciness and truth-telling had the desired effect. Charles, merciful by nature and easily persuaded when nothing but justice and custom were in question, gave Blood his life and an estate in Ireland worth five hundred a year.

Ossory and Arlington blamed Buckingham for this monstrous insult to the Duke of Ormonde and all loyal servants of the crown; but the triumph of Blood was simply the result of Charles's whim. Years later Buckingham's name was again associated with Blood's in peculiar and mysterious circumstances.

4

Lady Shrewsbury was now known to Buckingham's intimates

29 Carte: *Life of Ormonde*.   30 *Ibid.*

as "the Duchess" and his wife as "the Duchess-Dowager".
According to Gramont, "Lady Shrewsbury and the Duke of
Buckingham remained happy and undisturbed; never had she
been so constant; never had he proved himself so tender and
considerate a lover." "I feel the utmost of love's anger now," the
Duke wrote, "if he should bend it more, he'd break his bow"
—and he added one of his little rhymes which he may have
intended to set to music—

> "A thousand blessings on this gentle moon
> And on thy silver light,
> Thou mak'st my evening, morning and my noon,
> This sun begins my night."[31]

The Duchess of Buckingham made no more protests; her
father, who died in 1670, remained, till the end of his life, on
friendly terms with his son-in-law.[32] It is possible that Mary
managed to conceal her husband's worst behaviour from him.

In the spring of 1671 Lady Shrewsbury gave birth to a son
whom Buckingham acknowledged with all the publicity that his
circumstances afforded. He called the child Earl of Coventry—
one of the first Duke's titles—and persuaded the King to stand
godfather.[33] At about this time he began to build Cliveden which,
like almost every house he possessed, was destroyed within a
hundred years of his death. Cliveden, says a contemporary, who
visited it before it was finished, "is a noble building, *à la moderne*,
with a great terrace fronting the garden: under it twenty-six niches
in which the Duke of Buckingham designs to place statues bigger
than the life: and in the middle a pretty alcove with stone stairs
which ascend to the apartments."[34] Evelyn, visiting it in 1679,
gives a fuller description.

"I went to Clifden, that stupendous natural rock, wood and prospect,
of the Duke of Buckingham's, buildings of an extraordinary expense. The
grots in the chalky rock are pretty: it is a romantic object, and the place
altogether answers the most poetical description that can be made of
solitude, precipice, prospect, or whatever can contribute to a thing so very
like their imaginations. The stand, somewhat like Frascati as to its front,
and, on the platform, is a circular view to the utmost verge of the horizon
which, with the serpenting of the Thames, is admirable. The staircase is
for its materials singular; the cloisters, descents, gardens and avenue

---

[31] Commonplace Book.
[32] See Appendix II for Buckingham's *Epitaph on the Lord Fairfax*, one of his most
charming pieces.
[33] Marvell: *Correspondence*.   [34] Jesse.

through the wood, august and stately; but the land all about wretchedly barren, and producing nothing but fern. Indeed, as I told His Majesty that evening (asking me how I liked Clifden), without flattery, that it did not please me so well as Windsor . . ."

The comparison with Windsor gives some idea of the splendour of Buckingham's final tribute to his mistress; for there is no doubt that this, the latest thing in palatial architecture, was built for Lady Shrewsbury. Long before it was finished Buckingham's son was dead. In August, 1671, he caused the five months' old infant to be buried in the sepulchre of the Villiers in Westminster Abbey, registering it as the Earl of Coventry.[35] This was a wildly reckless gesture, for it infringed the most sacred privileges of the class to which Buckingham belonged. A mistress, however extravagantly and shamelessly entertained, was one thing, the burial of a bastard in a family vault another. Buckingham's enemies could do nothing to stop his desperate course while he was still in favour; but his defiance of all that mattered most in the closed circle of rank and power was to weigh heavily against him when the day of reckoning came. The murder of Lord Shrewsbury, the humil-iation of the Duchess of Buckingham, the acknowledgement of Lady Shrewsbury as Buckingham's paramour and of the short-lived proof of their stormy loves—all these breaches of conduct could be accepted by their contemporaries in the course of time; but the arbitrary bestowal of an hereditary title on an illegitimate child and the sanction of that title by the Abbey authorities implied that the Duke had taken upon himself the powers of royalty—and that was not to be borne.

Lady Shrewsbury's share in this assumption of prerogative must be considered. It was said that before the birth of their child she and Buckingham went through a form of marriage.[36] She may have wished to bring about a divorce and marry him: or she may have been tempting him to behave more and more reck-lessly in order to achieve a climax or even a conclusion to the relationship that had cost so much already. She had been faithful to him for five years: it is possible that she was beginning to look elsewhere, even when she accompanied Buckingham to New-market, two months after the death of their child. Here, Evelyn heard, the Duke was " in mighty favour " with his mistress, whom he entertained with a band of fiddlers and with " a luxurious and abandoned rout " of guests.

[35] Marvell: *Correspondence*.   [36] James II: *Life*.

During the remainder of this year the reports of Buckingham show him in the highest spirits; evidently his debts worried him very little, for he took Lady Shrewsbury and Sir Charles Sedley to look over Holland House, with a view to buying it, in spite of the fact that when Cliveden was paid for (perhaps it never was) his income would shrink to a mere twelve thousand a year. He was still able to entertain on the grand scale; from his lodgings in the Cock-pit he gave water-parties to all the Court; in gilded barges, accompanied by skiffs filled with musicians dressed as Turks, slaves and savages, his guests, in the consciously unsophisticated raiment of shepherds and nymphs, glided down the Thames to the sound of flutes, oboes and violins.[37] The Duke's talent for mimicry and what Pepys described as his "briskness" still delighted the King, with whom he spent hours alone, to the rage and alarm of the Duke of York.[38] Fortunately for Buckingham, Lady Muskerry, now seven months pregnant, returned to Court at one period of his ascendancy. She appeared at a ball given by the Queen, looking more ridiculous than ever—for she had tried to rectify the asymmetry of her figure by putting cushions underneath her dress; one of these fell off and was seized by Buckingham, who "tenderly picked it up, wrapped it in the skirts of his coat, and imitating the puling cries of a new-born babe, went among the Maids of Honour enquiring after a wet-nurse for poor little Muskerry".[39] Nothing could have been in worse taste, according to modern notions; but to the wits of the seventeenth century a pregnant woman who made a fool of herself was a natural victim. Buckingham followed this with an unprintable punning couplet in French on the King's relationship with Miss Winifred Wells[40] and some unrecorded witticisms about Pepys and his friend, Sir John Duncombe.[41] Pepys immediately assumed that the Duke "had a spite at" him. There was no spite in Buckingham's nature; but "he would rather lose his friend (nay, the King) than his jest."[42]

During Buckingham's days of power the King's chaplains had a hard time with their sermons; any reference to continence was received with smothered titterings from the maids of honour and punctuated by the snores of the gentlemen in waiting.[43] One divine, it is true, publicly rebuked the Duke of Lauderdale with "My Lord! My Lord! You snore so loud you will wake the

[37] Mme d'Aulnoy.   [38] Pepys.   [39] Gramont.   [40] *Ibid*.
[41] Sir John Duncombe succeeded Shaftesbury as Chancellor of the Exchequer in 1672.
[42] Ailesbury.   [43] *Ibid*.

King!", but most of the clergy were incapable of so adapting
themselves to their company.[44] One unfortunate young preacher,
having taken for his text, " I am fearfully and wonderfully made ",
suddenly developed, under Buckingham's eye, a nervous trick of
stroking his sweating face with his hand; his black gloves were
imperfectly dyed, with the result that the entire congregation, led
by Buckingham and the King, was soon in an uproar.[45] This was
very simple fun; but a country gentleman, meeting Buckingham
at dinner, reported his conversation as " nothing but quintessence
of wit and most excellent discourse ", and was deeply troubled to
hear that His Grace was on the verge of ruin. These were still the
years of gaiety: but they were numbered.

5

By the end of October 1671, Louise de Kéroualle had been living
under Charles II's protection for just over a year; she had not yet
consented to become his mistress, and he was getting impatient.
The French Ambassador told her that to hold out any longer would
be a tactical error; she therefore accepted the Arlingtons' invitation
to accompany the King to Euston and there, after a mock marriage
ceremony and a good deal of horse-play[46] the bargain was concluded and her position assured. It never occurred to Louise that
her influence over Charles was sometimes ineffective; during the
years that followed she appeared to be doing what was expected
of her, while all the time he pursued a policy of his own.

The Portsmouth – Arlington combination was extremely
dangerous to Buckingham, as he very well knew. Already he had
tried to weaken Arlington's power by suggesting that Charles
should break off the match between Arlington's daughter Isabella
and the Duke of Grafton, the King's second son by Barbara
Villiers; he could get the Percy heiress for the young Lord Harry,
Buckingham said; but Charles would not break his word to
Arlington.[47] Then Buckingham, after interviewing the French
ministers at Dunkirk, returned to find that the blow he so much
dreaded had fallen. The English military contingent was to be
reduced to two thousand four hundred men and the generalship
given to the Duke of Monmouth, with Ossory, Buckingham's
bitterest enemy, as second in command.

---

[44] Airy.   [45] Granger.   [46] Evelyn.   [47] *Life*: James II.

As soon as Colbert de Croissy broke the news to him, Buckingham asked for an audience of the King. He did not get it for a week; when he did, Colbert was present and sent an account of the interview to his master. The Duke was very angry and spoke with his usual freedom of manner. He accused Arlington and Montagu of double-dealing; he added that the diminution of the help he had promised was a breach of confidence and a slur on the national honour. He harangued the King violently and at length.

Charles listened with his customary air of good-tempered imperturbability. Then he said that Buckingham was not fit for such a command; in the circumstances he would not trust his own brother with it. Buckingham began to storm and protest. The King cut him short; his mind was made up; this was no time for discussion or argument; in such a matter he would consider Buckingham no more than he would his dog. Then, as Villiers stood silent and aghast, Charles added firmly that his ministers must learn to work peaceably with one another. Buckingham was dismissed.

A few days later Lady Shrewsbury, acknowledging the receipt of her allowance, asked the French Ambassador if there was a possibility of her lover's receiving a lieutenant-generalship in the allied army, and was told that this post would be his, subject to the approval of Count Schomberg, the Commander-in-Chief.[48] This was at the end of November. During the rest of the year Buckingham seemed to have forgotten his defeat, for he was absorbed in the production of *The Rehearsal*, that " posy made of weeds instead of flowers ",[49] that provoked astonished and satirical comment from Louis and his ministers; that a gentleman of breeding and a Minister of the Crown should condescend to scribble for the theatre was exceedingly droll: but then the Duke was known to be even more eccentric than most Englishmen.

Buckingham also found time, according to Arlington, to make mischief between the King and Louise. Arlington, Ossory (and through Ossory, Monmouth) Charles and Louise all appeared to be lined up against him. With considerable bitterness he must have recalled his casual recommendation of Louise to the King. " It was a decent piece of tenderness to his sister," he had said, " to take care of some of her servants."[50] But that had been before his disastrous negligence in France. Now he was beginning to realise that the demure and kittenish Madame de Portsmouth was a

[48] Mignet.   [49] Prologue to *The Rehearsal*.   [50] Burnet.

far more implacable enemy than the bad-tempered Duchess of
Cleveland.

In June of this year Buckingham and Arlington had a long—
and not very satisfactory—interview with the Dutch delegates at
Hampton Court; later on the Duke, accompanied by Arlington
and Brian Fairfax, went to the Hague; they supped with William
of Orange at his camp at Bodegrave and the next night with the
French King at Utrecht, staying with him three days. After a
month's tour of the Low Countries they returned to London,
having tied up the threads of their agreement over the partition of
Holland.

On the announcement of the war against the Dutch, Buckingham immediately went to sea in a craft of his own; he had no
intention of being sent home by the Duke of York this time. He
left nothing to chance. Before going into action he boarded York's
flagship and asked if he might speak to him alone; then he
announced that he intended to become a Catholic—could His Highness provide him with a priest? " Since we may engage the enemy
quickly I wish to make sure of another world," he explained. The
Duke of York produced his own confessor and Buckingham remained closeted with him a long time;[51] it is difficult to believe that
James took this conversion seriously: that he did so is proved by
the fact that a few weeks later he told Buckingham the secret of
the King's religious convictions.[52] Before the fleet went into action
at Southwold Bay, Buckingham had been recalled to London. On
May the Twenty-Eighth he spent from four in the afternoon till
eight in the evening putting out a fire that was raging round the
Tower wharf; he went out on the river in a lighter, blew up houses,
directed the engineers and himself paid the men working under
him.

Then, following upon the news of Southwold Bay, came the
reports of King Louis' sweeping advance in the Low Countries.
Buckingham and Arlington were instructed to proceed at once to
Holland.

6

The French armies seemed to be swallowing up the Netherlands
without any difficulty at all. Charles, who had no wish to be in

---

[51] Burnet.   [52] Christie.

the power of an unconquerable ally, began to consider withdrawing from the war; his sailors were weary of it and his soldiers
mutinous. His plan was to make a separate peace with the Dutch
and at the same time persuade them to accept terms that would
satisfy Louis. Buckingham and Arlington reached the Hague on
the Twenty-Fifth of June, to find that Charles's nephew, the
twenty-year-old William of Orange, had become the leader of his
people and that the de Witts had been imprisoned; they were
lynched a fortnight later. The English plenipotentiaries had been
instructed to propose the following terms to the States-General:
(1) Recognition of England's claim to be saluted by ships of
other nations, (2) a subsidy for war expenses, (3) control of the
ports of Flushing, Sluys and Brill, (4) favourable conditions for
William of Orange, (5) a subsidy for the herring fishing,
(6) regulation of Anglo-Dutch trade in the East Indies, and
(7) a year in which to evacuate the English merchants from
Surinam. The French agreed to these conditions; the Dutch
refused them in circumstances which must be fully described.

Buckingham, Arlington and the Duke of Monmouth, who was
then in his twenty-fourth year, were received with tremendous
enthusiasm from the moment of their arrival. "What I have seen
here," said Buckingham, "can be compared to nothing but the
burning of the Rump." He landed at Brill and proceeded at once
to the Hague, where he had rather a daunting interview with the
Princess-Dowager Amalia, William's grandmother, a lady "of
great wit and common sense".[53] She had guessed the real purpose
of his embassy and received him coldly. Buckingham, in his most
insinuating and friendly manner, told her that there was no cause
for fear: he and Lord Arlington were "good Hollanders". "That
is more than we ask," replied the old lady drily. "We only expect
that you should be good Englishmen." "We are not only so," said
Buckingham, "but good Dutchmen, too. Indeed," he added, with
one of those odd turns of phrase which made him such delightful
company, "we do not use Holland like a mistress, but love her like
a wife." The Princess-Dowager gave him a look: then she remarked, "Truly, I think you love her just as you do yours." For
once Buckingham was speechless.[54]

From the Hague he and Arlington and Monmouth went on to
the camp at Neuerbrugge to interview Willliam of Orange, whose
health, coupled with that of the English King, was the favourite

[53] Sir William Temple: *Memoirs*.   [54] *Ibid*. Echard.

O

toast of the deluded Hollanders. Buckingham's conversation with the young Stadtholder was characteristic of them both.

They had met in London some eighteen months before Buckingham's visit to Bodegrave. William, reserved, intolerant, delicate and melancholy, had made a bad impression at his uncle's Court. He did not care for the play, dancing brought on his asthma and he considered gambling a waste of time. What was to be done with such a young man? The King suggested that Buckingham should give a supper-party for his nephew; if he did not unbend with George Villiers he must be given up as hopeless. The host, seeing that there was only one thing to be done, managed to make William drunk; this was difficult, for the Prince " did not naturally love " strong liquor.[55] But " having once entered," says Reresby, " he was more frolic and merry than the rest of the company." The correct youth became noisy and pugnacious; he smashed a window trying to break into the apartments of the maids of honour and had to be held back by force.[56] No doubt he was as disgusted with Buckingham as with himself when he realised how he had behaved.

Buckingham's only recollection of their London meeting was that it had been a merry one; with the same fluency and pleasantness that he had used towards William's grandmother, he assured the stern and harassed young man that his uncle had " conditioned " good terms for him with the French King before consenting to go on with the invasion; the plan was that he should be acknowledged King of Holland by Great Britain and France, while accepting the French and English terms of conquest.[57]

William's reply was brief and uncompromising. " I like better," he said, " the condition of Stadtholder which the States have given me." He added, " I believe myself bound in conscience and honour not to prefer my interests to my obligations."[58] This conversation took place before supper. After supper, two of William's ministers, Van Beuning and Beverling, were summoned to the conference. Then William took the lead.

He pointed out the danger for England and her religion if Holland were to become a province of the French Empire, with himself as a puppet ruler and the tool of Louis. The French armies, having consolidated their conquests, would then be in the best position for invading England. It was better, surely, to combine now, before Louis held all Europe in his grasp. The taciturn

55 Reresby.   56 Burnet.   57 Foxcroft: *Life of Lord Halifax*.   58 *Ibid*.

William became so eloquent that Buckingham was deeply moved. "By God!" he exclaimed, turning to Arlington and Monmouth, "he is in the right!"—and as they stared at him, amazed, he went on to say that he was ready to sign a peace with William then and there.[59]

Monmouth took no part in the discussions; Arlington was appalled: but he knew better than to irritate Buckingham by frank opposition. He murmured something about rashness and suggested that they should sleep on the matter before making any further decisions. William instantly caused a peace treaty to be drawn up ready for signature.[60]

What passed between Buckingham and his colleagues during the next few hours will never be known. When they all met again the next morning he had gone back on his impulsive offer of the night before. He again tried to persuade William to accept the terms. William, swallowing his bitter disappointment, answered, "My country has trusted me, and I will never deceive nor betray her."[61]

Buckingham was full of pity and concern. He saw the poor young man, who had been his guest and whose cause he was beginning to support, rushing to his doom. "You are not to think any more of your country," he said gently, "for it is lost." Was he speaking with the recollection of Kingston and Worcester in his mind? As William did not reply, he went on, "If it should weather out the summer, by reason of the waters that have drowned great parts of it, the winter's frost will lay them open." Still William said nothing: he was worn out with anxiety and suspense: he may have been struggling with his tears. Buckingham, seeing his emotion, unable to believe that he was not convinced—for, after all, hero though he was, the Prince of Orange knew as little of war as he did of politics or women—thought he was wavering; he repeated urgently, "Do you not see that it is lost?" Then William made the retort that has become a catchword. "I see that it is indeed in great danger," he said, "but there is one way never to see it lost, and that is to die in the last dyke."[62]

The contrasting principles and beliefs of two generations are revealed in this dialogue. The middle-aged gambler, who had once lost everything he possessed and won it back by a combination of luck and intrigue, was using a different language from the young

---

[59] Oldmixon. Burnet.   [60] *Ibid.*
[61] *Ibid.*   [62] Oldmixon. Burnet. Temple.

soldier, who had acquired his statesmanship from the high-minded, painstaking genius of de Witt. William's reply has been extolled by countless historians. Buckingham's reasoning has been arraigned on the grounds of corruption, cynicism and disingenuous-ness. William, a prig, was in the right: Buckingham, veering from one attitude to another, was in the wrong, as usual. Neither appears, at this moment, at his best; but which of these two deserves our sympathy—the youth, with his desperate, copy-book formula and his victorious future, or the ageing diplomat, with his short-sighted remedy and his desire to make everything as pleasant as possible? Buckingham did not believe that the breaching of the dykes, that already historic Dutch defence, would keep away Louis' armies; he could not know that the states of Luneburg, Branden-burg and Münster were about to join William against the powers of France.[63]

There was no more to be said. The English deputation left Neuerbrugge and made their way towards Heeswick, where Louis was encamped. Here they were joined by Halifax, who had been sent from England with further instructions from Charles. The terms were again submitted to and refused by William of Orange. The land was flooded. A fortnight later, to the amazement of all Europe, Louis withdrew his armies and marched back to Paris.

The diplomacy of the Cabal in general and of Buckingham in particular was utterly discredited in the eyes of the English people. Buckingham and Arlington then sent in the account of their expenses for the expedition to Holland; it came to four thousand seven hundred and fifty-four pounds and a penny.

7

It was said that the failure of his embassy had made Buckingham unpopular with the King; but Burnet, who first came to know him at this time, perceived that Charles was still deeply attached to him; he believed that the Duke " had a deep root " with his old comrade, who " either loved or feared him ".

Burnet was brought to Buckingham's notice by Ellis Leighton. They got on very well; at their first meeting they " passed almost a whole night together ", with the result that Buckingham recom-mended Burnet to the King. Shortly after their pleasant evening

[63] Temple.

the Duke gave Burnet his celebrated definition of Charles and James. The King, he said, could see things if he would and the Duke of York would see things if he could. "It was the more severe, because it was true," commented Burnet. Buckingham then asked Burnet what he meant by being so much with the Duke of York, and as he got no satisfactory answer, he went on, " If you fancy you can change him in point of religion, you know him and the world very little." He added, "If you have a mind to raise yourself, a sure method is to talk to him of the Reformation as a thing done in heat and haste, and that in a calmer time it might be fit to review it all." Burnet must have protested at such a notion, for the Duke continued, "You need go no further, for such an intimation would certainly raise you." " I would not enter into such a compliance," replied the other indignantly. Buckingham seemed rather amused. " I know courts better than you do," he said. "Princes think their favours are no ordinary things. They expect great submissions in return, otherwise they think they are despised. You will feel the ill-effects of the favour you now have, if you do not strike into some compliances. If you are resolved against these," he concluded, " I advise you to withdraw from the Court, the sooner the better."

The conversation ended there. Burnet thought the Duke spoke out of hatred for James. " But I found afterwards," he says, " the advice was sound and good." It may therefore be assumed that the astute cleric followed the counsels his magnificent host let fall so lightly. The careless, semi-mocking tone is typical of Buckingham. He did not know the meaning of discretion; nor did he care if Burnet repeated what he had said to the persons concerned.

Buckingham (who was spending his time either at Cliveden with Lady Shrewsbury or in London with Buckhurst and Sedley) had received splendid presents in commemoration of the Treaty of Heeswick; Colbert de Croissy told his master that the Duke was very much in debt and could almost certainly be bribed; but there are no records of his having received anything in cash at this time.

The autumn meetings of the Privy Council were stormy; one member told another that " Buckingham and Arlington should be called to account for making this war with the Dutch." At St. Germains, Montagu was now speaking openly against the Duke, who had heard nothing of the lieutenant-generalship promised him under Schomberg. On the credit side there was Buckingham's alliance with Shaftesbury, who became Lord Chancellor in

November 1672, and the rise of his protégé, Sir Thomas Osborne, who was soon to become Earl of Danby and Lord Treasurer in place of Clifford. All the ministers of the Cabal now knew the secret of the King's religious convictions, although Croissy continued to warn his colleagues that Buckingham did not.[64] Then, after more than a year's prorogation, the Houses met in February 1673.

Charles declared his intention of sticking to his detested Declaration of Indulgence for recusants and dissenters in spite of the protests of the Commons, who saw it as an arbitrary assumption of personal power. York, Clifford, Lauderdale and Buckingham supported Charles and urged him to dissolve Parliament; Shaftesbury, who had just heard about the Dover Treaty from Arlington, took the side of the Commons; the French Ambassador, too, thought it wiser that the King should give in, and on March the Eighth Charles cancelled the Declaration. Three weeks later the passing of the Test Act made it impossible for any Roman Catholic to hold office, with the result that James resigned his commission as Lord High Admiral and Rupert took his place. Buckingham, with Lauderdale, Monmouth, Arlington and some other members of the Privy Council, was made a Commissioner of the Admiralty.

8

Buckingham, Arlington and Shaftesbury had become the representatives of Protestantism in England: but the Commons trusted Shaftesbury only. Arlington, whom Clarendon had described long ago as caring " nothing for the conditions and laws of England ", was the most suspect of the three. Buckingham's reputation was that of an unreliable eccentric.[65] In the spring of 1673 his hopes of serving under Schomberg revived and he went north with the intention of recruiting five thousand men. This expedition was a failure. His intimacy with Louis and the reports of the presents he had received during his visits to France and Holland brought him under suspicion of Popery. No one trusted

---

[64] Villiers's comments on the King's apostasy have not survived; but it is difficult to believe that he could have kept his feelings to himself when he realised that he had been more grossly deceived, more heartlessly used, more thoroughly made to look a fool, than any other minister of the Cabal.

[65] Question : " When shall Don Carlos (the King's son by Catherine Pegg, afterwards Earl of Plymouth) be made a Lord? " Answer : " At about two o'clock in the morning, when the Duke of Buckingham has dined." (From a contemporary news sheet.)

him now; even after he had taken the sacrament at York Minster he was only able to raise six hundred men. He then did the rounds of the principal churches in his Lieutenancy; "but the people," remarked one of his many enemies in London, "hearken as little to his devotions as (I believe) Heaven to his prayers."[66] Buckingham went on doggedly with his recruiting campaign; he took immense pains, righting the troubles and listening to the complaints of "the meanest soldier", but—deplorable and characteristic rashness!—he was overheard saying that he believed in neither heaven nor hell, and the number of his recruits began to diminish.

In June, Schomberg came over to organise the review of the troops at Blackheath. The King, the Duke of York, the Duke of Monmouth and all the Court were present. A few days later Schomberg refused to serve with Buckingham. This was York's doing; he had recommended Schomberg and warned him against his old enemy.[67]

Buckingham was hysterical with rage. He worked off some of his temper on Lady Shrewsbury's coachman, who was brought before him on a charge of murder (there was a rumour that he had broken the fellow's head and sworn to have him hanged). The censure that falls on a man who has failed oppressed him very little; he knew that it was useless to appeal either to Charles or to Louis about Schomberg's action. It was consoling that some of the regiments he had collected with so much trouble refused to serve without him—they described Schomberg as "too much Frenchified"—sent for their colours and drums from the warships that were to have carried them to Holland and went home. Naturally Buckingham was blamed for this insubordination. "I leave you to consider how I am to behave myself with this Lieutenant-General," was Rupert's sarcastic comment to Arlington.

All those who hated and feared George Villiers rejoiced; one member of the Privy Council wrote to another with dreadful facetiousness, "His Grace is a little out of humour at present, but as he comes in grace again, the good humour will return to His Grace." But the result of the slights inflicted on Buckingham was foreseen by no one, except perhaps the King; the Duke turned against France and towards Holland, to the alarm of Louis and his ministers, who at once instituted a system of bribery on a scale

---

[66] Sir J. Williamson.
[67] *Memoirs* of John Sheffield, Duke of Buckingham and Normanby.

hitherto unparalleled in Franco-British relations. Sessac, a disgraced gambler, was sent over with Ruvigny, a Huguenot nobleman, to work up Buckingham's loyalty. "C'est un sale tactic,"
was Ruvigny's comment on this assignment: but he carried it out
nevertheless. He and Buckingham administrated the five hundred
thousand pounds provided by Louis for the purposes of propaganda; a bribe of ten thousand was destined for Shaftesbury, but
he refused it. Meanwhile the Duke continued to fulminate against
his enemies and finally made Montagu—who returned to England
at the end of 1673—the scapegoat for all the wrongs he had
endured.

At a meeting of the Privy Council in the first week of December
1673, Buckingham had asked leave to impeach Arlington; the
request was refused and so his grounds of complaint remained
unheard. On the same evening Ralph Montagu took his place in
the circle standing round the King and Queen in the withdrawing-
room at Whitehall. Buckingham, entering late and hastily, tried to
get past him in order to speak to the King; as Montagu refused to
move he pushed him out of the way. "What do you mean?"
exclaimed Montagu. Buckingham replied, "I will come by."
Their voices had risen and everyone was looking at them. "You
shall not!" shouted Montagu, and Buckingham kicked him to
one side. Thereupon Montagu left the room, desiring the Duke
to follow him, "which he did," says a courtier who was present,
"and so they appointed to meet the next day."

It is quite possible that Arlington, not caring to reply to Buckingham's attack at the Council board, had instructed Montagu to
pick a quarrel with him. No one, not Charles himself, would be
able to protect the Duke if he became involved in another duel.
Unfortunately for Arlington, Montagu was arrested for challenging
a peer in the King's presence and sent to the Tower. Montagu
denied that he had ever made the challenge. What probably
happened was this: Montagu, primed by Arlington and relying
on Buckingham's irritable and hostile humour, brought on the
quarrel in the hope that the Duke would take the initiative. When
they left the withdrawing-room he must have been certain of
success; but by that time he was as angry as Buckingham, and the
giving and taking of the challenge was no doubt confused and
simultaneous; they had barely interchanged a few words before
the King, aware of the trap, had Montagu arrested.

There is no excuse for Buckingham's share in this undignified scene but that he was goaded beyond endurance and extremely anxious about the forthcoming session of Parliament. He expected impeachment and disgrace, and said so openly. He did not know that he was about to be attacked, not only as a Minister of the Crown, but as a private individual.

9

The Houses met in gloom and severity. Their bitterest resentment was against France and against those ministers who had supported French interests; they suspected themselves deceived over the French treaty and the military alliance with Louis. (Buckingham had been urging Charles to make the false treaty public, but without success.) The Commons observed with growing alarm Buckingham's intimacy with Sessac and Ruvigny, Shaftesbury's dismissal from office,[68] and Arlington's intrigues. The King's assurance that it was impossible for him to doubt their affection was received in silence, perhaps because he hesitated as he said the words. Both Houses requested a day of public fast, " to seek a reconciliation at the hands of Almighty God ", and it was then the turn of the Commons. They began with their general grievances, which were presented under twenty-seven heads; they spoke of " the unChristian war with Holland ", " the imprudent league with France " and the growing power of Louis XIV. They declared the King " traitorously ensnared by the pernicious practices " of Buckingham and Arlington and those ministers themselves guilty of high treason; with Lauderdale, they formed " a triumvirate of iniquity ". The Commons then attacked York and his new Duchess, Mary of Modena (whose marriage had taken place without their knowledge or approval) suggested that York's elder daughter, Mary, should marry William of Orange, and concluded by saying that " this Parliament, the only hopeful remedy for this dying kingdom " must be fully answered on the points they had raised. Of the ministers, Lauderdale was the first to be pilloried; his indictment followed. The House then turned its attention to Buckingham.

The Duke had made his preparations against these attacks by going to the afternoon service at St. Martin's in the Fields with

---

[68] He retired to the country in the autumn of 1673, having been Lord Chancellor for a year.

his wife[69] and by "courting all the ministers in town, the debauchees by drinking with them, the pious by sober discourses and receiving the sacrament at Westminster ". These tactics did not save him on the morning of January the Third, 1674, from being accused of "many high misdemeanours ". He was impeached for peculation of the public funds, breaking the Triple Alliance by the negotiations of 1672, raising troops in Yorkshire, speaking treasonously against the sacred person of His Majesty and negotiating secretly with Louis XIV.

Then followed charges of a more personal nature. Buckingham's relationship with Lady Shrewsbury and the murder of Lord Shrewsbury were touched on with disgust; "not only that, but he has attempted a horrid sin not to be named; not to be named at Rome, where their other practices are horrid . . . This Duke has given night and lanthorn councils, not to be owned by the rest of the Councillors." Villiers' past—the past of more than twenty years ago—was raked over for innumerable petty crimes. "When the King was at Windsor, because he would not stay so long as the Duke would have him—at a drinking-bout—he took the bridle from the King's horse, to the great danger of the King's person . . . In Scotland, did he not correspond with Argyll and ransack the King's close-stool for papers? . . . He has not common bowels of mercy . . . He laughs always at all religion and true wisdom . . ."

Buckingham, thinking to propitiate the Commons, had decided to give them his answers in person. Lauderdale had not done this; no doubt his ungainly appearance and "rough and boisterous manners" would have gone against him.[70] Buckingham backed himself to disarm the House by his graceful and gallant bearing and one of those skilful, apparently forthright speeches for which he was famous. In his Commonplace Book he had written, "I will not trust an orator who is not able to answer objections."

"I have written something," he began, turning over a paper in his hand, "but I will trust to my own present thoughts." He then replied in general terms to the accusations made against him, taking care to incriminate Arlington and protect Shaftesbury, who had now come out of his retirement to organise the Opposition. "I have been in as much danger," he went on, "for my respect to this House, as any man; have been turned out of all my places at

[69] Williamson.

[70] Burnet : "His tongue was too big for his mouth, which made him bedew all that he talked to."

Court; proclaimed traitor; witnesses hired to swear against me, and confessed so . . . I was not afraid of my enemies in the House of Commons, but of being tried for life, before you met . . ." While deploring the misfortunes that had fallen on his administration, Buckingham felt it his duty to point out the blundering ineptitude of those in authority over him. He did not actually name the King and the Duke of York; but he made it quite clear that he was referring to them when he reached his peroration. " I can hunt the hare," said His Grace, " with a pack of hounds, but *not with a brace of lobsters.*" He then bowed to the House and withdrew.

A brace of lobsters . . . the extraordinary picture created by this simile was remembered and repeated long after Buckingham's other witticisms on the Stuart brothers had been forgotten; but the Commons were not in the mood for jests, however striking and peculiar. Finding the Duke's discourse " loose and uncertain ", they decided to tie him down to a number of written questions and desired him to attend them on the following day at ten o'clock in the morning.

Buckingham arrived at the appointed hour, magnificently dressed and seemingly unperturbed. He addressed the House briefly; but he managed to insinuate into this second speech a mixture of bluntness, naïveté, patriotic indignation and scrupulous delicacy that bewildered—though it did not quite take in—the majority of his hearers. He said:

" Mr. Speaker—I give the House my humble thanks for the honour you have twice done me, especially expressing myself so ill yesterday. I hope you will consider the condition I am in, in danger of passing in the censure of the world, for a vicious person and a betrayer of my country; I have ever had the misfortune to bear the blame of other men's faults. I know the revealing the King's councils, and corresponding with the King's enemies that are laid against me; but I hope for your pardon if I speak truth for myself. I told you yesterday, if the Triple League had any advantage in it (I speak it without vanity) I had as great a hand in it as any man. Then, upon the instance of the French Ambassador, I was sent into France upon the sad subject of condoling the death of Madame, where I urged for the service of the King, that the French ought not to endeavour to make themselves considerable at sea, of whom we had reason to be more jealous than of the Dutch, because the French then would have power to conquer us. When I returned, I found all demonstrations that the French had no such thoughts, but that the King of England should be master at sea.[71] I do not pretend to judge whether I or other men were in

[71] i.e. the French were willing to give Charles maritime supremacy.

the right, I leave the judgement of that to this honourable House. At this time my Lord Shaftesbury and myself advised not to begin a war without the advice of the Parliament, and the affections of the people (for I look upon the King at the head of his Parliament, to be the greatest Prince in the world); this was my Lord Shaftesbury's opinion and mine, but not my Lord Arlington's. My next advice was, not to make use of French ships, half their value in money would have been much more serviceable. I alleged, they would be of no use to us, by reason of their want of experience in our seas, and there would be great danger in their learning the use of them, which advice my Lord Arlington opposed, notwithstanding the King was so desirous of avoiding a breach with France, that he sent me to Dunkirk, and my Lord Arlington to Utrecht, where I still endeavoured to get money instead of ships. At my first audience the King of France was willing to comply, but after some returns and letters from hence[72] he was altered; but I make no reflections upon persons, but merely state matters of fact. Then it was my Lord Shaftesbury's advice and mine, so to order the war, as that the French should deliver us some towns of their conquests into our hands; a useful precaution in former times. My Lord Arlington would have no towns at all for one year. And here is the cause of the condition of our affairs. We set out a fleet with intention to land men in order to the taking of towns. The French army go on conquering and get all, and we get nothing, nor agree for any. Pray consider who it was that was so often locked up with the French Ambassador. My spirit moves me to tell you, that we were to consider what to do, we were to advise with the French Ambassador! I will not trouble you with reports, but pray look not on me as a peer, but as an honest English gentleman, who has suffered much for love to my country. I had a regiment given me that was Sir Edward Scott's, I gave him sixteen hundred pounds for it; there is no Papist officer in it, nor any Irishman. I shall say nothing of my extraordinary gains, I am sure I have lost as much as some men have gotten (and that is a big word). I am honest, and when I appear otherwise, I desire to die. I am not the man that has gotten by all this; yet after all this I am a grievance! I am the cheapest grievance this House ever had; and so I humbly ask the pardon of the House for the trouble I have given."

Eleven questions were then put to the Duke by the Speaker. He was asked first whether he had received any " ill advices " as to the liberties of the administration or alteration of the Government, who were these hypothetical advisers and what they advised? To this quadruple question, Buckingham replied oracularly:

"There is an old proverb, Mr. Speaker, ' Over Boots, Over Shoes '. This reflects upon one that is not now living, and so I desire pardon for saying anything further, fearing it may be thought a malicious invention of mine, the person being dead. I have said nothing yet but what I can justify, but this I cannot."

"The person dead " was Clifford, who, it is believed, had committed suicide after his retirement to the country. The next question was—whom did Buckingham accuse of having received several thousands of pounds and from what source did the money come? Buckingham's answer must have caused a smile; but it did not help his case.

"I am not well acquainted by what means they got so much, being not at all acquainted with the ways of getting money. What the Duke of Ormonde has got is upon record, being about fifty thousand. My Lord Arlington has not got so much, but has got a great deal."

"By whose advice was the army raised and Monsieur Schomberg made General?"

"I cannot say by whose advice, but upon my honour, not by mine," replied Buckingham with genuine feeling, "I was told by a man that's dead [Clifford again?] that my Lord Arlington sent for him, and it will be easily proved."

Clifford came in handy for the next question. "By whose advice was this army brought up to awe the debates and resolutions of the House of Commons?"

"I must make to this the same answer as I did before; it was a discourse from a man that's dead, of one now living.[73] If I had deserved the honour I think I might have had the command of the army before him; but Schomberg was told, my Lord Arlington would have the government by an army."

After some further questions as to the French alliance, the Triple Alliance and the offensive against Holland, Buckingham spoke at some length in defence of the Treaty of Heeswick, saying:

"If we had made a peace [with Holland] then, we had been in a worse condition than before . . . the Prince of Orange hoped for a good peace with us upon that Treaty, but I would never consent that France must have all, and we nothing. The consequence would be that Holland must entirely depend on France, and I think it is a wise article, that the French were not to make peace without us."

The broken phrases of this speech denote some confusion; in his answer to the final question Buckingham was on firmer ground and he replied calmly and briefly:

"My Lord Shaftesbury and I were for advising with the Parliament and adverse to the Prorogation. I can say nothing, but I believe the Parliament will never be against a war for the good of England."

[73] i.e. Clifford told Buckingham that Arlington had recommended Schomberg.

Composure, frankness, gentlemanly reserve, conscious modesty, subtle allusion—all were thrown away on that stern and unsympathetic audience. The House asked the Duke to withdraw and then presented an address to the King, asking him to dismiss Buckingham and Lauderdale from his councils for ever. Two days later, they dealt with Arlington, who managed to escape condemnation by the mingled falsity, moderation and common sense of his replies. He took up the charges against Buckingham who was responsible, he said " for all the trouble ". As to his, Arlington's, alleged introduction of Schomberg—that was a matter of expediency. The General's military reputation was well known: he was " fitter to command " than Buckingham. " The Duke of Buckingham," Arlington added, with an assumption of scrupulous fairness, " is a person of as great a courage as any in the world, but none would say but he had less skill than Schomberg in military matters." Passing on to the negotiations with William of Orange, Arlington represented himself and Lord Halifax as inclining towards moderation in their demands—" but Buckingham," he said regretfully, " was absolutely against having them moderated." The Duke was also responsible for the French treaty, in fact, His Grace was to blame for everything.

The Commons accepted, or rather, swallowed whole, every one of Arlington's excuses. Buckingham lost his place, peace was made with Holland and the Cabal ceased to exist. Charles then deprived Buckingham of the Mastership of the Horse, which he gave to Monmouth; but George Villiers' misfortunes did not end there. A few days after his dismissal from the Ministry he was ordered to appear before the Lords to answer a petition brought against him by the guardians of the young Earl of Shrewsbury.

10

The strain of the attacks from both houses was too much, even for the Duke's resilience, and he broke down. His collapse was diagnosed as a fever by the doctors; but those who knew him thought him ill " more in soul than in body ", and believed that he would retire altogether from public life. It was not in Buckingham's nature to throw in his hand; he had not lost his instinct for power nor his zest for the political gamble. After a few days' rest, he appeared before the Committee of the Lords. Here, all his enemies (including Ormonde, Worcester and Bristol) had combined to destroy him.

Through his guardians the fifteen-year-old Earl of Shrewsbury accused Buckingham on two counts, the murder of his father and the "public debauchery" of his mother; to these the Lords added a third accusation, that of the christening and burial of the so-called Earl of Coventry in Westminster Abbey, adding "that they would not have done so, had the offenders employed the usual care to cover their guilt and shame."

Although Buckingham had received a pardon for the murder of Shrewsbury some six years ago, his security could no longer be taken for granted now that he had fallen from power. He summoned Shaftesbury to help him. The ex-Lord Chancellor, who had been violently irritated by Buckingham's indiscretions at an uproarious supper-party, decided that the Duke was, in spite of everything, too useful to lose.[74] He worked for Buckingham behind the scenes, with the result that the Duke received only "very gentle censure" from the Lords, to the disgust of the Arlington faction.

Buckingham began his defence in these words: "I admit," he said, "that my life has not been so regular nor so free from blame . . . on the other hand, I thank God I am not delivered up to so profane a temper of mind as to justify the least misdemeanour." He then threw himself on the mercy of the Lords and told them he intended "to deal frankly and openly". He denied that there had been adultery between him and Lady Shrewsbury before her husband's death, adding, "I believe that if the Earl had been left to the natural goodness of his disposition . . . he had not resented a thing so much for which there was such little ground." There followed a very glib account of the circumstances of the duel. According to Buckingham, Lady Shrewsbury left her husband and went to France because "her honour was not vindicated upon one who had done her a public and barbarous affront[75] . . . and . . . the Earl, upon a groundless jealousy of my having been the cause of her going away was much incensed against me. After the death of the said Earl," continued Buckingham, "*for which I had as sensible a grief as any of those gentlemen that subscribed to the*

---

[74] "After they had drunk very freely the Duke of Buckingham began to tell some of their secrets, which Shaftesbury had no way to prevent but by giving him the lie, which turned the discourse into a quarrel." (Lord Dartmouth's Note to Burnet's *History*.)

[75] Buckingham was perhaps referring to Killigrew's attack on his mistress. See p. 133.

petition, the Countess, returning into England and being disowned by her friends and relations . . . sent to me to desire my assistance, which no man of honour could have denied a lady in her condition." After hinting that it would be a difficult matter to condemn him for a crime for which he had long since been pardoned, Buckingham proceeded to give his peers some assurance for his future conduct. He made a " very submissive recantation . . . acknowledging the miserable and lewd life he had led with Lady Shrewsbury" and concluded, "Though it is a very heavy burden to be under the displeasure of the House and the sense of my transgressions, yet I have reason to give God thanks for it, since it has opened my eyes and discovered to me the foulness of my past life, which I am resolved . . . to amend." To this piece of supremely hypocritical eloquence, Buckingham added " several other pathetic expressions", asking pardon for his "incontinence" and promising to discontinue it.

Well aware of what these promises were worth, the House of Lords absolved Buckingham on all three charges, "upon promise never more to cohabit with my Lady Shrewsbury", and caused both parties to sign a bond of ten thousand pounds apiece to that effect. As further security Buckingham pledged his Irish pension of two thousand four hundred a year and a Committee of Bishops drew up the contract, "with all the caution and strictness imaginable". The body of the misnamed Earl of Coventry was, after some discussion, allowed to remain in the Abbey.

As soon as the bond was signed Buckingham approached the Lords again, with a characteristically impudent request. He asked that all mention of the Shrewsbury affair should be " taken out of the file, and razed out of the records." When this was refused, the Duke tried to retract his confession, with the excuse that he "had owned more than the petitions against him could prove". That this demand also was ignored is shown by the records, which contain the whole sordid story of his parting from his mistress. Henceforth her life had nothing to do with his. Two years later she married a Mr. Rodney Bridges and was again received at Court. She survived Buckingham by fifteen years and was buried in London at the Church of St. Giles in the Fields.[76]

It is just possible that Buckingham's physical collapse—which took place between his public disgrace and his private penalisation

[76] Her second son, John, was killed in a duel by the Duke of Grafton, the King's second son by Barbara Villiers.

—was caused, not by his fall from power, but by the realisation that Anna Shrewsbury had no further use for him. That it was she who wearied first is almost certain; it would have been both easy and convenient for her to get rid of a ruined lover by placing herself on the side of his enemies. But it was useless to plead with such a woman. " 'T'is not your tears will keep you from love," the Duke wrote in his Commonplace Book, " fishes that live in water feel that fire."

Buckingham marked his parting from Lady Shrewsbury by an access of ostentatious piety and by constant attendance on his wife who, selflessly devoted, had been in an agony during his ordeals. " C'est un étrange changement que celui de son humeur ", remarked Ruvigny as he saw them reunited and apparently happy together.

Buckingham now counted Halifax among his friends; in spite of the fact that he was one of Shrewsbury's trustees, Halifax was able to renew his early alliance with the Duke, who was looking round for supporters. Turning towards Danby, whose career he had partly created, Buckingham asked him to intercede with the Duchess of Portsmouth: there was no answer to this appeal. Danby, pitiless, able and ambitious, took no interest in the fortunes of the man who had helped to raise him.

One disaster followed another. The loss of the Mastership of the Horse was followed by that of the Chancellorship of Cambridge, which was given to Monmouth. The King, whose sense of humour had failed him over the lobster speech, complained to his equerries of Buckingham's inefficiency, and the complaints were repeated. Six hundred pounds' worth of plate was stolen from the Duke's lodgings in the Cockpit.[77] One of his chaplains, with a view, perhaps, to leaving the sinking ship, kept badgering him for the bishopric of Durham. But although Buckingham was, according to Burnet, " alone, hated by all and hating all the rest ", his private life was more varied than usual. Freed for ever from any permanent relationship, he went from one woman to another; Mme d'Aulnoy says rather wistfully, " He abandoned many mistresses without having just cause, and loved them without reason." The Duke's private opinion under the heading, " Fickleness ", is more succinctly expressed. " One mistress is too much, so that it is to be feared he will come to love

---

[77] The thief was caught and condemned to death, but reprieved at the request of the Duchess of Buckingham.

P

none . . . Nature and his fancy know nothing ugly . . . To love but one is the monastic life of love, and may justly be suspected of sloth."[78]

Buckingham's political career was by no means at an end. He was still admired and loved by the common people: and Shaftesbury was his ally; guided by the relentless energy of the "little Lord", he presently turned away from the Court to the City, the Green Ribbon Club and the New Country Party.

[78] Commonplace Book.

CHAPTER THREE

I

BUCKINGHAM and Charles were thus estranged again, apparently for ever. The King would not—perhaps he dared not —receive his dishonoured and broken Minister; York, Arlington, Danby and the Duchess of Portsmouth saw to that. Every sharp speech, every careless jest that Buckingham had let fall about his master was repeated; the little rhymes, the mocking expostulations that had been a part of their relationship were recalled in hatred and bitterness: above all, his ridicule of the King and his brother —ridicule that might have amused Charles if it had been spoken to his face in the equivocal privacy of the Bed-Chamber—was repeated by the circle that stood between him and Villiers with dire effect. The King's heart hardened: his displeasure crystallised; and Buckingham realised that he must retire to the country until his friends—Rochester, Buckhurst and Nelly—ventured to speak for him. Before he did so he wrote a long letter of remonstrance to Charles. Melancholy, sincere and dignified, it is one of the most effective of his compositions; indeed it is impossible to believe that the man who wrote of his master

> "Whilst in the State all things look smooth and fair,
> I'll dabble up and down and take the air,
> But at the first appearance of foul weather
> I and my Ducks will quack away together."

is also the author of the following lines:

"I am not in the least surprised at my having enemies about Your Majesty; but I wonder very much, after the many observations I have made of Your Majesty's good nature to all the world, that you can find it in your heart to use me with so much cruelty who have ever loved you better than myself . . . Pray, Sir, what is it I have done that should make you thus angry with me? Was it my fault that other men did really prejudice Your Majesty's affairs upon the hopes of doing me a mischief? Did I say anything in my defence which could possibly be wrestled to a reflection upon Your Majesty? Or if I was forced to reflect upon others, was it any more than what you yourself gave me leave to do? I beseech Your Majesty to examine your heart well upon this subject . . ."[1]

[1] Buckingham's excuse for the lobster speech was made to Burnet; he declared that he thus referred to Prince Rupert and Lord Arlington; but he had already used the simile for Charles and James in conversation.

Yet the courtier who received his King's fault-finding with this verse—

> " By hidden springs man's smallest actions move,
> Wound up by an unerring hand above.
> Why say you then, that this or that's amiss,
> Since nothing could be better than what is? "

now reproached him in grave and fluent prose with

" Your Majesty knows I have often told you that I would depend upon no man's favour in the Court but yours, and that nothing would make me desire to stay there but your kindness. These have always been my thoughts and are so still. If it be upon the score of the House of Commons' address to Your Majesty, that you are resolved to remove me from my place, I hope at least you will not be harder to me than the House of Commons were. And if it be only that Your Majesty has a mind the Duke of Monmouth should have it, even in that case I shall not complain of Your Majesty; neither I do not think it strange you should love him better than me: but I cannot believe Your Majesty would for his sake do anyone an injustice . . .

Consider, I beseech you, that I had the honour to be bred up with Your Majesty from a child: that I lost my estate for running from Cambridge where I was a student, to serve Your Majesty and your father, at Oxford, when I was not thought of an age sufficient to bear arms . . . That at the end of the wars, returning into England, and having my whole estate restored to me by the Parliament, without composition . . . there happening to be a design laid to take up arms for Your Majesty, my brother and I engaged in it, and in the engagement he was killed . . ."

The explanation of such contrasting attitudes as are here shown is not necessarily one of brazen and habitual hypocrisy, though Buckingham was capable of that also. A twisted thread of love and hatred, tenderness and scorn, sympathy and impatience, bound him to the King; in spite of his revolt, in spite of his contempt, the old Cavalier loyalty sometimes predominated; memory, the past, triumph and misfortune shared over thirty years streaked his irritation with and dislike of Charles; the derision of his rhymes was as strong, as genuine an emotion as the respectful subservience of his letter—and the result was that nobody believed in either. The King's enemies saw an underlying sycophancy in Buckingham's most insolent satires, and the King himself had no trust in his affection. That George Villiers was quite sincere in both expressions of feeling occurred to no one, very naturally. At times he felt extremely bitter about his position. " Men ruined by their princes and in disgrace," he wrote, " are like places struck with thunder, it's accounted unlawful to approach 'em," adding philosophically, "Princes' anger is like thunder, it clears the sky a great while after."[2]

Charles stood for everything that Buckingham enjoyed— mirth, extravagance, ease; Shaftesbury stood for all that he respected, admired and wanted, liberty of the mind and of the spirit, hatred of superstition and tyranny, the chance of great political power. For the next ten years he hesitated between these two loyalties, striking sometimes for one and sometimes for the other, giving his whole heart to neither; it became inevitable that the devotees of both sides should abuse and detest him. This fatal division of interests widened as he grew old, splitting and dissipating his energies; it probably had a worse effect on his health than the "wenching" and "whoring" of which he was often, and sometimes unjustly, accused.

2

Buckingham spent the year 1674–75 in retirement. He went first to his estate of Burley-on-the-Hill in Rutland and then came to Cliveden, so as to be near the Court in the event of a recall. He hunted all the winter; in the summer he occupied himself with music and writing; his laboratory, though moveable, had not yet been set up at Cliveden. In two letters to Rochester written from there he describes, with characteristic absorption, his latest hobby; the scribbled lines give an impression of his state of mind and of his way of life at this time.

". . . Mr. Powis . . . came hither the other day to see my building and give me some instructions about the breeding of carps . . . The circumstances of the matter are something long; but this in short is the sum of it. That you must be sure cleanse your pond very well, and let no fish be in it whatsoever but two carps, a male and a female; and that the next year you must take them out of that pond, and put them in to another, for fear of their being eaten by pikes. This he says will make them breed infinitely and grow very fat, though he has not as yet been pleased to tell me what they are to be fed with. I wish with all my heart that he and our grand politicians were always to go together in couples, for it is a very great pity that persons of such extraordinary parts should ever be parted . . . For he is a fool that only makes one laugh, the others make one cry too, which, that it may be their turn to do in God's proper time is the hearty wish, of my Lord, Your Lordship's most humble and obedient servant,
BUCKINGHAM."

2 Commonplace Book.

"I can truly assure your Lordship as my Lord of Bristol did the Duchess of Richmond,[3] that I have not contaminated my body with any person below my quality since I saw you . . . In the meantime I have sent you two of the civilest carps that ever I had to do with, and if they could speak they would infallibly (according to Mr. Boyle's way of moral reflections)[4] assure Your Lordship that I am, more than any man living, etc., etc."[5]

This second letter, with its private jokes and odd fancies, seems to show that Buckingham was getting over his depression. He was also beginning to forget Lady Shrewsbury. For a year after their parting he had written nothing; then, shortly after he and Rochester, disguised as publicans, set up an inn near Newmarket in order to have some fun with the local ladies,[6] his grief resolved itself into conscious artifice and he composed a formal complaint in the fashionable manner.

> Forsaken Strephon in a lonesome glade,
> By Nature for despairing sorrows made,
> Beneath a blasted oak had laid him down,
> By lightning that, as he by Love o'er thrown.
> Upon the mossy root he lean'd his head,
> While at his feet a murmuring current led
> Her streams, that sympathized with his sad moans;
> The neighb'ring echoes answered all his groans.
> Then as the dewy morn restored the day,
> While stretched on earth the silent mourner lay,
> At last into these doleful sounds he broke,
> Obdurate rocks dissolving whilst he spoke.
> "What language can my injured passion frame,
> That knows not how to give its wrongs a name;
> My suff'ring heart can all relief refuse,
> Rather than her, it did adore, accuse.
> Teach me, ye groves, some art to ease my pain,
> Some soft resentments that may leave no stain
> On her loved name, and then I will complain
> Till then to all my wrongs I will be blind,
> And whilst she's cruel, call her but unkind . . ."

[3] At this time Frances Stuart, who had no children, had been a widow for two years. She retired to Cobham, where she remained until her death in 1702, appearing at Court from time to time. A wax figure (of which the face is taken from her death-mask) in the robes she wore at the coronation of Queen Anne may be seen in Westminster Abbey.

[4] The Hon. Robert Boyle, seventh son of the Earl of Cork, who was a scientist and historian. Buckingham is referring to the theories expressed in Boyle's *Occasional Reflections*, in which he purports to draw moral lessons from the behaviour of animals and plants.

[5] From the original manuscript letters in the British Museum.

[6] St. Evremond: *Correspondence*.

and so on, for another twenty-five lines. The complete conventionality of this poem, with its carefully picturesque background, is in strong contrast to the colloquial, spontaneous style of the verses that Buckingham wrote for Lady Shrewsbury when he first fell in love with her.

> What a dull fool was I
>   To think so gross a lie,
> As that I ever was in love before.
> I have, perhaps, known one or two
> With whom I was content to be
> At that, which they call " Keeping company ".
>   But, after all that they could do,
>   I still could be with more.
> Their absence never made me shed a tear;
>   And I can truly swear,
>   That, till my eyes first gazed on you,
> I ne'er beheld the thing I could adore.
>
> A world of things must curiously be sought,
> A world of things must be together brought
> To make up charms which have the power to move,
>   Through a discerning eye, true love.
>   That is a masterpiece above
>   What only looks and shapes can do;
>   There must be wit and judgement too;
> Greatness of thought and worth, which draw
> From the whole world respect and awe.
>
> She that would raise a noble love, must find
> Ways to beget a passion for her mind,
> She must be that, which she to be would seem,
> For all true love is grounded on esteem.
> Plainness and truth gain more a generous heart
>   Than all the crooked subtleties of art.
>   She must be (what said I?) She must be you.
>   None but yourself that miracle can do;
>   At least, I'm sure, thus much I plainly see,
> None but yourself e'er did it upon me.
> 'T"is you alone, that can my heart subdue—
> To you alone it always shall be true!

A sea of varying emotions lies, uncharted, between these two pieces; the first, easy and mechanical, is almost without feeling; the second, jerky, adolescent, idealistic, reads like a cry for help. The eight years that separate them must have been years of agonising unrest and bitter ecstasy.

3

In April, 1675, Buckingham again took up his Parliamentary duties, though he was not received at Court. He returned to find Danby all-powerful. The Lord Treasurer had contrived to become the friend of the Duchess of Portsmouth while supporting William of Orange against France; he had instituted some sort of financial stability in the kingdom while organising a system of bribery—through money and titles—of the lesser members of the Commons, thus creating a " packed " Parliament. Ruthless in his persecution of Catholics and Dissenters, he was subservient to Charles, who was delighted with him; no minister had ever given him so little trouble or taken so much work off his shoulders; above all, Danby's good management enabled the King to achieve a modicum of independence while at the same time he was provided with funds for his pleasures. In fact Danby combined the old-fashioned, conscientious efficiency of Clarendon with the energetic, unscrupulous drive of the business man.

The slogan of Danby's new administration—Church, King and State—was expressed at the opening of Parliament in the Treasurer's Non-Resistance Bill, or Test Oath, described as " dark, intricate and perplexed " by Shaftesbury. The conditions of the Oath made any attempt to alter the laws or any criticism of the régime a treasonable offence; it prevented ecclesiastical reform, acknowledged dictatorship and was fiercely combated by the Opposition. The King, the Bishops and a majority in both Houses supported it; the Duke of York was nearly persuaded by Shaftesbury to join the New Country Party and fight it; in order to please him, Shaftesbury offered to strike out his primary contention in the forthcoming struggle, that Parliament had a right to alter the succession; but James withdrew at the last moment and allied himself with his brother, whom he did not trust, and Danby, whom he hated.

Shaftesbury's attack on the Test Oath was planned so that the speeches of his ablest supporters—Halifax and Buckingham—should be set off by the soberer eloquence of Lord Holles and Lord Wharton. Halifax made an even greater impression than had been anticipated by the coolness and common sense of his address. He pointed out that there was

". . . really no security to any state by oaths; so also no private person, much less statesman, would ever order his affairs as relying on it; no man would ever sleep with open doors or unlocked up treasure or plate, should all the town be sworn not to rob; so that the use of multiplying oaths had only been most commonly to exclude or disturb some honest conscientious men who would never have prejudiced the government."

Then it was Buckingham's turn. His criticisms were launched under a barrage of ridicule and fantastic satire; when the debates reached the question of ecclesiastical reform he took the Bishops as his victims. Marvell, who could not quite bring himself to approve of Buckingham, burst into unwilling admiration. "Never," he says, "were poor men exposed and abused, all the session, as the Bishops were by the Duke of Buckingham upon the Test: never the like, nor so infinitely pleasant;[7] and no men were ever grown so odiously ridiculous."

During the course of a debate on the punishment for defying the Test Oath, Buckingham made one of his best effects and " set the House a-laughing " as had been planned.

" By a Praemunire," he said, " we are to be stripped of all we have, and as we go along the streets, anybody may take our clothes from us, saying, You are in a Praemunire. If anyone in compassion should give a Lord a new coat to cover his nakedness, the next man he meets may take it away again, saying, You are in a Praemunire, and have a right to nothing. However, the stripped Peer has his seat in Parliament; he still may sit here without waistcoat or breeches."[8]

After an interval of two and a half centuries this peroration sounds rather childish and crude. It is necessary to remember that the word Praemunire had a colloquial meaning—"Here's a Praemunire!" meant "Here's a pretty kettle of fish!"—and that such a speech as this depends largely on intonation and timing.

Before the softened, relaxed mood which follows a good laugh had melted away Shaftesbury's livid face and golden periwig rose in the gloom, and with the deadly sweetness that was so familiar and so deceptive, he asked for a precise definition of the Faith about which they were disputing. The Lord Keeper Finch fell at once into the trap, and, with a satirical air, begged that " it might not be told in Gath or published in Askelon, that a Lord of so great parts and eminence, and professing himself a member of

[7] " pleasant " = amusing.   [8] Oldmixon.

the Church of England, should not know what is meant by the Protestant Religion." He was followed by Buckingham's former protégé, Dr. Morley, Bishop of Winchester, who, heavily informative, "condescended to instruct" Shaftesbury that "the Protestant Religion was comprised in the Thirty-nine Articles, the liturgy, the catechism, the homilies and the canons."[9]

This was what Shaftesbury had been waiting for. With the same equable and self-abnegating air he began upon a comparative analysis of the tenets of the Reformed Religion; he had the liturgy, the catechism and the Thirty-nine Articles at his fingers' ends: he quoted from the statutes of Henry VIII: he tied up the Bishops in the knots of their own creed, while declaring that "he hoped he should burn" for the faith that they were nailing to the cross of tyranny. "How must we again be priest-ridden, when the Church shall, by Act of Parliament and your Oaths, be there separate and set above the civil power? This does, indeed, set the mitre above the crown."[10]

The tropes, the subtlety, the close reasoning, the wide knowledge and the concerted influence of the three most brilliant men in the kingdom were of no avail against the Bishops and the solid ranks of Danby's bribed members. The Non-Resistance Bill was passed in the Lords, though by such a small majority that swords were drawn on the floor of the House and the opposing members spat in one another's faces. Before it could go up to the Commons, Parliament was prorogued until October, 1675.

4

During the six months of the prorogation Buckingham again retired into private life; although he retained his lodgings in the Cockpit he did not go to Whitehall. It is not unreasonable to connect this second retreat with the permanent estrangement from his wife that, long overdue, resulted at last in an informal separation. The disappointment caused by the failure of the Country Party's fight against Non-Resistance, his exile from Court, and the gap that the loss of Lady Shrewsbury had left in his life turned Buckingham towards other distractions—the distractions furnished by a voluntary descent in the social scale. From the time that he

[9] *A Letter from a Person of Quality to His Friend in the Country.* (1675)
[10] Christie.

parted from his mistress his name is never again connected with that of a woman of his own standing; but his contemporaries, Burnet in particular, continued to dwell on his "vices" and his "debauchery".[11]

No doubt Buckingham had begun to drink heavily, more heavily perhaps than was the custom of his circle. Furthermore, one must conclude that as he does not seem to have taken any interest in women of breeding, he found his pleasure among those whose business it was to minister to wealthy and privileged persons. Indeed it is possible that Lady Shrewsbury's behaviour and character caused him to turn in disgust from the amateurs to the professionals. In doing this he ran a slightly greater risk than if he had continued to frequent his own class. It is clear that venereal disease shortened the lives and sapped the energies of many who seldom, if ever, strayed beyond the confines of the Court; Danby, for instance, had not long given his eldest son a place there before both the young man and his wife died horribly, while another son had to be sent to France for a cure. The Duchess of Portsmouth openly blamed Charles II for her enforced retirement to the waters of Bath; and the Duke of York, though he himself lived to be sixty-seven, handed down the seeds of "the diseases of love" to many of his children.[12] While there was so much danger of a hideous end in the highest circles, infection was almost inevitable in the case of those who frequented the stews and bawdy-houses: that Buckingham was one of these is certain. He laughed at the fuss that was made of him in such places and was not in the least deceived by it. "I thought we had loved one another," he remarks to one unknown entertainer, "but I perceive we are both rivals in the love of my money. I promise you, you shall not exceed me in that passion." Under the heading "A Wench" he adds, "She goes purring up and down like a strok'd cat ... Her beauty is like a mountebank's medicine, the price of it falls every day ... Wenches are like fruits, only dear at their first coming in. Their price falls apace afterwards."[13] Buckingham's appetites led him towards many different sources of pleasure; his connection with the theatre was linked with the pursuit of those

---

[11] *History*. "He gave himself up into a monstrous course of studied immoralities of the worst kind. He was so full of mercury that he could not fix long in any friendship or to any design."

[12] Besides his illegitimate sons and daughters, James had fourteen children by his wives of whom only four, Mary, Anne, the Old Pretender and the Princess Louisa Mary lived to grow up.   [13] Commonplace Book.

who supplemented their earnings by exploiting their personal attractions.

As a man grows old—and Buckingham had now reached his forty-eighth year, a climacteric in that day—he tends to return to the influences of his youth. It may have been about this time that the young George Villiers who had been the guest and pupil of the Medici came to life in the body of the disillusioned and ageing Duke of Buckingham. When he deigned to visit the tiring-rooms of the Theatre Royal he was treated with the awe and admiration that the Privy Council and the House of Peers had denied him; in this dusty, tinsel world he appeared as a god: and as the choice of a god his favourites were envied and acclaimed. Strangely reminiscent, in this incongruous setting, were the face and figure of Edward Kynaston, then in his early thirties—for he was the reincarnation of those exquisite youths who, in skin-tight scarlet hose, stand holding beakers or balancing spears in the pictures of the Florentine Renaissance. No doubt Kynaston was aware of this resemblance, for he dressed to the part by wearing his own hair and letting it fall in thick golden waves on to his shoulders. Disdainful, heavy-eyed, his beauty was remarkably apropos at this idle interval in his patron's career. Many years later, when his triumphs had not yet become a memory, Kynaston married and became prosperous and obscure: in the sixteen-seventies he was as supreme in the theatre as Buckingham had been at Whitehall.

To Buckingham, as to most persons of developed intelligence and educated views, the pursuit of pleasure was not necessarily confined to the pursuit of the opposite sex: he believed one " divertisement " to be as good as another. He cared nothing for censure and would have been very much amused, if it had been possible for him to have come across such a thing, by any reference to the love that dares not speak its name. His arrogance despised and his sanguine temper ignored the laws of the seventeenth century which punished certain enjoyments by death. As a peer he ran very little risk—or so he believed—of endangering himself or anybody else; and to be, like Ormonde, " discreet even in his vices ", was beyond him. So, temporarily relinquishing politics and the accepted forms of gallantry, Villiers disappears from view down a long dark passage of private life . . . The only clue to his frame of mind lies in a dialogue, discovered among his papers after his death. It is called *The Militant Couple, or,*

the Husband may Thank Himself, and sums up the attitude of
a man who is resolved to run down what he cannot achieve. In
these few pages Buckingham gives a picture, not of himself and
his patient wife, but of those who subscribed to the conventions
and pretended to be satisfied with them. We see the Militant
Couple through the eyes of Bellairs, who is talking to Freeman,
much as Rochester may have gossipped to Buckingham about their
country neighbours.

Free. Is this their constant course of life?

Bell. Why, really, yes. Only with this difference, that what thou saw'st
yesterday was mere sport and pastime to the terrible tragedies I have seen.

Free. . . . I can't comprehend how the scene could possibly be worse.
Methinks Sir John and my Lady threw " Whore " and " Rogue " at one
another very plentifully.

    .   .   .   .   .   .

Bell. Yes I tell you, blows are more provoking and odious. What
signify a few angry words? . . . Mithridates, you know, by accustoming
himself to poison, brought his body to such a pitch at last that he could
regale himself with opium and feast upon ratsbane . . . By the same token,
a quarrel happened about dressing a dish of fish. Sir John swore the
cook deserved to be crucified for spoiling so noble a brace of carp . . . After
abundance of compliments had passed between 'em on this head, " Yes,
Madam," says he, " I must own you are in the right; my palate is very
vicious, and I showed it . . . when I married such a composition of pride,
malice and lust, as Your Ladyship."

Free. Ah, worthy Knight, that was spoke like a hero! But what reply
did my lady make to it?

Bell. " At least," says she, " I have something more to plead for myself
than thou hast. I knew thee to be a worthless sot, an empty, guzzling,
smoking wretch. But a devil of an uncle forced me to take thee for my
husband: otherwise I had sooner courted an infection, and bedded a leprosy
than suffered myself to be polluted with thy nauseous embraces." . . . The
cloth was no sooner removed than the war broke out with greater fury
than ever. Sir John . . . swore and blustered like a hero in one of our
modern tragedies. My lady, on her side, exercised her lungs with equal
vigour . . . At last the knight, unable to contain himself any longer, struck
off her commode,[14] which courtesy her Ladyship immediately requited by
throwing Sir John's periwig into the fire.

Free. That was doing business to some purpose.

Bell. With that Sir John pushes my Lady against a fine pendulum clock
that stood in the room, and broke the olive case all to pieces. My Lady soon
rallied and beat Sir John back upon a huge Japan looking-glass, which was
demolished in an instant; to retaliate which favour, the knight finished all
her china at three or four strokes of his cane. But now they came to a closer
engagement, distributing their blows to one another with incredible gallantry,
while I——

[14] Headdress.

Free. That is what I long to hear; for methinks I would have found myself *un peu embarrassé* how to behave myself in so nice a conjuncture.

Bell. Listen then. All this while I sat unconcerned upon my chair, keeping up to my old maxim of being neuter. . . . At last, after an hour's dispute . . . my Lady . . . retired triumphantly out of the parlour, and left her lord and master grovelling upon the floor with a brace of black eyes. . . .

Free. Well, 'tis a mystery to me, that married people, however they behave to one another in private, should not take care to preserve a fair outside at least before strangers. . . . But, prithee, Bellairs, how long have Sir John and my Lady been married?

Bell. Somewhat over five years. Sir John was the same numerical beast that you behold him now, but my Lady was one of the most agreeable, sweet-tempered creatures the sun ever saw . . . Alas! I know the whole history of their intestine broils, and what occasioned them. I was invited to the wedding. . . . There was a world of noise and impertinence, of scandal and bawdy, attended with dancing, fiddling, swearing, drinking, smoking and the like. . . . The bride's brother, who is a true country rake, without the least share of good sense or manners to atone for his vices, was pleased to tell all the company how he had consummated (but he used a more familiar expression for it) the night before with a farmer's daughter upon a haycock; and this he delivered in such beastly language, that I wonder none of the grave ancient matrons at the table did not rebuke him for it. . . . Had Sir John been a man of tolerable discretion, he would certainly have been the happiest man in the universe But I consider his behaviour upon the nuptial day gave me a vile omen of his future conduct.

After some further descriptions and a little moralising, Bellairs concludes, " 'T'is as natural for wives as for subjects to rebel."

In this dialogue we see Buckingham's impatience with provincial society; as long as he could feel this impatience he was able to pull himself together and exercise his talents where they were needed. When Parliament opened he returned to London and spoke with restraint, persuasion and common sense upon the subject nearest his heart—religious toleration.

5

Buckingham's second recorded speech on this subject, one of the shortest he ever made, begins slyly, " There is a thing called property, which (whatsoever some men may think) is that the people of England are fondest of . . ." The train of thought that guided the rest of his argument is now too obvious to bear quotation; in the speaker's day it was so iconoclastic as to be unacceptable to the greater part of his audience. Such satirical phrases as "niceties of religion", "zeal for every opinion that is held by those that have power in the Church" and "uncertainties of religion" were very shocking to Buckingham's contemporaries, to whom they indicated a frankly irreligious attitude. The Duke had learnt by this time that it was both useless and dangerous to come out into the open and ask for toleration of atheism; he was beginning to see that toleration of Dissent was almost as impossible to obtain: and when his Bill was thrown out and Charles prorogued Parliament again he returned to the country without any complaint or comment.[15] He had so much on his mind that he did not even protest when his laboratory was seized in payment of his debts. It was returned to him later.

During the weeks of the session of 1675 Buckingham had continued to besiege his master; but Danby and the Duchess of Portsmouth were still in control and Mrs. Gwynn could do nothing for her old friend.[16] Buckingham then took a step that removed him even further from the Court party; he leased a house in Upper Thames Street, Dowgate, at the same time that Shaftesbury moved to Aldersgate, so as to be nearer the City, where the Green Ribbon Club was the stronghold of the Country Party.[17]

The site of the Green Ribbon Club is at the corner of Chancery Lane and Fleet Street, overlooking Temple Bar. Here, in the early seventeenth century, stood the King's Head, a fashionable tavern with a sign of Henry VIII;[18] it was now the headquarters of Shaftesbury's Opposition. The most noticeable features of the club were the long oak-panelled dining-room and the double balcony looking out on to Fleet Street and Temple Bar; it was the centre of communication with other, similar clubs in the provinces and with the coffee-houses—those fortresses of the Opposition—in London.[19] The original members—about forty in number—

[15] Reresby.

[16] Mme de Sévigné says, " Mlle de Kéroualle has been disappointed in nothing . . . The King . . . takes up his abode with her every night in the face of the whole Court; she has had a son who has been acknowledged and presented with two Duchies " (this was the Duke of Richmond, born in 1672) " but she did not foresee that she would find a young actress in her way whom the King dotes on . . . he divides his time, his care and his health between these two . . . I love these original characters." *Letters* 1675.

[17] The Green Ribbon Club (the name derives from the sea-green ribbons worn at Rainborough's funeral) was not so called until 1679.

[18] Pepys. This was on the site of the house of Sir John Oldcastle, who was supposed by some to have been the model for Shakespeare's Falstaff.

[19] In later years the Court Party made a great many jokes about the coffee-swilling effeminacy of the Opposition, who replied that it was only by staying drunk that their enemies remained loyal.

were in constant touch with Parliament and encouraged the membership of young men from the country.

Informality was the custom of the Green Ribbon Club; gentlemen appeared on the balcony without hats or swords, sometimes without their periwigs, smoking long clay pipes and interchanging jokes and slogans with the crowd below when they were not directing the clerical work that their political activities entailed. Here the petitions for the reassembling of Parliament were drawn up, and here, on the long solid tables littered with bottles of claret and sherry, candle-snuffers, grease-droppings and news-letters, lists of subscribers were made and designs for cuts, caricatures and medals selected. (These pursuits sound harmless enough; but there were other schemes, discussed by a group of plainly-dressed men in a locked upper room that were not quite so innocuous.)

The majority of the Green Ribboners sat on backless benches; for the principal members—Shaftesbury, Buckingham, Halifax, Monmouth, Lord Howard of Escrick, Lord Grey of Werke, Baron Wharton and the Earls of Essex and Radnor—there were tall chairs with wicker seats and backs. Shaftesbury would sit in one of these, near the great open hearth, his pale eyes burning beneath the shadow of his hat with its " Monmouth cock " and huge green satin bow, his chin sunk on his breast;[20] and here, in five years' time, would be seen the monstrous bulk of Titus Oates, in his doctor's gown and bands.

With the people the most popular members of the Club were Monmouth and Buckingham. Shaftesbury had his adorers, his " brisk boys", his roaring apprentices and his few intimate dependents; but as the years went by and the great Achitophel became more powerful and yet more desperate, as his plans for constitutional reform changed into feverish dreams of revolution, his companions of the Opposition began to fear his poisoned tongue and his embittered fanaticism. Monmouth, fondly described as " the Revolting Darling "[21] had long been the idol of the crowds; warm-hearted, beautiful, not very clever, he pleased by his graceful bearing and his natural, engaging manners. George Villiers pleased because he was as unexpected as he was good-humoured and gay; to the thousands that stopped to stare up at those famous balconies, he stood for the extravagance, wealth and power that they could never enjoy; he had killed his man; it was

---

[20] From some contemporary woodcuts, reproduced in *The First Whig*, *The* " Monmouth cock " pushed the hat to the back of the head. [21] From a popular ballad.

said that the King could not do without him: that the Duke of York hated and feared him; best of all, nobody knew what he was going to say next, what daring jest or pleasant nonsense he would let fall with that negligent air in which mockery and magnificence were so strangely blended.

It was just as well that his admirers outside the Green Ribbon Club could not hear all that the Duke said about them inside it. Relaxed, amused, he listened to his companions' schemes for establishing their hold over the mob. " The follies of the people," he noted sarcastically, " are to be observed and obeyed as well as the rules of wise men. He that will sail in the ocean must observe the winds as well as the stars. . . . You can no more tell the value of men by the impression they make in people's minds than you can tell whether the seal be of brass or gold by the stamp it makes in the wax. . . . Popular fame is like a glass, not only for its brittleness, but because it is blown into any form. . . ."[22] As for Shaftesbury's violence, it got on his nerves—"They who have poison in themselves will always, like serpents, hiss at others "— while Halifax's aphorisms, witty though they sometimes were, held an undercurrent of seriousness that was not at all to his taste; and he was violently irritated by any discussion about the welfare of future generations. " We shall be revenged on posterity," he noted, " for let 'em think never so little of us, we shall think less of them."[23]

Buckingham was to be in close contact with Monmouth for the next seven years, and although they got on well enough he sometimes found the younger man rather silly. " He lives as if the world were made only for him," he wrote, " and truly the world is so foolish a thing, that I think it was so." As for Monmouth's circle of toadies—" When they praise you they take you for another man than you are, and so praise that other man, not you."[24] Involuntarily, Monmouth had supplanted Buckingham in many of his honours and seemed now to be taking his place as a dashing public figure. Although Buckingham liked the company of his juniors he really had little use for Monmouth's, for the Revolting Darling was no intellectual. Buckingham's dislike was generally irrepressible; yet among his many recorded jibes there is only one sarcastic reference to Prince Absalom. What did he feel, then— Boredom? Indifference? The answer is perhaps that no one, not even Shaftesbury, could associate with Monmouth without liking

[22] Commonplace Book.   [23] Ibid.   [24] Ibid.

Q

him—although Shaftesbury's treatment of him was entirely heartless and unscrupulous. In a world of cheats, climbers and cynics
Monmouth stands apart, emotional, generous, childishly simple.
Buckingham merely found fault with the rowdyism, to use no
severer word, of the Protestant hero's early days—it is noticeable
that Villiers himself may be entirely exonerated from the nose-
slitting, public obscenity and murderous horseplay of the younger
set—and expressed his disapproval in some verses, of which these
lines—

> " Nay, could we yet do grander things than these,
> Murder an harmless watchman on his knees,
> Go travel afterwards for more renown
> And then take Maestricht, hard by Windsor town."

—describe a crime committed by Monmouth when still in his 'teens,
his useless share in the visit to William of Orange and his reproduc-
tion of the siege of Maestricht for the benefit of his father's Court
at Windsor in the summer of 1677. But such satire as this—even
the conclusion—

> " There never was but one yet sot enough
> Could wish to live for such base silly stuff."

—seems to show Buckingham shrugging away the follies of the
next generation;[25] and there is no record of his quarrelling with
Monmouth. They had in common a love of music, sport and pretty
women, and a natural ease, very rare in those days, with the
common people. Buckingham's freedom of manner with persons
of all classes was incomprehensible and shocking to many,
especially to foreign visitors, who recoiled in horror and loathing
from the conversational advances and brutal insolence of the
watermen, hackney-coach drivers and apprentices of London;
they hardly knew which was the more offensive, the stone-
throwing and bawling of the apprentices or the attempted political
discussions of the watermen and drivers. " Tout le monde se croit
en droit de parler," was the disgusted comment of one French
nobleman. In vain Courtin, Louis' new Ambassador, implored
Buckingham to relinquish his low connections with the City.
Alderman George, as Charles now called him, continued to affiliate
himself with the Opposition. The Leader of the Country Party
was known as Alderman Shaftesbury; this is a good example of the

---

[25] For real venom and hatred, Buckingham's verses on Arlington and a prose piece
on an unnamed woman—probably the Duchess of Lauderdale—though unquotable, are
worth reading.

difference between his social attitude and Buckingham's; no one would have ventured to describe Little Sincerity as Alderman Anthony.

Sensitive readers will rightly shrink from the suggestion that the Duke accepted a bribe or two from Louis while continuing to support Shaftesbury; and yet he cannot be exonerated from conforming to the recognised custom on one or two occasions.

6

It was now a year since Charles had promised Louis to dissolve Parliament; while accepting payment for doing so he had merely prorogued the Houses for fifteen months. As the time for the opening drew nearer Louis, seeing his hopes of a French party in England diminish, paid Charles to sign a secret treaty in which both Kings promised not to help their common enemies nor to sign agreements with other countries without one another's consent. Danby was appalled by the lengths to which his master was prepared to go and declared that he himself would pay with his head if he countenanced such a document; so Charles had to make out the treaty with his own hand before he could send it off.

Meanwhile Government spies were watching Buckingham and his friends and reported on all their activities; already his and Shaftesbury's speeches against the Test Oath had been seized and a warrant issued for the apprehension of the printers; now, although the Country Party was trying " to make the Court odious to the people " and the question of Buckingham's arrest was still being considered, he behaved with provoking circumspection. At last the Duke was followed to a tavern at Edmonton, where he entertained a party of friends, among whom were several notorious republicans. But all this famous debauchee did was to pour himself out a dish of tea and drink a health to a new Parliament " and to all those honest gentlemen of it that would give the King no money ". This disappointingly mild gesture was not treasonable; nor could the rumours that Buckingham and Shaftesbury were estranged and that Buckingham had visited the Duke of York be verified. It was most unsatisfactory. The spies did not get hold of the facts; actually Shaftesbury was much tried by the Duke, who " blabbed out everything ". He complained that Buckingham was

" giddy-pated " and the criticism was, of course, repeated.[26] Nevertheless Buckingham, although he had a fit of the gout and could not leave his house, subscribed fifty pounds as his share of a banquet given by Shaftesbury to Lord Mohun, who was flirting with the Country Party.

The Court party hoped that Buckingham would be too ill to attend Parliament: but he recovered just in time. Giddy-pated or not, he was Shaftesbury's most valuable asset in the grand attack that had been planned. The Country Party was resolved, at whatever cost, to force a dissolution; and for this purpose Shaftesbury had gone so far as to ally himself, temporarily, with Louis XIV.

The House of Lords assembled on the morning of the Fifteenth of February, 1677. Shaftesbury, Buckingham, Baron Wharton and the Earl of Salisbury were in their places. As soon as the King and Lord Chancellor Finch had spoken, Buckingham, dressed in a magnificent suit of blue, " all diversified "[27] rose and in a " long set speech "[28] moved that, according to two statutes of the reign of Edward III,[29] Parliament, having been prorogued for more than a year, was automatically dissolved. He was supported by Salisbury and Wharton and denounced by Lord Frescheville and the Chancellor.

Buckingham's opening phrases are worth quoting; they assumed a hesitancy, and indeed a humility, in which he was entirely lacking.

" My Lords [he began] I have often troubled Your Lordships with my discourse in this House; but I confess I never did it with more trouble to myself than I do at this time, for I scarce know where I should begin, or what I have to say to Your Lordships. On the one side, I am afraid of being thought an unquiet and pragmatical man; for in this age every man that cannot bear anything is called unquiet; and he that does ask questions for which we ought to be concerned, is looked upon as pragmatical. On the other side, I am more afraid of being thought a dishonest man; and of all men I am most afraid of being thought so by myself. . . . He is most certainly a knave that takes himself to be so . . . and therefore, though I should be in the wrong . . . I shall behave myself like an honest man. For it is my duty as long as I have the honour to sit in this House to hide nothing . . . which I think may concern His Majesty's service, Your Lordships' interest or the good and quiet of the people of England."

Buckingham went on to recall the motion made by himself fifteen months before for a dissolution and the obstreperous behaviour of the Commons who, he said, perhaps with an eye or

26 Burnet.   27 Roger North : *Examen*.   28 James II.
29 Edward III, 3 and 30.

Danby, looked upon themselves " as a standing Senate ". He then compared the Commons with the little wheels in the mechanism of a watch and proceeded to declare the non-existence of Parliament according to laws more than three hundred years old. " And gives me leave to tell Your Lordships," he added, " that statutes are not like women, they are not one jot the worse for being old." After quoting the statutes, which contained a provision that "a Parliament shall be holden every year once and more often if need be ", and pointing out that they had not been repealed, Buckingham pronounced " the Kings of England bound by the Acts ... of Edward III, or else the whole government of England by Parliaments is absolutely at an end ". Then came the appeal to Magna Carta (shades of John Lilburne) and a denial of the recent prorogation, followed by these words:

" Now, if we cannot act as a Parliament, by virtue of the last prorogation, I beseech Your Lordships, by virtue of what else can we act? Shall we act by virtue of the King's proclamation? Pray, My Lords, how so? Is a pro-clamation of more force than a prorogation? ... I have heard, indeed, that two negatives make an affirmative: but I never heard before that two nothings make anything."

" Do we meet by accident? " went on Buckingham, after the full insolence of this *reductio ad absurdum* had sunk in. " That, I think, may be granted, but an accidental meeting can no more make a Parliament than an accidental clapping a crown on man's head can make a king."

This was defiance. But we may be sure that Charles's dark im-passivity never stirred as he heard his old comrade reach his climax thereby, tie up the legal threads of the argument, emphasise the limitations of the royal power and declare that the prorogation of fifteen months ago " might as well have put [Parliament] off till Doomsday. And then, I think," the Duke concluded, " nobody would have doubted but that had been a very sufficient dissolution."

Buckingham then reminded the Lords that Charles " was bound up by the laws of England, just as Almighty God was bound by his own decrees," and after a last appeal for dissolution suggested that the Peers should " humbly address themselves to His Majesty ... for his own sake as well as for the people's sake ... for the welfare, the safety and the glory of the English nation."

While Lord Frescheville was speaking the Duke " took a pen and wrote a syllogism " outlining his thesis and offering to dispute it with the Bishops and Judges. " He argued with great appear-ance of reason and greater wit," says one who was present at this remarkable session, "His Grace had a great mind to banter the Judges."[30]

Shaftesbury then supported Buckingham "largelier" and with "extraordinary vigour, courage and sharpness of application"[31] declaring that to call him to the Bar of the House, as Frescheville had suggested, would be taking away liberty of speech. When Finch had attacked the motion and Salisbury and Wharton had supported it, the debate was adjourned till the next day.[32] Shaftesbury and Buckingham then left the House, after " some high and bitter clashings " with Danby.

7

Next day the Lords decided that the four rebellious peers must ask forgiveness and retract their declarations. A distinction was made between the case of Salisbury and Wharton and that of Shaftesbury and Buckingham. The first two were acquitted of pronouncing the non-existence of Parliament: but all four were called to the Bar of the House to ask pardon in the following words, " I do acknowledge that my endeavouring to maintain that Parliament is dissolved was an ill advised action, for which I humbly beseech the pardon of His Majesty and this most honourable House." Salisbury and Wharton " peremptorily " refused to recant; Lord Anglesey beckoned Salisbury out and " persuaded his submission "—but he was followed by Shaftesbury, who " dissuaded it " and made him stick to his friends.

Shaftesbury's refusal should have followed Buckingham's; but when the Usher of the Black Rod went to look for the Duke he was not in his place nor anywhere in the House, although a few moments before he had been sitting near Shaftesbury. The three others lords were then committed to the Tower " for high contempt " and an order made for Buckingham's arrest. When it was discovered that he was not in the House, the ports were stopped in case he should try to leave the country.

These judgements and searchings took several hours. Then Buckingham was seen to be in his place once more and cries of " To the Bar! To the Bar! " arose. It was never discovered whether he left the House as a gesture of defiance or what he had been

---

[30] North. [31] *Ibid*.
[32] Shaftesbury's speech on this occasion has not been preserved.

doing. He was commanded to withdraw and so brought to the Bar. He knelt; then he was told to stand up and account for his disappearance.

"I beg Your Lordships' pardon," he said, "but you very well know what exact economy I keep in my family. I only went home to set my house in order." This mingling of impertinence and falsehood was surprisingly well received. The Lords required Buckingham to recant. He replied, "If I have offended His Majesty and this House in anything I have uttered, I ask their pardon. But I cannot ask pardon for thinking and speaking my thoughts, and I refuse to make the submission." He was then committed.

Before leaving the House, Buckingham announced that he had a favour to ask—could he take his cook with him to the Tower? At this point some of the more frivolous members of the House burst into roars of laughter. Although he afterwards, in accordance with Shaftesbury's instructions and example, declared that he was afraid of being poisoned—ostentatious terror of poison being a great feature of the Country Party's propaganda—Buckingham may perhaps have hinted at the horrors of the Tower cookery. He then remarked, rather as an afterthought, that he had felt his gout coming on again yesterday, and retired.

On the same afternoon he set off from the Mitre Tavern to the Tower in a state coach, his cook following in another. Permission had also been given him to take some of his servants; so his footmen (dressed in brand new liveries) came after him in hackney carriages. Crowds pursued him all the way, and the narrow alleys and streets echoed to shouts of "A Buckingham! A Buckingham!" as the coach lumbered by.

As soon as the peers arrived at the Tower Lord Salisbury asked for his wife and Buckingham for his laboratory; it is not known whether the Duke's request was granted. A close prisoner, he was not allowed to see any visitors without the King's order and prevented from communicating with the other imprisoned lords, although they all, after the manner of most prisoners, came to chapel and talked to one another during the service. Then Buckingham suddenly remembered his buildings at Cliveden; matters had got to a critical point and his presence was urgently needed. He wrote submissively to Charles and was given permission to visit Cliveden, going there under escort and returning within forty-eight hours.

Buckingham's imprisonment was not a long one; he, Salisbury

and Wharton were all released after a very short time; Shaftesbury,
an infinitely more dangerous rebel, was retained. As Buckingham
came into the courtyard, Shaftesbury, who was standing at the
window, leaned out and said in his soft, carrying voice: "What,
my Lord, are you leaving us so soon?" Buckingham looked up:
he had not quite forgiven Little Sincerity his strictures. "Ay,
my Lord," he replied, "You know that we giddy-pated fellows
never stay long in one place at a time." And so these ill-assorted
allies parted for a year; for although Halifax, who had voted against
Shaftesbury's motion, was allowed to visit him, we may be sure
that Buckingham was not.

9

From the moment that he was permitted to visit Cliveden
Buckingham must have known that his imprisonment was not to
be severe. He got his release by pleading that he had "contracted
several indispositions and needed a month's air". Immediately
his friends, Nelly, Rochester, Buckhurst "and the merry gang"
obtained his freedom; he was allowed to leave, as it were, on parole
"with presumption to make it an entire liberty". With characteristic boldness he at once went to Rochester's lodgings at
Whitehall. Danby and the Duke of York protested to the King;
such leniency was hard to bear. "It is to leap over all the rules
of decency," said the Lord Treasurer severely, "to suffer authority to be trampled on." For some days the battle between the
"Ministers of State and the Ministers of Pleasure" went on.
Then Buckingham was told that he could have his liberty but
must retire at once to Cliveden. During his stay at Whitehall he
had made no attempt to revenge himself on his enemies, and this
was considered very singular. Andrew Marvell gave the explanation. The Duke, he said, loved pleasure more than revenge;
"and yet this last," he added meditatively, "is not the meanest
luxury." Revenge was something that Buckingham often talked
about; but, unlike his contemporaries, he seldom carried it further
than a set of verses or an amusing letter to a friend.

And now, alone at Cliveden, he began to brood over his
relationship with the King; posted at Whitehall, pleaded for by
Nelly, he had hoped for reinstatement; but he had left the palace
after one brief cold interview with the man whose proclamation

and prorogation he had described as " two nothings ". What was to be done?

Buckingham was in correspondence with Rochester, who had been advising him as to the King's mood. At last, unknown to anyone else, Nelly and Rochester between them persuaded Charles to say that the Duke might return; but his recall must be preceded by a written apology. Immediately Villiers dashed off all that he felt, just as it came into his head; the result was one of the queerest communications that even Charles, that specialist in oddities, can ever have received. Buckingham was in too much of a hurry to sign or date his letter; but its content places it in this period of his disgrace. As his pen scrawled and blotted the words his thoughts rushed backwards and forwards, from the uneasy past to the clouded future. He made no attempt to defend his recent actions: he simply ignored them. A consciously false or calculating man might have tried to draw a line between his deep personal affection for the friend and his disapproval of the ruler. Such a differentiation did not belong to Buckingham's age: nor was he capable of the blind loyalty that he was obliged to profess. There was a link missing somewhere in the chain that bound him to Charles; he seems to be fumbling for the words that were to make everything clear between him and his master. He began in the middle of what he wanted to say, without any preamble:

" I am so surprised with what Mrs. Nelly has told me that I know not what in the world to say. The most sensible grief I had in being put away from Your Majesty was not the losing of my place, but the being shut out of Your Majesty's kindness . . . What has made this inclination more violent in me . . . is the honour I had of being bred up with Your Majesty from a child. . . . And therefore I beseech Your Majesty to believe me when I say that I have ever loved you more than all the rest of mankind . . . What shall I say? I am not one that pretends to preciseness in devotion, but yet I am sure Your Majesty never found me to be a knave, and I wish that all the curses imaginable may be upon me if I tell you a lie . . . I have lived long enough in this world not to care much for it, and have met with so much ungratefulness from almost all mankind that the pleasure of conversing with men . . . is quite taken from me. Yet I beseech Your Majesty to believe that the grief which in my whole life did ever sit nearest to my heart was the loss of Your Majesty's kindness. You that have been a lover yourself know what it is to think oneself ill used by a mistress that one loves extremely, and it is that only I can truly compare my past misfortune to. Yet . . . there was a great deal of art used to make me believe that Your Majesty hated me, and I can hardly forgive them that did it, since it was done with as much undutifulness to Your Majesty as ingratitude to me. But why should I say more of the matter? ... Could you make a question whether I love you or no? O Christ, Sir, for Heaven's sake, know that I would as willingly die to-morrow to do Your Majesty service as any of those about you would have me dead to satisfy their envy and their ill-nature.... Do with me what you please, I will be absolutely governed by you; but, I beseech Your Majesty, have a care of me ... for God's sake, Sir, don't look upon this as obstinacy I never was so towards a friend and can much less be so to my King and my master.... God in Heaven reward you ... and may he curse me whenever I am ungrateful to you. ..." [33]

Buckingham's letters to Rochester about himself and Charles give the same effect of sincerity; though they are less wildly written, they bear out the strange and tormenting duality of his feelings. His love and his contempt, his loyalty and his treason went hand in hand; the tone of injured resentment in which he writes of Danby's machinations and of his enemies' evil counsels to the King is almost artless. During this time Buckingham stayed with Rochester at Woodstock and may then have collaborated with him in those poems, too well known for quotation, that bear their joint names. Towards the end of the summer the merry gang carried him back to Court.

Buckingham's return was a ghastly blow to Danby. This time he had thought himself secure. He could not believe that the man who had openly insulted and mocked the Majesty of England would ever rise again; nor did it occur to him that Charles might have missed the wittiest and liveliest member of his Court and long for his company: nor that His Majesty might have been rather entertained than incensed by Villiers' dogmatisms in the House of Lords. When at last the friends were reunited and "supped at Nell's" Charles could indulge to the full his sardonic humour at the expense of Alderman George and the Protestant Whore; and his mockery did not spare Shaftesbury, still eating his heart out in the Tower. At the theatre, watching Hart as Macbeth, the King turned to the gentlemen in his box and exclaimed, "Pray, what is the meaning that we never see a rogue in a play but oddsfish! they always clap him in a black periwig, when it is well known one of the greatest rogues in England wears a fair one?" [34]

Danby's sole consolation was that Buckingham was given a private, semi-official pardon: he was permitted to kiss the King's hand in the Bed-Chamber only:[35] but worse was to follow. Shortly

[33] From the original manuscript letter in the British Museum.
[34] Montague Summers.
[35] Burnet.

after his return Villiers visited Oxford, of which he was still High Steward, and was there given a magnificent reception: there was even talk of his buying another house; by the autumn he was in the greatest possible favour and took the Duchess of Mazarin and a party of Court ladies to Bartholomew Fair.

The Lord Treasurer did not waste his time commiserating with the Duchess of Portsmouth. He determined to blacken Buckingham's character on an entirely new basis; three years later he found the weapon he needed.

CHAPTER FOUR

I

THE portraits of Buckingham give the impression that he could barely endure the tedium of sitting or standing still for more than a few moments at a time. In the family group he seems about to spring from his mother's arms; as a child of nine and as a boy in his teens he appears resentful and impatient; and the look of sulkiness and boredom is as noticeable in the mezzotint from Verelst as in the picture by Lely. These last two portraits are separated by an interval of nearly twenty years. Verelst's makes it easy to understand what Sir John Reresby meant when he described Buckingham as the finest gentlemen he ever saw, although even here the effect is that of beauty bruised and despoiled. Lely, having no need to flatter, shows Villiers at his worst, and the result is terrifying; here is no single trace of gaiety, distinction or good looks: all are submerged in pride, greed and disdain. Verelst's splendid man of the world has become a disagreeable, coarse voluptuary with a swollen nose and a double chin. One quality remains—intelligence. Although pouched and underscored, the eyes are piercingly bright, the expression keen and hard. Lely saw ruin, degradation and heartlessness beneath the Garter robes, the delicate lace and the silky wig: Buckingham knew what he saw, and did not care.

Was he too wrapped up in his schemes and his hobbies to realise that for some he had become an object of pity and disgust? "The Duke of Buckingham has a set of false teeth and wears a feather. I think when a fellow has come to that, it is no matter what he does or is," wrote Lady Harvey to Ralph Montagu in spiteful triumph.[1] Nell Gwynn, "his great friend and faithful councillor" also observed the Duke's growing carelessness and begged him, through a mutual acquaintance, "to buy new shoes, that he might not dirty her rooms, and a new periwig that she might not smell him stink two storeys high when he knocks at the outward door," while Henry Savile added

[1] " Wears a feather " is a slang term. A fop or a coxcomb was sometimes described as a feather. According to the *Gulls' Horn Book*, which dates from 1609, to wear a feather in one's hat was to draw attention to oneself, or to one's dress. Lady Harvey was Montagu's sister.

that Buckingham was " out at heels and stunk most grievously ".
What had happened to the only English gentleman Louis XIV
had ever met? The tone of Nell's criticisms is facetious; this
was the sort of joke in which she specialised: yet there must have
been an undercurrent of truth in her teasing. The explanation
lies perhaps in Buckingham's increasing predilection for low
company and in the general decline in manners—in his world, at
least—that made itself felt about this time. An etiquette book,
published in 1679, dedicated to the Duke of Monmouth and
written for the *nouveaux riches*, the players and the " cits " who
had broken into the Court circle and lowered its tone, gives a
picture of the habits that had to be put aside in order to achieve
social success. The anonymous author of *The Refined Courtier,
or, A Correction of Several Indecencies Crept into Civil Conversation* begins with an alarming description of Restoration
table manners, urging his readers not to ape

" . . . those who, more like so many swine than men, put their noses
into a mess of broth, and never once lift up their faces or eyes, much less
remove their hands from the dish; and that with their cheeks distempered
and swollen (as if they were sounding a trumpet or blowing a fire) don't so
properly eat as devour their meat . . . grease themselves up to the elbow and
make their napkins look like dishcloths, and yet are not ashamed to blow
their noses on them and sometimes to wipe off the sweat, which, it may be
through immoderate haste and eagerness in eating, trickles down their forehead and face to their necks."

Though we may shudder at the scene thus created we cannot
but applaud the sound sense of such remarks as—

" There are those who when they cough or sneeze do it with so shrill a
sound that they pierce through the heads of the standers-by and almost strike
them deaf; and (which is far worse) do not turn away, but after an incon-
siderate and immodest sort, all to bespatter the faces of those they talk
with. . . ."

and

" He who would be a well-bred man ought to refrain from loud and
frequent yawning (a crime the Romans severely punished)."

The author continues—

" We ought industriously to refrain from *singing*, especially if the voice
be *unmusical*, or if there are none to make a consort, or if we are not desired
to show our skill. . . . Beware of jeering instead of jesting. Take care
that your jests look not like the issue of labour and study . . . they must
be witty fallacies, subtle and artificial, prompt and sudden."

This is to set a high, an unattainable standard, especially when it is flanked by

" Make no loud expression of mirth or sorrow, for both are improper and tedious " and " Do not protract the time with empty preambles ", and preceded by the thoughtfulness of " When you are discoursing with anyone, you must not draw so near that your breath may reach him; for some can't endure another's breath, though it does not stink at all, but is a great deal sweeter than his own."

Quite so: but do we now realise that

" 'T'is uncivil when you are discoursing to fix your eyes steadfastly upon a man, as if you meant to put him out of countenance "—or that " 'T'is unseemly to break your bread into small morsels or to crumble it to pieces "?

Although we can afford to feel superior about the adjurations

" to be careful that no unsavoury rank smell shall come from you; and if you be now and then perfum'd, 'twill not be amiss " and to " refrain from spitting as much as you can . . . why can't we contain for a little time? "

But the standards of Restoration society held many pitfalls. It was inadvisable

". . . for any to put his nose towards a glass of wine . . . it being possible that some moisture may drop from his nostrils," and " an unseemly practice openly . . . to prepare for the easing of nature in public view, or to truss up our clothes before others when we return from performing that office."

What with curbing all these instincts and recalling what the Greeks and the Romans would have liked, there can have been little energy left for abjuring certain topics of conversation in the company of unmarried girls, deciding what dreams to recount and what not, and trying not to burst out with such conversational gambits as " Do you not know my friend Mr. Such an One? O then you can know no one! " In fact a thorough soaking in *The Refined Courtier* makes the state of Buckingham's shoes and perriwig seem trivial, or at worst a minor lapse of taste.

2

In 1678, Buckingham entered upon the final period of his public career. The course of his actions is sometimes obscured by the turmoil and the complication of the events in which he played a secondary part; in order to understand his position and his attitude it is necessary briefly to outline the political scene.

The battle for the control of the kingdom was waged by four antagonists—Charles II, Danby, Louis XIV and Shaftesbury. From time to time one or other of these four was forced to ally himself with an enemy in order to hold his own against the rest; but the aims of all were irreconcilable and may be roughly summed up as follows:

Charles, who continued alternately to blackmail, deceive and cajole Louis in order to obtain from him the money that every now and then ensured his independence of Parliament, had long ago thrown aside his old scheme of a dictatorship based on a national reconciliation with Rome. His private conviction, that the Catholic faith was the only religion for a Christian and a gentleman, was now subordinated to his secret plan—to give England religious toleration while binding her to the wheels of Louis' war-chariots and Louis' policy of European conquest. Only so could he achieve the absolutism which would bring him unlimited wealth, idleness and a firm seat on the throne. In order to cover up these designs he made, as it were, a number of Protestant gestures—the chief being his arrangement of the marriage of Mary, York's eldest daughter, to William of Orange, Louis' most formidable enemy. The wedding took place in November, 1678, and delighted the English people and a portion of the Country Party. Shaftesbury was not, of course, deceived by this tribute to popular feeling.

Danby, as the representative of the Church and State party, was determined to govern England by an oligarchy of which the King would be the nominal head, to enforce the tenets of the Church of England through a powerful prelacy and the persecution of recusants and dissenters and later, with the help of the Dutch, to beat the French at their own game of overseas trading and conquest.[2] A completely submissive, feudalised peasantry and a well-disciplined, enormously wealthy landowning class were essential for this scheme.

Louis' plans had changed very little since his nonage: conquest, empire and government through submission to Rome predominated. But his grasp on Europe was slipping, his expenses were greater than he could afford and he so much feared Danby's

[2] At a City banquet Danby publicly drank confusion " to all who were not for a war with France."

threats of a war with France that he allied himself, althougl temporarily, with Shaftesbury, on the principle of dividing before conquering, England and Protestantism.

Shaftesbury, with Buckingham as his second in command had one entirely disinterested aim—religious toleration. (Here he agreed with Charles and was at war with Louis and Danby.) He planned a constitutional monarchy, with himself as Prime Minister and Monmouth as a puppet ruler; with this end in view he succeeded in convincing a great many people that Monmouth was the legitimate son of Charles.[3] Later, as the struggle grew more desperate and he felt his health beginning to give way, his pressure on the Country Party and his galloping tactics divided it into two groups—the "fanatics", led by himself, Algernon Sidney[4] and William, Lord Russell,[5] who advocated a republic and a complete reversal of the existing order, and the moderates who were willing to substitute Mary or William of Orange for Monmouth, so long as James did not succeed. Buckingham's point of view is too variable to bear analysis; but he continued to stand for the restraint of monarchical power and for religious toleration.

The three main causes of dispute between these four antagonists were (1) the standing army, which, at the end of 167; had not been disbanded; (2) the dissolution of Danby's packed " Cavalier " Parliament; and (3) the succession. Charles was—rightly—suspected by Louis, Danby and Shaftesbury of retaining the army for sinister purposes of his own; Shaftesbury and Louis were allied in their determination that Danby's anti-French anti-toleration Parliament should be dissolved; Danby and Shaftesbury were thrown into one another's arms against Louis in their resolve that the Popish heir should not succeed.

To further the dissolution of Parliament, Louis allowed Charles

---

[3] It is possible that Charles and Lucy Walter went through some form of marriage during the exile; the first Mary of Orange, Charles's eldest sister, several times referred to his " wife " in her letters to him. She may have been speaking of Lucy: or she may have been referring to some private joke about Lucy or another woman. But in the late nineteenth century the Duke of Buccleuch found in the muniment room at Dalkeith Palace the marriage certificate of Charles and Lucy Walter which he, after some consideration, destroyed. E. D'Oyley: *James, Duke of Monmouth.* See also Lord George Scott: *Lucy Walter.*

[4] Algernon Sidney (1622–82) joined the Parliamentary army in 1642; he remained in exile till 1677, then returned to England as the advocate of a republic and, later, became the adversary of both Shaftesbury and Charles. See his *Discourses,* written in 1680.

[5] William, Lord Russell (1639–82) third son of the Duke of Bedford and an Exclusionist. He later turned away from Shaftesbury's policy and favoured the succession of William of Orange.

six million livres a year for three years and the Country Party ten thousand pounds for their election propaganda, at the same time promising to respect their religion in the event of his own success. Buckingham went over to France to make the necessary arrangements, thus causing Danby and his friends considerable alarm. In September, 1678, he visited the French Court incognito, " without his star and wearing a dark periwig ". For some time after his departure from England it was given out that he was ill or in the country, but Danby's spies traced him at last. The Duke had told Barillon—who succeeded Courtin as Ambassador in August, 1677—that he himself could not be bribed; nor was he. He had prepared for his mission by trying once more to establish himself as a serious character; he made a desperate attempt to put his money affairs in order and allowed himself to be " converted " by Burnet; but his conversion was greeted with a ballad in which he was described as " a damned atheist " and a teasing letter from St. Evremond, who begged him to continue with his economies and told him that if he returned home with a small retinue and a great deal of money in his pocket he would certainly be the wonder of the nation.

When Buckingham did come back from France he made a short stay at Cliveden, when he entertained the Duchess of Portsmouth. By the end of September, 1678, he was lodging at Nell Gwynn's house in Pall Mall; he had been spending a great deal of time with her and Charles, with whom " he advanced in conversation and merriment ", reducing the King to tears of laughter by his imitations of Lady Danby. The Court party looked very grave at this and told one another that " it was a bad sign for Danby ". They became graver still when they heard that both the Duke of York and the King were being " very civil " to Buckingham, in spite of the fact that the Duchess of York's summer visit to Cliveden had ended in disaster; entranced by Buckingham's company, she stayed so late that her servants got drunk and her coach was overturned. By February of 1679, Buckingham, Shaftesbury (who had been released from the Tower in February, 1678) Essex and Halifax were " governing men " in the House of Lords where Buckingham " spoke more pleasantly than learnedly " at a debate on war with France. Then it became known that Danby was preparing an attack on Buckingham; but it did not materialise.

The Lord Treasurer was wise in time. Some months before

R

Buckingham's ascendancy a weapon had been placed in the hands of the Country Party which made the dissolution of Parliament and the triumph of Shaftesbury certain. A group of men, whose reputations are for ever associated with evil, mystery and panic had already become famous. At this point in Buckingham's story the names of Tonge, Prance, Bedloe, Titus Oates and Sir Edmund Berry Godfrey are scrawled in red across the page.

3

"The English nation," said Charles I, "are a sober people." This celebrated summing up of the national temperament has been generally accepted and endorsed from Charles I's day down to the present time. That it is a short-sighted, superficial judgement—that the English people were, and are, tempestuous, fierce, hysterical and violent can be proved in the first place by studying the events of 1678–81 and in the second by an analysis of the correspondence columns in the popular press. No one gauged the English appetite for riot, cruelty and blood better than Shaftesbury or ministered to it more lavishly than Titus Oates, the son of a Norfolk clergyman who, after expulsion from two Jesuit colleges on the Continent,[6] came back to London in June, 1678, at the age of twenty-nine.

There were two Popish Plots. The first, described by Oates on five separate and famous occasions,[7] was almost entirely the work of "the Salamanca Doctor's" demonic and fecund imagination and embraced wholesale torture, murder and robbery;[8] it abounded in melodrama, contradiction and absurdity and was swallowed whole by all but a few. The Pope, according to Oates, had declared himself Lord of England and Ireland. From an Irish port a Franco-Irish army would arrive, burn down London, confiscate or destroy all property, murder the King (and the Duke of York, if he did not lend himself to their schemes) and begin a reign of terror, unparalleled since the days of Queen

---

[6] Valladolid and St. Omers.

[7] On August 1st, 1678, Oates informed the King, through Kirkby and Tonge, of the designs against his life and the Protestant religion: on September 1st he placed this evidence before Sir Edmund Berry Godfrey: on September 30th he was interviewed by the Privy Council: on October 23rd at the Bar of the House of Commons: and on October 30th at the Bar of the House of Lords.

[8] Although he had never been there, Oates asseverated that he had obtained his degree at the University of Salamanca.

Mary. This information, co-ordinated under eighty-one heads, by Oates and his jackal, the Reverend Ezrael Tonge, of St. Michael's, Wood Street, was never substantiated, except on one or two points.[9]

The second Popish Plot has already been outlined in this memoir as part of a scheme originated by Charles II, sanctioned by the *Traité de Madame*, and pursued by Louis XIV and his Catholic agents—of whom the Duke of York was the most important and the clumsiest—from the early years of the Restoration till the Revolution of 1688. This Popish Plot—the real one—was known to a few and suspected by many; that suspicion had been expressed on several occasions, most succinctly perhaps, in the House of Commons in 1674, by the placing of a pair of beads and a wooden shoe, painted with the arms of France and England, in the Speaker's Chair.[10] By the time Buckingham and Shaftesbury had become the heads of the Opposition, fear of Popery was at the back of the national consciousness and every misfortune—the great fire, the appearance of the Dutch in the Medway and even the plague—was attributed to Catholic intrigue. Four years after the episode of the wooden shoe, when the deposition of Oates was laid before a Justice of the Peace who had already got into trouble with Charles—when that Justice, Sir Edmund Berry Godfrey, was murdered in circumstances which to this day remain obscure—when the letters of York's secretary to Louis' confessor, Père de la Chaize, seemed to bear out all that Oates had prophesied—then the rage, the terror and the frenzy of the English people appear comprehensible and inevitable.[11]

It cannot be too much emphasised that a Catholic triumph was a genuine possibility, both from the point of view of those who desired and those who dreaded it. The very fact that not only the "old" Catholics, but also the modern, "Jesuited Papists" —a distinction keenly felt and widely recognised at this time— were hoping or working for a Catholic renascence, explains the rising disgust and horror with which Protestant England contemplated a Catholic *maîtresse en titre*, a Catholic Queen (not that she counted for much), a Catholic heir-presumptive, and

[9] Titus Oates: *True and Exact Narrative of the Horrid Plot and Conspiracy*, etc.
[10] Anchitell Grey: *Reports of the Debates in the House of Commons.*
[11] Sir John Pollock: *The Popish Plot.* This brilliant and fascinating analysis, first published in 1903 and re-issued forty years later, is still the most persuasive guide to the subject. That Sir Edmund Berry Godfrey was murdered by a Catholic gang, but not by those who were executed for his death, seems an almost inescapable conclusion, in view of the evidence of Miles Prance, and Sir John Pollock's explanation of that evidence.

Catholic nobles in high positions. From the April of 1676 when the Duke of York ceased to worship in the Church of England this terror so increased that the Pope himself advised James, outwardly at least, to curb his convert's zeal; he would have done better to have insisted on the removal of Edward Coleman, James's secretary. This young man, well bred, talented and fatally energetic, brought persecution, misery and ruin on thousands of innocent and loyal Catholics and a hideous death on himself by his fanatical and misguided intrigues. It was the publication of his correspondence with Père de la Chaize and its exploitation by Oates and the Country Party that sent the English people mad with hatred and caused one nobleman to declare that he would not have " so much as a Popish dog . . . nor so much as a Popish cat to purr or mew about the King."

On the waves of this mass hysteria, Buckingham and Shaftesbury were borne in triumph. All that they had been fighting for—the defeat of Roman Catholicism ("Popery and slavery, like two sisters, go hand in hand "),[12] the succession of a Protestant heir, the dissolution of Parliament and the standing army—seemed about to fall into their hands. Although they were perfectly aware of the depth and extent of Oates's perjury, they acclaimed him as the saviour of their cause. For a time Danby believed that he too might use Oates's revelations; but he had neither the power nor the skill to control the weapon that Shaftesbury had seized. Shaftesbury, through the elaborate organisations of the Green Ribbon Club, had the mass of the people (whom Danby despised) behind him; Danby and his bribed members were thus outnumbered. Charles, more cunning than either, stood aside, intervening only when he dared, to expose Oates's inventions or to protect the Queen.

For by the end of November, 1678, Oates, intoxicated with publicity, adulation and success, arraigned the Queen of England of planning the death of the King, at the bar of the House of Commons, in his hideous nasal drawl; Buckingham, springing to his feet, exclaimed, "This rascal Oates will spoil our business— it is not yet time to bring the Queen forward." He was referring to Shaftesbury's second line of attack, the divorce of the Queen, the re-marriage of Charles and the birth of a Protestant heir whose long minority would establish the rule of the Country Party. Shaftesbury held this alternative scheme in reserve till as late as

[12] Shaftesbury.

1679; during a Committee meeting in the House of Lords at which the King was present as a spectator, he rose and, pointing to Charles, said, "Can anyone doubt, if he looks at the King's face, as to his being capable of making children? He is only fifty. I know people upwards of sixty, who would have no difficulty in making children." As Shaftesbury sat down Charles joined in the laughter of the Peers.

The accusation against the Queen was Oates's first blunder; at the King's order he was confined and his papers seized. But already the depositions of Tonge, Prance and Bedloe, creatures of Oates's calibre, though not of his stature, had caused the execution of William Staley, a Catholic goldsmith who cannot be completely exonerated of conspiring to murder Charles, of Coleman and of fifteen perfectly innocent people. On the Second of November, 1678, Shaftesbury requested the Lords to dismiss the Duke of York from the Privy Council and, through William Sacheverell in the House of Commons,[13] asked whether the King and Parliament between them might not dispose of the succession. The Country Party's cards were thus placed on the table. Some other instruments of their anti-Catholic propaganda were now prepared—the "Protestant flail" (something between a knob-kerry and a "cosh") smart little pistols for ladies to carry in their muffs, and quilted silk armour, in which, Roger North remarks, "any man was a safe as in a house, for it was impossible to strike him for laughing."

All this time Buckingham, who was on the Committee dealing with Oates's depositions, alternated between his house in Upper Thames Street, the Green Ribbon Club and—for he was still a courtier—Whitehall. Charles's leniency had protected him during the whole of the preceding year. One of the Duke's dismissed servants, Henry North, condemned to death for highway robbery, had attempted to save himself by hinting at a plot organised by Buckingham against the King. "That heroic prince, my master," said North, "would not have engaged but by the frequent importunity of an eminent man." The Reverend William Silverton, who attended North and reported his statement, added that Buckingham was "led by a faction" and his actions misunderstood. Charles ignored the oblique hit at Shaftesbury and the attack on Buckingham, just as he ignored a prophesy that

---

[13] William Sacheverell (1638–1691), described as the ablest Parliamentarian of Charles II's reign. At the election of January 1679, he was returned as M.P. for Derbyshire. He retired into private life during the reign of James II.

" Protestantism should be delivered " by the Earl of Salisbury and the Dukes of Buckingham and Monmouth. During the summer and autumn of 1678 he retained Buckingham at Court, in order to keep an eye on him (this simple but ingenious policy was completely misunderstood by his brother and his courtiers) and instructed Sir Joseph Williamson, his Secretary of State, to "lay by " the evidence of another plot in which the Duke, with Halifax, Shaftesbury and Salisbury, was accused of planning to murder the entire royal family and bring in a republic. Charles, unlike his subjects, was perfectly able to distinguish between the real and the false in these matters; he must have sympathised with the desperate struggles of the injured Catholics to lay the blame elsewhere. When the five unjustly accused Popish Lords—Powis, Stafford, Petre, Bellasis and Arundel of Wardour—instructed Netterville, a prisoner in the Marshalsea, to "find some man to swear " that the Popish Plot really originated with Buckingham and Shaftesbury, the King said nothing; nor did he intervene when Atkins, Pepys' clerk, was examined on the grounds of privacy to the Plot by the Lords' Committee. Roger North was present at both the examinations of Atkins and has left an account of them.

4

During the last thirty years of the seventeenth century the art of the informer reached its highest point of development. The standard set by Oates and his satellites was never afterwards surpassed. The verbose, detailed, circumstantial accounts of plans that had never been formed, much less described, of threats and brutal treatment never used, were based on intimate knowledge of the men who were supposed to have practised them. The skill of the informer lay in his adaptations, rather than in his inventions..

The report on Atkins shows Buckingham and Shaftesbury at their worst, hectoring, dramatising themselves and their cause; stagey and exaggerated as their methods seem to-day, they are at least free from physical brutality. Shaftesbury began by "wheedling " Atkins to give the information he required on the Popish Plot; but Atkins refused to yield. "The Duke of Bucks," says North, " then came to [Atkins], and, laying his finger upon his forehead, ' I see,' said he, ' the great workings of thy brain—come, for thine own sake, declare what thou knowest!'"

It is easy to picture the scene—the sombre panelled room, the long table scattered with papers, and the plainly-dressed clerk facing the row of bewigged inquisitors—Shaftesbury's imperceptible glance at Buckingham as he relinquished his victim and Buckingham's frightening histrionics. But neither had the effect desired and Atkins was sent to Newgate. At his second examination shock tactics were employed. Shaftesbury began, with ogreish geniality—" I have good news for thee, but one way to save thy life; confess all you know and make discovery of this matter." Atkins replied, " No fear of death shall make me tell a solemn lie, to the prejudice of anyone." Shaftesbury's tone changed at once to bitter irony. " Since you are so gallant," he said, " you will certainly be either knighted or hanged. If the Papists rise and cut all our throats, thou wilt be knighted; if not, thou wilt be hanged." He then paused in his examination to sum up the evidence and added that " diverse others, well known to Bedloe, were concerned in the Plot." Buckingham remarked that " they were all in custody ", and Shaftesbury concluded, " If one of these swear you were in it, then all the world cannot save you." Atkins answered steadily, " I should be glad of discoveries, but I cannot suffer by things being misplaced." " O! he expects a pardon! " put in Buckingham, to which Shaftesbury replied grimly, " No—I'll secure him from that, I warrant you."

Unpleasant as the protagonists of this scene appear, their behaviour is mild indeed when we compare it with that in an imaginary examination, described by Francis Caryll or Corral, a hackney coachman of Gunpowder Alley, Shoe Lane, who was arrested on suspicion of having carried away Sir Edmund Berry Godfrey's body and later discovered to have been bribed by the Catholics to embroil and discredit the leaders of the Country Party. His evidence was eventually proved to be false from beginning to end.

Caryll deposed that he was taken from Newgate to Wallingford House, where he appeared before the Marquess of Winchester, Buckingham, Halifax, Shaftesbury and " another Lord ". In answer to questions, he said that he knew nothing of Sir Edmund Berry Godfrey's death, upon which Shaftesbury called him a " bloody-minded rogue and threatened him with a cruel death . . . but the Duke of Buckingham declared he should not be so long a-dying, for he would run him through presently; and so, first striking him and calling him bloody rogue and dog, he then drew his sword and ran it several times at Caryll's breast, but seemed to be prevailed with by the Earl of Shaftesbury not to kill him presently, but to preserve him alive for some more cruel death. . . ." According to his own account Caryll was racked and then taken back to the Lords at Winchester's house. "They told him that if he would confess he should have five hundred pounds and his pardon." He refused, was taken again to Newgate, loaded with irons, given no food or drink and kept in prison for six weeks.[14] He was then brought a third time before the Lords, apostrophied by Buckingham as "bloody dog, Papist and villain" and "hove by the hair, buffeted and pricked in the breast" by that nobleman. Caryll's evidence ends rather tamely with the statement that he was at last allowed to go free on bail.[15]

The verisimilitude of this description is remarkable; the leadership of Buckingham by Shaftesbury, the merging of threats into assault, the cat and mouse treatment, the melodramatic phraseology are excellently done. Our sympathy with the Catholics is enhanced by the realisation that they gave as good as they got on more than one occasion.

These two reports can be suitably placed against a third, which may be true or false: there is no means of knowing. It is suspect, because it was not submitted to the Privy Council until June 1682— two years after it was supposed to have taken place. It is credible because, although the threatening of the witnesses is as terrific as in the other interviews, no physical violence seems to have been employed. After hearing from another spy that Shaftesbury's and Buckingham's parties were divided and that Buckingham was opposed to the idea, emanating from one of his own men, that they should "stir up the people to go to Whitehall and demand justice", the Committee called upon Mrs. Pampling to give evidence as to her interview with Shaftesbury and Buckingham about Sir Edmund Berry Godfrey's murder. According to this lady, Shaftesbury called her "a damned woman", threatened her because she would not lay information against Mr. Pepys and said that she should be torn to pieces by the rabble or "worried as the dogs worry the cats". Buckingham then intervened. "If you were a man," he said, "I would sheathe my sword in your heart's blood, for you have undone all the business by endeavouring to

[14] Caryll adds a horrific touch by stating that he was forced, during this last period of imprisonment, to drink his own urine.

[15] For the disproval of Caryll's evidence, see Grey's *Reports of the Debates in the House of Commons* and Pollock's *Popish Plot*.

take off the report that Sir Edmund was murdered by the Papists."
At this point, in Mrs. Pampling's recollections, she was dismissed
and no more of her evidence, invented or otherwise, was taken
down.

5

The attitude of Louis XIV towards the Popish Plot was
entirely practical. Any immediate hope of guiding or forcing
England into reconciliation with Rome was abandoned; it only
remained for the Most Christian King to profit by the general
confusion and get rid of his enemies, of whom Danby was still
the most dangerous. If the Treasurer and his anti-French Parliament were disposed of, then the possibility of England making war
on France was temporarily removed. On this point Louis and
Shaftesbury were allies; and it is through the French King's correspondence with Buckingham that the nature of the alliance can be
perceived.

Buckingham was on excellent terms with Barillon, by far the
most notable and intelligent of Louis' ambassadors; in November
1678, the Duke told Barillon that the London citizens must be
armed against the militia, whom he described as being under the
control of Danby's party, and that Louis must be persuaded to
give the money for this purpose. Barillon refused; the citizens
were then armed, but from the funds of the Country Party. A
month later, when Godfrey's murder and Oates's depositions had
turned the terror of a Popish invasion into an obsession, Buckingham again asked Louis for money and sent a messenger to the
French Court with a long involved story about a plot, formed by
Danby and the Duke of York, to murder Louis.

" Several persons," the message ran, " had taken the sacrament on it
to assassinate Your Majesty. The Duke of Buckingham considered that
it was his duty to communicate the matter to Your Most Christian Majesty
and he begs Your Majesty to beware of strangers, and in particular of
Irishmen."

This report—in which Buckingham himself cannot possibly
have believed—was filed, but not answered. A month later Louis
succeeded in effecting the downfall of Danby and the dissolution
of Parliament by bribing Ralph Montagu to publish his latest

financial agreement with Charles, to which Danby had unwillingly subscribed. As soon as Louis, through Montagu (who received a bribe of fifty thousand pounds), gave this information away, Shaftesbury's party was able to force a dissolution, sweep the country at the elections of January 1679, and carry out a bill of attainder against Danby, who escaped with his life, but remained in the Tower for the next five years. At the impeachment of Danby Buckingham kept in the background—was this by Shaftesbury's advice?—and persuaded the Earl of Carnarvon, who had never yet spoken in the House, to be his mouthpiece. Carnarvon was rather nervous: Buckingham primed him with claret and told him genially to " display his abilities " against Danby by any means that offered. Owlish and portentous, Carnarvon rose, and made his first and last speech to the Peers.

" My Lords," he said, " I understand but little of Latin, but a good deal of English and not a little of the English history, from which I have learnt the mischiefs of such prosecutions as these, and the ill fate of the prosecutors. I could bring many instances, and those very ancient: but, my Lords, I shall go no further back than the latter end of Queen Elizabeth's reign, at which time the Earl of Essex was run down by Sir Walter Raleigh. My Lord Bacon, he ran down Sir Walter Raleigh, and your Lordships know what became of my Lord Bacon. The Duke of Buckingham, he ran down Lord Bacon, and your Lordships know what happened to the Duke of Buckingham. Sir Thomas Wentworth, afterwards Earl of Strafford, ran down the Duke of Buckingham, and you all know what became of him. Sir Harry Vane, he ran down the Earl of Strafford, and your Lordships know what became of Sir Harry Vane. Chancellor Hyde, he ran down Sir Harry Vane, and your Lordships know what became of the Chancellor. Sir Thomas Osborne, now Lord Danby, ran down Chancellor Hyde; but what will become of the Earl of Danby, your Lordships best can tell. But let me see that man that dare run the Earl of Danby down, and we shall soon see what will become of him."[16]

Although it had gone against him, the joke was too good. Buckingham exclaimed delightedly, " The man is inspired—and claret has done the business! " and turned his energies elsewhere. The election had been a period of tremendous activity for himself and Shaftesbury. They took no risks; the Green Ribbon Club was still their headquarters and from it they organised the campaign in which the voters were bribed, cajoled, intimidated and literally carried drunk to the poll.

While the elections were in progress a man called Prosser was accused by Prance of saying that Buckingham and Shaftesbury

[16] Echard.

" did not deserve to live " for their enmity to the Catholic religion. Nothing more was heard of the unfortunate Prosser, who may have been a personal enemy of Prance; but the gravity with which this unimportant piece of evidence was received shows the tenor of public opinion and the height of popularity attained by the two leaders. A month later Buckingham was publicly received at Court, to the dismay of his enemies at home and abroad. The sensation caused by this mark of favour affected even William of Orange, who wrote to his father-in-law for further details. The Duke of York tried very hard to make nothing of his brother's unaccountable behaviour; that it might be the result of applied tactics did not, of course, occur to him. He owned himself surprised, but added that Charles knew Buckingham too well to " let him do him any harm ".

The first session of Shaftesbury's Parliament, in March 1679, was shadowed by a division in his party. The debates on the Exclusion Bill—voted in May by the House of Commons—marked Halifax's withdrawal from the Country Party; he wished James to succeed, but as a constitutional monarch, with limited powers; Shaftesbury advocated his exclusion. Buckingham took no part in the discussions; but he later told Barillon that though he had always been the Duke of York's enemy, he would never consent to his exclusion in favour of Monmouth, in whose legitimacy he did not believe. On another occasion he burst out into a passionate speech against both York and Monmouth; " after he had cursed them both sufficiently, he in the end cursed himself if he was for either "; he was for no king, but a commonwealth.[17] But it scarcely mattered what Buckingham thought about the Exclusion Bill, for in April 1679 the King, advised by Sir William Temple, called a new Privy Council in which Villiers had no place. Charles solemnly promised to be guided by the advice of these thirty councillors, of whom half were his adherents and half Shaftesbury's; he made Shaftesbury President, and so partly tied his hands, although he could not prevent the passing of the Habeas Corpus Act, for which Shaftesbury was responsible, in May.[18] Six months later he was able to dismiss Little Sincerity; to his friend Lord Bruce he remarked, " Oddsfish! they have put a set of men about

[17] Burnet: *Correspondence.*
[18] Of this Act, Hallam says, " It was not to bestow an immunity from arbitrary imprisonment, which was abundantly provided for in Magna Carta . . . but to cut off the abuses by which the Government's lusts of power and the servile subtlety of Crown lawyers had impaired so fundamental a privilege." *History.*

me—but they shall know nothing, and this keep to yourself,"[19]
During these months Buckingham remained at Cliveden; in July,
when Parliament was dissolved, he came back to London.

In August the King fell seriously ill and was not expected to
live. The Country Party's hopes soared up again. Monmouth and
the armed citizens of London were ready for a *coup d'état*. The
Duke of York was summoned from his exile in Brussels. Buckingham, in common with many others, believed that Charles had been
poisoned, and told Barillon so; then, rather to Villiers' relief—
for he had begun to realise that in the present state of affairs
the sudden death of the King might mean civil war—Charles
recovered.

As soon as he was about again Charles took action; already he
was beginning to regain the territory that his enemies had taken
from him. Through another haggling deal with Louis he managed
—but only just—to keep Parliament prorogued until October,
against the advice of the Privy Council. He exiled James and Monmouth, one to Scotland, the other to Holland; in August he refused
to receive Buckingham, and in September there was a rumour that
he had ordered both Buckingham and Shaftesbury " to be
secured ". Shaftesbury was still too powerful to be struck down;
but on September the Twenty-Third a warrant was issued for
Buckingham's arrest " for treasonable practices in endeavouring to
alienate the hearts of the King's subjects from him and to stir up
sedition ".

The prosecution was based on Buckingham's remarks about
the Lord Chief Justice Scroggs, whom he had accused of " favour-
ing the Papists ". This accusation was phrased so as to imply that
Scroggs had received his instructions from the King. As soon as he
heard of the warrant, Buckingham " absconded ". He had already
declared himself " bound in conscience and duty to reveal . . . any
plot or conspiracy against His Majesty's sacred person " and had
thereby received a pardon for all his past misdemeanours; he was
right in thinking that this time a short absence was all that was
required of him, for no efforts were made to find him or to carry
out the terms of the warrant.

[19] Ailesbury.

6

Althought the year 1679 had been one of failure for Buckingham, he was still high in the people's favour; his rehabilitation after the quashing of the Meal-Tub Plot enhanced his fame. Through information given by Dangerfield, a convicted perjurer and coiner, and Mrs. Cellier—described by herself as a midwife and by others as a bawd[20]—the Catholics, headed by the Duke of York, claimed to have discovered a Protestant plot for murdering the King; some of the written evidence—afterwards found to have been placed there by Dangerfield himself—was hidden behind the bed in the house of Colonel Roderick Mansell, an employee of Buckingham, and some in Mrs. Cellier's meal-tub; when Dangerfield took fright and gave his confederates away the exposure of this attempt at Catholic retaliation increased Buckingham's popularity, the more especially because Mrs. Cellier's narration "reflected upon" himself and Shaftesbury; for Mrs. Cellier was a Catholic and the tool of Lady Powis, a Catholic Peeress, and everything the Catholics did was wrong.

The Meal-Tub Plot was disposed of by the end of March 1679. In November of the same year Buckingham's knowledge of the theatre was made use of in the planning and rehearsals of those weird and terrible pageants known as Pope-Burnings; these were organised and paid for by the principal members of the Green Ribbon Club and took place on the anniversary of Queen Elizabeth's accession[21]: for that sovereign had become the Protestant saint and her statue over Temple Bar was " decked out like a heathen idol ",[22] so that Catholics were heard to say that their enemies preferred Bess, Queen of England, to Mary, Queen of Heaven.

Of all George Villiers' many and varied activities his share in the presentation of the Pope-Burnings is the oddest and the most incongruous. That this man of the world, this self-acknowledged atheist, should cynically apply his power of invention and his talent for dramatic display to the incitement of cruelty, fear and hatred in what he and his contemporaries described as the *mobile vulgus*, adds a stinging irony to the record of his career. That the democrat,

---

[20] It was quite usual to combine these professions at this time.
[21] The 17th November, 1588 (Old Style).   [22] North.

the wit, the patron of the arts, should pander to the lowest form of superstition—that the author of *The Rehearsal* should turn his expert hand and graceful adroitness to such blustering showmanship as this, is typical, because it is so unexpected, so incredible; the incredible and the unexpected form the basis of Buckingham's character.

The procession which inaugurated the Pope-Burning began as soon as dark had fallen, at about five, and went on till ten o'clock. More than two hundred thousand people collected to see the slow, torch-lit march from Aldgate to Temple Bar where, under the windows of the Green Ribbon Club, it reached a melodramatic and —to them—satisfactory conclusion: for to the majority, the figures of the Pope and his minions were not mechanised puppets or hired actors, but real personages; each time he, his Cardinals and Jesuits fell into the flames they saw their enemies perish. So remarkable and thrilling were these pageants that even Catholics risked their lives to see them. On one occasion the King was said to have looked on from a goldsmith's window near Temple Bar; and Barillon, though warned that he would be lynched if the crowd discovered him, insisted on watching the spectacle from a friend's house in the Strand.[23]

Before the procession started claret was distributed by the stewards of the Green Ribbon Club and the Protestant slogans— " A Shaftesbury! " " A Buckingham! ", " Exclusion! No Popery and wooden shoes! ", " Long live the Protestant Duke! " echoed across the darkening streets. Then, from a side-alley in Aldgate, issued the first figure—a bell-man, dressed all in black, tolling his bell and calling out through a megaphone, " Remember Justice Godfrey! Remember Justice Godfrey! "—and again " Remember Justice Godfrey's death! You were the men that stopped his breath! " He was followed by a great white horse on which sat the blood-stained corpse of the murdered magistrate, his neck lolling to one side, his sword thrust through his breast; this figure must have appeared all the more horrible in that it was of wax, worked by machinery and having no life of its own. Sitting behind it and holding it up was an actor, dressed as a Jesuit, with a crucifix in one hand and a bloody dagger in the other. Then came a group of monks, cardinals and friars, followed by two priests, one distributing pardons and the other carrying a phial of poison, labelled " Jesuit powder ".

[23] Sir George Sitwell.

After these came the climax of the show—a sledge drawn by four singing boys on which swayed a huge golden chair; in it sat the Pope, dressed in white, wearing his triple crown and carrying a blood-stained sceptre; this ghastly figure was also of wax; but in the torchlight it seemed to grimace and leer, while the hidden machinery enabled it to raise one hand in jerky benedictions; behind it crouched the Devil, clad in scarlet and black with horns and tail, whispering his instructions in the ear of the Pope, who nodded stiffly, as if in answer.

Before the yells and curses that greeted these two had died down there passed a car full of waxen ladies, one very splendidly dressed; this was Donna Olympia Maldachini, Buckingham's old acquaintance (she had died of the plague more than twenty years before), with a company of nuns, labelled " Courtesans in Ordinary "; over her head floated a banner on which was written "The Pope's Whore". She was escorted by the "Inquisitor-General " and his attendants, bearing instruments of torture. The procession closed with a single gorgeously-dressed male figure, whose identity is obscure and was perhaps meant to be so: some thought it was the King of France, others the Duke of York, but whatever it was, it looked extremely disdainful and frightening.[24]

As the mob closed in round the last of the pageant its pace slowed down a little, so that as many as possible could overtake it to the enormous bonfire at Temple Bar. Here, in her niche, Queen Bess, the goddess of Protestantism, contemplated her devotees and her victims; the torches flared up and illumined her narrow face under its jewelled diadem, the shield on her arm and the spear in her painted hand. Then the figures of Donna Olympia, her attendants and the Pope were placed in a semi-circle round the fire. A mock trial, in crude rhyme, took place. At its conclusion the Devil sprang from the papal throne and "appeared to fly away ".[25] How this was done has not been revealed.

Then, at long last, came the most intoxicating moment of all. Amid the roaring of the flames and the shouts of the people " the mitred poppet from his chair they draw "[26] suspending him over the fires of hell; above the tumult rises his voice in defiant—but relentlessly rhyming—expostulation; he is unrepentant and dies game, as wicked people always must. He is flung into the bonfire.

[24] Memories of Bernini's *I Due Teatri* may have inspired Buckingham in his arrangement of this part of the procession.   [25] North.   [26] Dryden.

And an appalling, hob-goblin shriek arises, scream upon scream, ear-piercing, unforgettable, unbearable; for the Pope's belly has been stuffed with live cats, who are burning to death in hideous agony.[27]

It may well be believed that such a pageant as this was very expensive; indeed it cost just under a thousand pounds. First there was the claret, then the actors' fees, which were high, for they ran the risk of being torn to pieces by the crowd; then there was the elaborate machinery with skilled hands to work it and all the bills of the middlemen who provided the torches, dresses, sleighs, wax-works, and so on (the figure of the Pope, complete with cats, cost forty pounds). But from the point of view of those who supplied bread and circuses to the Protestant mob, it was worth while. Pope-Burnings were instituted in many of the provincial towns, and their fame reached the most desolate and ignored hamlets of the countryside. The realisation that Popery had been and could be destroyed before their very eyes gave the uneducated masses courage to go on with their resistance to tyranny.[28]

Paradoxically, the man who above all others was responsible for their fears remained popular and even beloved. The savagery of his people was never turned upon King Charles. When he walked with long strides in the Park to feed his ducks they cheered him, when he pulled off his hat to them they applauded, when his sombre look broke into a sardonic smile or a short harsh laugh, they were ready to fall at his feet: when he was ill they wept and despaired. Nothing that Shaftesbury could evolve, no sneer, no piece of evil gossip that Buckingham let slip affected their loyalty. They saw no inconsistency in a simultaneous worship of Absalom, Achitophel, Zimri, and a Stuart King.

7

In December 1679 Buckingham left for France; he told the King, who repeated it half-jokingly to Barillon, that his purpose

[27] Sitwell. The author of *The First Whig*, that unique historical study, cites the use of the cats as a typical piece of Puritan brutality and points out that the wailing of bag-pipes would have given the same effect. Surely no man-made instrument can ever achieve the eeriness in which the cry of these animals seems to excel? May we not look on the Green Ribbon Club cats as subsidiary martyrs to the Protestant cause?

[28] Barillon, says Danby, " wondered much when I told him no manner of mischief was done, not so much as a head broke, but in three or four hours the streets were all quiet as at other times. It would not have been so in Paris, he said."

GEORGE VILLIERS IN HIS LATE FIFTIES

From the portrait by Sir Peter Lely in the National Portrait Gallery

Reproduced by permission of the Directors of the National Portrait Gallery

was to effect an alliance between France and England. It is more probable that he went over to get funds for the Country Party. Charles added " that a man who had passed through Calais three days ago assured him that M. de Buckingham was staying in a house with Leighton and some ladies ". The Ambassador told Louis that Buckingham had now become rather an object of ridicule than of alarm.

During the course of this year the Popish terror increased as the blood of its victims flowed. In October Charles had prorogued Parliament for twelve months, and Shaftesbury began to organise petitions for its recall throughout the country. These petitions were followed by counter-addresses from those who " abhorred " them. Oates and the petitioners called the " abhorrers " Tories, a slang term for Irish Catholic highwaymen; the Tories counter-attacked by calling the petitioners Whiggamores or Whigs, after the Scottish fanatic Covenanters whose rebellion Monmouth had put down at Bothwell Brig in June of that year. So four new words, Whig, Tory, mob and sham[29] came into use during the winter of 1679-80.

Monmouth had returned without his father's permission for the Pope-Burning of November 1679; the Duke of York followed him on February the Twenty-Fourth, 1680. The excitement over the Exclusion Bill and the succession had reached its height when Monmouth and Buckingham gave an entertainment to their followers at a tavern in Wapping; they drank confusion to Popery and toasted the success of the Whigs for many hours; later, Buckingham, with a great company of guests, escorted the Protestant hero back to his splendid new house in Soho Square, the house that he inhabited for only six months after it was finished. Then all the publicity—publicity of a most unpleasant kind—fell on Buckingham. Danby, from the Tower, had struck at last, and raised a monstrous scandal about his former patron. Now, more than ever, Buckingham needed Shaftesbury's keen wit and widely spread power; but he was again at loggerheads with his chief, whom he had described to Barillon as incapable of leading the Opposition, and he stood alone. He had been ill during the debates on the Exclusion Bill, " worn to a thread by whoring " said some, merely of a fever which he cured by taking quinine, according to others. At the beginning of February he recovered, to find that

---

[29] " Sham " was heard of by 1677, but was not in common use till the Popish Plot had achieved general publicity.

S

Colonel Thomas Blood, with seven other men and women, all bribed by Danby, had joined together to accuse him of a horrible crime.

The course of Danby's attack on Buckingham follows the muddiest byways in the "underworld" of seventeenth century London. The plot against the Duke, planned by Blood, financed by Danby and, it was believed, supported by "greater persons" than the ex-Lord Treasurer, was an attempt on Buckingham's life; if he had been found guilty there would have been no hope of reprieve or even of exile or imprisonment. But Blood's distempered fancy led him to his own ruin in this affair; if he had confined himself to possibilities he might have succeeded in disgracing Buckingham and would have certainly brought his political activities to an end; as it was, his scheme failed, partly because he employed at least ten informers where two would have sufficed and partly because he accused Buckingham of a crime that he had never committed.

Blood and his accomplices attempted to destroy the Duke by accusing him of "unnaturally and wickedly using"[30] a woman called Sarah Harwood, the deceased wife or sister of Thomas Harwood, "a prisoner on the common side of Newgate" who, a year later, informed Danby and the Lieutenant of the Tower that he was receiving "very extraordinary cruelty" by the command of the Duke of Buckingham.[31] That Blood and his associates were aware of the weakness of their case is proved by the fact that they declared Sarah Harwood to have been sent overseas and then murdered, by the Duke's orders, in company with several other—unnamed—women whom he had similarly maltreated. Two of Blood's employees had been in Buckingham's service; others may have been used—and cast aside—by the Green Ribbon Club; that part of the evidence remains obscure. In February 1680, just after Buckingham had been received at Court—when indeed it was rumoured that he would again be granted the Mastership of the Horse, of which Monmouth had been deprived—Blood brought his case. The resultant sensation was terrific and—unfortunately for the Duke—prolonged. "The business of the Duke of Buckingham," said one news-letter, "is now become the only discourse of

---

30 *A True Narration of the Design Lately Laid by Philip Le Mar and Others, against George, Duke of Buckingham.* 1680.

31 Jenks, Buckingham's agent, did not deny this accusation; he said that it was done "only to keep the petitioner in awe, so that he would not speak or act anything against the Duke of Buckingham."

the town . . . and some are so confident to declare publicly that several persons of quality will be found to be encouragers or abettors in it. . . . Any who have . . . been . . . abetting to it will be made public exemplaries for . . . their ill practices."

Eight weeks later the bill against Buckingham was sent up to the Grand Jury, who found the evidence contradictory and inadequate. A verdict of *Ignoramus* was returned and Buckingham " came off with honour ". A few days later his lawyers took action and the principal witnesses—Philip Le Mar and his mother, Frances Loveland, a widow—were found guilty of subornation and perjury: the evidence against them was " very foul and reflected extremely upon other persons ". During the course of the trial Le Mar died in prison; his mother was fined and sentenced to stand in the pillory on June the Nineteenth, 1680, " where she was severely dealt with by the people throwing dirt and rotten eggs at her ".

It now remained for Buckingham to take action against the instigators of the plot. Nothing could be proved against Danby, who was " the promoter of it all ". But by July the Duke was able to sue Blood for *scandalum magnatum*. He won his case and received, in all, thirty thousand pounds' worth of damages. Meanwhile Blood continued to swear that he had had no hand in the case; all he had done, he said, was to check " the disloyal actions of the Duke of Buckingham and all the Commonwealth Party ". He was in need of his arrears of salary—six hundred pounds—and " a supply of thirty or forty guineas to bear the charges of disentanglement ", as he had had to pawn his plate, and was destitute. A few months later he wrote and caused to be circulated a pamphlet describing the plot and protesting his innocence and his loyalty to Buckingham. The warrant for Blood's arrest and the report of his trial not only support the charge of subornation but show that he spent several hundreds of pounds in bribing his witnesses, whom he promised " the friendship of some Peers " and places in the Customs.

As soon as Blood had been disposed of Buckingham found it necessary to submit to another " conversion " by the Protestant clergy. Lady Sunderland reported that he " pretended to have some trouble of conscience and talked of it to some fanatics; and they said he appeared to be in a good mind, and they were come to him again to finish the work; at the time appointed he could not be found: and afterwards they heard he was with a wench all day ". It may have been true; on the other hand, Buckingham may have taken refuge in his laboratory.

8

By the autumn of 1680 the gossip arising from the trials of Blood and his confederates had died down. After a short retire-ment Buckingham returned to London and kissed the King's hand; there was talk of his being sent as Ambassador to France, but nothing came of it. He was still Charles's friend, in spite of his alliance with the disgraced Monmouth and the hated Shaftesbury, in spite of his failure to secure the beautiful Miss Lawson, his sister's niece by marriage, for his master's harem. " She is another Papist ", said the Tories angrily. But the young lady was discreet and pious; she preferred the cloister to the gaieties of Whitehall.

In October of this year Buckingham told Barillon that when Charles was drunk his irritation with the Duke of York turned to hatred and was freely expressed; but the King continued to support his brother, just as Buckingham, while remaining on the best of terms with Charles in private, attacked him in a speech in the House of Lords, at the end of November, in which he suggested that a Committee drawn from both Houses should " consider the state of the nation with regard to Popery ". This motion was debated for two hours and then thrown out. Meanwhile it was observed that Buckingham looked very ill and people began to say that he was retiring altogether from the political scene. He took no part in the Lords' debates on the Exclusion Bill, in which Halifax defeated Shaftesbury and Monmouth; it is possible that he was at Oxford when Charles, backed by French bribes, made his celebrated surprise attack on the Whigs and dissolved his fifth and last Parliament. Although Buckingham was now completely estranged from Shaftesbury, he was still popular in London; in March 1681 he received the freedom of the City, and in May a Captain Bury was tried and sentenced to a fine of a hundred pounds and a year's imprisonment for " conspiring " against him.

During the summer the tide began to turn against the Whigs, a letter, denouncing Shaftesbury and saying that he had invented the Popish Plot in order to ruin the Government fell into Bucking-ham's hands, but he refused to let it be used against his former chief, who in the following month was arrested on a charge of high treason and sent to the Tower. During the weeks of Shaftesbury's imprisonment Buckingham became active again; he formed an association with a group of Protestant ex-officers and with their help collected a great many recruits, whom he armed at his own expense; Government spies reported that as soon as the King died Buckingham would be in a position to exclude the Duke of York by force. But some of the Whig Lords, Salisbury, Essex, Russell and Grey of Werke, did not trust him and subscribed, with the Tories, to the opinions expressed in the late Samuel Butler's *Character of a Duke of Bucks*, which made very popular reading at this time.[32]

Yet Villiers could still afford to laugh at this diatribe; when the Grand Jury returned a verdict of *Ignoramus* at Shaftesbury's trial and he was escorted back to Aldersgate by an hysterically vociferous crowd, Buckingham's coach followed his. The great Achitophel was reported to have said that " the Duke of Buckingham had as much right to the crown as any Stuart in England ". This was gratifying, to say the least; and so were the shouts of the people, who came down to St. Paul's churchyard towards Ludgate, waving their swords (the swords that Buckingham had given them) and calling out, "No Popish successor, no York! A Monmouth! A Buckingham! God bless the Earl of Shaftesbury!" Shute, the sheriff, " came out on a pretence to discharge the rout, and said, ' You keep me a prisoner here, too—pray depart '—smiling, and immediately waving his hat. ' Shout, boys,' says he, ' Shout! ' and they did so."

This was the last time that the people of the city of London shouted for Buckingham.

[32] See Appendix IV.

CHAPTER FIVE

I

IN 1682 Buckingham finally retired from political life. His health was believed to have broken down; indeed Burnet's last account of him gives the impression that he had only a short time to live.

"He also ruined both body and mind, fortune and reputation equally. The madness of vice appeared in his person in very eminent instances; since at last he became contemptible and poor, sickly and sunk in his parts, as well as in all other respects, so that his conversation was as much avoided as ever it had been courted."

That Buckingham survived for five more active and, on the whole, enjoyable years may perhaps be partly accounted for by his breaking off all connection with the Whigs at the age of fifty-four; at the same time he probably observed the warnings of his physicians and resigned himself to a less arduous, healthier course of pleasure. He still frequented the Court and was restored to favour with the King; but the greater part of his time was spent in the country; from there he watched the ruin of the "good old cause "[1] and the triumph of Charles and the Tory party as they put a stranglehold on local government and the civil and religious liberties he had so often defended.

A group of young, able, more single-minded but no less corrupt politicians than Buckingham now held the strings that he had disputed with Arlington and snatched from Clarendon—Godolphin, Mulgrave, "Lory" Hyde, and Spencer, Earl of Sunderland[2] —the Chits, as Buckingham called them. These set the fashions,

---

[1] Algernon Sidney.

[2] Sydney Godolphin (1645–1712) became Secretary of State in 1684 and Head of the Treasury. Charles II's celebrated description of him as being " never in the way and never out of the way " was justified by the suppleness of conduct which kept him in power during the reigns of James II, William and Mary, and Queen Anne.

John Sheffield, Earl of Mulgrave and First Duke of Buckingham and Normanby (1648–1721) was banished by Charles in 1682 because of his courtship of the Princess Anne, in whose reign he became President of the Council. His verses are not so readable or so vivid as his *Memoirs* and his *Character of Charles II*.

Laurence Hyde (1641–1711) second son of Clarendon, remained in office till his dismissal by James II in 1687. He became Lord Lieutenant of Ireland under William and President of the Council under Anne.

Robert Spencer (1640–1702) Second Earl, a superlatively brilliant turncoat and politician, became a Roman Catholic at the accession of James II, lived in Holland from 1688 till 1691 and became William's Lord Chamberlain in 1697.

patronised the artists and enjoyed the privileges of the Council and the Bed-Chamber. Lord Bruce, a newcomer in his early twenties, six feet of stalwart, simple fealty to the Stuart cause, recorded his disapproval of Villiers with two adjectives—flashy and vain—and passed on to more important matters.[3] For this generation of courtiers knew passages of *Absalom and Achitophel* by heart, and spoke of Buckingham and his circle accordingly; when the Whigs struck a medal to commemorate Shaftesbury's release from prison the result was another broadside from Dryden, of which the inspiration came from the King.

"One day," says Spence, who heard the story from Pope, "as the King was walking in the Mall and talking with Dryden, he said, 'If I were a poet, and I think I am poor enough to be one, I would write a poem on such a subject in the following manner.' He then gave the plan of *The Medal*; Dryden took the hint, carried the poem, as soon as it was written, to the King, and had a present of a hundred broad pieces for it."[4]

Buckingham, realising that he was outmatched, set Shadwell on to answer Dryden, although he himself was not pilloried in *The Medal*. Shadwell, who had recently dedicated his *History of Timon of Athens* to " the most illustrious Prince, George, Duke of Buckingham ", and drawn attention to the fact that he had had " the honour of being admitted sometimes into Your Grace's conversation, the most charming in the world "—did his best with some heavy satire and a *rechauffé* of the Duke's ten-year-old jokes about Mr. Bayes. But his arrows fell wide of the mark, as the Whig cause sank and perished in the confusion of the Rye House Plot, which was followed by the collapse of Shaftesbury, his flight to Holland and his death—" after having cast some very deep sighs "—in Amsterdam in January 1683.[5] In Dryden's stage directions for *Albion and Albianus*, the great Achitophel was held up to public ridicule for the last time and with perfect safety, for he had been two years in his grave.

"Fame rises out of the middle of the stage, standing on a globe; on which is the arms of England; the globe rests on a pedestal; on the front of the pedestal is drawn a man with a long, lean, pale face, with fiends' wings and snakes twisted round his body; he is encompassed by several fanatical rebellious heads, who suck poison from him, which runs out of a tap in his side."

[3] Thomas Bruce, Second Earl of Ailesbury (1640–1702) whose delightful *Memoirs* reveal an integrity, naïveté and forthrightness excessively rare in that age, became a Jacobite soon after 1688 and ended his days in Brussels. His great-grand-daughter, Louisa Maximiliana of Stolberg-Guedern, married the unfortunate Young Pretender, the great-nephew of Charles II.   [4] *Anecdotes.*   [5] Christie.

Shaftesbury's Council of Six—Monmouth, Russell, Howard of
Escrick, Essex, Sidney and Hampden—were dispersed, the plans
for seizing Whitehall and the persons of Charles and James were
revealed, together with Shaftesbury's Five Points for the Government of England;[6] and Buckingham saw that he had thrown in
his hand just in time. As Monmouth fled to Holland, Russell and
Sidney went to the block and Essex committed suicide in the
Tower, Buckingham's thoughts were drawn back to another,
almost forgotten execution—that of his father's murderer—and he
scribbled the following lines:

> " Here uninterred suspends tho' not to save,
>   Surviving friends th' expenses of a grave,
>   Felton's dead earth, which to the world will be,
>   Its one sad monument; his elogy,
>   As large as fame, which whether bad or good
>   I say not, by himself 't'was wrote in blood;
>   For which his body is entombed in air,
>   Arched o'er with heaven, set with a thousand fair
>   And glorious stars, a noble sepulchre,
>   Which time itself can't ruinate, and where
>   Th' impartial worm (that is not bribed to spare
>   Princes corrupt in marble) cannot share
>   His flesh, which oft the charitable skies
>   Embalm with tears, raining those obsequies,
>   So long to men shall last, till pitying fowl
>   Contend to reach his body to his soul."

Oddity rather than wit characterises this casual piece of verse:
but its composition seems to contradict the intellectual decline suggested by Burnet. Some entries from Buckingham's Commonplace
Book fill in the picture of a combatant who has retired gracefully
but unwillingly from the struggle; writing of " Solitude " and
" Greatness " respectively, he observed: " I'll have nothing to do
with the world, methinks spectators have more pleasure than
actors "—and " Great men cheat by gross and are cheated by

---

[6] These five points were submitted to Monmouth, who gave a slightly evasive but
on the whole favourable reply to them:
1. That the militia should be in the hands of the people.
2. That they should choose their own sheriffs in every county.
3. That there should be an annual parliament which should sit as long as it had
   anything to do.
4. That there should be liberty of conscience.
5. That the nobility of England that acted contrary to the interest of the people
   should be degraded from their hereditary rank.
(See Thomas Sprat's account of the Rye House Plot.) These " points " are clearly
derived from Lilburne's *Agreement of the People*, published more than thirty years before.

retail." Under the heading " Fortune " Buckingham adds, rather cryptically, " 'T'is as dangerous to slip in a very smooth way as to stumble in a very rough one."

But the King still supported him; they were old men now: and Charles, secure at last, could afford to indulge himself as much as he pleased.

2

By the beginning of 1683 Buckingham's income had sunk to six thousand a year—or so it was believed—and his debts had reached a staggering height; he was now reduced to borrowing from his trustees for his current expenses.[7]   Nevertheless he expostulated with Charles for relieving him of the Stewardship of York, which was given to James;[8] he had to conceal his hatred of his old enemy, whose influence had been re-established—so Villiers told Barillon— by the follies of Shaftesbury and Monmouth. If the Whig leaders had listened to him, Buckingham said, he would not have been forced to " leave them in the lurch ": but it was too late to think of that now. Meanwhile, he could afford to ignore the aspersions of the informers who continued to speak against him to the Privy Council. Buckingham " talked freely " still, they declared, to Anabaptists and republicans, had taken six hundred armed men to the Oxford Parliament and offered a Government agent three hundred a year for life to swear that Danby had instigated Sir Edmund Berry Godfrey's murder; these rather dated accusations left the Duke unharmed: but his domestic troubles increased. One of his servants stabbed another and his bailiff at Cliveden, John Goodchild, had the impertinence to sue him for assault, declaring that he had broken into his house with a party of men armed with blunderbusses. Buckingham replied that he had returned from a journey into Lincolnshire to find no hay for his horses and not a scrap of food for himself or his servants; he went to Goodchild's house, he added, " but only had a switch in his hand; and as for blunderbusses, he never did nor would willingly travel without them ". To his great indignation the Duke was bound over for fifteen hundred pounds to keep the peace with Goodchild.

In July Buckingham went into Wales and stayed with Lord Bridgewater at Ludlow Castle. There had been talk of his

[7] Ashley.   [8] Reresby.

becoming Viceroy of the West Indies—but what could he do in such a place? He was too old to start life again on the other side of the world, and the scheme came to nothing. Then he entered on a complicated legal squabble with his cousin, the Earl of Rutland, over a matter of tithes at Helmsley. The lawsuit dragged on for three years and was settled at last in Rutland's favour; instead of leaving the matter to his trustees, Buckingham was unable to resist attending the court in person and making fun of his own lawyers; "but his appearance," said one of Rutland's agents, "daunted neither counsel nor witnesses". The Duke's dilatory habits held up the proceedings and quadrupled his own and his cousin's expenses. "We cannot get the Duke's answer in respect of Privileges of Parliament . . . we find they give us all delay imaginable," was the report a year later.

At Nottingham, staying with the Duke of Newcastle, Buckingham had a long talk with Sir John Reresby about politics. Reresby noted that his old patron was pro-French again and much incensed with Lord Halifax for refusing to communicate with Barillon; the Duke added that Halifax's power "would never be considerable" if he persisted in this absurd policy. Villiers was still, in Reresby's eyes, "the wittiest, most handsome and best bred man of his age," but, as ever, "wholly addicted to his pleasures, and unsteady." In Nottingham, if he had cared to do so, Buckingham might have investigated the records of his ancestor, Pagan de Villiers, who had settled there after waiting to see the result of the battle of Hastings.[9] But Pagan de Villiers' descendant was apt to be rather derisive of those who took their ancient lineage too seriously. "He brags of his ancestors as if he had begot 'em," he remarked of one acquaintance, and added, "I had rather blush at my ancestors than have my ancestors blush at me."[10]

No doubt Buckingham's Norman ancestors would have blushed at some of his minor triumphs—at the continued prosperity of his glass-works at Lambeth, where Evelyn inspected the "huge vases . . . clear, ponderous and thick as crystal," and mirrors that were better than those of the Venetians; and they might not have understood the easy-going friendliness of Charles, whom the Duke accompanied in his yacht to Portsmouth in the summer of 1684; the King's brother and three of his sons, Richmond, Grafton and St. Albans were on board: the Duchess of Portsmouth went to

[9] A. Collins: *Peerage of England.*   [10] Commonplace Book.

meet them by road; guns, rockets and church bells greeted the royal yacht as she entered the harbour.

On such occasions as these Charles and Buckingham were at their best; they watched the young men play cards and amused them and one another with talk of old days, of women, horses and statesmen long dead, of the walking match that one of Buckingham's servants had won against a team from Cheshire, of an expedition to Ipswich which the Duke described as " a town without inhabitants, a river without water, streets without names and where the asses wore boots "[11] and of their adventures after Worcester. The older men may have recalled, but in silence, another yachting expedition to Harwich and Aldborough, with the youthful Monmouth, restless as quicksilver, charming everyone who saw him. He and Buckingham had breakfasted together while the King took his chocolate at Captain Silas Taylor's . . . but that was sixteen years ago. Captain Taylor was in his grave and the once adored Monmouth with his enigmatic mistress, Henrietta Wentworth, at the Hague; no one ever spoke of him or expected to see him again.

During the last months of Charles's reign Buckingham's health and appearance seem to have improved; his spirits must have risen accordingly. He did not expect to outlive his master: on the other hand, Charles must surely outlive James—that was the general opinion. As long as Charles was alive Buckingham had nothing to fear; he could keep down his expenses by paying long visits to his friends and return to Court whenever he pleased.

3

On the morning of the Second of February, 1685, King Charles had a stroke and fell back into the arms of Lord Bruce. Forty-eight hours later he received the sacrament from a Catholic priest. Another night passed and another day dawned; at eleven-thirty the next morning the Duke of York became King of England. In the following April, Buckingham made his last public appearance at the Coronation.

He had been deprived of all his places and most of his privileges. He was not therefore entitled to carry any of the regalia, as at the Coronation of Charles; but he walked alone in

[11] Jesse.

the procession and was as conspicuous, if a pictorial record of the ceremony can be trusted, as on many another occasion.[12] Eight Duchesses—among them his wife, his cousin Barbara and Frances Stuart—preceded him; he was followed by Clarencieux and Norroy Kings-of-Arms, the Lord President of the Council, the Lord Privy Seal and a number of other dignitaries. He wore his Garter robes and carried his coronet in his left hand; in Sandford's engraving the tallest of the Duchesses—is it Frances or Barbara? —is turning back to look at him over her shoulder.

Something about Buckingham's last appearance as a public figure seems to have caught the artist's imagination. All the other personages in the pageant, even the King and Queen, appear as dolls and no attempt has been made at a likeness, although dresses, orders, coronets and emblems are minutely and accurately treated. Villiers' appearance is that of Verelst's rather than of Lely's portrait, but considerably aged and fallen away. One may perhaps conclude that although he had by this time become the wreck of his former self, he was no longer puffy and swollen, as when Lely painted him. In Sandford's drawing the weight and solidity of ermine and velvet do not hide the fact that his figure is not now elegant or athletic; but his face, with its pencilled moustache, sunken eyelids and high-bred features, has fined down into a reminiscence of beauty. The expression, self-contained, sardonic and alert, is that of a man who finds his circumstances ridiculous but mildly enjoyable.

No matter what the inducement, Buckingham could not take James II seriously; a few weeks after the Coronation he outraged the King's sensibilities by writing an essay, in the form of a letter to a friend, entitled *Reason & Religion*, in which, for the last time, he pleaded for liberty of conscience.

The arguments that Buckingham employed are now commonplaces; but to many of his contemporaries they appeared, as before, dangerously subversive. *A Short Answer to His Grace of Buckingham's Paper* was produced by an anonymous employee of James, who told Barillon that he had decided to ignore the whole affair; nevertheless, the Ambassador added, Buckingham's publication was still causing a great deal of talk. Meanwhile the Duke demolished the *Short Answer* with an even shorter—and much more readable—reply.

At some point in this theological skirmish the Duke had an

[12] Francis Sandford: *Coronation of King James II and Queen Mary*. 1685.

interview with James; what passed between them will never be known; but two years later, when Buckingham had laid aside for ever such problems and temptations as these, the King told a cousin of Reresby's that Villiers had taken the sacrament with him " after the Roman " before he left London for the last time. Perhaps, encouraged by the Duke's effrontery and persuasiveness, James was concluding the scene that had been interrupted by the Dutch cannon fourteen years before on board his flagship in Southwold Bay. It is certain that James thought highly of his own powers as a saviour of souls: it is no less certain that Buckingham could never resist egging him on, whatever the consequences to himself. The final result of the interview was *A Conference*, an extremely amusing imaginary dialogue between the Duke and an Irish priest, sent to him, according to his own account, during an illness, by the King and Queen. This is one of Buckingham's best pieces; but the conventions of seemliness now obtaining do not, unfortunately, permit free or full quotation; and the miracle of the wicked old woman who, through divine intervention, " continued in mingent circumstances, from morning till night " must be passed over for the present. One passage, thrown in as make-weight for Buckingham's contemptuous " baiting " of the pompous James, allows of repetition; for it shows, quite inadvertently, the Duke's attitude towards an inferior and partly gives away the secret of his popularity with simple and uneducated persons.

" When I was sent Ambassador from the late King to Paris," he says, " in the year 1670, I took over with me a young blackamoor boy, who could just make a shift to be understood in English; and this boy one Holy-Day morning, went along with some of my gentlemen to see the curiosities of so remarkable a city, and all of them at last went into Notre Dame church, as the Priest was celebrating Mass, at the High Mass. The lad was perfectly surprised at their rich habits and fine music; and when the priest came to the elevation, he asked one of my gentlemen, what that white thing was, which the man in the parti-coloured coat held up in his fingers? ' Why,' replied he, ' these people believe it to be God Almighty.' Not long after he saw a priest giving the wafer to a parcel of people upon their knees, and putting it into their mouths. ' What? ' cries he to the gentleman, ' do they eat their God after they have so solemnly worshipped him? ' ' Yes,' answers he, ' this is their belief.' The boy was so strangely confounded at what he had observed, that he spoke not a syllable when he came home; but was moping and musing by himself. I could not but take notice of this alteration in him at dinner; ' So, Tom,' says I to him, ' what's the matter with thee, if thou'rt ill, go down to the housekeeper.' ' No,' cries he, 'I am not sick, but I have seen a very odd sight this morning; which I can't help thinking on. I saw a man in fine clothes show the people God, and they fell upon their knees and beat their breasts; and afterwards I saw this man put God into their mouths, and they swallowed him.' 'Well,' says I, 'and where's the harm of that, Tom?' 'I don't know,' says the boy, 'why they should eat God, since He does us no harm; but if they have the same power over the Devil, I wish we had a hundred or two of these fine men in our country, to eat the Devil for us; for we cannot rest for him o' nights, he pinches us in the arms, sours our palm wine, spoils our victuals, and is so plaguey mischievous, he and his young cubs, that we should be glad to get rid of him, at any rate.' And this reflection a poor ignorant lad just come from Guinea made of himself."

"*So, Tom, what's the matter with thee, if thou'rt ill, go down to the housekeeper*"—that is one of the most revealing sentences that George Villiers ever wrote; set against an age in which the average servant was treated like a piece of cheap machinery, the picture created of the puzzled little negro and his amused, friendly master is delightful, if only because the one shows no self-consciousness and the other no condescension.

The postcript to *A Conference* lies in a letter from Buckingham to Lord Dartmouth, recommending two of his oldest servants, Douty and Smith, to that nobleman; he would not dismiss them till he had found them good places elsewhere. Hopeless economies —how could they affect a deficit of a hundred and forty-one thousand pounds? But he struggled on with these and similar retrenchments while his trustees wrung their hands and his wife retired to Nun Appleton, which was all that was left of her inheritance.

While Buckingham's trustees were wrangling with his creditors over the sums charged on his estate by the plasterers, joiners and carvers who, still unpaid, had helped to make Cliveden one of the most splendid palaces in England, the last act of the struggle for democracy and constitutional government was played out at Sedgemoor.[13] The once radiant and alluring Monmouth, whose beauty had dwindled to a lean dark elegance, shadowed with the brooding melancholy that seems to have descended on all those of his blood in middle life, made his final attempt to carry out the schemes that Shaftesbury and Buckingham had long and vainly supported. Lured by Whig promises, deserted by the

[13] The aims of Monmouth and his followers were to establish and improve on Shaftesbury's plans for constitutional democracy. The so-called Glorious Revolution of 1688 merely brought into power a capitalist oligarchy whose grip on England was not to be loosened for more than 200 years.

great landowners of the West, who had sworn to stand by him
if he made one last effort to establish the people's cause, Monmouth
could yet command the loyalty of seven thousand followers,
great numbers of whom gave their lives and fortunes for their
adherence to " the old men's vision and the young men's dream ".[14]
While the dream and the vision perished on Tower Hill and in
the nightmare of the Bloody Assize, Buckingham stood apart;
neither side would have had any use for him, as he very well
knew.

He stood apart: but he did not keep silence. It must be
recorded that to his undying shame the man who had been the
protector of Lilburne and the ally of Shaftesbury saw fit to write
a sketch, *The Battle of Sedgemoor*, in which he used the most
tragic episode in our history as a theme for jest. It is something
that the jokes are too feeble, too half-hearted to bear quotation;
and in justification of this unworthy effort it may be admitted
that *The Battle of Sedgemoor* is merely a caricature of Louis
Duras, recently created Earl of Feversham, who took the
credit from Churchill for Monmouth's defeat and came within an
ace of losing the battle altogether.

So much Buckingham saw and no more—a foppish ninny,
describing, in broken English, the events of the day to a group of
tittering courtiers. These were the punishments, less heavy perhaps, but more degrading, than ill health, povery and disgrace,
for all his day and nights of reckless power—a withered heart,
an empty mind . . .

4

In November, 1685, Buckingham's sister died, having survived
her third husband, Colonel Thomas Howard. Her only child,
Mary, and her son-in-law, were also dead, leaving no heirs; and
so Buckingham's only remaining kinsfolk were distant cousins.
He was very much alone, except for Brian Fairfax who, with his
wife and five children, was now settled at Bolton Percy and had
a house at Bishopshill in York; but Buckingham's spirits were
sufficiently resilient for him to embarrass the King by a farewell
gift. James had expressed a wish to buy some of his deer; through
a friend the Duke replied:

[14] *Absolom and Achitophel.*

"I cannot bring down my mind low enough to think of selling red deer, but if you believe that His Majesty would take it kindly of me, I will present him with ten brace of the best that I have."

With this characteristic gesture Villiers retired to Yorkshire. All he had left of his many possessions were some scattered pieces of land, his father-in-law's riverside house in York and Helmsley Castle, once the greatest stronghold in England, now a mass of gigantic ruins enclosing a small portion of Elizabethan architecture in which the Duke made his home. He had inherited this property and the surrounding estate from his mother; shortly before he regained it by his marriage, his father-in-law, by Cromwell's order, had utterly destroyed the Castle itself, leaving the little sixteenth-century wing almost untouched; it consisted of a two-storied suite of rooms, attached to a thirteenth-century tower. Here, surrounded by piles of shattered stonework and a double moat beyond which stretched the hills and moors of the wildest and poorest county in England, Buckingham, with such companions as his circumstances afforded—seedy poor gentlemen, drunken fox-hunting boors—settled down to the life of a country squire.

He did his best to keep up the round of pleasures and hobbies to which he had been accustomed; he built an annexe to the house in York for his chemistry, a portion of which still exists; in a cupboard in the wall may be seen the little oven in which he heated his brews and distillations. All that is left of this great building is a tiny public house, registered as *The Plumbers' Arms* and known locally as "the Cock and Bottle". Here are the little rooms, the winding staircases, the heavy, undecorated oak panelling of the house in which Buckingham continued his hopeless search for gold. From the diamond-paned windows he could still see the wooden turret with its revolving lights that he had installed on the Minster Tower in the event of an invasion by the Dutch during the days of his greatness.[15] In the grounds below, with their "noble ascent out of Skeldergate, and gardens extending to the ramparts of the city walls beyond,"[16] he could walk up and down among the trees and the flowers of which his father-in-law had been so proud; and here, "according to his natural gaiety of temper, he set all those diversions on foot in which his whole life had hitherto been spent."[17]

[15] *A York Miscellany*: J. P. Pressly.
[16] *History and Antiquities of York*: F. Drake. *History of the City of York*: C. B. Knight (1944).   [17] Drake.

HELMSLEY CASTLE
*Reproduced by permission of the Ministry of Works
Crown Copyright reserved*

THE WATER GATE OF YORK HOUSE, LONDON
Reproduced from THE SURVEY OF LONDON, VOLUME XVIII, *by permission
of London County Council*

What diversions were these? Alternating between York and Helmsley, he who had once been the finest gentleman in England arrived one night at the Castle with a " company of ruffians "[18] and made a riot at an inn. Here, where he " never went out of his way to open a gate "[19] for all his land, stretching from Helmsley to the sea was still—and how characteristically—unenclosed, Buckingham threw himself into the last excitement that was left him. With his shoddy, toss-pot companions he hunted with the Stantondale, the Sinnington and the Bilsdale, the oldest pack in England, of which he was Master. The days were, perhaps, endurable and even happy; but when the weary hounds were whipped in for the journey home and dusk crept over Helmsley and rush-lights were set in cottage windows and the waters of the moat gleamed black and steely round the shapeless ruin—then, as he rode in under the shattered portcullis the long evening must have stretched ahead of him in deathly gloom. Then he had time to feel his age, his failing health, his loneliness, his obscurity, to recall the demands of his creditors, to wonder whether the remedies for his perpetual chills and rheumatism were doing him any good, whether his huntsman Foster was neglecting the hounds and whether that last combination was getting him any nearer the philosopher's stone . . . And yet, what use had he made of liberty and power? "Methinks thy body is not a prison, but rather a tavern or bawdy house to thy soul," he reflected.[20]

The rooms that Buckingham inhabited during the last months of his life are as time, not the hand of man, has left them; after he died they were never used again and fell into decay. The delicate panelling, the plaster frieze in which the Manners and Villiers arms are interspersed with dolphins, mermaids and fleur-de-lys, the Tudor roses on the ceiling, the glazed tiles on the floor are still there; among a heap of fragments half a silver sugar-sifter and a brass chessman stand out, reminders of uneventful days and quiet evenings. Colourless and worn, the decoration of this final refuge yet reflects a taste that must have seemed to Buckingham hopelessly old-fashioned and depressing. Cliveden, Owthorpe, Wallingford House, Burley-on-the-Hill, Barn Elms with its dark memories, Whitehall with its long galleries and innumerable doors, the house in Dowgate by the busy Thames—all, all were lost; and he was alone, in spirit if not in fact, in a little room with rats in the wainscoting, owls and curlews sweeping round the

---

[18] Oldmixon.   [19] Drake.   [20] Commonplace Book.

T

walls—and for neighbours and companions a set of Yorkshire squires, celebrated even then for their independence, their churlishness, their contempt for the polished manners and sophisticated outlook of which he had been the best example. A writer of the sixteenth century has summed up the atmosphere in which Villiers now moved in some lines which he may have read and would certainly have agreed with—

"They have no superior to court, no civilities to practise; a sour and sturdy humour is the consequence, so that a stranger is shocked by a tone of defiance in every voice, and an air of fierceness in every countenance."[21]

No possessions, no associations, could prevent Buckingham from being a stranger in such a circle. Brooding, remembering, he longed for sleep, "sound as death and swift as life"[22] and then started from it, because it "torments me with such dreams that it is rather the imagination of hell than of death."[23] Then he wrote these two lines, the last of all his verses:

"In all those mighty volumes of the stars
There's writ no sadder story than my fate."

On another page of his note-book he put the heading "Tears" and wrote beneath it—
"You must water your life well, if you would have it grow again."

5

But he was not entirely forgotten. One day, riding across the moors and the flat country where the Danes had landed, came a messenger, bearing a letter. It was from Etheredge, "gentle George", the friend of his prosperous days. Elegant, urbane, Sir George wrote from Ratisbon, in terms that indicated his determination to impress posterity. He expostulated with Buckingham for "leaving the play at the beginning of the Fourth Act", and declared his amazement that

". . . the Duke of Buckingham, who never vouchsafed his embraces to any ordinary beauty, would ever condescend to sigh and languish for the heiress-apparent of a thatched cottage in a straw hat, flannel petticoat, stockings of as gross a thrum as the Bluecoat Boys' caps at the Hospital

[21] James Rither.　　[22] Commonplace Book.　　[23] Ibid.

and a smock (the Lord defend me from the wicked idea of it) of as coarse a canvas as ever served an apprenticeship to a mackerel boat. Who would have believed that Your Grace . . . would, in the last scene of life, debauch his condition in execrable Yorkshire ale? and that he who all his life-time had either seen princes his playfellows or companions would submit to the nonsensical chat and barbarous language of farmers and higglers? "

To Etheredge or to some other correspondent (his letter bears no address or date , but is ascribed to this period) Buckingham explained that

" I neither am nor desire to be out of the world, but I confess I am grown old enough to be unwilling to lose my time, and therefore . . . I thought it better to do nothing by myself than to play the fool in company."[24]

Did he not think of Frances Stuart and her card-castles as he wrote the last words? He then gave an extremely guarded and purposely obscure account of the political situation as he had left it and spoke of himself as

". . . intent about looking after my farm . . . in order to the securing every man in England his religion and liberty and estate (things which we conceive to be of some importance, though they have not of late been much talked of . . .) "

Broken, old and ill, George Villiers could still dream of a free England; but he had been so busy nailing his colours to the mast that he had let the ship sink beneath him. This is his last surviving letter.[25]

His fifty-ninth birthday was now behind him, and he was again at Helmsley for the hunting. On the Fourteenth of April, 1687, the meet was held in the courtyard of the Castle. Foster, with one of his sons as whip, was there, their charges, Dido, Spandigo, Truelove, Bonnylass, Dairymaid, Ruler and the rest, made a moving patch of brown and black and white between the grey stone and the pale spring flowers.[26] The Bilsdale had formerly hunted both fox and red deer; the only deer now left in Yorkshire wandered at ease within park walls.

Presently the hunt, the tall figure of the Master at its head, rode past the scattered cottages below the moat and away beyond

[24] From the original manuscript in the British Museum.

[25] A long, maudlin letter, purporting to be written by Buckingham to Dr. Barrow, may be dismissed as the interpolation of a later age; its style bears no resemblance to the Duke's nor to that of any writer of the seventeenth century, and its origin is obscure.

[26] A hound descended from the Bilsdale and one of the descendants of Foster hunted as recently as 1898; the Bilsdale ceased to exist in 1912; the names of Buckingham's hounds were handed down from one pack to another. (*Victoria County History*.)

the ring of the hills. The Castle was empty and silent. Morning sank into afternoon. The light began to fade from the portraits of Villiers and Manners ancestors and from the painted emblems of past glories. Darkness covered the wild country and the birds of night swept over the broken battlements and roofless towers. Still there came no sound of hoofs beneath the archways, no faint echo of the huntsman's horn from the moors or the forest. Eighteen miles away, at an inn in York, James Douglas, Earl of Arran, was resting on his way into Scotland. Presently news came to him that the great Duke of Buckingham was dying—was perhaps already dead—at Kirkby Moorside, six miles from Helmsley.

6

Lord Arran, now in his thirty-first year, was Buckingham's second cousin once removed.[27] Respectable, high-minded, not very clever, he could not but deplore the course of life which had brought his magnificent relative into the squalor and obscurity that now surrounded him. He had kept in touch with the Duke's trustees in the hope that something might have been saved out of his ruined fortunes; after the Duchess of Buckingham, Arran was next of kin, and he could not help thinking that he must be mentioned in the Duke's will, even though there was so little to leave. It would be unfair to suggest that he wished to profit by the confusion of Buckingham's affairs; but where there had been so much there might still remain, unknown to the Duke himself, some little property or possession worth having. So Lord Arran went to Kirkby Moorside as quickly as possible.

Where the Bilsdale found and what area they covered during the morning and afternoon of the Fourteenth of April is not known; but they ended with a three hours' run. The climax was reached, for Buckingham, when his horse dropped dead beneath him at a cross-roads called Chop Gate, some twelve miles from Helmsley. Here the fox went to ground, and huntsman and whip began to dig. Meanwhile Buckingham waited, presumably sending for another horse, and helped with the digging.[28] He

---

[27] See Genealogical Table, Appendix I. Arran, who became Duke of Hamilton in 1698 and was killed in a duel by Lord Mohun in 1712, has been immortalized in Thackeray's *Esmond*. He was no relation to the other Earl of Arran, Ormonde's fifth son, who had married Buckingham's only niece, Mary, and died in 1686.

[28] Drake.

was exhausted and very hot; he probably threw off his coat as he
sank back on the grass, which was soaking; several hours passed
before his groom arrived with fresh horses.[29]

Of all George Villiers' " excesses " this, a prolonged sitting
on damp ground, is the one that has caused most comment among
his contemporaries. To be incapably drunk every night, rotten
with disease and frequently subject to the languor that follows
extreme self-indulgence—all this was the natural concomitant of
wealth, position and breeding. But to sit on the wet grass—that
was a folly that shocked as much as it bewildered them: only a
madman would do such a thing; and Buckingham's sudden and
fatal sickness was always ascribed to this last piece of eccentricity.

By the time the Duke was able to leave Chop Gate and the
stone, ever afterwards called Buckingham's Stone, where his horse
had fallen, it became plain that he was too ill to go very far. At
Kirkby Moorside he decided to dismount and rest at one of his
tenants' houses—the best in the town—in the market-place; he
would stay the night and move on to York the next day: Helmsley
was too draughty and uncomfortable for a man in his condition.
A few hours later he changed his mind and sent a messenger to
Brian Fairfax to ask for a bed at his house in Bishopshill.

Kirkby Moorside was an exposed, lonely little town. Strag-
gling groups of stone houses sloped upwards to the market-place
on one side and to the churchyard on the other, with the heather-
covered dales above and the flat country stretching away below.
" The King's Head ", with its gaily-painted sign of Henry VIII,
stood next to Tinley Garth, a two-storied building with four
square rooms on each floor, twisting oak staircase and small leaded
windows. Each room was panelled in the same heavy, unorna-
mented style; the ceilings were low, the atmosphere close, smoky
and cold.

Here, in the largest of the four upper rooms, Buckingham was
put to bed. The rheumatism which had been hanging about him
for so long had now turned to an aching fever; he was in great
suffering and discomfort from swelling and inflammation of the
stomach; no one seemed to know what remedies to apply for this,
for there was no doctor handy, and the Duke ordered fomentations
to relieve the pain.[30] He was not much perturbed about himself

[29] Drake. *Victoria County History*.

[30] For Buckingham's symptoms and for details of the ensuing scene see Lord Arran's
long account to Bishop Sprat, written a few hours after the Duke's death. (*Fairfax
Correspondence.*)

but distressed at not being able to leave so dreary and uncomfortable a refuge.

After a miserable day and a night which brought an increase
rather than a diminution of his sufferings, Buckingham was told
that Lord Arran had come from York. He roused himself, and
greeted his cousin with something of his old grace and energy.
But as soon as Arran drew near the bed he saw that the Duke was
dying. Buckingham told him of his symptoms and said that
when the swelling went down he would be at ease; as Arran
looked doubtful he declared emphatically that so far from being
dangerously ill, he would be about again in a few days—he had
been on horseback only two days earlier—but the ague that had
long hung about him had made him weak. " I am sure," the
sick man added hastily as he saw his kinsman's swarthy face
lengthen, " I am in no danger of my life." " His understanding
was as good as ever," says Arran, " and his noble parts were so
entire that though I saw death in his looks at first sight, he would
by no means think of it."

Arran then sent his groom back to York for Dr. Whaler;
Buckingham suggested that his cousin should stay until he was
able to move and Arran, consenting, had time to observe the
" miserable condition " the Duke was in and in what a " pitiful
place " he was. " I confess it made my heart bleed ", he said
afterwards. As soon as Dr. Whaler, accompanied by another
physician, arrived, he saw that the Duke's case was desperate, and
told Arran so. His Grace now felt some relief from pain; this was
due, not to the remedies he had been taking, but to the morti-
fication that had set in and was rapidly ascending; though he
" enjoyed the free exercise of his senses, in a day or two at most,
it would kill him ".

But there was something about the Duke's alertness and his
commanding manner that made it impossible for them to tell him
of his condition. Arran, who believed that the end was near,
agreed that his cousin should be told, and by him; but it was
hard. Very much discomposed, he left the doctors and again
entered the bedroom.

7

Arran began by warning Buckingham as gently as possible of
his danger; he was sharply contradicted. " It is not as you

apprehend," said the Duke, "In a day or two I shall be well."
Again Arran withdrew; this time he sent for a clergyman, not the
local incumbent, but the Reverend Mr. Gibson, who was a neigh-
bour of Buckingham and lived only a mile away. Then, remarking to Gibson that it was high time His Grace "began to think
of another world, for it was impossible for him to continue long
in this," Arran again approached Buckingham and told him
bluntly that he was dying.

At this point, no doubt, Mr. Gibson let fall one or two of
those scriptural aphorisms with which he had primed himself on
his journey across the moors. But Villiers seemed not to hear him.
His expression altered: he was overcome: he could not face death.
Arran was sympathetic; but, as he said to Gibson, they would not
have discharged the duty of honest men "or I of a faithful
kinsman," he added, "if we had suffered him to go out of this
world without preparing for death, and looking into his conscience."

So the grisly work began. For the next six or seven hours,
until the Duke began to lose consciousness, Arran and Gibson
took it in turns to urge him to make his peace with God and
declare his heir; for a long time he would do neither. It would be
unjust to blame the upright, intensely conscientious Arran for
this badgering; he saw his once splendid cousin in danger of
everlasting punishment and the wrangles over his estate prolonged
indefinitely; but it is certain that he made Buckingham's last
hours of consciousness a torment and a misery; instead of sinking
peacefully into oblivion he was bothered and bullied about a
number of things that had long ceased to concern him.

Who, Arran began, should be "an assistant" to his cousin,
"during the short time he had to live?" Buckingham made no
reply; he was still adjusting his mind to the idea that life was
slipping from him. Arran considered a moment and recalled the
gossip he had heard about a conversion, and one of the King's
Jesuits—was it Father Petre?—visiting Buckingham before he
left London. Should he send for a priest? he asked. "No, no
—I am not one of that persuasion," replied the Duke angrily,
"I will hear no more of it, I will have nothing to do with
them——" and he muttered something about a "parcel of silly
fellows".[31]

Rather relieved, Arran suggested that he should send for Mr.

[31] Thomas Davies: *Dramatic Miscellanies.* Brian Fairfax.

Gibson or the parson of the parish, Mr. Shepherd. Buckingham refused. A Presbyterian, then? "No," said Villiers wearily, "those fellows always made me sick with their whine and cant."[32] "I thought," added Arran, in extenuation of his own lack of orthodoxy, "any act that should be like a Christian was what his condition now wanted most." So the night went by.

At seven o'clock the next morning the tireless relative was at the bedside again. Surely it was now time to send for the parson of the parish? To his immense gratification, the exhausted Duke consented. "Yes, pray send for him," he said quietly.[33] He was feeling very low, very weary; perhaps he was dying, after all, though somehow he could not believe it, for his mind was still perfectly clear.

Mr. Shepherd then arrived, and began to read the prayers for the dying; before continuing however, he felt it his duty to ask a question. The answer to one of the most absorbing, most discussed secrets of the day was within his grasp. "What is Your Grace's religion?" he enquired respectfully.

There was a pause. The watchers round the bed were on tenterhooks for the answer. At last the dying man gasped out— "It is an insignificant question." Then, aware perhaps of the thrill of horror which greeted the words, he added feebly, "I have been a shame and a disgrace to all religions—but if you can do me any good, do."

Mollified, Mr. Shepherd began the prayers again; and Buckingham joined in them "very freely". Dying as he had lived, he desired to adapt himself, and succeeded in doing so. There was, surely, no more ironic moment than this in all his long life.

Arran, Gibson, Shepherd and the weeping servants were now joined by Colonel Liston, an old friend of Buckingham's. During the course of the afternoon Mr. Gibson asked the Duke about his will—had he made one? "None", was the answer. At this point Arran found it prudent to withdraw and the clergyman, no doubt instructed to find out all that he could, continued his enquiries on worldly matters. Who was to be His Grace's heir? Buckingham said nothing. Heir to what? he might have answered: but his strength was going.

Gibson then named various persons in order, as it were, of probability. "My Lady Duchess?" "No." A long list of cousins and collaterals followed, with the same result. "The Earl of

[32] Davies.   [33] Brian Fairfax.

Purbeck?" By no means. "Who, then?" Still there was no answer, and Gibson, in despair, applied to Lord Arran for further advice.

Arran, hearing that his name had met with the same negative as all the others, began to lose his patience. He told the Duke sternly that it was "absolutely fit, during the time he had the exercise of his reason" (for Buckingham now showed signs of nearing collapse) "to do something to settle his affairs." But Villiers remained firm. He had nothing to settle on anyone, and nothing to say.

Very much disturbed, Lord Arran then pointed out the desirability of a Christian death. "Since you call yourself of the Church of England," he said coldly, "the parson is ready here to administer the sacrament to you." "I will take it," said Buckingham, and Arran left him to give the necessary orders.

Meanwhile Brian Fairfax had received a second message—the Duke was dying. In spite of the fact that they had drifted apart during these last years, he loved his old patron and friend with all his heart. As he hurried towards Kirkby Moorside, riding post for greater speed, the afternoon wore away into evening and, in the little room above the silent street, Buckingham was receiving the last sacraments of the Church of England, Gibson and Colonel Liston receiving with him. As the prayers were begun he called out, very loudly, three or four times, in protest, as Arran seems to imply, for he was not yet willing to "take death to him". A few moments later he became perfectly composed and received the sacrament "with all the decency imaginable". Again Arran felt a twinge of pity.

Gibson, who seems to have shared the Earl's passion for correctness, was "somewhat doubtful of [the Duke's] swallowing the bread because of his weakness and pain." But long afterwards he remarked on the dying man's "seeming devotion" and added modestly, "So far as I ever had any discourse with His Grace, he was always pleased to express a love for good men and good things, how little able soever he was to live up to what he knew."

At this moment Brian Fairfax hurried into the room, thrust aside the bed-curtains and grasped the Duke's hand; but Buckingham was speechless now, and could only look "very earnestly", as if he wanted to say something; he held on to Brian's hand. Lord Fairfax of Gilling then arrived: but the Duke did

not recognise him. So the evening passed into night. At eleven
o'clock, without a struggle or a sigh, George Villiers ceased to
breathe.[34]

8

Early the next morning Lord Arran wrote to Dr. Sprat,
giving a detailed account of the Duke's last hours. Then he
turned to financial matters. It was all far worse than he had
imagined: the wreckage was appalling. He could hardly bring
himself to believe that there was no will, for the servants now
declared that there was, somewhere, "a sealed parchment"
which they thought contained it. Had Buckingham destroyed
this paper? Had he entrusted it to some one else? Nobody was
sure. "But my Lord himself said positively in the presence of
several that he had no will in being; so what to make of this I
cannot tell you," Arran concluded. He took care to point out
that he himself had done nothing covertly; Mr. Gibson and
Mr. Brian Fairfax had been witnesses of all his proceedings. "The
confusion he has left his affairs in will make his heir, whoever he
be, very uneasy," he added, ". . . there is nothing here but confusion,
not to be expressed." Not a farthing was left for the expenses of
the funeral, although Buckingham had, at intervals, entrusted his
stewards with "vast sums". Upon opening the Duke's strong-
box in the presence of Gibson and Brian Fairfax, Arran found it
empty, save for some "loose letters of no concern; but such as
they are, I have ordered them to be locked up and given to my

---

[34] Pope's incorrect but celebrated description of Buckingham's last hours are as
follows:

> " In the worst inn's worst room, with mat half-hung,
> The floors of plaster, and the walls of dung,
> On once a flock-bed, but repaired with straw,
> With tape-tied curtains, never meant to draw,
> The George and Garter dangling from that bed
> Where tawdry yellow strove with dirty red,
> Great Villiers lies—alas! how changed from him,
> That life of pleasure and that soul of whim!
> Gallant and gay, in Cliveden's proud alcove,
> The bower of wanton Shrewsbury and love;
> Or just as gay as council, in a ring
> Of mimic statesmen and their merry king.
> No wit to flatter, left of all his store!
> No fool to laugh at, which he valued more.
> There, victor of his health, or fortune, friends,
> And fame, this lord of useless thousands ends! "
>
> *Moral Essays*

Lady Duchess." Lord Fairfax of Gilling had consented to take charge of the small amount of the Duke's plate and linen until the Duchess's wishes were known.

Arran's thoughts turned then to the tall figure lying in the little room upstairs. He had already given orders that the body should be embalmed, and soon the experts from York would be at their work: the intestines would be buried at Helmsley. Meanwhile, as the nearest male relative, he had taken the liberty of giving His Majesty a full account of the last hours and his own share in them, at the same time, sending to him, under separate cover, the Duke's George and blue ribbon, " to be disposed of as His Majesty shall think fit ". The body would, of course, remain at Helmsley until the Duchess's pleasure was known. As the correct and painstaking nobleman signed and sealed the letter he might well reflect that he had fulfilled all the duties of a relative, a man of honour and a Christian. What now remained? Only to leave Kirkby Moorside and its melancholy associations as quickly as possible. One detail escaped him. Buckingham's death was entered in the register of Kirkby Moorside as that of " Gorges Vilaus, Lord Dooke of Bookingham " and his intestines never reached the parish of Helmsley.[35]

No expression of the Duchess of Buckingham's grief has been recorded; she may have thought it best to destroy the letters that Lord Arran sent on to her, for they have not survived. But there was one memento that she cherished until her death seventeen years later—a love-letter from her brilliant husband, ironically enough, the only love-letter of his that has been preserved. It was not even written to poor plain Mary herself (" Love in writing is only compliment," he had said once),[36] but to one of her servants; its contents place it in the period of their courtship. The marks of the ribbon and the seal are still there. The writing is elegant and clear.

" The little ribbon I received from you last night instead of binding up my wound has made it greater, and though I have kept it ever since as near my heart as I could I can find no other effects by it than the being much less at my ease than I was before. I have not slept one wink, never since I saw you, neither have I been able to think of any other thing than how to find a means of speaking to your dear Mistress for I dare not without her leave presume to call her mine, though it be already out of my power ever to call rightly so anybody else. If I were less concerned I should perhaps be more successful in my endeavours to wait upon her, but the truth is I am not now in a condition to design anything well myself, the passionate desire of seeing her running so much in my head, that it does not give me leave to contrive a way how I should be able to compass it. I do therefore most humbly beg your assistance, since I am utterly unable to afford any to myself, and do hope that if your good nature be not sufficient to persuade you to do it, at least your curiosity will, to see how great a charge it will be in your power so suddenly to work upon me for one minute's conversation with that dear Mistress of yours (if you could order it so as that her answer would not make me absolutely despair) would, from as troublesome an estate of mind as ever creature was in, settle me in a condition not to envy the happiest man living. This is the only request I have to make to you, or indeed that I have to make in this world, the gaining of your dear Mistress' good opinion being the utmost ambition of your most humble and obliged fellow-servant."[37]

9

For more than six weeks the body of the Duke lay at Helmsley Castle. Then he began his last journey to the city that had seen his greatest triumphs and his bitterest failures. At midnight, on June the Twenty-First, after a splendid funeral, more elaborate and costly, it was said, than that given to His late Majesty, the Second Duke of Buckingham came to rest for ever by the father he had never known, the brother he had lost and the bastard infant that had helped to cause his ruin. His place in the family vault bears no monument or effigy.[38]

His reputation lives on in a confusion of echoes, from the "wonderful man" of Echard to the sonorous condemnation of Oldmixon—"and may all fortunes and honours so acquired so expire"; from the far-off whisper of Sir Edward Nicholas's first judgement, "But I doubt he wants ballast"—to the sour comments of Burnet, the mutterings and boomings of Clarendon, the sighs of Mme d'Aulnoy and the acidities of Shaftesbury—". . . unusual and ungrave . . . good-for-nothing . . . wholly given up to mirth and pleasure . . . giddy-pated . . . born for gallantry and magnificence . . ." Above these rise the voices of Frances Stuart—"Send all over the town for him"—of Anna Shrewsbury "I will make him comply in all things"—of Brian Fairfax lamenting the "tragi-comedy of his life"—of Mrs. Aphra Behn declaring that "Wit

[37] From the original manuscript in the British Museum.
[38] Westminster Register. James II supplied the funds for the funeral.

and wit's God for Buckingham shall mourn "—and of the Yorkshire country people, whose jingle

> "O! with the Duke of Buckingham
> And other noble gentlemen,
> O! but we had some fine hunting!"[39]

has survived into the twentieth century. But the most fitting conclusion to the story of George Villiers is the epitaph that he wrote
for himself:[40]

> "Fortune filled him too full, and he run over."

[39] *Victoria County History.*   [40] Commonplace Book.

APPENDIX I

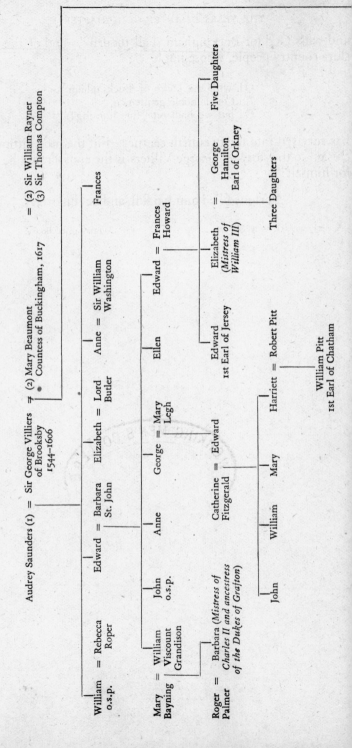

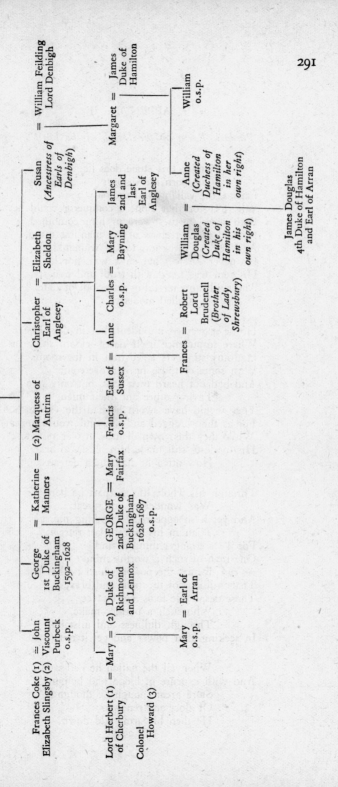

Frances Coke (1) = John
Elizabeth Slingsby (2) Viscount
Purbeck
o.s.p.

George = Katherine = (2) Marquess of Antrim
1st Duke of Manners
Buckingham
1592–1628

Christopher = Elizabeth
Earl of Sheldon
Anglesey

Susan
(*Ancestress of
Earls of
Denbigh*)

Margaret = James
Duke of Hamilton

William Feilding
Lord Denbigh

William
o.s.p.

Lord Herbert (1) = Mary = (2) Duke of
of Cherbury Richmond
and Lennox
Colonel
Howard (3)

GEORGE = Mary
2nd Duke of Fairfax
Buckingham
1628–1687
o.s.p.

Francis
o.s.p.

Earl of = Anne
Sussex

Charles = Mary
o.s.p. Bayning

James
2nd and
last
Earl of
Anglesey

Mary = Earl of Arran
o.s.p.

Frances = Robert
Lord
Brudenell
(*Brother
of Lady
Shrewsbury*)

William
Douglas
(*Created
Duke of
Hamilton
in his
own right*)

= Anne
(*Created
Duchess of
Hamilton
in her
own right*)

James Douglas
4th Duke of Hamilton
and Earl of Arran

APPENDIX II

A Pindaric Poem on the Death of the Lord Fairfax

Under this stone does lie
One born for victory;
Fairfax the valiant, and the only he
Who e'er for that alone a conqueror could be:
Both sexes' virtues were in him combined,
He had the fierceness of the manliest mind,
And yet the meekness too of womankind:
He never knew what envy was, nor hate;
His soul was filled with truth and honesty,
And with another thing quite out of date,
    Called modesty.

He ne'er seemed impudent, but in the place
Where impudence itself dares seldom show its face;
Had any strangers spied him in the room
With some of those he had overcome
And had not heard their talk, but only seen
    Their gesture and their mien,
They would have sworn he had the vanquished been:
For as they bragged and dreadful would appear,
While they their own ill luck in war repeated,
His modesty still made him blush, to hear
    How often he had them defeated.

Through his whole life the part he bore
    Was wonderful and great,
And yet it so appeared in nothing more,
    Than in his private last retreat;
For it's a stranger thing to find
One man of such a worthy mind
As can dismiss the power which he has got,
Than millions of the polls and braves;
Those despicable fools and knaves,
    Who such a pudder make
    Through dullness and mistake
In seeking after power and get it not.

    When all the nation he had won,
And with expense of blood had bought,
    Store great enough he thought,
    Of glory and renown,
    He then his arms laid down,

With just as little pride
As if he had been of his enemies' side,
Or one of them could do that were undone:
    He neither wealth nor places sought:
    He never for himself, but others fought:

    He was content to know,
    (For he had found it so)
That, when he pleased to conquer, he was able.
And left the spoil and plunder to the rabble.
    He might have been a king,
    But that he understood
  How much it was a meaner thing,
To be unjustly great, than honourably good.

This from the world did admiration draw
And from his friends, both love and awe,
Remembering what he did in fight before:
    And his foes loved him too,
    As they were bound to do,
Because he was resolved to fight no more.
So, blessed by all, he died; but far more blessed were we,
  If we were sure to live, till we could see
  A man as great in war, as just in peace as he.

U

APPENDIX III

I, *Kings*, 16.

8. In the twenty and sixth year of Asa, King of Judah, began Elah the son of Baasha to reign over Israel in Tirzah, two years.

9. And his servant Zimri, captain of half his chariots, conspired against him as he was in Tirzah, drinking himself drunk in the house of Arza, steward of his house in Tirzah.

10. And Zimri went in and smote him and killed him, in the twenty and seventh year of Asa, King of Judah, and reigned in his stead.

11. And it came to pass, when he began to reign, as soon as he sat on his throne, that he slew all the house of Baasha: he left him not one that pisseth against a wall, neither of his kinfolks, nor of his friends.

12. Thus did Zimri destroy all the house of Baasha according to the word of the Lord, which he spake against Baasha, by Jehu the prophet.

. . . . . .

16. And the people that were encamped heard say, Zimri hath conspired, and hath also slain the king; wherefore all Israel made Omri, the captain of the host, king over Israel that day in the camp.

17. And Omri went up from Gibethon, and all Israel with him, and they besieged Tirzah.

18. And it came to pass, when Zimri saw that the city was taken, that he went into the palace of the king's house, and burnt the king's house over him with fire, and died,

19. For his sins which he sinned in doing evil in the sight of the Lord, in walking in the way of Jereboam, and in his sin which he did, to make Israel to sin.

20. Now the rest of the acts of Zimri, and his treason that he wrought, are they not written in the book of the chronicles of the kings of Israel?

APPENDIX IV

CHARACTER OF A DUKE OF BUCKS

By Samuel Butler

"Is one that has studied the whole body of vice. His parts are disproportionate to the whole, and like a monster he has more of some, and less of others than he should have. He has pulled down all that fabric that Nature raised in him, and built himself up again after a model of his own. He has dammed up all those lights that Nature made into the noblest prospects of the world, and opened other little blind loopholes backwards, by turning day into night, and night into day. His appetite to his pleasures is diseased and crazy, like the Pica in a woman that longs to eat that which was never made for food, or a girl in the greensickness that eats chalk and mortar. Perpetual surfeits of pleasure have filled his mind with bad and vicious humours (as well as his body with a nursery of diseases) which makes him affect new and extravagant ways, as being sick and tired with the old. Continual wine, women and music put false values upon things, which by custom become habitual and debauch his understanding so, that he retains no right notion nor sense of things. And as the same dose of the same physic has no operation on those that are much used to it: so his pleasures require a larger proportion of excess and variety, to render him sensible of them. He rises, eats and goes to bed by the Julian account, long after others that go by the new style; and keeps the same hours with owls and the Antipodes. He is a great observer of the Tartars' customs, and never eats till, the great Cham having dined, makes proclamation that all the world may go to dinner. He does not dwell in his house, but haunts it like an evil spirit, that walks all night to disturb the family and never appears by day. He lives perpetually benighted, runs out of his life, and loses his time, as men do their ways in the dark; and, as blind men are led by their dogs, so he is governed by some mean servant or other, that relates to his pleasures. He is as inconstant as the moon, which he lives under; and although he does nothing but advise with his pillow all day, he is as great a stranger to himself as he is to the rest of the world. His mind entertains all things very freely that come and go; but, like guests and strangers, that are not welcome if they stay long, this lays him open to all cheats, quacks and imposters, who apply to every particular humour while it lasts, and afterwards vanish. Thus with St. Paul, though in a different sense, he dies daily, and lives in the night. He deforms nature, while he intends to adorn her, like Indians, that hang jewels in their lips and noses. His ears are perpetually drilled with a fiddlestick. He endures pleasures with less patience than other men do their pains."

BIBLIOGRAPHY

Acton, Harold, *The Last of the Medici.*
Ailesbury, Lord, *Memoirs.*
Airy, Osmund, *Charles II.*
Airy, Osmund, *The English Restoration and Louis XIV.*
Albion, C., *Charles I and the Court of Rome.*
Arlington, Lord, *Correspondence.*
Arundel, Dennis, *Essay on Dramatic Poetry.*
Ashley, Maurice, *John Wildman.*
Ashmole MSS., Bodleian Library, No. 807.
Aubrey, John, *Lives.*
Aubrey, John, *Natural History and Antiquities of Surrey.*
d'Aulnoy, Madame, *Mémoires de la Cour d'Angleterre.*
Baker, C. H. C., *Lely and the Stuart Portrait Painters.*
Barbour, V., *Henry Bennet, Earl of Arlington.*
Bath MSS.
Bathurst MSS.
Bayley, J., *History of the Tower of London.*
Beaufort MSS.
Behn, Aphra, *Works.*
Beresford-Chancellor, E., *Lives of the Rakes.*
Bertrand, Louis, *Louis XIV.*
Besant, W., *Westminster.*
Biographica Britannica, Vol. IV.
Birch, J., *Court and Times of James I and Charles I.*
Birch, T., *History of the Royal Society.*
Blencowe, R. W., *History of England.*
Boyle, The Hon. Robert, *Moral Reflections.*
Bremond, S., *Hattigé: ou les Amours du Roy de Tamaran.*
British Museum Addenda MSS.
Brown, L. F., *The First Earl of Shaftesbury.*
Bryant, Arthur, *Charles II.*
Bryant, Arthur, *Samuel Pepys.* (3 Vols.)
Buccleuch MSS.
Buckingham, George Villiers, First Duke of, *Correspondence.*
Buckingham, George Villiers, Second Duke of, *Works and Correspondence.*
Buckingham and Normanby, John Sheffield, Duke of, *Works.*
Burghclere, Lady, *George Villiers, Second Duke of Buckingham.*
Burke, *Extinct Peerages and Baronetcies.*
Burnet, Gilbert, *History of My Own Time.*
Burnet, Gilbert, *Memoirs of the Dukes of Hamilton.*
Burton, Thomas, *Parliamentary Diary.*

Butler, Samuel, *Works*.
Cambridge Modern History, Vol. III.
Cammell, A. J., *The Great Duke of Buckingham*.
Carey, Sir L., *Memoirs of the Civil War*.
Carleton, Sir Dudley, *Correspondence*.
Carte, Thomas, *Life of the Duke of Ormonde*.
Carte, Thomas, MSS.
Castlehaven, Earl of, *Memoirs*.
Character of a Tavern (Anonymous).
Chester, A., *Westminster Register*.
Chesterfield, Philip Stanhope, Second Earl of, *Works and Correspondence*.
Christie, W. D., *Life of Shaftesbury*.
Cibber, Colley, *Works*.
Clarendon, Edward Hyde, First Earl of, *History, Life and State Papers*.
Clarendon, Henry Hyde, Second Earl of, *Correspondence*.
Clark, G. N. *The Seventeenth Century*.
Clarke MSS.
Cleveland, Duchess of, *The Battle Abbey Roll*.
Cleveland, John, *Works*.
Clifford, Martin, *Works*.
Cobbett, E., *State Trials*.
Collier, J., *Short View of the Immorality of the English Stage*.
Collins, Arthur, *Peerage*.
Collison-Morley, L., *Italy after the Renaissance*.
Commons' Journals.
Conway MSS.
Cooper, A., *Annals of Cambridge*.
Cotton, Charles, *Games and Gamesters of the Restoration*.
Cowley, Abraham, *Works and Correspondence*.
Crowne, John, *Works*.
Dalrymple, Sir John, *Memoirs of Great Britain and Ireland*.
Davies, Thomas, *Dramatic Miscellanies*.
Denbigh MSS.
Dennis, John, *Original Letters*.
Dictionary of National Biography.
Dobree, Bonamy, *Restoration Comedy*.
Dobree, Bonamy, *Restoration Tragedy*.
Domestic State Papers.
Downes, John, *Roscius Anglicanus*.
Drake, Francis, *History and Antiquities of York*.
Dryden, John, *Works*.
Echard, Rev. Laurence, *History of England*.
Ellis, J., *Letters*.
Essex MSS.

Etheredge, Sir George, *Works*.

Evelyn, John, *Diary and Correspondence*.

Evelyn, John, *Life of Mrs. Godolphin*.

Fairfax, Brian, *Life of George Villiers, Second Duke of Buckingham*.

Fairfax Correspondence.

Fanshawe, Lady, *Memoirs*.

Fea, Allan, *King Monmouth*.

Fea, Allan, *Flight of the King*.

Fea, Allan, *James II and His Wives*.

Feiling, Keith, *British Foreign Policy*.

Feiling, Keith, *History of the Tory Party*.

Ferguson, J., *Robert Ferguson, the Plotter*.

Finch MSS.

Firth, C. H., *Last Years of the Protectorate*.

Firth, C. H., *Stuart Tracts*.

Firth, C. H., *Arber's Reprints*.

Firth, C. H., *Percy's Reliques*.

Fitzherbert MSS.

Fonblanque, E. B. de, *Annals of the House of Percy*.

Forneron, H., *Louise de Kéroualle*.

Fox, C. J., *History of James II*.

Foxcroft, C., *Life of Lord Halifax*.

Foxcroft, C., *Supplement to Burnet's History*.

French State Papers.

Gardiner, S. R., *History of England*.

Gardiner, S. R., *Charles II and Scotland in 1650*.

Gooch, G. P., *English Democratic Ideas in the Seventeenth Century*.

Goodman, A., *History of the Court of James I*.

Gosse, Sir E., *Seventeenth-Century Studies*.

Gourville, Comte de, *Mémoires*.

Granger, G., *Historical Biography*.

Green, J. R., *Short History of the English People*.

Grey, Anchitell, *Debates of the House of Commons*.

Grey of Werke, Lord, *Secret History of the Plot*.

Guizot, E., *Life of Monk*.

Halifax, Lord, *Works*.

Hallam, Henry, *History of England*.

Halstead, Henry, *Succinct Genealogies*.

Hamilton, Anthony, *Memoirs of the Comte de Gramont*.

Hamilton MSS.

Harleian Miscellany.

Harley MSS.

Harrington, James, *Oceana*.

Hartmann, C., *Charles II and Madame*.

Hartmann, C., *Clifford of the Cabal*.

Hartmann, C., *La Belle Stuart*.

Hartmann, C., *The Vagabond Duchess*.

Hatton MSS.

Herbert of Cherbury, Lord, *Autobiography*.

Hill, C., *The English Revolution*.

Historical Commission MSS.

Hobbes, Thomas, *Leviathan*.

Hodgkin, Eliot, MSS.

Hutchinson, Lucy, *Life of Colonel Hutchinson*.

James II, *Memoirs* (ed. Clarke).

James II, *Memoirs* (ed. Macpherson).

Jesse, J. H., *Memoirs of the Court of England*.

Johnson, Samuel, *Lives of the Poets*.

Jonson, Ben, *Dramatic Works*.

Jusserand, J. J., *A French Ambassador at the Court of Charles II*.

Kennet, White, *History of England*.

Kenyon MSS.

Lafayette, Madame de, *History of Madame*.

Lafayette, Madame de, *Memoirs of the Court of France*.

Lambeth MSS.

Lang, Andrew, *The Valet's Tragedy*.

Larrey, Isaac de, *Histoire d'Angleterre* (Vol. IV).

Lauderdale MSS.

Le Fleming MSS.

Le Mar, Philip,
>   *Declaration concerning George Villiers, Duke of Buckingham.*

Lilburne, John, *A Defensive Declaration*.

Lindsey MSS.

Locke, John, *Works and Correspondence*.

Lords' Journals.

Louis XIV, *Works and Correspondence*.

Ludlow, Sir T., *Memoirs*.

Luttrell, Narcissus, *Diary*.

Macaulay, Lord, *History of England*.

Macaulay, Lord, *Essays*.

Macpherson, James, *Original Papers*.

Magalotti, Lorenzo, *Travels of Cosimo III*.

Malet MSS.

Manley, Mrs., *The New Atalantis*.

Manning and Bray, *History of Surrey*.

Markham, C. R., *Lord Fairfax*.

Marvell, Andrew, *Works and Correspondence*.

Masson, D., *Life of Milton*.

Mathew, Fr. D., *The Jacobean Age*.

Mazarin, Duchess of, *Memoirs*.

Mercurius Publicus (1660–63).

Mignet, E., *Négociations Rélatives à la Succession d'Espagne*.

Miscellanea Aulica.

Montpensier, Mademoiselle de, *Memoirs*.

Mordaunt, Viscount, *Letter-Book*.

More, L. T., *Life and Works of the Hon. Robert Boyle*.

Morton, A. L., *A People's History of England*.

Motteville, Madame de, *Memoirs*.

Mullinger, J. B., *Cambridge Characteristics of the Seventeenth Century*.

Newcastle, Duchess of, *Life of the Duke of Newcastle*.

Nicholas MSS.

Ogg, David, *England in the Reign of Charles II*.

Oldmixon, T., *History of the Stuarts*.

Ormonde MSS.

Orrery, Earl of, *Works*.

Osborne, Dorothy, *Letters*.

Osborne, Thomas (Duke of Leeds), *Correspondence* (ed. Browning).

Otway, Thomas, *Works*.

d'Oyley, E., *The Duke of Monmouth*.

Oxinden and Peyton Letters (ed. Dorothy Gardiner).

Pease, T. C., *The Levellers' Movement*.

Peck, Francis, *Desiderata Curiosa*.

Peerage, The Complete.

Pepys, Samuel, *Diary and Correspondence*.

Petrie, Sir Charles, *The Stuarts*.

Petrie, Sir Charles, *Louis XIV*.

Poems on Affairs of State (1699).

Pollock, Sir John, *The Popish Plot*.

Pope, Alexander, *Works*.

Portland MSS.

Pressley, J.P., *A York Miscellany*.

Quarterly Review (No. 373, Jan. 1898).

Quennell, Peter, *Aspects of Seventeenth-Century Verse*.

Ralph, T., *History of England*.

Ranke, L. von, *History of England*.

Ravaisson, H., *Archives de la Bastille*.

Rawdon MSS.

Refined Courtier, The (Anonymous).

Renier, G., *William of Orange*.

Reresby, Sir John, *Memoirs*.

de Retz, Cardinal, *Memoirs*.

Rochester, Laurence Hyde, Earl of, *Diary and Correspondence*.

Rochester, John Wilmot, Earl of, *Works and Correspondence*.

Rushworth Collections.

Russell, Lord John, *William, Lord Russell*.

Rutland MSS.

Ryan, P. F. W., *Stuart Life and Manners*.

St. Evremond, Seigneur de, *Works and Correspondence*.

Sandford, Francis, *History of the Coronation of James II*.

Savile MSS.

Scott, Eva, *Travels of the King*.

Scott, Lord George, *Lucy Walter—Wife or Mistress?*

Scott-Thomson, G., *Life in a Noble Household*.

Scudéry, Mademoiselle de, *Works*.

Sedley, Sir Charles, *Works*.

Settle, Elkanah, *Works*.

Sevigné, Madame de, *Letters*.

Shadwell, Thomas, *Works*.

Sheppard, J. E., *The Old Royal Palace of Whitehall*.

Shrewsbury MSS.

Sidney, Algernon, *Discourses*.

Sidney, Henry, *Correspondence*.

Sitwell, Sir George, *The First Whig*.

Sitwell, Sacheverell, *British Architects and Craftsmen*.

Sola, Pinto V. de, *Sir Charles Sedley*.

Somers, Baron, *Tracts*.

Somerset and Ailesbury MSS.

Sophia, The Electress, *Memoirs*.

Spence, J., *Anecdotes*.

Sprat, Thomas, *Life of Abraham Cowley*.

Sprat, Thomas, *History of the Royal Society*.

Sprat, Thomas, *History of the Rye House Plot*.

Stanley, The Very Rev. A. P., *Historical Memorials of Westminster Abbey*.

Steinman, George, *Althorp Memoirs*.

Steinman, George, *The Duchess of Cleveland*.

Steinman, George, *Mrs. Myddelton*.

Strickland, Agnes, *Lives of the Queens of England*.

Strickland, Agnes, *Lives of the Tudor and Stuart Princesses*.

Strype, T., *Survey of London*.

Summers, Montague, *The Restoration Theatre*.

Summers, Montague, *The Theatre of Pepys*.

Sunderland, Lady, *Correspondence*.

Sutherland MSS.

Swift, J., *Works and Correspondence*.

Tanner, J., *Constitutional Conflicts of the Seventeenth Century*.

Tanner, J., *Correspondence of Pepys*.

Temple, Sir William, *Memoirs and Correspondence*.
Thurloe MSS.
Traill, H. D., *Life of Shaftesbury*.
Treasury Papers.
Trevelyan, G. M., *England under the Stuarts*.
Trevelyan, G. M., *History of England*.
Trevelyan, G. M., *Social History of England*.
Vanburgh, Sir John, *The Relapse*.
Venetian State Papers.
Verney, Family of, *Memoirs and Correspondence*.
Vernon, Mrs. H. M., *Italy (1494–1790)*.
Verville, M. de, *Memoirs of the Court of England*.
Victoria County History of Rutland.
Victoria County History of Yorkshire.
Walker, Clement, *History of Independency*.
Walker, Sir E., *Journal* and *Works*.
Walpole, Horace, *Royal and Noble Authors*.
Warren, Albertus, *An Apology*.
Warwick, Sir Philip, *Memoirs*.
Welwood, J., *Memoirs*.
Westminster Abbey Guide (1942).
Wheatley, C. *London Past and Present*.
Wheatley, C., *Pepysiana*.
Whitelocke, B., *Memorials of English Affairs*.
Willcock, J., *The Great Marquess*.
Willey, Basil, *The Seventeenth-Century Background*.
Williamson, Sir J., *Correspondence*.
Willis and Clarke, *Architectural History of the University of Cambridge*.
Winstanley, Gerard, *Works*.
Wood, Anthony à, *Athenae Oxoniensis*.
Woodhouse, A. S. P., *Puritanism and Liberty*.
Wycherley, John, *Works*.
Young, Colonel, *The Medici*.

INDEX

Absalom and Achitophel (Dryden), 64, 171*n.*, 267

Absalom Senior (Settle), 171*n.*

Achitophel, Shaftesbury as Dryden's, 143, 145, 152, 228, 260, 265, 267

Agreement of the People, The, Levellers' tract, 37, 268

Airy, Osmund, 53

Albemarle, Duke of: *see* Monk

Albion and Albianus (Dryden), quoted 169–70, 267

Amalia, Princess-Dowager, 197

Anabaptists, 134, 269

Anglesey, Earl of: *see* Annesley, Arthur; Villiers, Christopher

Anne of Austria, 110

Annesley, Arthur, 1st Earl of Anglesey (1661), 234

Antrim, 2nd Earl, 1st Marquess of, 11

Argyll, Earl of: *see* Campbell, Archibald

Arlington, Earl of: *see* Bennet, Henry

Arran, Earl of (Ormonde's 5th son), 125, 130, 280 *n.*

Arran, Earl of: *see* Douglas, James

Arras, siege of, 79, 80, 124

Arundel of Wardour, Henry, 3rd Baron, 152, 156, 250

Arundel House, 146

Astrée, L' (d'Urfé), 168

Atkins, Samuel, Pepys' clerk, and the Popish Plot, 250–1

Aulnoy, Comtesse d': *see* Mothe, Catherine de la

Aylesbury, William, 29, 33, 34, 39, 49, 51

Bacon, Sir Francis, 17

Bamfield, Colonel, 91

Banqueting Hall, Whitehall, 107

Barillon, Paul de, Marquis de Branges, French Ambassador, 245, 253, 255, 258, 260 *and n.*, 261, 264, 269, 270

Barlowe, George, 69

Barn Elms, duel at, 112, 146, 277

Battle of Sedgemoor, The (Buckingham), 165, 275

Beauclerk, Charles, 1st Duke of St. Albans, son of Charles II, 270

Beaumont and Fletcher, 165

Beaumont, Mary: *see* Villiers, Mary

Bedloe, William, and the Popish Plot, 246, 249, 251

Behn, Mrs. Aphra, 288

Bellasis, John, Lord (Belasyse), 250

Bellasis, Sir Henry, 127, 129

Bellings, Sir Richard, 156

Bennet, Henry, 1st Earl of Arlington: displaces Nicholas as Secretary of State, 115; and Frances Stuart, 120; member of the Cabal, 150; rivalry with Buckingham, 182, 194, 195, 204; in Dutch negotiations, 196–200; attacked in Commons, 205, 210; minor references: 121–4 *passim*, 132, 135–8 *passim*, 140, 152, 156–61 *passim*, 186, 190, 201–9 *passim*, 215, 230*n.*, 267

Berkeley of Stratton, John, 1st Baron, 154

Berkshire, Lord, 112, 168

Beverling (Minister to William of Orange), 198

Black Prince, The (Orrery), 171

Blagge, Henrietta, 117 *and n.*

Blood, Captain: attempts to murder Ormonde, 189–90; plots against Buckingham, 262–4

Bodegrave, 196, 198

Bolton Percy, 89, 90, 275

Bothwell Brig, 261

Bowles, Rev. Mr., 101

Boyle, Hon. Robert, 218 *and n.*

Boyle, Roger, 1st Earl of Orrery, 171 *and n.*

Brandenburg, 200

Braythwaite: Buckingham's Steward, 135

303